The Nation's Largest Landlord

The Nation's Largest Landlord

The Bureau of Land Management in the American West

James R. Skillen

 University Press of Kansas

Chapter three incorporates some text originally published in "Closing the Public Lands Frontier: The Bureau of Land Management, 1961–1969." *Journal of Policy History* 20, no. 3 (2008). Copyright © 2008 by the Pennsylvania State University.

Published by the University Press of Kansas (Lawrence, Kansas 66045), which was organized by the Kansas Board of Regents and is operated and funded by Emporia State University, Fort Hays State University, Kansas State University, Pittsburg State University, the University of Kansas, and Wichita State University

Library of Congress Cataloging-in-Publication Data

Skillen, James.
    The nation's largest landlord : the Bureau of Land Management in the American West / James Skillen.
        p.   cm.
    Includes bibliographical references and index.
    ISBN 978-0-7006-1671-8 (cloth : alk. paper)
    1. United States. Bureau of Land Management. 2. Public lands—West (U.S.)—Management. 3. National parks and reserves—West (U.S.) 4. National monuments—West (U.S.) I. Title.
    HD243.W38S55 2009
    333.730978—dc22   2009009675

British Library Cataloguing-in-Publication Data is available.

Printed in Canada

10 9 8 7 6 5 4 3 2 1

The paper used in this publication is recycled and contains 30 percent postconsumer waste. It is acid free and meets the minimum requirements of the American National Standard for Permanence of Paper for Printed Library Materials Z39.48 1992.

For Bethany

Contents

Preface

This project began with a simple set of questions. First, why don't the lands managed by the Bureau of Land Management have a name? Or rather, why didn't they have a name until December 2008, when Interior Secretary Dirk Kempthorne designated them as the "National System of Public Lands"? Throughout this project I refer to them as "the public lands" because this is the title that Congress uses in the BLM's broadest statutory authority, but Congress does not use this as a proper name. Second, why is the Bureau of Land Management so different from the U.S. Forest Service when the two agencies have virtually identical missions in their primary authorizing legislation? Third, why was the federal land agency that manages the largest number of acres also the weakest agency politically during the twentieth century?[1]

To answer these questions, I initially set out to locate a definitive, or at least moderately comprehensive, history of the BLM and was surprised to find very few book-length treatments of the agency as a whole.[2] It was only as I pieced together the agency's complex and fascinating story that I began to understand the dearth of historical literature on the BLM compared to the National Park Service and the U.S. Forest Service. First, the BLM's history is bound more closely than the other agencies to the broader narratives of the American West: western settlement and the closing of the frontier, western sectionalism, and the struggle over federal versus state or private control of the original public domain. Second, the BLM has always been a highly decentralized and fragmented agency, so its story is the sum of many independent, overlapping, and conflicting resource programs such as those covering minerals, forests, and above all, range.[3]

Faced with the complexity of the BLM's history, I relinquished my initial impulse to identify a single narrative thread that holds the agency's story together. Perhaps more deeply, I relinquished the search for a teleological account of the BLM and the public lands. The BLM's story may have looked as though it had a clear trajectory in the 1960s, when it became clear that the public lands would remain in permanent federal ownership and the great public lands historians such as

Paul Gates and Vernon Carstensen emphasized the triumph of public ownership. By the end of the twentieth century, however, political and ecological crises such as the Sagebrush Rebellion and the Northwest Forest Plan made it difficult to see public ownership itself as a triumph. Without a central narrative thread, I chose to follow the many narratives that rise and fall throughout the BLM's story in search of some kind of unity.

One of these threads is the basic question of public and private property rights. Ranchers in particular have argued that they hold a common-law right to use the public lands range based both on the long history of public lands grazing and on the investments that they have made in their grazing allotments. The courts have consistently rejected these claims, yet with the protection offered by western members of Congress, grazing privileges have looked like and in many ways functioned like property rights for almost a century.

Another thread that runs through the agency's history is the contentious issue of federalism. Constitutionally, the federal government holds authority to regulate federal lands as both a proprietor and a sovereign, and given the concentration of federally owned land in the West, this authority has made the federal government a de facto land-use planner for the region. The federal government has attempted to ease tensions with western states by giving them payments in lieu of property taxes and by showing deference to state governments in administrative decision making. Still, tension between the federal government and state governments has flared repeatedly over the last century. The Sagebrush Rebellion of the late 1970s and early 1980s—discussed in chapter six—is but one example.

Still another thread is the rise of environmental values and management goals in the 1960s and the evolution of those values during the second half of the twentieth century. All federal land and resource agencies have adopted new environmental values and management goals, but the BLM's initial response lagged behind those of the Forest Service, National Park Service, and U.S. Fish and Wildlife Service, in large part because it did not have an environmental constituency to support its work.[4]

In tracing these and other threads through the BLM's history, I began to see that perhaps *ambiguity*—political, social, and economic—is itself a central narrative thread that holds the story together. The very questions that prompted this project suggest as much, for the BLM is an agency of limited political power that manages a collection of nameless lands in the American West. There have been moments of consensus—admittedly fleeting—over the purpose and meaning of national forests and national parks, but there has never been any consensus over the *federal* purpose of public lands managed by the BLM. This has had an enormous impact on the BLM, and for the last sixty years it has been an agency in search of a mission.

During the BLM's first two decades, the level of ambiguity in its mission set it apart from other federal land agencies. The U.S. Forest Service, for example, still enjoyed considerable autonomy, professionalism, and esprit de corps during these decades, and conservationists often measured the BLM by Forest Service standards. However, from the early 1970s through the end of the twentieth century, the differences between the BLM and the Forest Service faded considerably. The shift came in part because the BLM became more professional and independent—that is, more like the Forest Service—but the deeper reason that the agencies are more similar today is that the Forest Service lost much of its autonomy, professional homogeneity, and clarity of purpose.

By the beginning of the twenty-first century, the main thrust of federal land and resource conservation had little to do with heroic, professional, and autonomous federal agencies speaking for the public good, which is the model that the Forest Service pursued for most of its history. Federal land and resource agencies—floating on a sea of litigation, financially handicapped in congressional appropriations, and beset by urban and exurban expansion in public lands states such as Nevada, Arizona, and Utah—could no longer aspire to professional independence. Instead, planning and management processes had become increasingly cross-jurisdictional, collaborative, site-specific, and court mediated. As odd as it may sound, the BLM's chronic struggle for clarity of purpose had in many ways prepared it for the new climate of federal land management, whereas this same climate created nothing less than an institutional crisis for the U.S. Forest Service.

As much as federal agencies, environmentalists, industry, state and local governments, and others may lament the political complexity of federal land and resource issues, they agree that there is no escape to the past. Most understand that no federal agency, environmental group, resource industry group, or state government will be able to control federal land and resource decisions in any stable sense. There will be more give-and-take in twenty-first-century resource battles, if for no other reason than the fact that the federal land and resource debate is more crowded than ever before.

It is for this reason that the BLM's story is so timely. The BLM has more experience dealing with an ambiguous mission and hostile clientele than any other federal agency; it is the underdog of federal land agencies.[5] The BLM's story provides, I think, a cautionary tale to anyone who is still searching for a "final solution" to federal land and resource conflicts. No executive reorganization or congressional statute will ever be able to wipe the federal land and resource slate clean and rebuild it from the ground up. Solutions to the inefficiencies, the hostilities, and the environmental dilemmas of federal land and resource issues will always be incremental, contextual, and specific. Indeed, while new policies and management strategies may deal effectively with particular political and ecological problems, they cannot eliminate the underlying dynamism that leads constantly to new problems and new challenges.

The BLM's story serves as a reminder that federal land management can improve, but it also serves as a reminder that the very criteria by which improvement is judged change significantly over time. The story that follows is an account of the BLM's search for a clear mission and identity in this dynamic political environment; it is also, therefore, the story of Americans searching for consensus or at least of some Americans searching for hegemony over the definition of public lands conservation and protection.

Acknowledgments

My interest in the Bureau of Land Management is rooted in a variety of experiences with federal lands in the American West. I therefore owe an enormous debt of gratitude to those who made those experiences possible: to my parents, who first took me to national parks; to Jack Lewis with the Rio Grande National Forest, who supervised me as a seasonal forestry technician during the summers of 1996 and 1997; to Dave Willis, who taught me much of what I know about the practical politics of wilderness conservation; and to my wife, Bethany, who walked with me over many miles of federal lands during thru-hikes of the Colorado Trail and the Pacific Crest Trail.

I owe an equal debt of gratitude to the faculty at Cornell University, who guided me through the research on which much of this book rests. I am particularly grateful to Richard Baer, Theodore Lowi, Richard Booth, and to Jim Tantillo. I am also grateful for the financial support provided by the Department of Natural Resources, the Cornell Science Inquiry Partnership, and the H. B. Earhart Foundation.

The book in its present form was made possible by the time and financial support I enjoyed as a Lilly Postdoctoral Fellow at Valparaiso University from 2006 to 2008. I am grateful to the Lilly Fellows Program and to my postdoctoral mentor, Andrew Murphy, who saw the book through several drafts.

The book rests substantially on archival sources from ten different archives or special collections, and I am grateful to all of the archivists who assisted in my research. I am especially grateful to James Muhn, a retired BLM land law historian and coauthor of *Opportunity and Challenge: The Story of BLM*. He played a significant role in getting this book off the ground, and I have drawn extensively on the unofficial BLM archive he compiled at the BLM Library.

Throughout the research and writing process, I have been astonished by the generosity of BLM employees and retirees, who have given freely of their time and knowledge. There are too many individuals to name, so I offer my thanks to the Public Lands Foundation, an organization of BLM retirees dedicated to public lands protection, and to the staff of the BLM's National Operations Center in Denver, CO, and the National Training Center in Phoenix, AZ. Stewards of a vast national heritage, these individuals work tirelessly to find the illusive balance between public lands use and protection.

Abbreviations Used in the Text

ACEC	area of critical environmental concern
AMP	Allotment Management Plan
ANWR	Arctic National Wildlife Refuge
AUM	animal unit month
BLM	Bureau of Land Management
CMUA	Classification and Multiple Use Act (of 1964)
CEQ	Council on Environmental Quality
EIS	environmental impact statement
EMARS I	Energy Minerals Allocation Recommendation System (plan 1)
EMARS II	Energy Minerals Allocation Recommendation System (plan 2)
EPCA	Energy Policy and Conservation Act
ESA	Endangered Species Act (of 1973)
FLPMA	Federal Land Policy and Management Act (of 1976)
FWS	(U.S.) Fish and Wildlife Service
FY	fiscal year
GAO	General Accounting Office
MFP	Management Framework Plan
MMS	Minerals Management Service
MUSY	Multiple Use Sustained Yield Act (of 1960); multiple use, sustained yield
NEPA	National Environmental Policy Act (of 1969)
NEPDG	National Energy Policy Development Group
NLCS	National Landscape Conservation System
NPR	National Partnership for Reinventing Government
OCLA	Outer Continental Lands Act (of 1953)
OCS	Outer Continental Shelf
PLAA	Public Land Administration Act (of 1960)
PLLRC	Public Land Law Review Commission
PLLRCA	Public Land Law Review Commission Act (of 1964)

PLSA   Public Land Sales Act (of 1964)
PPBS   (the Bureau of Budget's) Planning, Programming, Budget System
PRIA   Public Rangelands Improvement Act
RCA   Resource Conservation Area
RMP   Resource Management Plan
SMCRA   Surface Mining Control and Reclamation Act (of 1977)
TGA   Taylor Grazing Act (of 1934)

1

Enduring Tensions of
Public Lands Management

Next to the federal government as a whole, the Bureau of Land Management (BLM) is the nation's largest landlord. President Harry S. Truman created the agency in 1946 by merging the Department of the Interior's General Land Office (1812–1946) and the U.S. Grazing Service (1934–1946), initially giving the BLM responsibility for over 400 million acres of public domain lands—usually called the public lands. Today, the BLM still manages 256 million acres (Figure 1.1) and is responsible for the federal government's 700 million acres of subsurface mineral estate.[1]

The BLM is also a uniquely western land agency. The public lands are located almost exclusively in eleven western states and Alaska, where the BLM manages 23 percent of the surface land and 58 percent of the subsurface mineral estate. In some western states the BLM is a majority land or mineral estate manager (see Appendix A: Public Lands by State). In Nevada, for example, the BLM manages 68 percent of the state's surface land and 84 percent of the subsurface mineral estate (Figure 1.2).[2] Furthermore, unlike the fairly well defined national forest and park units, the public lands are scattered and intermingled with state and private lands, and in some areas the BLM manages every other square mile of land or small isolated tracts. As a result, the BLM is an important and hotly contested agency in the American West, but it is still virtually unknown in the East.

The BLM is a multiple-use agency, mandated to protect the public lands while encouraging natural resource development and recreational use.[3] Its core resource programs are grazing, mining, and logging, which generate millions of dollars for the U.S. Treasury and western economies, but tens of millions of people also recreate on the public lands each year, especially on the national monuments, national conservation areas, wilderness areas, wild and scenic rivers, and national scenic trails that make up 17 percent (43 million acres) of the public lands. The

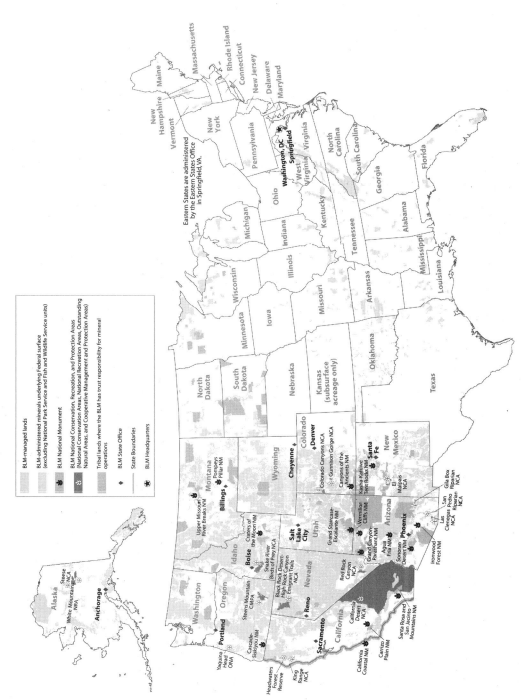

Figure 1.1. Public lands managed by the Bureau of Land Management, courtesy of the Bureau of Land Management.

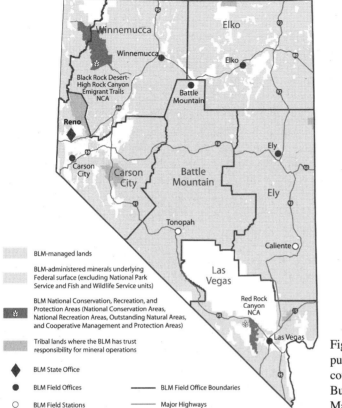

Figure 1.2. Nevada public lands, courtesy of the Bureau of Land Management.

BLM also manages millions of acres in areas of critical environmental concern (ACECs), herd management areas for wild horses and burros, national natural landmarks, and so on.[4] In fulfilling these diverse and often conflicting responsibilities, the BLM has the smallest number of dollars and staff per acre of the four primary federal land agencies. In this sense, at least, the BLM is the true underdog of federal agencies.[5]

The BLM's manifold and conflicting responsibilities evolved over time, and they reflect rich and important aspects of American history. Whereas the young Forest Service represented the values of the conservation movement and the young National Park Service represented the values of the preservation movement, the young BLM represented the values of the livestock and mining industries and of the western states in which the public lands are located. More than any other federal land agency, then, the BLM's history reflects the changing regional values and relationships of the West. Indeed, environmental goals and values were slower to take root in public lands policy and management compared to the national parks, national forests, and national wildlife refuges not only because of opposition from resource development industries, but also because the agency lacked any kind of supportive national constituency during the twentieth century.[6]

Two sets of questions have dominated BLM history: questions about the purposes and goals of public lands administration and questions about the decision-making processes that govern the public lands. Questions of purpose include the most basic question of public lands ownership and management: should the federal government retain ownership of the public lands, including isolated 40-acre plots surrounded by state or private lands? And if these lands are retained in federal ownership, to what end should they be managed? Questions about the BLM's decision-making processes include the most basic questions of democratic representation and decision-making power: who should have the most influence in public lands decision making? Should ranchers, who have a direct economic stake in the public lands, hold sway over tourists from the East Coast? Should the western states hold sway over midwestern states? Should the BLM privilege the practical, local knowledge of public lands users over "scientific data" and professional opinions? Although the specific articulation of these questions has varied throughout BLM history, they have remained fundamental points of conflict and debate.

The two sets of questions are obviously intertwined; those who control the decision-making process determine the purposes or goals of public lands administration. Nevertheless, focusing only on the purposes of public lands administration flattens analysis of public lands politics. Struggles over decision-making power and procedures are important in their own right because they rest upon distinct claims to social and political justice and raise fundamental questions about the appropriate place for democratic representation in administrative decision making.[7]

THE PURPOSE OF PUBLIC LANDS OWNERSHIP AND ADMINISTRATION

Why should the federal government own almost one-third of the United States, and to what end should the public lands be used? Answers to these questions have varied as much as the federal lands themselves. Most federal land agencies can point back to the original congressional statutes or presidential proclamations that reserved their lands and reinterpret them in light of current conflicts. For the BLM, however, these questions of ownership and purpose are more difficult to answer, because the public lands were not permanently reserved until 1976, exactly thirty years after the agency's formation.[8]

The federal government's ambivalence placed the public lands in a curious position, particularly in the first half of the twentieth century: the federal government held clear legal title to the public lands and clear constitutional authority to regulate their use for the public good, yet Congress chose to exercise that authority in very limited ways, essentially treating these lands like an open commons for ranchers, miners, and loggers.[9]

The ambiguous character of the public lands received its clearest articulation during the Hoover Administration (1929–1933), which tried to resolve questions of public lands ownership and purpose permanently. At this point, Congress had not expressed any clear interest in permanent federal ownership, yet experience had shown that the federal government would never be able to sell or give away the remaining public lands under existing land disposal laws. President Herbert Hoover recommended that Congress settle the matter by granting the remaining unreserved public lands in the American West, roughly 235 million acres, to the states in which they were located.[10] In August 1929, he wrote to western governors to promote the idea: the remaining public lands "bring no revenue to the federal government. The federal government is incapable of adequate administration of matters which require so large a matter of local understanding. . . . Therefore, for the best interest of the people as a whole, and people of the western states and the small farmers and stockmen by whom they are primarily used, they should be managed and the policies for their use determined by the state governments."[11] In other words, President Hoover described federal ownership of these particular lands as fundamentally illegitimate.[12]

President Hoover then established the Committee on the Conservation and Administration of the Public Domain in 1930—known as the Garfield Committee after its chair, the former interior secretary James R. Garfield—to conduct a full review of public lands policies and consider his land grant proposal.[13] In light of public lands deterioration, particularly from overgrazing, the committee argued that "all portions of the unreserved and unappropriated public domain should be placed under responsible administration or regulation for the conservation and beneficial use of its resources," and accomplishing this would require dividing the public lands into three distinct categories of ownership and administration.[14] First, the federal government should reserve and manage "areas important for national defense, reclamation purposes, reservoir sites, national forests, national parks, national monuments, and migratory-bird refuges," that is, areas in which the federal government had a clear national interest.[15] Second, the remaining unreserved public lands that were valuable chiefly for grazing should be given to the states. Third, assuming that some states would refuse to accept these lands, the president should designate the unreserved public lands as a national range to be managed like the national forest rangelands.[16]

The choice was clear: transfer ownership of the public lands to the states, which would presumably take a proprietary and regulatory interest in their management, or take responsibility for range regulation. If federal management proved necessary, the committee recommended a system of administration closely resembling that of the national forests, namely discrete areas of national rangeland managed for a common purpose.[17] Yet even in recommending regulatory management, the commission continued to express a certain ambivalence about the federal interest in the public lands. Despite the fact that the U.S. Forest Service had an active and moderately successful range management program, the commission did not recommend Forest Service administration. It reported that the public rangelands needed a federal agency made up of "men who are intimately familiar with the conditions of the ranges, wisely established customs of stockmen, the needs of contiguous areas, and the movement of herds and flocks from summer and winter ranges, regardless of political or topographic divisions."[18] In other words, the committee seems to have implied, they require an agency more sympathetic to the livestock industry than the Forest Service.

The main political hurdle in the president's and committee's plan was that it offered only the surface lands to the states and retained all federal, subsurface mineral rights. The message seems to have been that minerals served the national interest because they could generate substantial revenue to the U.S. Treasury. Since the public lands range generated no revenue to the U.S. Treasury but generated income for private ranchers, the committee and the president viewed these rangelands as a private, agricultural matter best administered by the state and local governments.[19]

It is important to emphasize that President Hoover and the Garfield Committee were not taking a radical, states' rights position in the matter, as their insistence on retaining subsurface mineral rights indicates. When Garfield was challenged during a congressional hearing as to the legitimacy of federal ownership, he responded, "the Federal Government owns so many acres of land. It can do with it as Congress sees fit. . . . We are not willing to let you have the subsoil, because we feel we can develop that subsoil and make enough money out of it to pay some of our debts, or do *whatever we want*."[20] And by the 1930s, the courts had provided substantial support for Garfield's position. As the Supreme Court explained in *Camfield v. United States* (1897)[21] and again in *Light v. United States* (1911), "The Government has with respect to its own land the rights of an ordinary proprietor to maintain its possession and prosecute trespassers. It may deal with such lands precisely as an ordinary individual may deal with his farming property. It may sell or withhold them from sale."[22]

The president's and the committee's proposals encountered strong opposition at two levels. Federal bureaucrats and some eastern congressmen opposed the wholesale grant of land, primarily because they feared that it would include some of the reserved lands in the national forest system.[23] The strongest opposition, though, came from the states themselves. State representatives argued that the federal government surveyed the original federal estate, reserved everything of value, and offered only scraps to the states. They were angered especially by the recommendation that the federal government transfer ownership of the surface land but retain the subsurface mineral rights. Senator William Borah of Idaho complained that the land grant was "like handing [the states] an orange with the juice sucked out of it."[24] The governor of Utah explained, "The States already own . . . millions of acres of this same kind of land, which they can neither sell nor lease, and which is yielding no income. Why should they want more of this precious heritage of desert?"[25] What the western states did want, the governor went on to explain, was federal range rehabilitation: "our ranges are being very seriously depleted and deteriorated, and they have got to be built up, and built up right away, or else they will be beyond repair."[26]

Thus, rather than resolving the public lands questions once and for all, President Hoover's failed proposal highlighted the intractable policy dilemma before Congress. The president had publicly insisted that federal ownership of the public lands did not serve any national interest, yet the commission he appointed insisted that the federal government had a custodial duty to regulate public lands use for their long-term conservation. In other words, Congress was asked to fashion a system of public lands regulation without any clear national purpose, which, to a considerable extent, is what Congress did.

The federal government's ambivalence was codified when Congress and western ranchers finally passed the Taylor Grazing Act of 1934 (TGA), which gave the interior secretary two mandates: stabilize the western livestock industry *and* improve range conditions.[27] To carry out the new responsibilities, the interior secretary first created a Division of Grazing within the General Land Office (1934–1939) and later created an independent agency, the U.S. Grazing Service (1939–1946). It is possible to imagine ways in which the TGA's two mandates might have complemented one another, and the early Division of Grazing certainly acted as if stabilizing the livestock industry would lead directly to range improvement. As time went on, however, the Division of Grazing and then the U.S. Grazing Service clearly experienced the two mandates as conflicting responsibilities. Stabilizing the livestock industry generally meant giving public lands ranchers greater security in their grazing privileges, whereas improving the range conditions, in many cases, required significant cuts in grazing levels. Where these mandates conflicted, stabilizing the livestock industry generally won out over range improvement, and this pattern continued unchecked during the BLM's first decade of operations.

Beginning in the 1960s, however, the BLM began to address noncommodity or amenity values, largely in response to the rise of public lands recreation, and by the 1970s, new environmental laws and pressure from environmental groups were forcing the BLM to broaden this focus to more comprehensive environmental protection.[28] The National Environmental Policy Act of 1969 (NEPA) forced the BLM to evaluate the environmental impacts of its decisions; the Wild and Free Roaming Horse and Burro Act of 1971 forced the BLM to preserve herds of wild horses and burros on the public lands; and the Endangered Species Act of 1973 (ESA) forced the agency to modify its management to protect many other plants and animals. These laws also began to change the BLM's culture by permitting— or in some cases forcing—the agency to hire new staff for recreation, wildlife, cultural resources, and planning.[29] Finally, in 1976, Congress passed new authorizing legislation for the BLM, which at least rhetorically placed environmental protection mandates on a par with resource development mandates.[30] Public lands politics since 1976 has been a struggle to balance these "equal" mandates.[31]

Today, some sixty years after the BLM's formation, questions of purpose remain as divisive as ever. The question of ownership has been resolved for the most part, yet the meaning of federal ownership—that is the rights, privileges, and responsibilities associated with ownership—are far from settled. Some western congressmen continue to argue that since the public lands are a uniquely western phenomenon, they should be managed primarily to benefit the economies of western states in which they are located through natural resource development. Others insist that the public lands should be managed primarily for ecosystem preservation, even if this means drastic cuts in resource outputs. Still others argue that the public lands belong to all Americans and must therefore serve the full diversity of public demands.

DECISION-MAKING PROCESSES

Who makes public lands decisions? As noted above, this question is closely related to questions about the purposes of public lands administration, because those who make public lands decisions have the greatest influence over the purposes of public lands administration. Debate on this second set of questions has taken many forms in the BLM's history—state/private vs. federal control, congressional vs. executive control, patronage vs. regulation, self-regulation or "home rule" vs. professional scientific management—but it can generally be understood as a conflict between decentralized and centralized systems of decision making. Advocates of decentralized decision making insist that BLM field managers and public lands users need freedom to respond to local land and resource issues. Advocates of centralized decision making, or at least systematic decision making and centralized accountability, argue that centralized decision making and accountability are necessary to protect the national interest.

By the time the BLM was formed in 1946, the public lands had a long history of self-regulation by ranchers and miners. Farrington Carpenter, the first director of the Division of Grazing in 1934, developed what he called a "split control system." Working with a skeleton budget and staff, Carpenter set up advisory boards made up of grazing permit holders, to which he deferred on many day-to-day management questions. He held legal authority, yet for practical and principled reasons he granted decision-making power largely to the ranchers themselves.[32]

Carpenter's experiment highlighted the federal government's lack of proprietary interest in the public lands, and it fit well into the patterns of congressional patronage. The public lands range was something that western congressmen, through the Taylor Grazing Act and ongoing oversight, could disaggregate and distribute as tangible benefits to particular clientele. It is therefore not surprising that Carpenter's vision of self-regulation by grazing advisory boards received strong support from western congressmen like Senator Pat McCarran (D-NV) and Representative William Barrett (R-WY), who fought to build and maintain the boards' power.

Oddly enough, Interior Secretary Harold Ickes initially supported Carpenter's system of self-regulation for grazing permit holders, despite the fact that it flew in the face of his ideological commitments to federal leadership and professional management.[33] As time passed, however, Ickes routinely chastised Carpenter for giving grazing permittees too much power and for failing to take control of public lands grazing: "you have not developed sufficient personnel even to protect the Government's interest let alone develop an adequate range conservation program."[34] Ickes also fought with McCarran and Barrett over funding, staffing, and the role of the grazing advisory boards, arguing that sanctioning the boards violated principles of sound administration, because it meant "control by beneficiaries."[35] In other words, Ickes fought to take decision-making power away from grazing permittees, and in a very real sense from Congress, and vest it in the Department of the Interior and the U.S. Grazing Service.

It is not necessarily clear that Ickes saw the public lands as particularly valuable or important, but as a conservation reformer, he clearly assumed that the fact of federal ownership implied a proprietary interest in the public lands and a responsibility to place them under professional administration. Ickes's opposition to the split control system that the Taylor Grazing Act and Farrington Carpenter established appears in a number of important debates, but it is perhaps most clear in his bid to create a Department of Conservation. In Secretary Ickes's vision of conservation, a comprehensive American land policy was possible, but it required the coordinating oversight of a single department and a single secretary who could rationally balance competing demands on federal lands and natural resources.[36]

In 1938 Ickes announced an ambitious proposal for a new Department of Conservation.[37] The new department, Ickes argued, would have the necessary authority to ensure both complete conservation, that is regulated use, and complete development of the nation's vast resource base.[38] The United States was at a turning point in its land policy, he declared: "The former plan of disposing of resources to anyone who would take them has proven unwise in many respects and is being abandoned."[39] Since Congress had not yet provided comprehensive statutes to guide agencies in the new direction of conservation, "there should be close association and cooperation between all the principal agencies involved in the formulation of public land policies and in the administration of public land use. The objective should be a balanced administration of the resources so that each can be given its proper place."[40] In other words, centralizing all federal land and resource administration in a single department—under a single secretary—could fill in the gaps left by disjointed congressional statutes and sporadic congressional leadership.[41] Although Secretary Ickes was driven in part by his ambition to control the

U.S. Forest Service, the public lands were a central issue in his argument. It was in the case of the public lands, most clearly, where the old disposal policies were slowly coming to an end but where the future was still largely uncertain.

Congress, however, was not prepared to relinquish its patronage power and its control over the public lands. From 1941 until 1947, Senator McCarran of Nevada held hearings on the administration of the public lands in order to reinforce the system of self-regulation that ranchers enjoyed, and in 1947, Representative Barrett held what amounted to a continuation of those hearings.[42] Indeed, McCarran, Barrett, and other western congressmen staunchly supported self-regulation by ranchers, and they rebuffed all attempts to centralize and professionalize range management. Thus, when President Truman created the BLM in 1946, the agency's leaders and field managers had clear legal authority but no political power to regulate grazing privileges and use without the support of grazing permittees.

Even though western congressmen and the BLM's commercial clientele continued to fight for decentralized management, two different centralizing pressures, one internal and one external to the agency, punctuated the BLM's history. The first pressure came from leaders in the executive branch who wanted to integrate and coordinate the agency's planning and management activities. These leaders were steeped in the Progressive Era and New Deal conservation tradition that emphasized shielding public lands decision making from political pressure. They pressed for more rational, scientific planning and management programs that would give the agency greater control over its commercial clientele. Although BLM field managers did not necessarily admire the U.S. Forest Service, agency leaders were laboring under its shadow and reaching for the kind of professional autonomy and control that it enjoyed from its formation in 1905 until at least the early 1970s. BLM leaders argued, far less successfully than the Forest Service, that they needed greater professional autonomy and discretion in order to achieve the best mix of resource uses on the ground.[43]

The second centralizing pressure came from various interest groups. Commercial land users had long demanded decentralized management, because historically this had favored liberal resource patronage. Conservation and environmental groups, on the other hand, generally advocated more centralized, professional management, arguing that this would favor the public interest over private economic interests.[44] This pattern grew out of circumstances, particularly until the 1970s, in which the relevant conservation and environmental groups represented interests that were largely eastern and/or urban. These groups did not have a strong presence near BLM field offices, where important decisions were made. Consequently, they demanded stronger decision-making accountability and coordination in Washington, where they could more easily influence the process. Furthermore, they demanded greater reliance on scientific data and analysis conducted by federal professionals, arguing that this would shield decision making from local commercial interests.[45]

As the American West became more densely populated, more urbanized, and less dependent upon resource development, however, western cities and communities frequently called for stronger environmental protection.[46] Furthermore, conflicts over competing commercial resource uses, particularly grazing and mining, led to new, though limited, alliances between ranchers and environmentalists.[47] Particularly in cases where policy debate in Washington was gridlocked, local and regional environmental organizations called for decentralized control. They also took the initiative to seek private and third-party agreements with public lands ranchers, and they collaborated with the BLM on the management of certain sensitive public lands areas. At times, local environmental chapters even broke ranks with their national organizations in an effort to reach compromises with commodity interests over land and resource use. It would seem, then, that commodity and environmental interests each advocated local control when they believed they have greater influence at the local level.[48]

As the BLM comes to terms with the new political dynamics of the West, the agency's culture of collaborative decision making and its resistance to centralized control are both a weakness and a strength. They are a weakness in that the BLM still struggles to assert itself over its clientele on a number of key conservation issues; they are a strength in that the BLM has had considerable practice being a mediator rather than a dictator in public lands decision making.[49]

At the beginning of the twenty-first century, the two basic sets of questions about the purposes and decision-making process that govern the public lands still animate public lands politics, and they still shape the BLM's mission and culture. The BLM's core mission is still open to conflicting internal and external interpretations, and public lands management promises to be fragmented along geographic and resource program lines well into the future. Calls today for ecosystem management and other comprehensive approaches to land management cannot overcome the precedents found in public lands history to provide a unified, cohesive, and comprehensive system of public lands management. Lacking a clear purpose and historical trajectory, the BLM's history confirms what Charles Lindblom argued in 1959, namely that federal land and resource management rest upon "The Science of Muddling Through."[50]

PRIMARY PERIODS IN BLM HISTORY

While the BLM has wrestled continuously with the basic questions of purpose and process, its history can be divided into three main periods based on changes in the patterns of public lands politics. The first period extends from the agency's formation in 1946 to the end of the 1960s. During this period, public lands politics were dominated by an iron triangle made up of the livestock industry, congressional committees, and the BLM, and this triangle maintained a status quo in which resource development occurred under minimal federal supervision and control.[51] During this period, many BLM leaders and field managers fought to exert more professional, regulatory control over public lands policy and management, which put them at odds not only with ranchers but also with the prevailing patterns of congressional patronage. Many of these leaders looked to the U.S. Forest Service model of agency-led, professional management.[52]

The second major period in BLM history may be dated more or less from January 1, 1970, to January 20, 1981—that is, from the day that President Nixon signed the National Environmental Policy Act (NEPA) into law to President Ronald Reagan's inauguration. NEPA marked the entrance of both environmental groups and the courts into public lands politics. Following NEPA, environmental groups became important voices for public lands regulation and protection, and the BLM became a mediator between two loosely knit armies of competing interest groups: resource developers and environmentalists. Political scientist Hugh Heclo labeled the new political forces issue-networks, by which he means groups of activists and experts organized around a particular issue through information exchange. Policy scholars Paul Sabatier and Hank Jenkins-Smith took Heclo's work further in developing the advocacy coalition framework, in which they trace policy change over time back to the issue- and information-based political coalitions that influence decision makers.[53] The new dynamics of interest-group politics are also what political philosopher Mark Sagoff recently called a four-sided triangle, made up of Congress, the BLM, the livestock and mining industries, and environmentalists.[54]

The third period in BLM history, from President Reagan's inauguration through the present, has been largely a period of gridlock over the BLM's multiple-use mission. Although each presidential administration, and each Congress, has pushed the BLM in a particular direction, they have been sufficiently polarized so as to negate one another's efforts. This political pendulum has taken a toll on the BLM, but it has also encouraged more grassroots collaboration and negotiations in order to break the national gridlock, in many ways rejuvenating civic engagement in the public lands debate.[55]

What is more, other federal land agencies, especially the U.S. Forest Service, are increasingly facing the same political challenges and identity crises as the BLM. In this respect, the BLM's history is more important and instructive for the Forest Service today than it has ever been, because the Forest Service must learn to function without a clear mission or supportive national constituencies.[56] The political debates over federal lands and resources have simply become too crowded and polarized to support consensus management strategies on the national level.

The chapters that follow are organized around significant periods in the BLM's history that involve new legislation, new administrative initiatives and reorganizations, new participants in public lands debate, and new presidential agendas. Priority is given to the events that have shaped the BLM's overall mission, organization, and culture and have shaped the larger patterns of public lands politics. These events highlight the durability that questions of purpose and process have had in all three main periods of BLM history, explaining why the BLM's search for a mission and a supportive constituency has continued for more than half a century.

2

Born into Controversy

The Bureau of Land Management (BLM) was formed on July 16, 1946, by Reorganization Plan No. 3.[1] Created by merging the General Land Office (GLO) and the U.S. Grazing Service (Grazing Service), the new agency was responsible for more land than any other federal agency, including 190 million acres in the western United States, 330 million acres in Alaska Territory, and additional subsurface mineral estate.[2] The BLM inherited diverse and conflicting responsibilities for range and forest conservation, wildlife conservation, food and fiber production, and land and mineral disposal. Some of these responsibilities required active management, while others were purely clerical in nature, so it was much easier to integrate the new agency on paper than in practice.

Despite the BLM's vast landholdings and far-reaching responsibilities, Congress,[3] public lands users, and the press virtually ignored the agency's formation. Congress dedicated no public hearings specifically to the merger, and trade magazines like *American Cattle Producer* and *National Wool Grower* made almost no mention of the new agency in 1946. Even later public lands literature has remained largely silent about details of the BLM's formation.

The main reason that the BLM's formation drew so little attention is that it had virtually no immediate effect on the basic policies, political relationships, or missions of its two predecessors.[4] Nevertheless, the BLM merger is important historically because it forced Congress and the nation to deal with the public lands in a single political arena rather than separating the grazing districts from the rest of the public lands.[5] The merger also heightened the tension between Congress and the executive branch over decision-making authority and power. Western congressmen continued to defend the patterns of congressional patronage, while the executive branch emphasized the need for administrative discretion and regulation so that dispassionate public servants could coordinate land and resource use in a system of rational, scientific management.[6]

Amidst the agency's conflicting responsibilities and the congressional/executive stalemate, the story of the BLM's early years is primarily one of survival.[7] Close examination of the BLM's formation illuminates some of the deepest problems of purpose and decision-making process that have haunted the agency for more than sixty years, and it explains why later attempts to either privatize the public lands or apply the Forest Service model of professional administration to public lands management both failed.

THE CALL FOR REORGANIZATION

The initial push for reorganization appears to have come from Clarence Forsling, the Grazing Service director from 1944 to 1946. Forsling set out in 1944 to reform range management in a way that reflected his prior training in the Forest Service: the BLM was to become a corps of technical experts regulating resource use according to its professional judgment. Compared to forestry, though, range management had few professional resources to draw upon, since in the early 1940s range management was still an enterprise that rested on practical rather than professional experience. For example, the U.S. Grazing Service was still staffed primarily by ranchers, since there were few university graduates with degrees in range science. As a result, Forsling was not only challenging stockmen and western congressmen with his proposed reforms, he was challenging the Grazing Service's staff and culture as well.[8]

To increase the Grazing Service's professional control, Forsling directed his staff to conduct new range surveys to replace the initial estimates made by ranchers on the grazing advisory boards; he advocated reductions in livestock numbers where range condition was poor; and he advocated increases in grazing fees to reflect something closer to the market value of the forage sold.[9] If Forsling had still been working for the Forest Service, none of these initiatives would have seemed radical, but in the Grazing Service context of "home rule" by permit holders, Forsling's initiatives ignited a storm of controversy. He was pushing the Grazing Service to act as a proprietor of the grazing districts, or at least as the primary representative of the federal government's proprietary interests, whereas ranchers still believed that they *owned* their grazing privileges and that the U.S. Grazing Service therefore ought to act as a trustee on behalf of livestock interests.[10]

Forsling argued that he was following the true spirit and intention of the Taylor Grazing Act of 1934, which he believed authorized far more than the system of self-regulation his predecessors had developed. Quoting directly from the act, Forsling reminded the powerful Senate Committee on Public Lands that under the TGA the interior secretary held authority "to make such rules and regulations and establish such service, enter into such cooperative agreements, and do any and all things necessary to . . . insure the objects of such grazing districts, namely, to regulate their occupancy and use, to preserve the land and its resources from destruction or unnecessary injury, to provide for the orderly use, improvement, and development of the range."[11] Essentially, Forsling argued that the TGA asserted the federal government's unrestricted sovereign and proprietary interests in the public lands range, and that it gave the Grazing Service, by delegation from the interior secretary, authority to interpret and defend those interests as it saw fit. Forsling's lecture clearly challenged many western congressmen, who argued that ranchers held a common-law right to the range that preceded and therefore trumped the TGA.[12]

As Forsling fought to professionalize the Grazing Service in the face of staunch opposition from both stockmen and western congressmen, he became increasingly frustrated not only with external political opposition but also with his limiting administrative boundaries, which he argued exacerbated the problems with public lands range management. When the U.S. Grazing Service was created as an independent agency in 1939, it was given responsibility for all grazing districts established and administered under the Taylor Grazing Act. But section 15 of the TGA permitted the interior secretary to lease public lands range that lay outside of the grazing districts, and responsibility for section 15 remained in the GLO.[13]

As a result of different provisions in the TGA as well as different cultures in the two agencies, administration of the grazing districts and "section 15 lands" differed dramatically. The Grazing Service issued renewable permits to ranchers, allowing them to graze a specified number of livestock within allotments of their local grazing district. The permits were tied to base property or water rights that the permittees owned and used to sustain their livestock in the off season. The Grazing Service regulated livestock grazing by establishing grazing seasons for each district and adjusting the terms of the permits in accordance with range conditions. Because the Grazing Service deferred substantially to the grazing advisory boards in the decision-making process, however, ranchers had considerable control over permit regulations. While the initial permits varied in duration, the Grazing Service planned eventually to renew all permits on ten-year terms. Whatever the term, permit renewal was almost guaranteed, allowing ranchers to treat their permits like private property and even borrow money against the value of their permits.[14]

In contrast, the GLO leased scattered tracts of rangeland located outside the grazing districts to individual ranchers. The leases, which were based on prior use of the land, were issued for only a three-year period and came with less assurance of renewal. While the leasing system offered less security and did not involve grazing advisory boards, it did have certain benefits for ranchers. Principally, it provided outright contractual leases with no ongoing oversight. As explained in one hearing: "One of the main points of section 15 [of the TGA] is . . . that it enables the stockman to use [public rangeland] as he would his own land . . . in an advantageous manner in his operations."[15] In short, the leasing system provided less long-term security but greater short-term autonomy.

Since section 15 of the TGA applied to all public lands range outside of organized grazing districts, it served as the default grazing system. Discussions over the creation of new grazing districts, therefore, represented a choice between the two systems. Even though the TGA permitted the interior secretary to establish new grazing districts with or without support from the affected stockmen, western congressmen insisted that the Grazing Service gain support from the stockmen before recommending a new grazing district. In effect, congressional oversight provided stockmen with veto power over the creation of each new grazing district, and this gave stockmen an enormous amount of leverage against the U.S. Grazing Service and Forsling's plans for regulatory reform.[16]

The issue came to a head during the 1940s in Nevada, where stockmen still grazed 19 million acres of public lands outside of the grazing districts. The Grazing Service had proposed grazing districts there in 1937, which the GLO supported, but Senator McCarran stalled the proposal in order to ensure that it would not restrict grazing operations.[17] McCarran even introduced a bill in 1945 that would have given ranchers the power to dissolve grazing districts by a majority vote, just in case Grazing Service administration inhibited their operations.[18] Given Forsling's insistence that the Nevada range needed tighter regulation and oversight, McCarran continued to oppose the formation of grazing districts throughout Forsling's tenure.

Forsling and Interior Department officials began to explore various consolidations and reorganizations in 1944 in order to standardize range management in the districts and the section 15 lands. Without standardization, Forsling argued, stockmen could play the two agencies off of one another, flaunting their political power and undermining federal range conservation.[19] Forsling recommended a limited and gradual reorganization because a complete reorganization "would undoubtedly be misunderstood and objected to in the West."[20] The primary goal would be to separate the major functions—that is both the purposes and processes—of surface resource management from the major functions of land disposal, exchange, and surveying.[21] TGA responsibilities would still be split between the GLO and the Grazing Service, but the Grazing Service would gain responsibility for all range administration and the GLO would gain responsibility for all land classification and sales associated with the TGA. Essentially, Forsling wanted to separate all regulatory responsibilities of range management from the clerical functions of land classification and disposal.

Congress created new opportunities for administrative reorganization through the Reorganization Act of 1945, under which the president could propose organizational changes in the executive branch that would become law unless both houses of Congress passed concurrent resolutions opposing a proposal.[22] President Truman signed the act in December 1945 and immediately requested reorganization proposals from each department. Secretary Ickes and Assistant Secretary Oscar Chapman initially focused on transferring the Forest Service to the Interior Department and gaining the power to create regional administrative authorities, and Forsling's reorganization request was a low priority.[23]

On January 16, Forsling wrote to Secretary Ickes reemphasizing the need for consolidation of grazing administration. Without unified administration, he argued, Senator McCarran and the livestock industry would undermine sound conservation of the public range by continuing to play the GLO and the Grazing Service against each other. Whether it was Forsling's plea for consolidation or other considerations, Secretary Ickes sent reorganization proposals to the Bureau of Budget on January 24 that included the full merger of the Grazing Service and the GLO.[24]

In justifying the BLM merger, Secretary Ickes first emphasized the benefits of increased efficiency that would come through the merger, but he also conveyed more substantive policy concerns about split administration: "If the policies which apply to public domain within grazing districts are sound, they should apply to the public domain outside grazing districts [i.e. section 15 lands], and vice versa." Unifying all TGA responsibilities in one agency, Ickes promised, would improve the Interior Department's "long-term program of husbanding one of our vital natural resources."[25]

With the BLM proposal pending, the Interior Department began preparing for the merger, but two important events handicapped the planning process. First, on February 15, 1946, Secretary Ickes resigned abruptly, and the Interior Department lost a powerful political leader. Furthermore, the GLO, the Grazing Service, and Interior officials had to spend time briefing a new interior secretary, Julius Krug, on the merger.[26]

Second, and far more important, it was at this very moment that conflict over range management exploded in Congress, eliminating whatever political power and discretion Forsling and Ickes had hoped the merger would create. Specifically, a fierce battle over grazing fees split the Congress, and the Grazing Service was caught in the crossfire. Both the House and Senate appropriations committees demanded that the BLM become a self-sustaining agency, which Secretary Ickes had promised during the TGA hearings in 1934, but the two committees recommended very different strategies for accomplishing this goal. The House Appropriations Committee demanded that the Grazing Service raise grazing fees high enough to cover operating costs; the Senate Appropriations Committee, led by McCarran, demanded that the Grazing Service cap or reduce grazing fees and reduce its staff and operating expenses commensurately. The conflict over grazing fees reached a stalemate, and the only thing the two committees could agree upon was to slash the Grazing Service's budget. The Grazing Service's reduced FY 1947 appropriations meant a personnel reduction of nearly 80 percent, so the agency was cut to a paper organization at the very moment that President Truman proposed the BLM merger.[27]

On May 16, 1946, with no reference to the Grazing Service crisis, President Truman submitted Reorganization Plan No. 3 to Congress, which included the BLM proposal. Curiously, despite the bitter battle over grazing fees, the proposal drew little attention in Congress, perhaps because it was reviewed by the House Committee on Expenditures in the Executive Departments and the Senate Judiciary Committee rather than the Appropriations or Interior and Insular Affairs committees. Furthermore, the BLM proposal was just one of many proposals in Reorganization Plan No. 3, and Congress had to accept or reject the entire plan. The House committee passed a resolution rejecting the plan, but their report and hearings made no specific objection to the BLM proposal. The Senate committee, which included McCarran, discussed the BLM proposal at greater length, but it voiced no specific objection either. After the Senate failed to vote on a concurrent resolution opposing Reorganization Plan No. 3, it became law on July 16, 1946.[28]

It is possible that Congress accepted the justification that consolidating existing "functions of the Grazing Service and the General Land Office in the Department of the Interior [would result] in improved service to the public as well as in economies and increased efficiencies,"[29] and increased economy would clearly be important given the Grazing Service's FY 1947 appropriations. It is more likely, however, that western congressmen like Senator McCarran were confident that they could control public lands policy and administration through oversight and appropriations committees no matter how range management was organized in the executive branch. After all, McCarran and other western congressmen had succeeded in keeping grazing fees low, giving ranchers a functional veto over grazing district organization, and cutting the Grazing Service appropriations so deeply that it would be unable to truly regulate or manage the grazing districts. Indeed, historian Karen Merrill argues that "McCarran saw this reorganization as a victory for western stock growers, believing it would check the growth of federal grazing management."[30]

If McCarran was satisfied with the reorganization, he didn't rest for long because Reorganization Plan No. 3 did include one provision that increased the interior secretary's discretion. The plan changed the status of twenty-five district land office managers from political appointees to civil servants, giving the interior secretary control over these appointments. Senator McCarran complained that transferring these positions to civil service status "is another evidence of the desire to reorganize and to remove, as far as possible, the participation of the Congress in the selection of officials who carry out the laws that Congress makes."[31] Early in 1947, he introduced a bill to reestablish the land office positions as political appointments and to convert the BLM director and associate director positions to political appointments as well. Although the bill failed, McCarran had sent a clear message to the Interior Department: as far as he was concerned the merger did not give the Interior Department any more power over range management and conservation. According to McCarran, the purpose of public lands administration was supporting western economies, and decisions should be made by western congressmen and their constituents rather than by professional bureaucrats.[32]

REORGANIZING WITHOUT A CLEAR MISSION

Given the abrupt departure of Secretary Ickes and the bitter range battle that impoverished the Grazing Service, it is perhaps not surprising that organizing the BLM turned out to be a slow process. Given the competing visions that Forsling and Ickes on the one hand and McCarran on the other had for the BLM, it wasn't entirely clear what the agency was organizing *for.* The Senate had made it very clear that range administration was to honor the system of self-regulation that Farrington Carpenter had established, yet from an administrative perspective, the new agency needed greater oversight, accountability, and coordination across program areas if it was to achieve any kind of integration.[33] Echoing Ickes, Secretary Krug testified: "The administration of the public lands presents not a single problem, but a series of problems . . . [and] the policy of Congress with regard to the public domain is not yet finally developed."[34] In the absence of clear statutory guidance, Krug suggested, the new BLM director and the interior secretary needed greater control over the BLM's various resource programs.

Here, McCarran once again undermined any ambitions of administrative discretion and control on the part of BLM and Interior leaders. He insisted that Forsling and Archie Ryan, the director and associate director of the Grazing Service who had sought to professionalize range management, have no top leadership roles in the BLM.[35] Instead he supported the decision to place Fred Johnson, the GLO commissioner, in charge of the new agency. Johnson was on the verge of retirement, and he represented the GLO's service rather than management orientation. Between Johnson's appointment and the FY 1947 appropriations cuts, then, the BLM's range program had virtually no staff, no leadership, and no political power. In many ways, the combined events of 1946 set the clock on range management back ten years to the early days of TGA administration.

With the BLM's range program in chaos, Secretary Krug turned to stockmen for guidance and support. In September 1946, he appointed a California businessman named Rex Nicholson to study the reorganization plan and to recommend an appropriate organizational strategy for the merger. Although Nicholson was responsible for studying the full organization of the BLM, the purview of his work was largely grazing, since this was the dominant political issue at the time, and his interlocutors were largely from the livestock industry. As Kenneth Reid from the Isaac Walton League would later complain to the department, the Nicholson report came after consultation only with "the livestock interests and their advisory boards. As a result, it is too confined in its viewpoint and shows considerable bias in a number of places."[36] Senator McCarran endorsed Nicholson warmly, promising ranchers that "if he gets a free hand you will benefit 100 per cent."[37]

Nicholson's report, "Reorganization Plan No. 3 as Proposed to J. A. Krug Secretary of the Interior," which he issued two months later, provided an interpretation of the merger that stockmen must certainly have endorsed: "The primary objects of the amalgamation are to establish a *closer, more practical working relationship between the Federal Government* and the *industries* which use the public domain, to provide a more *uniform* and *efficient* management of the federally owned lands throughout the public-land states, and to achieve a substantial reduction in the administrative costs of the joint operation." At the same time, Nicholson wrestled with the tension between having a close working relationship with the commercial public lands users and developing a uniform, "clearly defined, carefully thought-out, and well-planned operating program."[38] Industry, Nicholson explained, relies on individual initiative, resourcefulness, and entrepreneurship, whereas government requires controls over individual initiative in order to coordinate a complex bureaucratic structure. The report was not always clear as to which should prevail: individual initiative or administrative control.

Favoring individual initiative, particularly by the livestock industry, Nicholson recommended decentralizing all existing programs in the new agency, arguing that both the Grazing Service and the GLO concentrated too much of their staff and workload in Washington. He also recommended that the BLM keep grazing fees commensurate with the cost of administration, and recommended that the Branch of Range Management have a staff of 242 and an annual budget of $1,147,896—essentially the staffing and budgetary levels of the Grazing Service prior to its drastic FY 1947 appropriations cuts.[39]

At the same time, Nicholson repeatedly pleaded for a comprehensive land use policy: "A clearly defined, long-range land policy is basic to the proper administration and final disposal of the publicly owned lands throughout the United States. We strongly recommend that such a policy be established as quickly as possible."[40] Here, Nicholson was critical of the stockmen's insistence that they *owned* their grazing permits. The stockmen, he argued, misunderstood the nature of the market in which they operated. They needed to accept the fact that the government was doing voluntary business when it issued grazing permits, and that it was unrealistic to think that they were *entitled* to their grazing allotments: "You want the same sort of security in your business I want in mine but I don't have it and I don't expect to have it."[41]

On balance, the Nicholson report favored the status quo in range administration, because neither he nor the interior secretary could establish "a clearly defined long-term land policy" on his own; this was congressional territory, and Congress had already demonstrated that it could not provide such a cohesive and unified policy. Armed with the Nicholson report, Secretary Krug made decentralization the dominant theme of the BLM's reorganization plans. Since the BLM lacked any cohesive mandate, decentralization appeared to be the only way to effectively meet the agency's multiple responsibilities and the demands of its clientele. The decentralized operations were to be overseen by seven regional offices, although it wasn't clear how much authority and influence those offices would have.[42]

Even with the basic plan in place, reorganization was painfully slow. Reeling from the 1947 budget cuts, the grazing program was struggling to survive. It was in such a desperate financial situation during the fall of 1946 that the grazing advisory boards paid many of the range staff's salaries out of the revenue they received from grazing fees.[43] In the GLO, efforts to decentralize and reorganize along the regional system were blocked by an appropriations amendment preventing the movement of personnel and work from Washington to the field, most likely because McCarran was attempting to convert land office registers back to political appointments.[44]

By the end of FY 1947, frustrations with the BLM's progress had grown on all sides, and Representative Barrett began a series of hearings to give the livestock industry a chance to voice its concerns.[45] Barrett explained to BLM leaders that their primary objective was to "establish a sound working relationship with three of the major industries in the West; namely, the stock raising, petroleum, and mining industries,"[46] and he judged the agency's progress based upon the industries' satisfaction. Barrett also demanded an explanation for the slow pace of reorganization. The BLM's assistant director responded, "It is harder in my opinion to integrate . . . existing organizations than to start building a brand new one. . . . Furthermore, a program of merger and decentralization combined required [attention to] aspects of detailed administration that just cannot be done overnight."[47]

In reality, the problem was not simply the administrative detail and complexity of the merger; rather the problem was conflict over the basic purpose of public lands administration and the distribution of decision-making power between the agency and its clientele. Gordon Griswold, president of the National Advisory Council, put it this way: "The issue here . . . is that of whether the [TGA] shall be administered, as we feel the Congress intended, primarily for the benefit of the economies of the local regions concerned and in turn the national economy or whether it is to be administered instead primarily for the purpose of enlarging the powers and extent of the administrative bureaus in charge."[48] Secretary Krug countered that the livestock industry was myopic in its reading of the law and in suggesting that the struggle was between economic development and bureaucratic aggrandizement; rather the struggle was between a single interest and the national interest: "The natural resources which abound in the public domain are the property of all the people, and are intended for the benefit of all the people . . . these gifts of nature will be increasingly and more significantly the balance between the abundant life we want [future generations] to have and the skimpiness which waste and profligacy today would inevitably bring."[49] Reorganization required answers to these questions; it would not, in itself, resolve them.

The Barrett hearings gave Secretary Krug a new sense of urgency to complete the BLM merger and decentralization, and he needed support from the livestock industry to get the range program back on its feet. Rex Nicholson warned BLM leaders that so far the reorganization had "been badly handled. The stockmen feel they have been misled in the range-management program."[50] Secretary Krug met with representatives of the livestock industry in September 1947 to hear their complaints and to gain support for supplemental appropriations. The stockmen praised Nicholson's report as a true and accurate representation of their interests and complained that it was not being carried out. The chief problem, they argued, was not the organizational plan but the personnel being appointed to the range program. They demanded the appointment of "men who are familiar with the questions of the west, men who are sympathetic with the questions of the west; not men who are acquainted with bureaucracy and who are sympathetic with the plans of bureaucracy."[51]

The conflict continued, and at the end of 1947, the deadline that Secretary Krug had set for the completion of reorganization activities, the BLM was still in shambles. Although most of the BLM's new regional administrators had been appointed, there was little to do without staff or appropriations. Marion Clawson, the regional administrator in San Francisco, summed up the year this way: "During calendar year 1947 . . . there really was not too much for a regional administrator to do. One of my fellow administrators, in frustration, used his GI training money to learn to fly. Many days I would go to the office, open and read mail, maybe dictate a few letters, confer with Favorite or others as needed, and then take annual leave for the rest of the day, and go home."[52] Clawson used his free time to revise his doctoral dissertation on the western livestock industry for publication.[53]

Frustrated with the progress or lack of progress in the BLM, and perhaps acting on complaints from the livestock representatives, Secretary Krug appointed Marion Clawson as the new BLM director in 1948.[54] Clawson was a Harvard-trained economist and a proponent of professional public administration, which did not endear him to the BLM's constituents, but he was from Nevada and knew the livestock industry well, which gave him standing among public lands users and western congressmen.[55]

When Clawson assumed the directorship in 1948, "the merger of the General Land Office and the Grazing Service had been made nominally, but the joint was clearly visible."[56] As result, Clawson's task was immense: "shaping the agency into a single, functioning organization, improving internal efficiency, regaining the confidence of both Congress and the various user groups, decentralizing routine operations, and achieving a reasonable budget for the agency's programs. The most important [task] was unifying its activities."[57] In reality, it might be more accurate to say that Clawson's primary task was keeping the new agency alive, and in this respect Clawson's tenure was a success. But Clawson made other contributions to the agency, and in many ways his appointment marks the BLM's functional birth.

Clawson's first major action was cleaning house, especially reducing the former GLO's dominance over BLM operations. He arranged for the retirement, transfer, or dismissal of a number of former GLO officials and replaced them mainly with economists from the Department of Agriculture. This represented a clear shift toward professional administration. Clawson also completed the agency's basic administrative organization, which followed the original plan for decentralized administration in district offices, seven regional offices, and overall coordination through a small Washington staff. Most important, Clawson began to build the agency's appropriations in creative ways. He gained a 30 percent increase in the range program's appropriations to control halogeten, a noxious weed to domestic livestock, and to reseed depleted range. He also gained the BLM's first appropriations for road construction in the BLM's Oregon forests.[58]

For Clawson, the BLM's basic policy problems "were concentrated, as before, on questions of allocating publicly owned lands to specific uses."[59] Clawson recalls that the three big issues were grazing, oil and gas leasing, and forestry in Oregon, although the agency also dealt with land disposal, wildlife forage, and, in very rare cases, recreation. These program areas overlapped geographically, and no amount of administrative reorganization could change the fact that the agency's fundamental statutory authority created conflicts among resource uses in the field—for example, mining and homestead claims on grazing lands.[60]

Clawson emphasized the BLM's de facto multiple-use mission and interpreted the BLM's primary statutes as a conservation mandate for the public lands, but he and the BLM staff were limited in their ability to move from rhetoric to action. Clawson recalls, "Our objective in those years was a simple one: achieve efficiency in operation. We did seek more conservation on the federal lands but we intended to push that harder later."[61] The BLM simply did not have authority or funding to develop the kind of multiple-use planning programs necessary to direct the agency's activities toward a unified conservation goal.[62]

In light of these conflicts, Ickes's vision of resolving policy problems through administrative reorganization seems both more and less plausible. On the one hand, there is no question that the policy problems of the BLM were not and could not be solved by streamlining the agency's administration and decision-making structures. On the other hand, and likely what Ickes envisioned, the struggle to organize the new agency without a clear mission highlighted the complex problems and contradictions of public lands policy, bringing Clawson, the Interior Department, public land users, and Congress into a new round of debate over the public lands.

THE HOOVER COMMISSION: ORGANIZATIONAL CRITERIA

Most scholars writing about the BLM's formation have focused, appropriately, on the livestock industry's influence over the BLM's early organization. It is also important to recognize, however, that the BLM was created at a turbulent time for congressional delegation of regulatory authority and at a time when Congress was beginning to check growth in the executive branch that had occurred during the Depression and World War II.[63]

In 1947, just one year after Secretary Ickes resigned and the BLM was formed, Congress created the Commission on Organization of the Executive Branch (or Hoover Commission, after the commission's chair, former president Herbert Hoover) to undertake a complete review of the organization and operations of the executive branch. Its primary task was to recommend changes to the executive branch that would allow for more efficient and better coordinated administration, although the commission recognized that it was impossible to separate administration from substantive policy.[64]

Two of the Hoover Commission task force committees dealt with public lands issues, and their January 1949 reports reflected very different views of public lands administration. Indeed, the two reports prompted an important debate in Congress over the basic purposes and decision-making processes of public lands administration. The Task Force Committee on Agriculture dealt with public lands range and forestry programs, viewing them as essentially agricultural activities and urging Congress to separate these programs from land disposal and minerals. For the committee, agricultural activities were primarily matters of local rather than national concern and ought to be administered as such. The committee recommended consolidating all agricultural activities, including forest and range management, in the Department of Agriculture.

The Task Force Committee on Natural Resources addressed all federally owned land and resources. Although it recognized some validity in separating agricultural from nonagricultural activities, it insisted that the type of program mattered less than ownership of the resources it managed. Whereas the federal government had some sovereign power over privately owned land and resources, it had both sovereign and proprietary power over federally owned land and resources: "the committee feels strongly that both agriculture as a way of life, and the trusteeship of our great natural resources under special conditions of government ownership or control should have separate representation at the top level."[65] As a result, the committee urged consolidation of all responsibilities for federally owned land and resources in a new Department of Natural Resources, which would provide more uniform execution of the federal government's proprietary power and responsibilities.[66]

Reorganization, the committee argued, would transform the Interior Department from a "'holding company' of numerous bureaus, somewhat 'fortuitously thrown together,'" to an "instrument able to enforce consideration of balanced and integrated multiple-purpose development and conservation commensurate with the span and unity of its responsibilities."[67] The committee reiterated Ickes's argument that centralizing administrative authority and discretion would allow the executive branch to overcome the conflicts, contradictions, and tensions that Congress had written into law and continued to write into appropriations.

Insisting that federally owned lands be managed in a way that reflected the federal government's proprietary interests and power did not eliminate difficulties with administrative decision making, however, and the committee struggled with the tension between centralized accountability and decentralized operations: "what is also needed is the sense of total responsibility that consolidation in a single department would give," yet administration "cannot be soundly conceived unless [it is] based upon the specific peculiarities of the resource and its situation."[68] To achieve this balance, the committee recommended countervailing forms of representation: "It is important to make a place in the administrative structure . . . for the advisory participation of the local consumers of the resource materials or services," but "as a corrective safeguard to regional or local pressures . . . the Committee proposes a central reviewing and coordinating board in the Executive Office of the President."[69]

The Hoover Commission was divided in its analysis of the arguments, but the majority sided with the agriculture committee in its final report on the Interior Department, issued in March 1949, recommending that the BLM's range and forestry responsibilities be transferred to the Department of Agriculture and merged with the Forest Service to create a new, comprehensive forest and rangeland agency.[70] This recommendation sent a mixed message to stockmen and other public lands users. On the one hand, it seemed to support the fact that public lands range and timber were already managed as matters of local agricultural interest. On the other hand, ranchers had long feared that consolidation with the Forest Service would lead to increased regulation and administrative control. The BLM's other responsibilities for subsoil, water, and construction would remain in the Interior Department.

A minority of the commission, however, sided with the natural resources committee, arguing that transferring BLM to the Department of Agriculture defied the underlying *purposes* and *proprietary responsibilities* of federal land ownership. They insisted on a new Department of Natural Resources to oversee all federally owned land and resources: "the problems of private lands are basically different from those relating to public lands. The division of functions we recommend should permit the Department of Agriculture to focus its responsibility on harmonizing the producer interest in private lands with the need for conservation of the soil resources."[71] Furthermore, the dissenting minority argued that unlike private agricultural land, federally owned land provided special opportunities for multiple land and resource uses, which served the broader national interest. A Department of Natural Resources, the commission argued, would preserve "these resources to the people and insur[e] their development in the interest of all," and it would rescue the Forest Service from its existing location in a "department of farms."[72]

The Hoover Commission's final recommendations to Congress, then, raised critical questions about the purposes and decision-making processes of federal land and resource ownership. Whereas the majority categorized federal programs based on their functional connection to agriculture, the minority categorized federal programs based on land and resource ownership. The minority followed the Supreme Court in *Camfield v. United States* (1897) and *Light v. United States* (1911), which asserted that the federal government "has with respect to its own land the rights of an ordinary proprietor to maintain its possession and prosecute trespassers. It may deal with such lands precisely as an ordinary individual may deal with his farming property."[73] The minority recognized that this did not eliminate the problem of representation, but it did resolve questions of final purpose.

The Hoover Commission's report and the ensuing debate highlighted rather than resolved the basic struggles of public lands management, particularly range management. Although the courts consistently recognized that the federal government had proprietary rights identical to those of a private property owner, the courts did not and could not dictate how Congress exercised those rights. As long as western congressmen controlled public lands policy, they could treat the public lands programs as matters of private, local, and agricultural interest. As other scholars have noted, ranchers and land managers did not negotiate land use privileges through the courts but through Congress, where western livestock interests dominated the public lands subcommittees.[74] This left BLM managers in a difficult position if they tried to advance interests contrary to local economic demands.

Interior officials responded quickly to the Hoover Commission's recommendations, denouncing the majority opinion. To treat the public lands range and forests as matters of agricultural interest only, officials complained, ignored the federal government's obligations to protect the land's productive capacity for future generations and to distribute the benefits of nationally owned resources equitably. Interior officials asked Congress to follow the minority recommendations and create a Department of Natural Resources, which would finally allow for comprehensive conservation management of all federal land and resources.[75]

The BLM's main constituent groups—grazing, mining, and timber—also opposed the majority report, although for a variety of different reasons. The mining industry opposed the Hoover Commission's recommendations for fear that splitting surface and subsurface responsibilities for federal land between two departments with radically different missions would inhibit mineral development. The timber industry supported the Forest Service, which wanted to maintain its autonomy in the Department of Agriculture. The livestock industry opposed the merger for fear that the new forest and rangeland agency would follow the Forest Service patterns of regulatory management and threaten existing grazing privileges.[76]

Furthermore, representatives of the Nevada livestock industry argued that the reorganization would violate the congressional intent of the Taylor Grazing Act of 1934. Forest Service statutory authority was rooted in timber management, making range management a secondary concern. In forest administration, the Forest Service had created "a landlord agent dictatorship system under *day to day bureau-made regulations* . . . with practically no chance for the tenant group to avail itself of the protection of the courts against the possible whims of the federal officials."[77] The Taylor Grazing Act, they argued, had established a "system of landlord-tenant relationships *by law* with the tenants placed in a position to protect in the courts . . . the economic fate of their enterprises against the possible whims of the government landlord's agents."[78] Put more simply, the system practiced under the Taylor Grazing Act established something akin to property rights to the range, whereas the Forest Service insisted that all resource uses were privileges.

In 1951 these arguments came together in a single debate when the Senate Committee on Expenditures in the Executive Department considered S. 1149, "A Bill to Provide for the Reorganization of the Department of Agriculture in Accordance with the Recommendations of the Commission on Organization of the Executive Branch of the Government." Senators on the committee demanded control over the reorganization itself; the Bureau of Budget representative argued that the executive branch should control reorganization; conservationists argued for consolidation along the Forest Service model of resource management; the Forest Service argued that a unified conservation program for renewable resources was impossible unless it encompasses private and public lands; the Interior Department argued that a single department of natural resources was the only defensible solution, because it would produce uniform "administrative policies and regulations, facilitation of a program to eliminate conflicts of laws, changes in boundaries of administrative units to reduce costs of administration, and simplification of dealings with the public";[79] and the livestock industry argued that it would support some kind of consolidation as long as Congress made inviolable the Taylor Grazing Act system of range management.[80] The debate ended in a draw, and S. 1149 failed. Conflicting ideas about the federal government's proprietary interests in the public lands, the rivalry between an older system of public lands patronage and professional management in the Forest Service, the irreconcilable tension between service and management functions within BLM, and the basic rivalry between Interior and Agriculture all conspired to defeat S. 1149. The failure of S. 1149 left the young BLM in a difficult position. The S. 1149 debate had demonstrated that there was just enough conflict to maintain the status quo, and just enough conflict to keep the BLM from articulating an independent vision for public lands management.

SNAPSHOT OF THE EARLY BLM: A LOOSE CONSORTIUM OF RESOURCE PROGRAMS

Without a clear statutory or administrative mission the early BLM operated as a loose consortium of resource programs rather than as a unified, mission-driven agency. The BLM's main resource programs—forestry, range, minerals, and lands

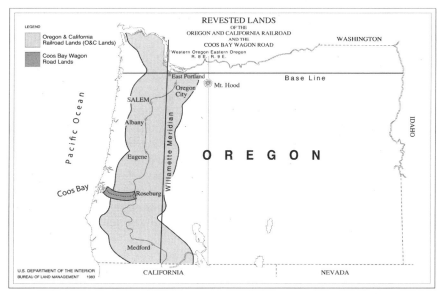

Figure 2.1. Revested lands of the Oregon and California Railroad and the Coos Bay Wagon Road (O & C lands), courtesy of the Bureau of Land Management.

and real estate—continued to operate under their own statutory authorities, their own clientele relationships, and their own administrative cultures.

The BLM's most discrete resource program in the 1940s and 1950s was the management of roughly 2.5 million acres of forestland in western Oregon, known as the Oregon and California lands (O & C lands, Figure 2.1). The O & C lands were old land grants to the Oregon and California Railroad Company and the Coos Bay Wagon Road Company that Congress reconveyed in 1916 and 1919, respectively. At that time, the timber industry and Oregon counties were concerned primarily with rapid timber development and property tax revenue, and they were staunchly opposed to Forest Service administration. As a result, Congress placed responsibility for the O & C lands with the GLO. Over the next twenty years, the Forest Service argued vigorously for administrative control of the O & C lands and the estimated 50 billion board feet of timber they contained. The Interior Department, particularly Interior Secretary Ickes, was not about to yield such valuable land to the Forest Service and fought just as vigorously for permanent administrative control. The timber industry and Oregon officials remained equally opposed to Forest Service control, pressing instead for a statutory mandate that the GLO offer O & C timber at a sustained yield rate. Ickes and his allies prevailed in 1937, when Congress made GLO responsibility permanent in the Oregon and California Revested Lands Act.[81]

The 1937 act directed the interior secretary, and by delegation the GLO's O & C

Administration, to manage the O & C lands for sustained yield timber production in order to sustain local timber economies, protect watersheds, and provide opportunities for recreation. Although this echoed the Forest Service Organic Act of 1897 in important ways, it placed much greater emphasis on sustaining local timber economies. In particular, the act required the O & C Administration to determine the "annual productive capacity . . . as promptly as possible" and to sell "not less than the annual sustained yield capacity."[82] Thus, sustained yield was not only a ceiling on annual timber harvests; it was the threshold as well.

By 1946, when the O & C Administration became part of the BLM, it had fulfilled the first part of its sustained yield mandate, producing extensive inventories of forest productivity within the gross boundaries of the O & C lands and organizing them into twelve master units for sustained yield planning. Still, it fell far short of its mandate to sell the estimated sustained yield annually. O & C managers hoped to remedy its shortfall by establishing 100-year cooperative leases for O & C timber. They planned to issues leases only to those who owned private timberland within the gross O & C boundaries in exchange for a contractual agreement that both the private and federal timber would be harvested on a federally established sustained yield basis. The leasing proposal, if successful, would have accomplished what the Forest Service had long sought: sustained yield forestry across both public and private lands. Furthermore, the leases would essentially have fixed the region's timber economy for a century.[83]

The BLM's formation in 1946, however, led to a very different sustained yield timber program. The slow pace of BLM organization first delayed hearings on cooperative leases, diminishing momentum generated by the O & C Administration. Furthermore, reactions were mixed when the BLM finally did hold hearings for its first O & C cooperative lease in 1947.[84] Many private landowners supported the concept, but many small timber operators and the Association of O & C Counties were strongly opposed to 100-year leases because they feared it would create timber monopolies and eliminate small mills and logging operations.[85] In essence, many local governments and citizens were not willing to accept economic stability because of the economic trade-offs it entailed. In 1948, the BLM officially abandoned the cooperative lease approach, and with it the hope of 100-year forest planning. BLM Director Marion Clawson removed the existing regional administrator and replaced him with Dan Goldy, a forest economist who emphasized the need for competitive timber sales.

With the competitive sale approach, however, the BLM faced an additional challenge to meeting its full sustained yield harvesting mandate: road access. The O & C lands, due to the terms of the original land grants, lay in a perfect checkerboard pattern of square-mile sections across western Oregon. Since the BLM managed every other square mile of land, it could not access federal land without crossing private land. This gave private timber owners considerable leverage in negotiating timber sales, because they could deny the BLM access to the federally owned sections. The 100-year leases that the O & C Administration had been developing were intended both to advance sustained yield forestry and to resolve this basic legal and political issue. The BLM's access problems were compounded by the fact that it did not have appropriations for road construction, so even if it were not limited by private property restrictions it would still have been forced to rely on private roads to get O & C timber to market.[86]

The BLM managed to resolve rights-of-way and road construction issues between 1948 and 1950. First, BLM leaders forced private landowners to accept reciprocal rights-of-way at section corners and reciprocal road use agreements by threatening to block private road construction where it crossed federal lands and threatening to close public roads to private timber operations. Second, the BLM gained appropriations for road construction beginning in 1950, arguing that private roads were insufficient to access the old-growth timber that forests viewed as "overripe." The BLM's road construction appropriations increased dramatically a year later after massive fires and blowdowns, because the burned and downed trees would decay beyond merchantable quality without immediate road access and timber sales. After the BLM gained reciprocal rights-of-way agreements and appropriations for road construction, its competitive timber sales increased dramatically.[87]

The early BLM, then, focused primarily on increasing timber sales on the O & C lands to their designated sustained-yield levels, and this left little time or funding to meet other mandates under the O & C Act of 1937. As Marion Clawson explained: "The dense Douglas fir forests on the O&C lands are splendid producers of trees and logs, but not much good for recreation, almost useless for grazing, and lacking in significant minerals."[88] Furthermore, the narrow focus on timber production on the O & C lands meant that the BLM's early forestry program operated in almost total isolation from other resource programs in the late 1940s. Only after the Materials Act of 1947 and forestry appropriations in 1949 expanded the BLM's forestry program beyond the O & C boundaries did the agency even begin to integrate forestry with other resource programs.

If O & C forestry was the early BLM's most discrete program, range management was without question its most important program and most significant challenge, in part because the BLM had virtually no control over its range clientele during the late 1940s. As political scientist Philip Foss explains, the livestock industry dominated the BLM through grazing advisory boards and through its influence over congressional oversight and appropriations committees.[89]

The livestock industry's political monopoly on the western rangelands in the late 1940s stemmed from a number of important factors over which reform-minded BLM leaders and field managers had little control. First, the BLM had no national or even regional conservation constituency to defend it when it challenged the livestock industry and its advocates in Congress.[90] The agency's narrow constituency stemmed in large part from the fact that public lands range was neither economically nor recreationally valuable in the 1940s and 1950s. Certainly ranchers valued their use of the range, but even most ranchers did not consider the range worth the cost of purchase and taxation when they could use it for a modest fee. Similarly, outdoor recreation may have been growing rapidly on national forest and park land after World War II, but very few people drove to the BLM's desert lands for a vacation.[91] Conservation groups in general supported professional conservation management and decried the livestock industry's influence over the BLM, but these groups focused their real political energy on the national parks and forests rather than the public lands. As a result, BLM managers who desired greater autonomy from the livestock industry fought for professionalism in an exceedingly hostile environment, opposed by both the livestock industry and fellow managers who were not willing to accept the costs associated with this battle.[92]

Second, the BLM had very few scientific resources with which to bolster its professional autonomy. The agency was formed during a time of upheaval in plant ecology and the budding field of range science. The ecological paradigm that had dominated the 1920s through the 1940s was coming under withering criticism, raising new questions about the proper foundations for range management. Most ecologists continued to argue that quantitative, professional ecology still provided the best way to determine range conditions and grazing levels, but range scientists were still struggling to develop methods of range evaluation that the livestock industry would accept as a basis for determining grazing levels.

In 1951, for example, the Forest Service unveiled a new method of range survey that minimized individual bias and variation and that it hoped would win support from the livestock industry. New survey methods, no matter how accurate, did little to address the livestock industry's more fundamental opposition to scientific management, as the *National Wool Grower* made clear: "To base decisions on scientific facts alone has seldom proven entirely satisfactory in any field of agriculture."[93] Scientific facts were important, but the industry argued vociferously that the ranchers' practical range knowledge was more appropriate for applied questions of range management. Supporting the livestock industry, a number of range specialists at state universities likewise rejected any narrow commitment to professional authority: "Perhaps the best method of determining proper stocking is a study of the history of the stocking over a period of years, together with a very careful study of its effect upon the range. This requires training and knowledge of plants, but it is nothing that the observant stockman cannot master."[94] What is more, the first society of range management and the *Journal of Range Management* appeared in 1948, at the height of upheaval in range ecology and science, and it focused primarily on technological and practical questions of range management that range professionals and ranchers shared.[95]

If the Forest Service, with its considerable professional autonomy and political power, struggled to build a system of scientific range management, prospects for the Bureau of Land Management were even more limited. When Clawson became BLM director in 1948 and set out to institute a professional system of range management, for example, he discovered that most of the existing range survey and range condition research in the nation had been conducted for more productive grasslands and not for the BLM's arid range. Clawson jokes that debates over range condition, the basic foundation for management decisions, were fairly sloppy affairs: "you say, 'ahh, this range is better than it was' and he says, 'like hell it is, look at it, how bad it is.'"[96] In short, the range program lacked public interest and a foundational science.[97]

Without a conservation constituency and with limited scientific tools, the BLM's range program did little initially to change grazing levels, challenge grazing advisory boards, or coordinate its activities with the agency's other programs. Marion Clawson—director from 1948 to 1953—had to focus instead on laying the foundation for future conservation management. During Clawson's tenure, the agency finished organizing grazing districts, settling the disputes that had prompted Grazing Service Director Forsling to call for reorganization in the mid-1940s; it recovered and then expanded the appropriations that Congress had eliminated in 1946, giving the BLM funding to expand its range operations; and it raised grazing fees from eight cents to twelve cents per animal unit month (AUM) to support the expanded range program.[98]

By the early 1950s, the BLM's growing range program had staff and funding to conduct controversial new range surveys to determine range condition and capacity so that range conservationists no longer had to rely on range capacity estimates provided by the grazing advisory boards. Furthermore, as a number of World War II veterans used their GI Bill funds to earn degrees in range science, the agency could hire range conservationists from a growing pool of trained, professional range managers rather than hiring ranchers.[99] In short, during the 1950s, the BLM began developing a professional esprit de corps in its range program, expanding the agency's ambition for professional autonomy in range management.

Moving from forestry and range to the BLM's other programs illustrates just how complex and at times contradictory the agency's responsibilities were at its formation—and why they continue to be so contentious today. Even though these programs overlapped spatially, they differed significantly both because of the types of resources they oversaw and because of their diverse statutory authorities. Whereas the BLM clearly had *management* responsibilities for forests and range—whether or not it fulfilled them all—it had only *clerical* responsibilities for minerals and real estate.

The BLM's minerals program was complicated and dynamic, changing in the 1950s because of both new legislation and the changing demands for minerals. The minerals program was clearly a clerical rather than a managerial operation for a number of reasons, giving the agency relatively little discretion and control over mineral activities. First, minerals are nonrenewable, so the sustained yield paradigm that applied to forest and range conservation and required managerial discretion could not be applied to minerals. In other words, it was impossible to tie the rate of mineral extraction to the rate at which minerals are formed—generally an administrative and discretionary task. Second, geologists can never identify the full extent or exact location of federal mineral reserves, making it impossible to regulate the rate of mineral extraction in light of a mineral's total extractive potential. In the case of minerals, then, conservation meant something very different from sustained yield, although all definitions involved the criterion of efficiency: "Sometimes it has meant avoiding waste in handling products; sometimes, avoiding an unduly rapid rate of oil extraction; and at other times, reserving minerals for later use."[100]

Second, unlike the BLM's forestry and range programs, which were each grounded in a primary authorizing statute, the sale and development of minerals were governed by a variety of statutes that split minerals administration into two very different programs—patenting and leasing—and, though it won't be explained here, subdivided these programs further in a variety of ways. The patenting program was shaped primarily by the Mining Law of 1872, which permitted prospectors to claim unreserved public lands and take title to them if they could prove the presence of valuable hard rock minerals. If they could prove their claim, they received title to the surface and subsurface of their claim for between $2.50 and $5.00 an acre, and they paid no royalties for the minerals they extracted.[101]

The patenting program presented the BLM with serious records and planning problems. The BLM kept very detailed records of all final mineral decisions and patents that it issued. However, since the Mining Law of 1872 did not require prospectors to notify the BLM when they staked their claims—only when they wanted to prove and patent their claims—the BLM's district offices never knew the locations of all unpatented claims under their jurisdiction: "Short of a search of county records," Clawson explained after his tenure as BLM director, "the Bureau has no way of knowing exactly how many mining claims have been filed against the public domain."[102] For example, of the estimated 20,000 claims located on O & C lands in 1948, only 1,200 were on file at the district land offices and only 900 of these could actually be located on the ground.[103]

The BLM's incomplete records raised one of the most basic problems for long-range planning, namely that the agency had no assurance of public lands tenure in any area open to hard rock mining claims. The system also produced severe adjudication problems for miners and the BLM. When miners staked overlapping claims in a given area, the BLM did not have the records on hand to determine who had prior rights to his or her claim. Figure 2.2 provides an extreme case of overlapping mining claims in Colorado.

Whereas the BLM administered a patenting program for hard rock minerals under the Mining Law of 1872, it administered a leasing program primarily for oil, gas, and coal under the Mineral Leasing Act of 1920. Here, the federal government maintained ownership of the surface lands, leasing them for mineral development. Lessees paid application fees, maintenance fees, and royalties on the minerals they extracted. Although the BLM had complete records of mineral lease applications, it still had no control over the pace and location of these applications and struggled to deal with leasing booms and lulls.[104] Furthermore, Congress passed the Outer Continental Lands Act (OCLA) in 1953, giving the BLM

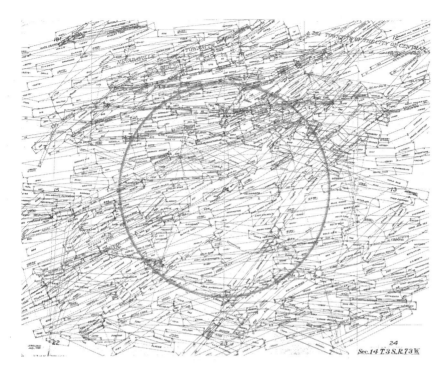

Figure 2.2. This map is of an area about 30 miles west of Denver in the 1950s. It depicts the surveyed boundaries of overlapping mining claims, some of which date back almost 100 years. Image courtesy of the National Archives and Records Administration, Rocky Mountain Region.

leasing responsibilities for all federal offshore oil and gas. Partly as a result of the OCLA, BLM mineral leasing jumped from 5,000 leases at the end of World War II to 130,000 leases in 1960.[105]

Third, the BLM's minerals program was almost exclusively clerical and not managerial because the BLM's primary decision-making responsibilities were for patenting and leasing minerals, not for regulating actual drilling and mining. Once the BLM issued a lease, the U.S. Geological Survey took over and monitored mineral extraction.[106]

Like the minerals program, the BLM's lands and realty program was largely a clerical operation, governed by a dazzling array of land disposal laws—literally thousands of laws. The program was a constant reminder to the BLM of the tenuous nature of public lands ownership; even though the Taylor Grazing Act gave the BLM authority to manage and regulate the range, it did so provisionally, according to the act, "pending final disposal."[107]

As with the mineral patenting system, the BLM had no administrative control over the rate or location of land applications, nor did it maintain any inventory concerning the suitability of its lands for various forms of disposal. In some ways, the lands and realty program was in no better position than the GLO's initial grazing division, whose first director, Farrington Carpenter, described the problem this way:

> I rushed over to the General Land Office and said, "I am going out there to handle 140,000,000 acres of land and I would like to know where it is. You have all the records. I'd like a map." "We haven't any map." "What? No map?" I said. "You've been administering this land a hundred years longer than the Department of the Interior has existed and you don't even have a map! What kind of an outfit is this?" Well, the fellow looked at me like a bull at a bastard calf. He said, "You don't know much, do you? We can't map the public domain. We have seventeen land offices in the West and they are open as the sun goes around. Every minute of the day, some bird is walking in and homesteading a piece. . . . So it changes every minute. We never know where it is."[108]

With no systematic inventory of disposable lands and with no national or state maps of the public lands, the BLM reviewed applications for homestead grants, land sales, and land exchanges on a case-by-case basis, and BLM field managers had no way of anticipating when areas of land under their jurisdiction would be transferred from federal to private or state ownership.

What is more, the BLM had no systematic land appraisal system or criteria. This was in part because land appraisers had virtually no professional training, but it was due even more fundamentally to the fact that the appraisers often didn't know what they were appraising for. The BLM administered so many different land disposal laws that appraisers often didn't know if they should appraise the land as valuable primarily for grazing, urban development, recreation, or forestry. As one BLM retiree explained, "We were appraising by the seat of our pants."[109]

The BLM's lands and realty program represented the agency's nineteenth- and early-twentieth-century policy roots in land disposal rather than the kind of professional conservation mission that some agency leaders and field managers sought. Furthermore, since the lands and realty program was primarily clerical and responsive to land applications, it could not provide the BLM with the one thing that might have advanced the agency's professional ambitions, namely consolidating the public lands holdings into discrete units and eliminating private and state inholdings.

CONCLUSION

It should come as no surprise, after a brief survey of the BLM's main program areas, that the Grazing Service and the GLO merger did not immediately produce a cohesive, professional, and mission-driven agency. The reorganization had con-solidated all of the GLO's and Grazing Service's responsibilities in a single agency, but it did not provide any guidelines for prioritizing or integrating them. Whereas vague statutory missions had advanced the Forest Service's and the National Park Service's administrative discretion and autonomy, the BLM's organization had left political power exactly where it had been under GLO and Grazing Service ad-ministration: with the livestock industry, the mining industry, the timber industry, and western states. Political scientists Samuel Dana and Sally Fairfax summarize the situation nicely: "Thus, the bureau had no coherent mission, no authority, and no statutorily defined existence. It was rather like the lands it managed, a residual category, assigned to administer the loose ends of over 3,500 statutes randomly enacted of the previous 150 years."[110]

The early BLM thus found itself in an ambiguous position in the late 1940s and early 1950s. The remarkable fact of the BLM, based upon its history and cre-ation, is that it survived at all. Indeed, the BLM crept along under withering attack from both conservationists and industry. Conservationists such as Bernard De-Voto launched salvo after salvo in *Harper's,* condemning the livestock industry, western members of Congress, and range managers, often by name.[111] Livestock industry advocates in Washington, particularly Congressman Frank Barrett, con-tinued to challenge the BLM at every turn through oversight and appropriations hearings, protecting the livestock industry's political power.[112] Even more remark-ably, despite the extreme hostility of the BLM's political environment and despite the swirling questions of purpose and decision-making process that plagued the agency, the BLM's staff and appropriations actually grew in these early years. During Clawson's tenure from 1948 to 1953, the BLM's staff increased from 1,382 to 1,557, and its budget rose from $5.8 to $14.2 million, and these numbers continued to rise throughout the 1950s, allowing the BLM to continue building a foundation for future professionalism and regulatory control.[113]

3

The New BLM

The early 1960s marked a new chapter in BLM history; public lands policy and management shifted far more dramatically during this period than in the agency's first fifteen years. The story of the BLM during these years is marked by a renewed quest for a cohesive and comprehensive public lands policy and a rational system of planning and managing the public lands, and through new legislation, new responsibilities, and new administrative organization agency leaders pieced together an official multiple-use mandate.[1]

In 1960, the BLM looked very much the same as it had during Marion Clawson's tenure in the late 1940s and early 1950s. Its functional programs in range, timber, minerals, and lands operated independently with almost no long-range planning or coordination; the livestock industry dominated the agency's range management program through the grazing advisory board system; and the BLM still had no legal basis to assume that the public lands would remain in permanent federal ownership.[2]

By 1966, however, the BLM had moved toward the Forest Service model of professional management and away from the legacy of nineteenth-century land disposal and political management. The BLM was developing a system of comprehensive land use planning; it had been reorganized to increase coordination among its functional programs; it had achieved unprecedented, if still quite limited, independence from the livestock industry; and it had implemented a classification program to identify public lands that should remain in permanent federal ownership. The BLM's workforce had grown from 2,500 to 4,000 employees and its budget from $35 million to $88 million.[3]

The BLM's transformation occurred during a period of unique political opportunity, generated in part by the broader upheaval of the 1960s. Secretary of the Interior Stewart Udall and BLM directors Karl Landstrom (1961–1963) and

Charles Stoddard (1963–1966) took advantage of, and to a limited extent shaped, a new context for public lands administration in which the federal government asserted a stronger proprietary interest in the public lands. In symbolic terms, they tried to nationalize the public lands—to abstract them from their integration in the economic, social, and political landscapes of the American West and recast them as a landscape of their own. They also tried to integrate BLM management programs through a system of rational planning and scientific management in order to overcome the political power of the agency's established clientele groups and achieve a comprehensive conservation focus. These efforts illustrate the fundamental tension between the Progressive Era ideals of rational, scientific management and the system of self-regulation that had been established under the Taylor Grazing Act. Looking to the U.S. Forest Service as an example, BLM leaders tried to equate the fact of federal land ownership with the need for agency control. Although they fell far short of their nationalizing ambitions in the 1960s, their efforts were significant steps in the BLM's evolution, and the issues they wrestled with remain controversial today.

SHIFTING CONTEXT OF PUBLIC LANDS ADMINISTRATION

A federal bureaucracy's broader political, social, and economic context—its relationships with Congress, with the chief executive, and with constituents; its social systems, organization, and command and control structures; and ideological forces in the academy and popular culture—shapes and constrains the choices that its leaders make. Charismatic leaders can reshape an agency's policy and management, but they are constrained by these contextual limits.

To understand the BLM's transformation during the early 1960s, it is important to recognize several key internal and external forces that were at work on the agency in the 1950s and 1960s. Internally, the agency grew increasingly professional, which provided skills and motivation to exert greater control of policy and management decisions. Externally, a growing body of academic literature condemned the BLM for being "captured" by the livestock industry while praising the BLM's counterpart in the Department of Agriculture, the U.S. Forest Service, for upholding the ideals of professional, scientific management; a sudden rise in outdoor recreation led to increased noncommercial demands on the public lands; and a new conservation philosophy, articulated in part by Secretary of the Interior Udall, began to influence public lands administration. Together, these forces created opportunities for the BLM to evade capture by a single clientele group, to develop a more systematic approach to land use planning and management, and to reshape its mission.

When Secretary Douglas McKay removed Marion Clawson from the BLM in 1953, the agency was still clientele driven, particularly by the livestock industry. The new director, Edward Woozley, worked primarily in the interests of the

BLM's three basic commercial user groups—ranchers, miners, and loggers—and was essentially "antagonistic to . . . the idea that the technicians of the Bureau knew more than the applicants."[4]

For the BLM multiple use was more a description of reality than a prescriptive system of management: "the concept of multiple use [arose], not out of a carefully drawn system of mixed land management, but rather as a practical response to the experience of accommodating a variety of users who are willing to share their use of the land but not surrender it."[5] As one scholar writes, "no mechanism existed for determining the appropriate mix of resource uses from a public policy standpoint or ensuring that the resources were harvested in a manner that would provide a long-term sustained yield."[6]

Despite these centrifugal forces at work during the 1950s, the BLM's overall professionalism grew because of changes in the agency's range staff. Whereas the Grazing Service and the early BLM hired ranchers from public lands states with only practical experience in range management, the BLM in the late 1950s hired men with professional degrees in range science and professional affiliations in the Society for Range Management. They were by no means antagonistic to grazing, but they brought more critical, scientific tools to range management.[7]

Emphasizing its growing professional expertise, the BLM began to reevaluate the grazing allotments on the basis of their own range surveys rather than on the basis of the local advisory board's recommendations, struggling with grazing advisory boards and individual permittees over range adjudication for nearly fifteen years: 1953–1967. This process has received very little detailed study, but it represents one of the most striking achievements of the BLM's range program.[8] As a result of the process, the total number of animal unit months (AUMs) permitted on the public lands dropped from an average of 15 million in the years 1946–1959 to an average of 11,750,000 in the years 1960–1970, a 20 percent reduction.[9] Sally Fairfax summarizes it this way: "In this period of relative calm, the Bureau appears to have begun to view itself as a land-management agency. Although it had not met with overwhelming success in its 1950s efforts to readjudicate the range and reduce allotments, neither was it content to merely plod along as the invisible handmaiden of a domineering industry."[10]

Furthermore, passage of the Public Land Administration Act in 1960 gave the BLM greater authority to initiate studies, investigations, cooperative management agreements, and certain land improvements.[11] The BLM initiated important scientific inventories of its lands and resources, including a 1964 inventory of frail watersheds. The inventory, suggested and led in part by the ousted Grazing Service director Clarence Forsling, identified the watershed areas in greatest need of protection and restoration. These types of studies also supported the BLM's grazing fee increases in 1958 and 1963, which allocated more money to range improvement projects.[12]

It is difficult to gauge the direct influence that public administration scholarship had on the BLM during this period, yet it is clear that scholars helped solidify certain public and congressional perceptions of the agency. Public administration theory had undergone substantial revisions in the late 1940s and the 1950s, led principally by the work of Herbert Simon. Traditional public administration scholars had emphasized the need to separate politics from professional administration in order to achieve rational, scientific management. They used the phrase "scientific management" somewhat broadly to mean a systematic approach based upon the supposed neutral competency of professionally trained managers. They tended to favor executive leadership in day-to-day decision making in order to shield it from the political fray of congressional, and particularly patronage, politics, and they emphasized the tasks and the organizational structure of a bureaucracy. Luther Gulick was representative of this traditional approach, and his work was highly influential during the New Deal years.[13]

Simon offered a powerful critique of the traditional approach, and the "Carnegie school" alternative he led changed the course of public administration. Simon focused on decision making as the primary activity of a bureaucracy. He argued that administrators are not capable of making fully neutral, rational, or optimal decisions; rather they make contextual, expedient decisions that support the agency's internal needs, a process that he called "satisficing."[14] By this, Simon meant that administrators seek solutions to management problems that meet the minimum criteria of acceptability: "To optimize requires processes several orders of magnitude more complex than those required to satisfice. An example is the difference between searching a haystack to find the sharpest needle in it and searching the haystack to find a needle sharp enough to sew with."[15]

Simon's pioneering work was followed by a number of important studies of federal land and resource agencies, which reinforced the "Carnegie school" of organizational behavior. In 1949, for example, Philip Selznick published his study of the Tennessee Valley Authority, entitled *TVA and the Grass Roots: A Study in the Sociology of Formal Organization*, in which he emphasized the importance of "informal and covert" relationships in the agency's overall decision making.[16] Chris Argyris, whose work influenced the BLM during the 1960s, studied the social systems and processes that shape an agency's identity and mission.[17]

Public administration scholars focused increasingly on the clientele relationships of federal land and resource agencies, arguing that patronage agencies like the BLM are invariably "captured" by their dominant clientele, which control the agency both directly through informal relationships and indirectly through Congress. In his influential 1960 study, *Politics and Grass,* Philip Foss described the BLM as the quintessential example of a captured agency.[18] Dominated by the livestock industry directly, through grazing advisory boards, and indirectly, through the House and Senate Committees on Interior and Insular Affairs, the BLM was powerless to control grazing on the public lands. Foss provided thorough descriptions of the advisory boards' power to make range management decisions and veto agency decisions they disagreed with. He also described in detail the role of western members of Congress in maintaining the livestock industry's dominance, using the devastating Grazing Service budget cuts for FY 1947 as a prime example of the Grazing Service/BLM dilemma. The capture explanation of public lands management dominated the public lands literature for the next twenty years, receiving perhaps its most popular articulation in Grant McConnell's 1966 study *Private Power and American Democracy.*[19] Academic consensus that the BLM represented an unmitigated abrogation of federal responsibility placed new pressure on Congress, the livestock industry, and the BLM to shift control of the public lands out of private hands and into the agency.

Condemnation of BLM management frequently took the form of a negative comparison between the BLM and the U.S. Forest Service.[20] Where the BLM failed to protect its resources and bowed to the interests of its clientele, scholars and popular authors argued, the Forest Service succeeded. The Forest Service was quick to promote this view, beginning with disputes between the Forest Service and the BLM's predecessors, the General Land Office and the U.S. Grazing Service. Gifford Pinchot, the first Forest Service chief, had condemned the GLO as corrupt and incompetent, particularly when compared to the professional model set by the Forest Service.[21] Soon after Congress passed the Taylor Grazing Act and gave the Interior Department responsibility for public lands range management, the Forest Service issued a report that lauded its own professional range management and condemned the failure of range management in the Interior Department.[22]

In 1960, this comparison received new attention in both the academic literature and Congress. That year Foss's study, *Politics and Grass*, appeared alongside an equally influential study of the Forest Service by Herbert Kaufman, *The Forest Ranger.*[23] In contrast to Foss's condemnation of the BLM, Kaufman provided a detailed explanation of the Forest Service's successful, professional administration. He argued that the Forest Service avoided capture despite its decentralized organization because of appropriate command and control systems and, more important, because the agency's social systems enforced uniformity of professional judgments. His study reflected both the influence of his advisor, Luther Gulick, and the influence of Herbert Simon. Kaufman's book reflected and reinforced admiration for the Forest Service's professionalism and autonomy.

Congress brought the disparity between the Forest Service and the BLM to statutory light in 1960 with the passage of the Multiple Use Sustained Yield Act (MUSY) in June and the Public Land Administration Act[24] (PLAA) in July. In MUSY, Congress declared that the Forest Service should administer the national forests for "outdoor recreation, range, timber, watershed, and wildlife and fish purposes . . . in the combination that will best meet the needs of the American people," essentially validating the Forest Service's broad exercise of discretionary authority in determining the appropriate combination of land and resource uses in the national forests.[25]

The public lands bill that Congress passed one month later, by contrast, only granted the BLM authority for studies and investigations, cooperative agreements, protection of public lands, forest rehabilitation, and a variety of other specific activities. This was a paltry delegation of authority by comparison, and BLM leaders lobbied Congress to grant them a statute similar to MUSY. Assistant Secretary John Carver explained in 1961 that MUSY was "the envy of most of the whole profession of land managers. If you don't think so, I invite you to consult almost any official of the Bureau of Land Management in my own Department. They recognize a tour de force when they see one, and they want in. We've been practicing multiple use all these years, too, they say—but we *need* this bill."[26]

BLM leaders and their predecessors in the U.S. Grazing Service had made numerous attempts to bring particular resource programs into line with the ideals of professional, scientific administration as they were practiced by the Forest Service, but this meant waging an open battle against the agency's well-entrenched clientele and the established decision-making structures. Best illustrated by the 1946 Grazing Service appropriations cuts discussed in the last chapter, the agency lost most of these battles in the 1940s and 1950s. Indeed, the BLM and its predecessors remained trapped between public/congressional criticism for their failure to live up to the Forest Service precedent and public/congressional criticism for trying to replicate the Forest Service model.

This leads to the third, and perhaps the most important, external influence on BLM policy and management: outdoor recreation. Recreation had been a principal force in shaping management in the national forests, but in the first half of the twentieth century it had little influence on public lands management. In the late 1950s, a sudden rise of outdoor recreation on public lands brought an entirely new political force into public lands debate, which both challenged the political power of the BLM's commercial clientele and highlighted the limits of the BLM's statutory authority and appropriations priorities.[27]

Outdoor recreation on federally owned lands had exploded after World War II, as more and more Americans gained the income, leisure time, and automobiles to travel. The Forest Service and the National Park Service initially absorbed the increased recreational visitation. But by the mid-1950s, there was growing public concern that these agencies did not have the land or resources to meet all of the future recreation demand. Visits to the national park system went from 33 million in 1950 to 79 million in 1960, and visits to the national forest system rose from 27 million to 93 million in that same period.[28]

In 1958, Congress established the Outdoor Recreation Resources Review Commission to (1) complete a comprehensive inventory of recreational resources and demand, (2) estimate future recreational demands, and (3) propose new strategies for dealing with outdoor recreation.[29] Scholars, including Marion Clawson and later BLM director Charles Stoddard, contributed to the growing research on outdoor recreation, addressing what Clawson called in 1959 "The Crisis in Outdoor Recreation."[30] They and the commission warned that outdoor recreation would continue to rise, that the existing infrastructure was insufficient to meet the demand, and that without new federal efforts recreational usage would degrade the federal lands.[31]

Curiously, very few people in the 1950s anticipated that recreational use would spill significantly onto the public lands, or perhaps they assumed that wherever this did occur, the land would be transferred to the National Park Service or to state, county, or private ownership. Even Marion Clawson, a former BLM director, assumed into the late 1950s that the BLM lands would not attract major recreational use.[32] As a result, the BLM was totally unprepared for the outdoor recreation rush at a number of levels, including funding, staffing, and statutory authority.[33]

Under Director Woozley, the BLM approached outdoor recreation primarily as a land disposal rather than land management issue. With the exception of the Oregon & California Revested Lands (the O & C lands), the BLM's only statutory authority for recreation was the Recreation and Public Purposes Act of 1926 and its 1956 amendments, which directed the BLM to sell or lease land chiefly valuable for recreation to local governments or to private groups. Furthermore, even on the O & C lands, Congress provided no funding for recreation. Marion Clawson recalls a budget examiner warning him in the early 1950s, "Don't you fellows ever come in here looking for money for recreation. We won't give you a cent."[34] In the early 1950s, the BLM signed an agreement with the National Park Service that when it discovered "public land areas having scenic, scientific, historical, archeological, or other recreation resources which should be protected and made available for public use," it would "look to the Service for technical advice and consultation in this field."[35] But without any recreation funding, it is not clear how extensively the BLM inventoried its land.

As recreation continued to rise on the public lands, the BLM was forced to take administrative steps to deal with the demand. Local governments and community groups identified a host of public lands recreation areas, and in 1958, Woozley reluctantly signed a new recreation policy.[36] The policy differentiated between lands valuable only for recreational use, which the BLM would sell, and lands with multiple-use values, which the BLM would only lease. This is significant, because it acknowledged recreation as an important use on federal land that remained in BLM ownership, even if the BLM would not manage the activities. BLM field managers also took matters into their own hands and built picnic and camping areas without any specific authority or appropriations. In 1960, the BLM exercised its authority to manage for recreation under the Oregon and California Revested Lands Act by constructing its first developed campground on the O & C lands in Oregon, and in 1961, the Oregon State Office issued a recreation handbook and began hiring landscape architects to work on recreation planning.[37]

After President John F. Kennedy's inauguration in 1961 and the Outdoor Recreation Resources Review Commission's (ORRRC) scathing report on the BLM in 1962, recreation vaulted to a much higher priority for the BLM. Secretary of the Interior Udall claimed, "Plans are to give recreation the same degree of attention as is given the more traditional management programs for such resources as range forage, commercial timberland and hardrock minerals."[38] While this lofty rhetoric was not realized in the 1960s, President Kennedy and Secretary Udall did place considerably more emphasis on the recreation potential of the public lands.

In 1961, Udall increased the area a local government or community group could buy/lease from 640 acres to 6,400 acres, and he announced a new pricing schedule for public purpose land sales at $2.50 an acre. By 1962, recreation leases had gone from 12,388 acres to 90,541 acres.[39] President Kennedy further promoted recreation development of the public lands in late 1962, when he launched thirty-one projects to build public recreation facilities under the Accelerated Public Works Program. These projects, which brought outside funding, manpower, and legal justification, sidestepped the agency's limited authorizing statutes and congressional appropriations.[40] By 1963, the BLM had surveyed 50 million acres of its land and found some 10,000 intensive recreation areas. BLM leaders argued that the sites could not be sold or leased to local governments and desperately needed active management, not primarily to promote recreation, but to protect the public lands from damage by uncontrolled use.[41]

Finally, in 1964, Congress acknowledged the BLM's responsibility for recreation management in the Classification and Multiple Use Act (CMUA), which stated that the BLM should identify lands with multiple-use values including outdoor recreation, wilderness preservation, and preservation of public values. In debate, Senator Frank Moss explained: "This legislation . . . will give clear authority to Bureau of Land Management to develop needed recreational facilities on public lands [, and] it will be possible for the Bureau to have a more comprehensive [recreation] program."[42] Recreation had arrived as a significant political pressure on the BLM, and by the late 1960s, the BLM had regular appropriations for recreation management and specially designated recreation and primitive areas.[43]

The rise of recreation supported a broad reinterpretation of conservation priorities for federally owned lands, and the Kennedy administration was undoubtedly a principal catalyst for this change. In particular, President Kennedy's secretary of the interior, Stewart Udall, became a popular spokesman for the evolving conservation movement.

When John F. Kennedy entered the 1960 presidential race, he was hardly a champion of public lands conservation, but he recognized its political importance and created a natural resources committee to advise him during the campaign.[44] What his committee developed was a conservation platform worthy of the progressive era. Freedom itself depended on wise use of the nation's natural resources, he warned, and without federal leadership "this Nation is going to be left behind."[45] Attacking President Eisenhower's record of limited federal initiative, particularly in the area of reclamation, Kennedy consistently emphasized federal, and in particular executive, leadership. In his "new frontier" campaign, he promised a return to New Deal and Fair Deal approaches to government.[46]

President Kennedy's broad affirmation of executive leadership in conservation set the stage for Secretary Udall, who provided energetic leadership for conservation in the Kennedy and Johnson administrations. Udall was a New Deal liberal who viewed the two Roosevelt presidencies as the high points of American conservation history,[47] and he was determined to create, as he told President Kennedy in their first cabinet meeting, a conservation legacy "that would equal or excel that of Theodore Roosevelt."[48] As he wrote in his first annual report, the Kennedy administration was engaging in "one last great effort" to fulfill the programs of preservation and conservation first established by Theodore Roosevelt and Gifford Pinchot and developed by Franklin Roosevelt and Harold Ickes.[49]

Udall took office with a progressive emphasis on efficient resource use and scenic preservation. Over the course of his tenure, however, he increasingly merged this utilitarian conservation philosophy with newer ecological and environmental ideas advanced by recreation interests and the environmental movement.[50] As one scholar writes, Udall "seemed torn between the traditional progressive position which was man-centered and the emerging, postwar perspective which was earth-oriented. The former sought both to balance resource development and preservation. The latter downplayed development. . . . Udall had difficulty straddling the two positions."[51] What emerged was a complex philosophy of conservation that Udall and others called the "third wave" of conservation.[52]

Although Udall was often disappointed by Kennedy's lack of personal enthusiasm for conservation issues, he certainly received public support from the President. After only one month in office, President Kennedy issued a "Special Message to Congress on Natural Resources," in which he called for a return to natural resource conservation based on "the progressive principles of national leadership first forged by Pinchot and Theodore Roosevelt . . . backed by the essential cooperation of State and local governments." The message covered a range of issues, including the public lands, which Kennedy called "a vital national reserve that should be devoted to productive use now and maintained for future generations."[53] Throughout the message, the President emphasized the need for more comprehensive planning and federal leadership.

On March 1, 1962, President Kennedy issued another message to Congress in which he once again emphasized the need for federal leadership in conservation. Just two months later, Udall organized and President Kennedy hosted a White House Conference on Conservation at which Kennedy pledged his support for both development and preservation. In the summer of 1962 and again in the summer of 1963, President Kennedy accompanied Udall on national conservation tours intended to raise publicity for conservation legislation that Udall was trying to push through Congress and general support for the administration's conservation program.[54]

After Kennedy's assassination, President Lyndon Johnson provided similar support for Udall's program. His "Special Message to Congress on Conservation and Restoration of Natural Beauty" and the White House Conference on Natural

Beauty provided public support for conservation efforts, particularly the protection of aesthetic resources.[55] President Johnson also advocated legislative reform of public land laws.

Even with strong presidential support, Udall faced a serious challenge in winning congressional support for reform of the BLM's statutory authority and appropriations priorities. Congress as a whole was torn between receiving fair market return for federal resources and sustaining western natural resource industries, and the BLM's legislative oversight committee generally favored the latter.[56] In pressing for stronger executive leadership and broader conservation of the public lands, Udall challenged these committees and clashed in particular with the chairman of the House Committee on Interior and Insular Affairs, Wayne Aspinall (D-CO). Aspinall agreed that public lands administration needed reform, but he insisted that Congress lead the way. As Aspinall reminded Udall and BLM leaders repeatedly, Congress, and Congress alone, held the constitutional authority to create policy; the executive branch could only recommend and implement policy.[57]

This was not simply a battle over constitutional principles; rather Aspinall objected to the application of Udall's new conservation philosophy to public lands administration. Aspinall took a fairly narrow reading of Pinchot and Roosevelt's utilitarian framework when it came to the public lands. To him, conservation, "was the antithesis of waste."[58] Conservation of the public lands meant something like sustained yield, or maximum resource production over the long term; it did not include preservation of wilderness and open space. Aspinall complained in 1962, "I do not know when, where, or how, the purist preservationist group assumed the mantle of the conservationists. . . . It is a disservice to the conservation movement that many people have come to think of conservation as meaning preservation alone, to the exclusion of other uses."[59]

These issues came to a head during the "Conservation Congress" of 1963–1964. In a letter to President Kennedy on October 15, 1962, Aspinall wrote, "we have reached a point where it is essential to establish clear cut legislative guidelines concerning the management, use and disposition of our public lands." The core of the controversy, he argued, "is the degree of responsibility and authority to be exercised by the Legislative and Executive branches." He called for a creative solution that would allow Congress to control public lands policy without "hamper[ing] the effective administration of that property in accordance with the time honored conservation principle of effecting the maximum good for the maximum number."[60]

Kennedy responded with deference: "I wish to assure you that we are fully mindful of and sincerely respect the constitutional prerogative of the Congress to make rules for the management and disposal of the public lands." At the same time, however, he argued that public lands administration had become highly technical and complex, and "the Legislative Branch is not equipped to engage in the kind of detailed consideration that must attend the hundreds of individual land use decisions inherent in effective management of the public lands."[61] He welcomed broad legislative reforms from Congress but insisted that executive agencies would have to guide and shape congressional policy in their day-to-day operations.

Aspinall's commitment to public lands reform, his debate with the Kennedy administration over executive discretion, and his larger objection to the new wave of conservation led to the passage of a complex package of federal land legislation in 1964, including the Public Land Law Review Commission Act (PLLRCA), the Wilderness Act, the CMUA, and the Public Land Sales Act (PLSA).[62]

The Public Land Law Review Commission (PLLRC) was Aspinall's answer to what he viewed as a serious abrogation of Congress's constitutional responsibility for the public lands and years of "public-land policy making by administrative caprice."[63] The commission, which Aspinall chaired, spent five years and $4.5 million reviewing every aspect of public lands legislation and administration, and it released a final report in 1970.[64] Aspinall hoped that the commission would finally develop comprehensive public lands legislation that would centralize control of public lands administration more narrowly in the House and Senate oversight committees. There, he believed, it would not be "unduly influenced by the emotional environmental binge" of the 1960s.[65]

Support for Aspinall's bill was far from unanimous, since many members of Congress objected to this time-consuming and expensive approach to federal land law reform. In the end, Aspinall cut a deal with sponsors of the 1964 wilderness bill to support wilderness legislation in exchange for the PLLRC. Aspinall had opposed the wilderness bill both because it would inhibit natural resource development and because as originally drafted, it permitted the executive branch to designate wilderness areas. Aspinall's support for the wilderness bill was contingent on an amendment making Congress the sole designator of wilderness areas.[66] The Wilderness Act was also limited to lands in the national park, national forest, and national wildlife refuge systems and did not apply to BLM lands. While there certainly were people inside and outside the agency who advocated extending the wilderness act to BLM lands, such an amendment would almost certainly have killed the wilderness bill.

The CMUA and the PLSA originated as legislative requests from the Department of the Interior, and they certainly had the greatest immediate impact on the BLM. The CMUA provided the BLM with temporary authority—set to expire with the PLLRC—(1) to classify areas of the public lands for disposal through various nonmineral land laws or for federal retention and multiple use management, and (2) to manage lands retained in federal ownership for a mix of values to achieve the highest and best use of the land, including grazing, fish and wildlife, industrial development, mineral production, occupancy, outdoor recreation, timber production, watershed protection, wilderness preservation, and other beneficial uses. This was the broadest delegation of discretionary authority ever given to the BLM, and it provided a temporary copy of the Forest Service's Multiple Use and Sustained Yield Act of 1960. The PLSA replaced a number of existing land disposal laws and gave the BLM broader, temporary authority to sell lands to states, counties, and municipalities for public purposes and to citizens, corporations, and partnerships at fair market value. Taken together, the CMUA and the PSA permitted the BLM make important decisions about land disposal, retention, and management.[67]

Aspinall introduced and supported the CMUA and PLSA as a stopgap measure until the PLLRC could complete its investigation and make comprehensive legislative recommendations. He assumed that the commission's report would override any administrative actions taken in this interim period. Ultimately, however, the wording of the statutes gave the BLM more authority than Aspinall seems to have intended. As the statutes were later interpreted, the BLM had a limited time period in which to exercise its authority, but the decisions made during this period were permanent unless Congress specifically revoked them.[68]

The CMUA helped redefine the BLM and the public lands. It signaled an end to the disposal orientation of earlier public lands legislation and administration, and it confronted the most basic land tenure problem the BLM faced: ambiguity over the future disposal or federal retention of the public lands. The act did nothing to address the agency's second basic land problem, which was the tenure pattern of intermingled federal, state, and private landholdings, but BLM leaders hoped to use the CMUA as a foundation to begin consolidating its landholdings. The CMUA was also important because it extended the rhetoric of multiple-use management to the public lands as a whole. Beyond the descriptive reality that the public lands supported many different and overlapping uses, multiple use was important symbolic language that pointed to the kind of administrative discretion that the Forest Service held to balance competing land and resource uses, and BLM leaders quickly used the statute to assert the agency's proprietary interest in the public lands. As Marion Clawson explains, the CMUA "gave the Bureau a psychological lift that has led to its taking the initiative more and more often."[69] The CMUA, despite the House subcommittee's emphasis on the act's ephemeral nature, helped set in motion a new and lasting, if limited, pattern of BLM discretion.[70]

CLASSIFICATION AND PLANNING: REDEFINING THE BLM AND THE PUBLIC LANDS

Seeing a window of opportunity created by the agency's shifting political context, BLM leaders, particularly directors Karl Landstrom (1961–1963) and Charles Stoddard (1963–1966), sought to redefine the public lands as a national land system and to reshape the BLM's management role. They struggled to define a clear national purpose for the public lands and a clear mission for the BLM in the face of conflicting demands from Congress, from public lands users, and from the American public. The new BLM that emerged was not something they designed out of whole cloth; rather it was an ongoing struggle between their ambitious vision of a comprehensive public lands conservation program and the complex political realities and property rights regimes embedded in public lands management.

Director Landstrom and Charles Stoddard, who served from 1961 to 1963 as Secretary Udall's director of resources program staff, started in January 1961 with the basic assumption that something was fundamentally wrong with public lands policy and management. Landstrom was fed up with the BLM's complex statutory and administrative program for land classification and disposal, and Stoddard complained that the BLM lacked any meaningful framework to guide the agency's programs.[71] They echoed Udall's complaints that the BLM was in administrative chaos and that the "statutory set up for administering these lands reminds me of a ghost town that time has passed by. We are being forced to use horse-and-buggy statutes in a guided missile age."[72] Or, as their immediate supervisor, Assistant Secretary John Carver, put it, "The crazyquilt patchwork of public land laws, altered and mended and embroidered to meet the exigencies of the moment, does not add up to a national land policy and program."[73] These leaders had their eyes fixed on a systematic approach to public lands conservation and management, and this was at odds with the catalogue of congressional patronage policy that had accumulated over the previous century.

Addressing these issues, however, meant confronting once again the legacy of the awkward General Land Office/U.S. Grazing Service merger that had produced the BLM. Fifteen years after the merger, the BLM remained two agencies: a land disposal agency in the General Land Office tradition and a land management agency in the Grazing Service tradition. BLM leaders hoped that land classification and new land disposal legislation would finally clarify the public lands' national importance and the proprietary interest that the federal government had in these lands. In other words, they hoped to redefine the public lands as a national landscape worthy of careful, professional management. If the BLM accomplished this, the leaders believed, it could then confront more clearly the ambiguity in its management mission and the tension between "home-rule" and professional management. They hoped ultimately to initiate the kind of professional, multiple-use management championed by the Forest Service.

Udall, Landstrom, and especially Stoddard argued for nothing less than a new Bureau of Land Management. The BLM's role, they believed had become "essentially a passive, adaptive one, in which meeting the needs of the clientele— through either direct or covert means—was emphasized."[74] This fit with the image of the old public domain lands of the nineteenth century, over which the General Land Office had served as a temporary custodian. The time had come, they argued, for the BLM to become a goal-driven land and resource manager, a role that fit the new definition that they were trying to give to the public lands.

One of the best indications of the identity that BLM leaders were trying to forge was the new emblem that they released in 1964. It challenged both existing images of the public lands as places of unrestricted economic development and the agency's fragmented organization and culture that had developed as a result.[75]

The agency's old emblem (Figure 3.1) emphasizes private initiative, natural resource development, and human progress. It depicts a miner, a rancher, an engineer, a logger, and a surveyor standing shoulder to shoulder against the backdrop of covered wagons, train tracks, and industrial development, and it is significant that only the surveyor is a BLM employee. It celebrates not so much the public lands themselves, but the public lands users; it was issued in 1952 with these words: "BLM stresses the importance of the human factor in the transition from a western covered wagon economy to that of modern industrial development."[76]

The 1964/current emblem (Figure 3.2), by contrast, emphasizes the public lands as landscapes that transcend any particular resource user. It depicts simply a mountain, a tree, and a river valley: as the BLM director explained, "This triumvirate of soil, water, and vegetation are the elemental constituents of the public lands. They were chosen to depict multiple use with unimpaired productivity."[77] The new emblem represents an attempt to erase or at least weaken the historical identity that ranchers, miners, loggers, and homesteaders had given to the public lands. Here, the public lands are depicted as a wilderness or park that is free from human presence or impact; they are represented as a blank slate upon which BLM leaders hoped to rebuild the agency's management role from the ground up.[78]

Directors Landstrom and Stoddard also tried repeatedly to redefine the public lands by renaming them, and these efforts proved more controversial. Many people in the early 1960s, including the president on several occasions, referred to the public lands as the "vacant, unappropriated, and unreserved public domain lands."[79] BLM leaders complained that this misrepresented the public lands in important ways. It suggested that the federal government had no interest in the public lands and that they were open to unrestricted use. It was also technically inaccurate, since the Taylor Grazing Act and two executive orders in the 1930s had withdrawn or reserved all BLM lands in the lower forty-eight states.[80] As Director Landstrom argued in 1961, "the so-called 'unreserved public lands' in the Western States are not 'unreserved' at all."[81] He acknowledged that the BLM still accepted and processed land applications, but he insisted that these were technically petitions for the BLM to reopen specific areas for entry and settlement. Landstrom argued that the legal status of the public lands was much closer in character to that of the national forest system than to the nineteenth-century unreserved public domain, and he believed that the public lands had been "reserved for conservation of natural resources."[82]

In 1961 Landstrom wanted a title that would convey national significance and distinguish the public lands as a permanent land system on par with the national park and forest systems. Citing a speech in which President Kennedy used similar language, Landstrom began calling them the "the National Land Reserve" even though he had no legal authority to do so. The new title would have had no immediate effect on public lands policy and management, but the ambition behind

Figure 3.1. Image
courtesy of the Bureau of
Land Management.

it alarmed many western congressmen. Wayne Aspinall in particular wanted to
protect western interests from this type of executive or administrative caprice. He
was not about to let a BLM director reshape the public lands identity, even rhetorically, and he forced Landstrom to drop the new title.[83]

After Charles Stoddard became the BLM Director, he tried other approaches
to renaming the public lands. In 1963, for example, Secretary Udall approved
the designation of eighty-five Resource Conservation Areas to highlight particular conservation priorities, and Stoddard intended to use the Resource Conservation Areas (RCAs) to demonstrate the BLM's new start in multiple-use planning
and management.[84] The RCAs were to serve as "an expanded program properly
planned, organized, and directed, calculated to yield maximum results for the dollars invested."[85] Most important, the RCAs were intended for tourists, tour groups,
and professional groups, rather than traditional commercial public lands users, so
they were intended to reach a national, rather than regional, audience.[86]

In 1964, Stoddard urged Secretary Udall to give each of the BLM's most consolidated management areas a name based upon a significant natural or historical
feature and to give these areas a general title, such as national conservation area
or national resource area, which would set them apart and indicate their national
value: "The general term 'public lands' is not sufficiently specific for this purpose.
Citizen awareness of public lands comes about by boundaries, colors on maps,
names such as National Forest and National Park, signs at entrances . . . etc."[87]
Udall rejected the request, perhaps thinking back to the controversy surrounding
Landstrom's use of "National Land Reserve."

U.S. DEPARTMENT OF THE INTERIOR
BUREAU OF LAND MANAGEMENT

Figure 3.2. Image courtesy of the Bureau of Land Management.

Finally, in 1965, Stoddard initiated a search for areas of natural wonder on BLM land, and Secretary Udall designated sixteen public lands sites as scientific natural areas.[88] These areas, like national parks, national monuments, and certain areas within the national forest service, emphasized preservation of natural beauty and objects of scientific interest and attracted tourists, scientists, and other non-commercial users. The resource conservation areas and the scientific natural areas allowed BLM leaders to redefine the purpose and value of some specific public lands areas in lieu of renaming the public lands as a whole.

Amidst this war of symbols, Directors Landstrom and Stoddard focused much of their attention on two immediate obstacles to creating a more cohesive and comprehensive system of public lands management: existing land tenure patterns and the BLM's almost total lack of long-range planning. Land tenure, both the uncertainty surrounding the future of public lands ownership and the checkerboard pattern of land ownership, was perhaps the more widely recognized problem, and land tenure questions were the agency's first priority in 1961. The second problem, the lack of planning, received less attention outside of the executive branch, but to BLM leaders it was the obstacle to professional maturity. Rational planning was the highest ideal of professional resource management, and for many leaders it was the agency's best hope of gaining control over land use decisions.

LANDSTROM'S INITIATIVES

Karl Landstrom assumed his position as BLM director soon after President Kennedy's inauguration. He had started with the BLM as regional chief of land planning in Portland, Oregon, in 1949 and became the BLM's chief of research and analysis in 1953. Immediately prior to his appointment, Landstrom spent two years as a legislative consultant for the House subcommittees on Public Lands, National Parks, and Mining, where he interacted with a broad range of interest groups and worked closely with Congressman Aspinall on a number of issues.

Landstrom, then, was familiar with the agency's land classification and disposal problems, and he was familiar with the land disposal scandals that the House and Senate Committees reviewed on a regular basis. He was determined to tackle land classification and disposal problems head-on by reducing the agency's backlog of land applications and clarifying the agency's policies governing land disposal. Ambiguity in the BLM's land tenure pattern, he argued, reflected the heart of the agency's dilemma. With a split disposal/management mission, the agency did not have clear direction as either a temporary caretaker or permanent proprietor of the public lands. Until the agency could clearly separate future disposal and management responsibilities, he told Congress, it would be impossible for the BLM to establish clear, long-range management plans.[89]

On February 14, 1961, Secretary Udall issued an eighteen-month moratorium on all nonmineral land applications so that the BLM could reduce its backlog of more than 45,000 nonmineral applications and Landstrom could begin to formulate a new approach to land disposal. On the same day, he issued a policy statement that established what Landstrom called the public interest test for all land disposal and exchange: (1) the government should receive full compensation for its property; (2) federal/private land exchanges must serve a federal interest; and (3) lands that cannot be developed under existing laws would be retained.[90]

The moratorium and policy statement were probably the first major point of tension between the BLM and Congressman Aspinall, because they raised the question of control over the disposal and retention of the public lands.[91] Congress had passed literally thousands of public lands laws over the past century, which provided for the sale or grant of public lands for a variety of reasons. Application of the public interest test, however, asserted that the secretary of the interior ultimately held discretionary authority to approve or reject each application, and it implied that the BLM had a proprietary rather than simply custodial responsibility for the public lands. Udall's actions were a bid to reshape public lands decision making, giving the executive branch greater control over public lands disposal and management.

Efforts to reshape public lands policy and tenure gained momentum when the president issued a "Special Message to the Congress on Natural Resources" on February 23, 1961. Coauthored by Charles Stoddard, the message advanced the BLM's goals for land inventory, classification, and planning. President Kennedy directed the BLM to (1) accelerate an inventory and evaluation of the nation's public domain holdings to serve as a foundation for improved resource management; (2) develop a program of balanced usage designed to reconcile conflicting uses—grazing, forestry, recreation, wildlife, urban development, and minerals; and (3) accelerate the installation of soil-conserving and water-saving works and practices to reduce erosion and improve forage capacity and to proceed with the revegetation of range lands on which the forage capacity has been badly depleted or destroyed.[92] The president's message provided political support, particularly in the appropriations process, to start or accelerate a number of programs.[93]

Stoddard worked with Landstrom to translate the president's mandate into specific appropriations and legislative requests. They proposed increased appropriations for land classification and range conservation, and they proposed legislation to broaden the Taylor Grazing Act beyond its existing livestock focus, to grant the president greater authority to regroup natural resources agencies as he deemed necessary, and to create a larger program of acquisition of parks and recreation areas. This marked the beginning of a major rise in BLM appropriations, and it was a clear bid for greater executive or administrative control of public lands policy and management.[94]

Pending new legislation, but with increased appropriations and a temporary moratorium on new land applications, Landstrom immediately tackled land classification and disposal problems. In 1962, the BLM launched the Master Unit Classification Program that Robert Jones and Irving Senzel had already been developing for the lands and realty program.[95] The thrust of the new program was comprehensive classification. Instead of responding to each petition to open a tract of land to entry, the BLM would conduct a systematic review of all public lands and identify lands suited to disposal in advance of land applications. This would give the BLM a more secure foundation for long-range planning and make land classification an agency-led rather than applicant-led process.

Under the classification system, the public lands were first divided into geographic study units, or master units, of various sizes (Figure 3.3). The areas were small enough that they could be analyzed as a coherent unit but large enough to allow for comprehensive classification. BLM employees then analyzed the physical, economic, and social characteristics of each unit, classifying them as (1) lands suited for disposal, (2) lands well suited to BLM management, and (3) residual areas that could not be placed in the first two categories.[96]

Distinguishing between lands best suited for private, city, or state ownership and lands best suited for federal ownership and multiple-use management asserted the federal government's proprietary interest in the public lands and the BLM's role in professional administration. In many ways, this classification was a symbolic substitute for the kinds of withdrawals, reservations, and classifications that had created the national park and forest systems. The BLM, in other words, emphasized in action what Landstrom had been arguing during his first year as BLM director: the BLM lands were a national land reserve that Congress and President Franklin Roosevelt had withdrawn for multiple-use management in the 1930s. Nonmineral land disposal, though still a statutory mandate, was a discretionary responsibility based upon the BLM's professional assessment of the highest and best use of its lands.

President Kennedy had also directed the BLM to develop a "program of

Figure 3.3. Robert A. Jones, "Master Unit Classification,"*Our Public Lands* 11, no. 3 (1962): 9.

balanced usage" for the public lands. The president's mandate to balance "grazing, forestry, recreation, wildlife, urban development and minerals" echoed the Forest Service's Multiple Use Sustained Yield Act of 1960. It was an invitation for the BLM to begin a planned program of multiple use in marked contrast to the unplanned or de facto multiple uses that existed. Udall and Landstrom prepared a legislative proposal for a BLM multiple-use act, which Secretary Udall forwarded to Congress in early 1963.[97] Landstrom explained: "Under the Department's proposal, all of the lands were to be brought under multiple use principles unless otherwise provided. Techniques of applying the principles, as in the 1960 Act, were left to administrative regulation."[98]

As the BLM developed its multiple-use proposal and waited for Congress to act, Landstrom worked to build the BLM's professional autonomy and discretion. This included inventories and initiatives in new areas like recreation, but it focused primarily on neutralizing some of the power that the grazing advisory boards held in public lands decision making. First, the BLM accelerated its range inventory and range adjudication program to reassess grazing levels in all grazing allotments, which Landstrom explained to the House Committee on Interior and

Insular Affairs would serve as the foundation for an entirely new, professional, and scientific approach to range management: "The objective is to complete adjudication of grazing privileges at the earliest date prior to July 1, 1967, to increase range use supervision in keeping with a substantially increased development and conservation program, to improve and refine management plans, and to accelerate range evaluation and economic studies."[99]

Second, in December 1961, Landstrom and Udall reshaped the BLM's advisory boards to broaden the agency's collaboration with public lands users. While the BLM's grazing advisory boards at the district level remained unchanged, the state and national boards were reorganized as "Multiple-Use Advisory Boards." Under the new rules, the state advisory boards would have the same number of livestock representatives, but they were expanded to include up to seven representatives from the areas of forest products, minerals, soil conservation, outdoor recreation, urban and suburban development, county and state government, and wildlife. The National Advisory Board would also maintain the same number of livestock representatives, but it would be expanded to include three to ten wildlife representatives and ten representatives of other interests.[100] President Kennedy followed this up in 1962 with an executive order that regulated the activities of the advisory boards. The new regulations required that federal employees call all advisory meetings, prepare the agenda, and hold the power to adjourn meetings.[101]

Third, Landstrom and Interior Department officials worked continuously to articulate a new vision of agency-led multiple-use management that would serve a broad range of competing interests and replace the old home-rule model of range management.[102] Multiple use, Assistant Secretary Carver explained to the American National Cattlemen's Association in January 1962, "is far from a refuge for the cattleman. Indeed it is the gate through which competing uses enter what was his domain." Recreation, he warned, was a real challenge to the dominance of the livestock industry: "The national forests had nearly a hundred million visitors last year. If collection of a ten cent entry fee had been made, recreation use of the forests would have returned more than three times the grazing fee proceeds from BLM lands."[103]

Fourth, after a two-year study of grazing fees, the BLM raised the fees by more than 50 percent, from 19 cents per animal unit month (AUM) to 30 cents per AUM, and the portion of the grazing fees designated for range improvement projects rose from 25 to 33 1/3 percent. In combination, this doubled the funds available for range improvement projects and reduced the BLM's dependence on the advisory boards.[104]

The BLM was taking broad, and in many cases purely symbolic, actions to demonstrate a new professionalism in range management and a new independence from the grazing advisory boards. To demonstrate this "new start" in more concrete terms, the BLM launched four special range management projects. The most widely touted project was located in the 4.6-million-acre Vale district in southeastern Oregon, an area of rich history in the Grazing Service/BLM range wars of the 1940s and 1950s.[105] Bob Wolf, who initially organized the Vale Project and later became assistant to the BLM director, recalls that despite very poor range conditions, the BLM had been unable to reduce grazing levels and had no money for range improvement.[106] Wolf and a member of the National Advisory Board Council convinced local permittees to accept reductions in grazing levels in exchange for the promise of additional range improvement funds and increased forage. In June 1962, Congress approved special range improvement appropriations for the Vale Project, and the BLM went to work making the Vale district a model set of grazing allotments. As Landstrom explained to the National Advisory Board Council, "We are hoping that these projects will demonstrate what can and should be done elsewhere. We are concerned with . . . the programming, scheduling and funding of a program that will achieve benefits within justified costs, and with public understanding and participation."[107]

Landstrom also tried to build the agency's professional stature and capabilities through long-range planning. As noted in the previous chapter, planning under Clawson had amounted to two-year appropriations plans for each of the agency's main programs. Woozley had taken the next step in 1960 with the BLM's first long-range management plan, "Project 2012." The plan was modeled to some extent after the Park Service's "Mission 66"—a comprehensive, long-range, and largely successful plan that outlined a strategy for revamping the agency's antiquated visitor services. Project 2012 provided a fifty-year plan for all BLM programs in a concise sixty-three pages, suggesting an overhaul of the BLM's antiquated custodial management. As Sally Fairfax notes, the plan was vague and lacked specific directions, but it was an important symbolic step in the Bureau's leadership and management ambitions.[108]

Landstrom, who viewed Project 2012 as a failure in terms of real program planning, went to work immediately on a more concrete planning program for the public lands. In May 1962, the BLM released a "Program for the Public Lands and Resources." With a flourish of multiple-use and conservation rhetoric, the document unveiled "a completely new effort to provide needed direction and guidance in the administration and development of public lands and their resources."[109] Although equally short—the document provided a two-phase plan covering 1962–1980 in a mere forty pages—"Program for the Public Lands and Resources" provided far more concrete planning by tying cost and benefit estimates to each projected program.

The plan reflected Landstrom's faith in professional multiple-use management: "Balanced use in an orderly manner provides for the best and most effective uses of all available public lands and resources—with due concern for the total availability of these resources regionally and nationally, the conservation of resources, and a reconciliation of conflicting demands for use of the public lands."[110] Multiple-use management, Landstrom argued, often appeared vague and confusing to the layperson, but it had clear professional meaning developed by Gifford Pinchot and the Forest Service. This faith in professional management and rational planning is, in part, what exacerbated tension between Landstrom and his immediate supervisor, Assistant Secretary Carver. Carver maintained that multiple-use management was still essentially political management, because it did not provide any formula to solve resource use conflicts.[111] When it came down to resolving conflicting uses, then, Landstrom argued for greater administrative discretion and Carver argued for congressional prerogative and responsibility. Ultimately, Landstrom's conflicts with Carver, the livestock and mining industries, and the BLM's congressional oversight committees became too great a liability for the Interior Department, and Secretary Udall removed Landstrom from the BLM directorship.[112]

When Landstrom left after two and a half years, the BLM was already moving in a new direction. As a result of Landstrom's actions and the broader contextual shifts noted above, the BLM had come to take greater control of its management decisions and serve a broader range of interests. Indeed, Carver later recalled that by the time Landstrom left the BLM, "he had already established a position as kind of a patron saint of the more militant conservationists, as being the best BLM chief that they'd ever had."[113]

STODDARD'S APPROACH: A STRATEGY OF BECOMING

Charles Stoddard assumed the position of BLM director in June 1963. With a background in forestry and experience with the Forest Service, the Bureau of Agricultural Economics, and Resources for the Future, he was well acquainted with federal land policy and management. Having worked on President Kennedy's natural resources committee during the 1960 election, on the president's "Special Message to Congress on Natural Resources," and as Secretary Udall's director of Resources Program Staff, Stoddard was also deeply immersed in the Kennedy administration's approach to conservation.[114]

Stoddard was extremely reluctant to leave his job on the Resources Program Staff and enter the fray of BLM administration, and he accepted the position with deep reservations that he expressed in a May 1963 memo to Udall:

> I have been extremely reluctant to accept this new appointment . . . [b]ut I have done so because you asked me to do so and because there is a long-shot chance of getting a much broader conservation program established on the public lands. I am fully aware that the BLM Directors are, by the nature of the job, the most expendable and vulnerable people in the Department, if not the Government—caught as they are between the cross fire of the Hill Committees, the booby traps laid by special interest groups and archaic laws which tie their lands. I have known all four recent Directors and worked for

Clawson and Forsling so I know full well what dandy plank I am about to walk. . . . *I know in any case my job expectancy will probably be two years at the outside even if I run only a purely custodial operation.*[115]

Stoddard had no intention of running a "purely custodial operation" in the BLM, and perhaps this pessimism about the duration of his tenure encouraged him to pursue change aggressively in the face of conflict.

By the time that Stoddard became director, Secretary Udall's conservation program was in full swing. What had begun as a traditional conservation agenda of balancing development and preservation had become for Udall a more comprehensive philosophy of the relationship between humans and the natural world.[116] Stoddard also inherited a number of new initiatives from Landstrom, including land classification, changes in range management, and legislative requests for broader land sales and multiple-use authority. Stoddard saw the momentum of Udall's conservation program and Landstrom's initiatives as an opportunity to transform the BLM's overall mission and culture and to redefine the public lands as a federal land system comparable to the national forests, national parks, and national wildlife refuges.

Above all, Stoddard pushed the BLM toward more integrated system-level analysis and planning. In this, he relied increasingly on academic scholarship in public administration and land use planning, eventually establishing a special program at the University of Wisconsin's Department of Urban and Regional Planning to ground BLM planners in current planning theory and practice.[117] This approach reduced some of the field managers' flexibility in dealing with local interests and gave the Washington office greater influence over the agency's planning and management.

After only ten days as the BLM director, Stoddard met with Dr. George Shipman from the University of Washington's Institute for Administrative Research. Landstrom had contracted Shipman and his doctoral student David Paulsen as research consultants to evaluate the BLM's organization and operations and to recommend ways that the Bureau could improve its effectiveness and efficiency. Landstrom initiated the study in response to ongoing demands from Congress to improve the agency's economy, to Udall's broad conservation goals for the public lands, and to the agency's ongoing problems of coordination across functional areas.[118] Shipman described the agency's "divided, uncoordinated, unilateral structure . . . [its] case-by-case orientation, its custodial (as opposed to managerial) approach and its lack of a mission or goal." Shipman went on, Stoddard recalls, "to say, 'Unless you can spell out a goal, a set of objectives, I can't be of much value to you nor can I come up with any organizational recommendations. Organization must be tailored to mission.'"[119]

In their first report on the Washington office, Shipman and Paulsen gave a more detailed but equally dismal assessment of the BLM's predicament:

The Bureau's mission is clouded with ambiguity. . . . It is apparent in the legislation the Bureau administers, and the relationship of formal legislative objectives to the realities of today's American society and its economy. It is apparent in the attitudes of interested public groups and of the Congress. It is manifest in the Bureau's own work processes. Given this ambiguity, it is not surprising that there is more than one interpretation of the Bureau mission. In the traditional view, the Bureau is charged simply with administering the transfer of the unreserved public domain from federal to non-governmental ownership. . . . This approach reserves initiative and, in effect, critical decision-making to the private sector of the society. . . . [In the emerging view] the central objective is promotion of the total public interest by wise and prudent use of federally-owned land and land-related resources.[120]

Shipman's assessment was hardly novel. Clawson, Landstrom, Stoddard, and a host of other federal administrators and public administration scholars had complained about this fundamental tension in the BLM's mission that began with its formation in 1946.

Shipman argued that in order to "live responsibly and effectively . . . the Bureau needs to develop a basic administrative and organizational design that will enable it to come to its full maturity. . . . In all respects, the Bureau must gird itself to take a leading role in national resource development."[121] Here, full maturity undoubtedly meant something like the Forest Service model of agency-led conservation. This idea had been proposed numerous times in the past, generally with detrimental effects on the agency's budget and congressional relations. However, Shipman's proposal focused on organizational and procedural changes rather than confrontational policy changes: "The primary need of the Bureau at this time is . . . an organizational environment in which the competence, the loyalties, and the enthusiasms of its people can be put productively to rewarding and self-respecting program accomplishment."[122]

In the second report on BLM field operations, Shipman and Paulsen explained that the basic problems of ambiguity and segmentation pervaded the entire agency. In the absence of any clear public consensus on the purpose of the public domain, they argued, "it appears that activities regarded as professional, on or related to the land, become directed to the long-range maximization of a single resource as a value in itself."[123] Thus, each professional group worked in isolation with its own authorizing legislation and its own appropriations priorities.[124]

Stoddard wanted the BLM to move beyond this segmented, adaptive management posture to become a "vigorous, goal-seeking organization oriented to conservation values and objectives,"[125] and this was no simple task. The BLM did not enjoy any clear public or congressional mandate, and the agency itself reflected diverse opinions on the best national policy for the public lands. In this environment, Paulsen wrote, "a doctrinaire conservationist position . . . would undoubtedly create great social strains, and undoubtedly be politically disastrous to the Bureau," both externally and internally. The two scholars recommended instead an approach they called a "strategy of becoming," which emphasized experimentation and incremental internal change. Rather than tackling conflicts and ambiguity in the BLM's external political environment—clientele groups, Congress, state and local governments, and so on—they recommended that Stoddard focus on achieving greater consensus within the agency: "a strategy of becoming requires that careful attention be given to the organizational environment within which substantive changes in attitudes and relationships can occur. The strategy of becoming refers, then, to a process of constant adjustment and reappraisal of guidelines to substantive changes and analysis of the organization's social environment."[126]

A strategy of becoming, the scholars argued, would require a number of broad steps in the BLM. First, the Washington office should provide greater clarity and leadership in articulating the agency's policies, so that the field managers clearly understood their role in relationship to their client groups. Second, the BLM should continue to modify its appropriations requests to emphasize conservation programs. Third, the BLM should build "system capacities" to record and analyze information, which would provide the agency with a common language. In particular, the BLM should develop a comprehensive planning process. Fourth, the BLM should put considerable effort into building a more positive public relations program, both to convey its new conservation focus and to anticipate public/clientele demands. The individual professional groups in the BLM, Shipman and Paulsen argued, were "in a very real sense . . . the center—the defenders—of the present system. . . . They legitimize the present processes and the character of adaptive management." All four of the recommended steps were designed both to diminish the dominance of individual professional groups and to create a new cultural, social, and intellectual core for the BLM.[127]

The incremental and indirect strategy was intended to avoid another showdown with Congress and clientele groups, but it also presented certain risks. The adaptive strategy itself might "degenerate into a continuation of the Bureau's present adaptive posture, but with a slightly different label."[128] BLM leadership, they argued, would have to provide the ongoing direction and commitment to change over an extended period of time.

Stoddard adopted Shipman and Paulsen's basic plan. In May 1964 he reorganized the Washington office, integrating the agency's previous functional divisions—timber, range, engineering, adjudication, classification, administration—into three main branches: resource management for renewable resources, lands and minerals, and administration. He also established the Office of Program Development to help coordinate the agency's planning and management programs. The central purpose of the office was to "create a system consciousness in the Bureau that things were related to one another,"[129] even while Congress continued to isolate functional programs in the appropriations process. The reorganization,

Stoddard wrote, was one step toward redefining "the whole personality of the organization."[130] This was, like the new BLM emblem that Stoddard released just two days later, an attempt to shift the focus from the agency's individual resource programs and uses to conservation of the public lands as a whole.

Stoddard eventually reorganized the state offices along the same line-and-staff model to increase coordination at the state level and improve cooperation with the states, and he relied on Shipman's evaluation of the BLM's state directors to make a number of personnel changes. After Assistant Secretary Carver rejected his proposal to reinstate three regional offices, Stoddard established two service centers in Portland and Denver to provide coordinated technical services to the state and district offices. While Stoddard did not immediately reorganize district offices (the district manager remained the only line officer in charge of multiple-use coordination at that level), he anticipated division of each BLM district into five or six management areas. Each area manager, working under the district manager, would be responsible for all functional programs in that space, bringing integrated management down to a smaller geographic area. In addition, Stoddard attempted to reorganize the BLM's career ladder, shifting control of hiring and promotion away from the agency's dominant professional groups and providing advancement opportunities for general managers.[131]

At the same time that Stoddard reorganized the BLM and tried to reshape its social systems, he accelerated the BLM's classification and planning efforts. When Stoddard assumed the BLM directorship, Secretary Udall had already submitted the BLM's legislative request for classification and multiple-use authority, and he directed Stoddard to prepare the BLM for this new statutory authority and multiple-use mission: "As a first step," Udall wrote in December 1963, "you are hereby directed to identify and classify those concentrations of public lands having multiple use values which must receive a long-term public management program in order to make their best contribution to local and national growth."[132] Stoddard asked Bob Jones and Irving Senzel to reshape the Master Unit Classification Program as a foundation for multiple-use planning and management.

In April 1964, Stoddard and Carver held a meeting of all the BLM's state directors and district managers to kick off the new classification program, discussing the issues in the Shipman report, the new definition that they hoped to give to the public lands through classification, and the new culture they hoped to build in the agency. The BLM, Stoddard insisted, had to answer basic questions about the "identity of the Bureau and of the lands which we administer."[133] Stoddard explained, the BLM faced a choice: "The first thing we are to do is to clarify our goals: are we active managers or passive custodians?"[134] Land classification would help to articulate the national importance of the public lands, and reorganization would help the agency to take more comprehensive steps toward active management.

After summarizing the Shipman report, Bob Jones explained the new classification program. The first step was a thorough inventory of the BLM's 256 master units. Next, the agency would classify its land into one of three categories: (1) resource management areas suited to intensive multiple-use management in federal ownership; (2) cooperative areas with intermingled private and public ownership; and (3) transfer parcels. The areas slated for retention would then be subdivided into individual multiple-use planning units. The new emphasis on geographic area rather than program function would give clearer identity to specific tracts of BLM land and would advance more integrated multiple-use management.[135]

Based on limited transcripts from Bob Jones's presentation, the state and district managers were concerned about the new direction the BLM was taking, not so much in classification but in coordinated planning. Chiefly, they feared loss of discretion and flexibility at the field level, coordination between states, funding, and the relationship between the comprehensive planning process and the existing planning processes within each functional area.[136]

Stoddard asked district managers to size up their land and recommend areas for retention under multiple-use management. In the meantime, Bob Jones, whom Stoddard appointed head of the newly formed Office of Program Development, Irving Senzel, and Ed Zaidlicz took the field managers' input and began to draft classification procedures. They settled on a system that the University of Wisconsin's College of Agriculture developed in 1928. The Wisconsin program began with a land inventory and analysis followed by planning, classification, and zoning, all of which involved public participation. Wisconsin succeeded, Stoddard believed, because it relied heavily on local government and citizen participation, which in turn built strong political support. The Wisconsin program, in other words, accounted for the interests and investments that local people had in the land and made them partners in the classification and planning process.[137]

The choice to use the Wisconsin program is instructive, because it was a program that the college had developed for use on tax-delinquent lands that were at that time reverting back to public ownership. Legal claims to these lands were unambiguous, for the state held a clear legal right to condemn private property for back taxes. Yet politically, the legacy of private ownership continued to influence the identity of these lands. Similar ambiguity surrounded the public lands, where the federal government held clear legal title, but ranchers, miners, loggers, and states had gained privileges to use the public lands, which were akin to common-law property rights.

By the end of the summer of 1964, the BLM had developed a more nuanced classification system consisting of five land categories: (1) well-blocked areas of 50–100 percent federal ownership; (2) scattered areas where BLM holdings made up 30–50 percent; (3) concentrated federal holdings where management was divided among different federal agencies; (4) BLM lands necessary for urban or industrial use; and (5) BLM lands so scattered that they made up less than 30 percent of the area. Although the percentage of federal ownership was not the only factor in the final classifications, it was an important indicator of the property rights regimes that the BLM had to consider. Lands well blocked in federal ownership would generally allow the BLM more freedom in planning and managing an area, whereas areas with a low percentage of federal ownership required greater dependence on and deference to state and private land owners: "The object of the classification effort, then, was to bring the local and national interests, plus the BLM technical knowledge, together in the decision-making process."[138] This process would give the BLM an opportunity to eliminate lands too integrated with private and state property interests to allow for clear federal control.

On September 19, 1964, President Johnson signed the CMUA and the PLSA, giving the BLM broader classification authority. The act gave the BLM a statutory foundation for what it was already doing administratively. The BLM's Office of Program Development was able to issue draft classification procedures just five days after the act was signed, and Stoddard met with Secretary Udall and Assistant Secretary Carver in early October to brief them on the BLM's plans.[139] Secretary Udall supported the BLM's basic approach but stressed the political sensitivity of the situation. The BLM was operating under administrative initiative and temporary statutory authority, and the agency worked in the shadow of the PLLRC. Udall and Carver insisted that the BLM run its draft classification regulations by members of Congress before taking them to the public. It was made clear that the BLM's new initiatives needed to harmonize with the current attitudes and work of the PLLRC, or it would most likely be counterproductive once the PLLRC released its report.[140]

Having worked on developing the classification program for three years by the time President Johnson signed the CMUA, the BLM moved far more quickly on classification than many members of Congress had anticipated. BLM field managers, who had been working on tentative classification boundaries, began to meet with local advisory boards and local government officials for advice on final classification. The BLM also met with representatives of the National Association of Counties, the U.S. Conference of Mayors, the National League of Cities, and the Council of State Governments. The agency selected eighteen counties from the eleven western states to test the classification process. By March of 1965, when the BLM hosted a conference on Urban and Regional Planning in Reno, NV, the test programs were up and running. By the time Secretary Udall signed the final classification regulations in October 1965, the BLM had presented them at more than sixty-five public meetings and made numerous changes as a result of public participation.[141]

Stoddard had initially estimated that the BLM would classify most of its lands for retention and multiple-use management, and yet the public support that the agency received for multiple-use retention still came as a surprise. After years of complaints about burdens of federal land ownership in the West, the BLM found almost unanimous support for multiple-use management of virtually all public lands:[142] "For decades, there have been urgings that the public lands be sold and placed on local tax roles. One of the surprising occurrences of the classification effort was the virtual disappearance of this recommendation when specific lands were under consideration."[143] Ranchers, timber companies, mining companies, and recreational users all enjoyed rights or privileges to the public lands, but none of them could afford to own the lands outright. Western counties, which often complained about their limited tax base, received far more in federal investment and shared revenues than they would from property taxes.[144] Indeed, support for federal ownership was so strong that the BLM often faced strong opposition when it tried to sell lands classified for disposal.[145] Clearly, then, debate over formal property rights and tenure was really less important than debate over informal property rights and privileges in the public lands.

By the time the CMUA expired in 1969, the BLM had classified approximately 131 million acres for retention under federal ownership and multiple-use management and roughly 3 million acres for disposal.[146] In other words, in five years the BLM classified almost 80 percent of its lands in the lower forty-eight states and found less than 2 percent suitable for disposal according to current resource values and under existing public lands disposal laws.

BLM leaders had hoped that identifying lands for retention and multiple-use management would provide the BLM with a fresh start in professional management. The day before President Johnson signed the CMUA in 1964, for example, Stoddard argued, "It all comes down to this: the public lands were neglected as a resource base because permanent, intensive management was not part of their tradition."[147] Stoddard argued that multiple-use management "meets the 'final disposal' dilemma head-on without destroying worthwhile traditions. It does not repeal or alter existing laws; it does not prevent disposition; it does not forbid mineral entry or development; it does not affect State jurisdiction or responsibility. What it does affirm, clearly, is that those public lands which can best serve the public should be managed up to their full capacities."[148] In other words, classifying public lands for retention and multiple use would provide a new rhetorical lens through which to view the agency's traditional resource programs.

What became apparent, however, was that the classification program did little in the short run to increase the BLM's professional autonomy from its clientele. Indeed, the BLM received broad support for federal retention of the public lands and for multiple-use management, not as a vote of support for professional autonomy and scientific management, but as a vote in defense of the status quo; ranchers, miners, recreational users, and western county and state officials all voted for retention to protect their own interests in and control of the public lands. These groups even opposed sales of some areas that the BLM classified for disposal, because this would grant all property rights and privileges to a single owner.[149]

The classification program, it appears, formalized what BLM leaders had known for some time, the fact that the vast majority of the public lands would remain in federal ownership, even though the federal government's proprietary interest in these lands was still ambiguous. Landstrom and Stoddard had both fought to redefine the public lands as a national land system on par with the national forest system. Stoddard in particular wanted to create a system of well-blocked areas of public lands to replace the checkerboard pattern of land ownership that typified the public lands, for this physical distribution of the public lands was reflective of and reinforced the complex patterns of private claims—be they legal claims or merely politically protected claims—to these lands.

This issue of consolidating public lands areas has continued to plague the BLM. Frank Gregg, BLM director under President Jimmy Carter, would complain in 1982 that the real problems of land tenure and land distribution had never been settled, and he would argue that until the BLM disposes of land poorly suited to federal ownership and multiple-use management, it will never overcome the basic political problems that have dogged the agency since its formation in 1946.[150]

With the public lands classification program under way, including the designation of individual planning units, Robert Jones and other BLM leaders struggled with a more difficult problem: joining the BLM's disparate activities in a single, comprehensive planning system. Whereas the BLM approached land classification as an open, political process—that is, it encouraged public participation, and it relied significantly on information from local governments and public lands users—BLM leaders saw the agency's new planning system as a way to build professional decision-making processes—that is, processes that rely on systematically collected data and professional expertise. Said another way, the BLM's classification program harkened back to Ferry Carpenter's approach to organizing the grazing districts, which involved going out to the field and inviting local public lands users and government officials to draw lines on a map.[151] By contrast, the proposed planning system was intended to be the BLM's first major step toward the kind of scientific management that was celebrated in the Progressive Era. Indeed, Bob Jones and his staff wanted to escape pressure from the livestock industry and other powerful clientele by establishing a planning process that rested on "objective" analysis rather than on the advice of grazing advisory boards and other public lands users. They wanted truly professional, rational planning.

BLM planners faced two major obstacles: one internal and one external. First, they faced the internal problem of coordinating and integrating planning activities, which Shipman had addressed. The CMUA gave the BLM a temporary foundation for planning, but it did not spell out a planning system or eliminate other specific planning responsibilities. The problem, according to one BLM employee, was that the BLM had seventeen planning systems located in various functional programs and within various professional groups. For example, the range program had a planning process for allotment management plans, the soil and water conservation program had a watershed planning process, and the lands program had a Master Unit System planning program.[152] The problem was not that the BLM lacked any multiple-use planning in the mid-1960s, rather that "each function in the Bureau had been developing a multiple use coordination system, where they would look at everybody else, and then figure out what they should do."[153]

To integrate all of these processes into a comprehensive system, Jones and his staff broke planning down to a number of levels. First, in the *Initial Analysis*, BLM managers established individual planning units to create clear planning boundaries. Second, the managers compiled what was called a *Program Policy Guide*, which was a compendium of all resource program policies that were operative within a given planning unit. Third, in what was called the *District Summary*, they collected social and economic data to determine specific resource values in each planning unit. Finally, BLM managers would draw up *Unit Plans*, with established management goals within each planning unit.[154] This was an important step, for it emphasized decision making within spatial boundaries rather than within resource programs, and it forced managers from each resource program to work together more directly. Nonetheless, the complexity of this process required difficult spatial and temporal coordination for which the BLM was unprepared.

The second and even more difficult problem was establishing a mechanism or formula for determining the most appropriate trade-offs among competing resource uses. This was, after all, the unanswered question of natural resource planning. Jones and his staff wanted to standardize resource valuation decisions to shield field managers from the powerful political pressures they faced.

The first set of draft regulations, released on October 7, 1964, directed BLM managers to establish "'resource values' as a common denominator measure to judge the merits of various resource proposals against their cost as well as against each other when they conflicted."[155] Rather than determining resource values politically in consultation with public lands users, the regulations directed BLM managers to define resource values in terms of local market prices, if available, or to use the standardized values that President Kennedy's Water Resources Council had developed in 1962, which were published as Senate Document 97 in the 87th Congress.[156] This version of economic planning stood in stark contrast to the classification process and to the historical processes of the BLM and its predecessors. Local communities would still participate in the planning process, but they could not determine the relative value of different resources or resource uses.

BLM field managers saw this as a direct attack on their expertise. It created a mechanical system of resource valuation that could essentially be run by someone in Washington who had no locally conditioned expertise. Faced with overwhelming opposition from field managers, the first draft planning system floundered. Jones argues that BLM field managers opposed this approach for two reasons: "The given reason was failure of end product market values to reflect *all* the values (social, environmental, etc.) inherent in each resource. The underlying reason was often fear that a specific resource could not compete in so tough an analytical arena."[157]

The second round of planning efforts followed the same basic approach, and it was further complicated in 1966 by the Bureau of Budget's Planning, Programming, Budget System (PPBS). The PPBS was intended to produce uniform planning procedures for all executive agencies and to tie planning with budgeting, and the new PPBS requirements consumed an enormous amount of the BLM's planning time. Bob Jones recalls that at this point he was essentially working on the BLM's planning program alone, because his staff was dedicated to the Interior Department's PPBS requirements. On March 31, 1966, BLM planners released a second draft planning manual for review, although the BLM's planning program had been reduced to a "PPB Support System."[158]

Despite the workload constraints imposed by PPBS implementation, the PPBS should not be blamed for failure of the BLM's second draft planning manual. Both the first and second drafts failed because they followed a highly analytical approach to resource valuation and decision making, which BLM field managers opposed. As Jones recalls, "the possibility of much more centralized and detailed program planning bothered the field greatly—how could they possibly indicate, in a program package write up, all of the subtle factors that should be considered in a decision on funding a package?"[159] Field managers believed that the new system would trap them into planning and management decisions made mathematically on the basis of standardized resource values, eliminating their flexibility in dealing with local resource users. As Robert Nelson writes, the system failed, both because it would limit field managers' ability to meet local demands and because it would, in many cases, challenge the dominance of a particular resource program.[160]

BLM leaders tried to reduce the direct political influence that traditional resource users had over field managers by developing an analytical system of resource valuation and a more systematic way of resolving resource conflicts. This attempt at rational planning simply reached too far in failing to appreciate both the durability of private claims to public lands and resources and the highly decentralized character of the agency. Ironically, BLM leaders pressed for rational planning at a time when the model of rational, scientific management championed by the Forest Service was coming under unprecedented attack, and the Forest Service was coming to terms with the inherently political character of forest management.[161] As scholars have pointed out, this does not necessarily reflect problems with the principles of planning, but rather the intractable problems of joining planning and democracy.[162] These problems have continued to haunt the BLM and other federal land management agencies.

CONCLUSION

Talking about the "new" BLM in the 1960s is perhaps misleading. It could imply that the BLM made a clean break from its complex past, and, more important, that the BLM succeeded in forging a clear new identity and mission. This would overstate the BLM's development. These were the *goals* that animated the BLM's leadership rather than the agency's *accomplishments* during this period.

The BLM did move, however, in a radical new direction: it moved away from uncoordinated land disposal and "home-rule" management and toward a new model of professional, scientific management of the public lands. This cut against the status quo for the agency's traditional clientele and its field managers alike, as indicated by Landstrom's attack on the livestock industry's influence and Stoddard's attack on the autonomy of professional groups within the agency.

While dismantling some of the key components of the "old" BLM, Landstrom and Stoddard worked to articulate a new multiple-use mission and identity for the agency. The problem was that the new mission still had to embrace the agency's scattered pattern of land ownership, overlapping resource demands and clientele, and complex statutory and appropriations tools. The BLM confronted some of the same recurring problems: political ambiguity of federal ownership, tension between local and national interests, and tension between Congress and the executive branch.

First, the BLM faced serious problems as it sought to clarify the political meaning of public lands ownership. BLM leaders hoped to use the classification program to assert the agency's proprietary responsibility for most of the remaining public lands in the lower forty-eight states and thereby bolster its autonomy in making multiple-use decisions. The BLM's classification program, validated in the CMUA and the PLSA, was an attempt to settle formally what the BLM had known for some time: despite the fact that Congress had still not claimed permanent ownership of the public lands, it was politically unrealistic to imagine that Congress would ever accomplish a large-scale transfer of ownership to the states or private parties. This settled some of the formal property rights issues, but it also highlighted the political strength of the property rights regimes that had developed over the previous century of public lands policy and management.

Second, the BLM wrestled with the problem of balancing local and national interests in the public lands. The sudden rise of recreation and the claim that recreation represented a broader public interest over against special commercial interests[163] gave the BLM new leverage in its dealings with its traditional clientele,[164] but the BLM still had no formula for resolving the tension among competing resource uses and values or the tension between professional and political management. BLM field managers felt these tensions acutely, which came to a head when the BLM began to draft a planning system.

Third, the BLM operated throughout the 1960s in the shadow of the PLLRC, highlighting the ongoing battle over congressional versus executive control. Aspinall, who created and chaired the PLLRC, granted the BLM temporary legislation—the CMUA and the PLSA—only as an interim measure while he reasserted congressional control over the public lands. The BLM developed new capabilities and gained greater power during this period, which worked to some extent against congressional policy control. Nevertheless, the real seat of congressional control and power remained the appropriations committees.

BLM leaders, then, never achieved a clear new mission for the agency; they simply pushed the BLM toward a new, more complex mission of multiple-use management. However, the growing complexity of BLM responsibilities and con-stituents made it more difficult for any one group of clientele or any one member of Congress to control public lands management. Although BLM leaders did not gain clear control over public lands policy and management, the agency became a more significant participant in the public lands debate. This was the "new" BLM.

4

BLM Enters the Environmental Decade

In the late 1960s, visions of professional administration—including centralized control over the public lands policy and integrated land use planning—were well established in the BLM's Washington office. Agency leaders had numerous initiatives under way to check clientele power over the BLM's management decisions and to integrate its multiple responsibilities in a more coherent way: raising grazing fees to fair market value, adjusting O & C timber harvesting to sustained yield levels, increasing environmental regulation of mining operations, hiring professional staff for recreation management, and gaining permanent statutory multiple-use authority that emphasized administrative discretion. Most significant, by the end of the decade the BLM had classified almost 200 million acres of public lands for retention and multiple-use management and had launched a formal multiple-use planning system.[1] It appeared, then, that despite ongoing resistance from clientele and some field managers, BLM leaders were making progress in achieving their professional goals.

At the beginning of the 1970s, however, two things changed the BLM's administrative opportunities dramatically. First, the statutes that had authorized the BLM's land classification and planning programs—the Classification and Multiple Use Act (CMUA) and the Public Land Sales Act (PLSA) of 1964—expired in 1970 following publication of the Public Land Law Review Commission's report, *One Third of the Nation's Land*.[2] This quickly shifted momentum from administrative to congressional politics, where the BLM's commercial clientele enjoyed clear political advantage.

Second, in the early 1970s a sea change in federal land and environmental politics began to realign the fundamental political patterns that had dominated public lands administration for half a century. The environmental movement had reached political maturity during the 1960s and demanded fundamental reform in environmental policy. Combining the preservation movement's romantic aesthetics, the conservation movement's faith in science and rationality, and the emerging popularity of participatory democracy, environmental groups demanded ecosystems-oriented management and direct access to federal decision-making processes. Congress responded in the early 1970s with a wave of new legislation, including the Clean Air Act, the Clean Water Act, the National Environmental Policy Act, and the Endangered Species Act.[3]

The most powerful new statutory tool for the environmental movement was without question the National Environmental Policy Act of 1969 (NEPA), which required federal agencies to consider the potential environmental impacts of their actions. As other scholars have noted, Congress passed NEPA without a clear understanding of its potential impact on federal land and resource management, and federal agencies generally responded slowly to the act as they waited for the courts to define the act's requirements. Environmental groups, however, saw NEPA's power immediately. Armed with NEPA and considerably more liberal standing requirements in the courts, they burst into decision-making arenas that had once been occupied primarily by the BLM and its commercial clientele. For the first time in its history, the BLM had a conservation constituency, but BLM leaders found that it was as hostile to their bid for professional autonomy as it was to unchecked industrial development. The BLM was caught between two powerful groups who were both equally frustrated with the agency's progress in conservation management, recalling the tension that had devastated the U.S. Grazing Service in 1946.[4]

Although the U.S. Forest Service also struggled to meet the new demands imposed by NEPA and the environmental movement, it still enjoyed support from the timber industry, recreational groups, and traditional conservation groups. Forest Service Chief Richard McArdle could say that "being in the middle is exactly where we ought to be,"[5] because for the Forest Service this was a position of considerable power. The BLM, by contrast, had almost no political support, so being in the middle simply meant political attack from two sides instead of one. Indeed, the environmental movement fulfilled one of the BLM's professional goals by challenging the dominance of commercial interest groups, but this did not lead to the kind of agency autonomy that BLM leaders wanted.[6]

ADMINISTRATIVE CONFLICTS IN THE LATE 1960S

In the late 1960s, the BLM had its sights set on permanent multiple-use authority modeled after the Forest Service's Multiple Use Sustained Yield Act (MUSY) of 1960 and its own temporary CMUA. This commitment to multiple use, Richard Behan noted in the late 1960s, rested on three assumptions: land has a fixed or limited production capability, demand for resources exceeds this capability, and the single use of resources cannot meet such overwhelming demand.[7] The BLM argued, as the Forest Service before it, that these conditions justified *both* permanent federal ownership of the public lands and greater professional autonomy for the agency in order to balance competing land uses. The BLM found broad support for federal ownership but continued to struggle in its quest for professional autonomy. Controversies in the late 1960s focused on the relative position of the BLM's existing resource commitments within an expanding multiple-use mission.

Range management remained the BLM's most important and contentious political arena. Although the BLM had successfully reduced grazing levels in the 1950s and 1960s and checked the dominant role of grazing advisory boards in day-to-day management decisions, it had not effectively resolved the underlying debate in public lands range management: permit ownership and value. As noted earlier, the federal courts had consistently found that ranchers had no legal rights to graze the public lands, yet grazing permits continued to *function* like private property. First, and foremost, grazing permits were bought and sold like private property. Grazing permits were issued to ranchers who had base property—that is, private land or water rights necessary to sustain livestock when they were not grazing on federal land—and the privately appraised value of a rancher's base property included the associated grazing permit. So even if the permits were not legal property, they functioned economically as property. Second, western congressmen defended ranchers' interests in the public lands *as if* they were common-law rights. So even if the grazing permits were not legally protected interests, they were politically protected interests. The BLM and the Interior Department engaged this contentious issue again in a battle over grazing fees during the late 1960s and early 1970s, winning a symbolic if not substantive victory.[8]

Throughout the 1960s pressure had mounted for significant reform of federal range policy, particularly grazing fees. Conservation and environmental groups, the General Accounting Office, the Bureau of Budget, BLM and Forest Service leaders, and conservation advocates in Congress all denounced the BLM's existing grazing fee of $0.33 per animal unit month (AUM). Virtually all critics of the fee complained that it was an abdication of the federal government's proprietary interest in the public lands. Some critics emphasized the federal government's responsibility to serve the national interest by returning more money to the U.S. Treasury. Others, such as environmental groups, were outraged not strictly because the grazing fee constituted a subsidy but because the federal government was subsidizing the ecological destruction of its property. They argued that charging fair market value for grazing permits would reduce overgrazing and improve range management.[9]

In 1968, just after the BLM finished its range adjudication process, the BLM and the Forest Service completed a joint, six-year study of grazing fees. In the final phase of the study, the USDA Economic Research Service collected and analyzed information from 218 financial institutions, 10,000 interviews, and 14,000 questionnaires to determine the fair market value of federal grazing permits and to determine whether or not fee increases would harm the livestock industry economically. In November 1968, representatives from the Statistical Reporting Service, the Economic Research Service, the Forest Service, the BLM, and the Bureau of Budget reported that the Forest Service and the BLM should have a uniform, market-based fee and that the approximate fair market value of grazing in the West was $1.23 per AUM—almost 400 percent higher than the BLM's existing fee.[10]

The livestock industry, represented by the BLM's National Advisory Board Council, the American National Cattlemen's Association, and the National Wool Growers Association, denounced the fee increase. They chose not to dispute the fair market value level of $1.23; rather, they challenged the federal government's claim to *own* the rangeland in an absolute sense and therefore its right to capture the full market value of range forage. Having paid a premium on the private market to acquire their base property, ranchers argued that they had, in economic fact, already paid a portion of the fair market value for their grazing permits. Consequently they argued that the real fair market fee ought to be adjusted to reflect the premium already paid for base property. Otherwise, livestock representatives argued, increasing the grazing fee to full market value would devastate the livestock industry by suddenly lowering the market value of ranchers' base property by 35 to 50 percent.[11]

The livestock industry's argument is fascinating because it separates two legal issues that are most often closely associated: property ownership and constitutional takings. The livestock industry sidestepped the fact that ranchers did not legally own their grazing permits and were therefore not legally entitled to compensation under Article V of the Constitution. Instead, by pointing to ranchers' economic investment in base property and historical control over grazing operations, the livestock industry argued that the $1.23 fee amounted to a metaphorical taking that violated the constitutional principles of American government.

Throughout the 1960s, Interior Secretary Udall and Agriculture Secretary Orville Freeman acknowledged that ranchers paid a premium to acquire base property, but they refused to concede a metaphorical taking. Indeed, they argued that they were legally constrained from considering the permit value recognized in private transactions. To do so, they explained, would violate congressional intent and judicial precedent by acknowledging or granting a property right to federal grazing lands. It would, in other words, legitimate a metaphor at the expense of law. In 1969, for example, BLM Director Boyd Rasmussen (1966–1971) testified that "giving the permittee credit for the interest on the permit value in computing fees would recognize that the permit gives the operator a proprietary interest in the public lands. This is clearly prohibited by the express provisions of section 3 of the Taylor Grazing Act."[12] The secretaries also rejected the ranchers' equity complaint, arguing that the livestock industry had exaggerated the financial impact of the fee increase, which would occur gradually over a ten-year period.[13] On January 14, 1969, in the very last days of the Johnson administration, the secretaries of Interior and Agriculture announced the new grazing fee schedule that would phase in a uniform grazing fee of $1.23 per AUM for both Forest Service and BLM permits over a ten-year period.[14] In the first incremental hike, the BLM's fee rose from $0.33 to $0.44 per AUM.

The new fee schedule was a symbolic victory for the BLM, capping a decade of expanding professional autonomy and power. However, the substantive value of the new fee schedule was less clear in subsequent years as western congressmen reasserted their power over public lands policy and management. Just two weeks after the Interior and Agriculture secretaries announced the new fee schedule, western congressmen began to undermine it during Walter Hickel's grueling Senate hearing on his nomination as President Nixon's secretary of the interior.[15] Hickel essentially agreed to postpone the FY 1971 fee increase until the PLLRC released its final report, deferring the issue to congressional prerogative. In the coming months, western congressmen reminded Hickel of their position: Senator Gale McGee of Wyoming introduced legislation (S. 716) calling for renewed consideration of the grazing permit value that ranchers had paid in acquiring their land; Senator Joseph Montoya of New Mexico introduced legislation (S. 1063) postponing fee increases until the commission's report; and the Senate Committee on Interior and Insular Affairs adopted a resolution calling on the secretaries of Interior and Agriculture to review the new fee schedule. Hickel also faced two immediate lawsuits, although the Circuit of Appeals later upheld the fee schedule in both cases.[16] Under this ongoing pressure, Hickel announced in November 1969 that the Interior Department would postpone grazing fee increases for one year, and the Department of Agriculture was forced to follow suit.[17]

The PLLRC report did nothing to resolve the issue, and Secretary Hickel faced a difficult decision the following year under even greater pressure from both sides. The White House insisted that he raise the grazing fees, and other agencies supported this position. Environmental groups remained adamant that increased grazing fees were essential to proper range management: "We are firm in our conviction that the Federal Government should receive fair market value for its forage, as with all other *commodities*, and many of the ills which have plagued the Bureau of Land Management for many years will be overcome once the Federal fees are on a par with those which are charged by private sources."[18] The livestock industry and western congressmen continued to press Hickel, warning that a fee increase would devastate the livestock industry. This time, however, Hickel supported the fee increase, and both Interior and Agriculture raised their fees for FY 1972—the BLM fee rose from $0.44 to $0.64.[19]

The grazing fee debate would continue for another decade, reflecting the pendulum of political pressure for and against grazing fee increases.[20] In principle, fair market value was established as the grazing fee standard, and the BLM continued to exclude the private value of grazing permits in its calculation. In substance, the livestock industry effectively blocked the application of fair market value to annual grazing fee increases on a number of occasions. Nonetheless, fee increases became an annual debate during most of the 1970s, and the outcome was no longer a foregone conclusion. The livestock industry was beginning to lose its determinative place in public lands politics; grazing was slowly becoming *a* multiple use rather than *the* dominant use of public rangelands.

O & C forest policy in the late 1960s and early 1970s was another proving ground for the BLM's growing multiple-use mission and the expansion of internal and external demands for broader environmental protection. Under the Kennedy administration, the BLM had established a new allowable cut that emphasized increased timber production as the dominant use of O & C lands, thereby following the Forest Service's early model of professional forestry. By 1966, however, the dominant-use model of forest production had given way to a multiple-use paradigm of forest management.[21]

In 1967, following review by the O & C Advisory Board and the Office of Management and Budget, the BLM completed an intensive, computer-assisted study of timber production on the O & C lands that provided detailed analysis of the sustained yield potential in light of new environmental concerns. Historian Elmo Richardson writes, "In the most momentous redirection of federal forestry policy since the adoption of sustained-yield management thirty years before, the BLM concluded that productivity must be balanced by policies to protect and maintain the environmental quality of the O&C lands."[22] The BLM's new allowable cut was slated for reduction from a projected 1,323 million board feet to 1,172 million board feet.

Like the new grazing fee schedule, the allowable cut hit a number of political obstacles during the Nixon administration. Representatives from the Oregon Association of Counties challenged the proposed reductions, and in 1970 Secretary Hickel agreed to postpone the allowable cut reduction until an Oregon state committee reviewed it. There were other postponements and modifications to the reduction schedule after Secretary Rogers Morton replaced Hickel late in 1970. The Oregon committee demanded a new inventory of the O & C lands and a reassessment of the allowable cut. The battle most likely contributed to BLM Director Rasmussen's resignation in 1971.[23]

Nonetheless, debate over the revised allowable cut indicated the growing importance of ecological analysis, environmental protection, and recreation in public lands politics. Under the revised cut, the BLM asserted its responsibility to manage the O & C forests not just for perpetual timber supplies, but also for the overall values that the forests provided. The agency remained committed to increasing timber production through intensive management, thereby supporting local Oregon economies, but it had reframed this commitment within the broader rhetoric of environmental protection.

Changes in the BLM's grazing fees and timber harvesting suggest that new environmental concerns were supporting the BLM's professional goals in range and forest management. However, BLM managers were also frustrated by some of the new, public attention the agency received in the late 1960s and the new responsibilities this gave the agency. Perhaps the best example of this was the BLM's program to protect wild horses and burros.

In the 1950s and early 1960s BLM managers viewed wild horses and burros—essentially feral horses and burros of European descent—as a threat to both livestock and wildlife, since they competed for scarce forage resources. To maintain livestock grazing levels and to support game species on the range, the BLM had issued permits for companies to round up and destroy wild horses and burros by the thousands.

The BLM faced growing criticism in the late 1950s not for permitting horse removal but for the way that the horses and burros were treated on their way to slaughter. Velma Johnston—"Wild Horse Annie"—and other activists convinced Congress to pass the Wild Horse Protection Act in 1959, which prohibited the use of motorized vehicles in rounding up horses and burros. From this initial step, however, public support for wild horse protection grew dramatically. Over the next decade, public opposition shifted from concerns about animal cruelty to calls for wild horse and burro preservation.[24]

The issue came to a head in the mid-1960s in the Pryor Mountain area along the Montana-Wyoming border. Wild horses were contributing to ongoing range degradation, and the state of Montana asked the BLM to remove wild horses to improve deer habitat. The BLM responded with a plan to remove and dispose of almost three-quarters of the existing herd. In 1966 and 1967, however, the agency was swamped by a national letter campaign opposing the plan, and the Humane Society sued the agency to stop the removal. Director Rasmussen appointed a seven-member wild horse study committee to review the situation, but it was clear that the BLM would need to change its approach to wild horses and burros management.[25] In 1968, Secretary Udall created the Pryor Mountains Wild Horse Range, and the BLM pledged to maintain a herd of 125–145 horses. This was not enough to convince activists that the BLM would protect wild horses and burros administratively, and the BLM lost administrative control of its wild horses and burros program in 1971 when Congress passed the Wild Free Roaming Horse and Burro Act.[26] The act directed the BLM to protect and manage numerous wild horse and burro herds in the western United States.

The 1971 act was a blow to the BLM, not so much because it required protection of wild horses and burros, but because it limited the BLM's discretion in balancing wild horse and burro needs with those of domestic livestock and wildlife. For example, the act authorized the BLM to remove excessive horses and burros by relocating them, destroying them humanely, or putting them up for adoption, but it did not specify how and when the BLM could choose to destroy the animals or even what exactly constituted an excessive number. In the face of strong public opposition to killing wild horses and burros, BLM managers felt handicapped by the law. Furthermore, Congress did not grant the BLM its desired authority to use aircraft to round up the animals, making the process more difficult and costly.[27] Range conservationists were pinched between ranchers who had political power to block grazing reductions and environmentalists who had the political power to stop the BLM from killing excess horses and burros. The result was continuation of existing grazing levels, continuation of existing wild horses and burros grazing, and little protection of rangeland health and quality.

The 1971 act also concerned the livestock industry, which had enjoyed dominant use of most public lands range. Whereas in the past, wild horse and burro needs would have been balanced against livestock needs in favor of livestock, the new act made wild horses and burros the top forage priority in a number of areas. The 1971 act led to numerous court battles, and it gave wildlife advocates, humane societies, and environmentalists a powerful tool with which to attack the BLM's grazing program.[28]

As the BLM's constituencies and goals expanded, so did the complexity of multiple-use management. It is important to note that the Forest Service faced a similar challenge forty years early when recreational use in the national forests challenged the agency's exclusive focus on timber.[29] However, the Forest Service had enjoyed far greater administrative discretion and political power in navigating the new public demands.[30] Apart from the temporary classification and land sales authority that the BLM received in 1964, Congress had not given the agency any new statutory authority or discretion. Without new statutory direction and without any new political support, BLM leaders looked increasingly to the procedural promise of comprehensive planning to resolve growing multiple-use conflicts.

The first two sets of draft regulations, discussed in the previous chapter, had floundered on vocal resistance from BLM field managers. The real problem with the first two planning systems is that they contained not only procedural requirements but also substantive requirements about what kinds of decisions field managers should make. Without statutory or political support for these substantive requirements, BLM leaders had little hope of implementing the previous planning systems.

BLM leaders in Washington—Director Rasmussen and BLM planners such as Robert Jones and Irving Senzel—continued to embrace the idea of comprehensive planning, but they were forced to abandon their substantive criteria in favor of a purely procedural system that essentially formalized the BLM's existing decision-making patterns. In the summer of 1969, BLM leaders published final regulations for a system that combined the goals of uniform planning with the decentralized reality of BLM resource programs and politics.[31]

Under the new system, planning progressed in three phases. The first phase involved amassing economic and social data in documents called economic or district management profiles. These profiles calculated present and future resource production and consumption, along with the potential impact of local, state, and regional planning activities that were currently under way. BLM planners broke this information down geographically for planning units that were generally 50,000 to 1,000,000 acres in size in a process called Unit Resource Analysis. Each Unit Resource Analysis provided the current status and maximum future potential for seven resource categories: lands, energy and minerals, livestock forage, timber, watershed, wildlife habitat, and recreation.[32]

The next phase had two distinct steps. First, each resource program would create a proposal to maximize its own resource values without consideration of the other resource categories. This reflected a continuation of the BLM's traditional approach to planning and management, in which the agency operated as a loose constellation of independent resource programs. The innovation of the planning system came in the second step, when representatives from all the resource programs would sit down and compare their proposals to determine overlaps and conflicts. The BLM developed a system of map overlays for the resource programs so that field managers could see graphic representations of overlapping and conflicting resource uses.[33] As Robert Nelson explains, this was "an explicitly adversary process in which BLM employees designated as proponents would advocate these resource-specific proposals to the extent of their persuasive powers."[34] Presumably each resource specialist could appeal to the strength of his constituency in this process. BLM field managers would resolve resource conflicts through this process, either immediately or through more in-depth analysis, and produce a final planning document called a Management Framework Plan (MFP).[35]

In a third and final phase, district or state managers who did not represent any single resource program would review each MFP against the BLM's broader statutory obligations for things like environmental protection. If approved, specialists in each resource program would then use the MFP as a foundation for more detailed planning and management decisions and appropriations requests.

The third and final planning system was an important symbolic achievement for the BLM, because it emphasized multiple-use rather than dominant-use management. Yet even as the new planning system reflected the BLM's growing professionalism, it also highlighted limits that the BLM faced in public lands politics and administration. Congress, the BLM's clientele, and BLM field managers all permitted the agency to establish a formal process for decision making, but they refused to allow the Washington office to dictate the substantive goals of decision making, such as economic efficiency or economic value.

As a result of its limited procedural requirements, it isn't clear that the new planning system had any great impact on the agency. One critic writes, "From one perspective the new BLM planning system was a success because it did not greatly disrupt existing arrangements and thus was likely to be accepted. From another perspective the planning system was a failure because, on the bottom line, it did not really change very much."[36] The new system simply formalized the existing dynamics of interest-group politics that governed the public lands, with resource specialists in each of the agency's resource programs representing a specific clientele. And to the extent that the agency was still dominated by range, mineral, and forestry staff, the new planning process did little to shift the BLM's focus from commercial resource development to a broader vision of conservation or environmental protection.

While BLM state and district managers accepted the new planning regulations officially, it also became increasingly clear in the initial round of planning that many of them did not view the planning system as their primary decision-making process. The initial plans that field managers produced in the early 1970s range widely in their specificity and hence their decision-making value, and the new planning process had to compete with several other decision-making systems, such as budgeting and program management systems, for influence.[37] One critic has likened it to the early urban comprehensive land use plans that emerged in the 1960s, which have "the pretense rather than the reality of rational decision making, lack of any great impact on traditional decision making modes and performance of mainly a symbolic function in that land use plans could said to be done."[38]

ONE THIRD OF THE NATION'S LAND: THE PUBLIC LAND LAW REVIEW COMMISSION

The BLM developed its planning system under the PLLRC's shadow, and as the commission neared the end of its five-year investigation, BLM and Interior leaders increasingly called for repeal of outdated public lands statutes and passage of broad, new multiple-use authority. The BLM's struggle for professional autonomy in the 1960s had highlighted the fact that agency leaders held limited power for direct attacks on the substantive policies governing the public lands and that their real opportunities for discretion came through indirect and procedural reforms.[39]

BLM and Interior officials complained that the agency was handicapped by scattered, overlapping, and contradictory statutes, which were difficult to reconcile in planning and management decisions. These statutes, they argued, reflected "the social and economic conditions of the nineteenth and early twentieth century and thus are predicated on essentially obsolete concepts, are of special purpose, and of limited scope."[40] Statutes such as the Taylor Grazing Act, which indicated that the public lands range management was temporary "pending final disposal," and the Mining Law of 1872, which encouraged unregulated mineral exploration, simply did not match the reality of the BLM's mission in the late twentieth century. For example, in an age of multiple demands on the public lands—grazing, mining, logging, recreation, wildlife, and so on—the Mining Law of 1872 undermined the very possibility of multiple-use management because it gave the BLM virtually no control over the most basic planning and management questions: "1. To whom is the resource to be disposed? 2. When and at whose initiative is it to be disposed? 3. At what price shall the disposal take place? 4. How are the conflicting uses of the land to be handled?"[41]

BLM and Interior leaders knew that they could not win direct legislative battles against the livestock and mining industries. In lieu of new substantive direction, then, they essentially requested greater procedural autonomy to resolve multiple-use conflicts through comprehensive planning. As Secretary Udall explained, under this type of procedural discretion, "the Secretary would be enabled legally and financially to conduct active [mineral] management operations under general statutory standards, rather than passive adjudication under inflexible statutory strictures which inhibit progressive management."[42] The PLLRC seems to have agreed with the BLM's complaint about the state of public lands legislation, but it was not prepared to turn public lands management over completely to administrative discretion.

The PLLRC released its final report in June 1970 in a small ceremony at the White House.[43] The report, *One Third of the Nation's Land*, was the most comprehensive treatment of public land law to date. Supported by 33 individual studies and hundreds of testimonies, the report covered a vast array of issues related to the public lands. In all, the Commission's report contained 405 recommendations: 18 basic principles, 137 numbered recommendations, and 250 unnumbered recommendations.

Despite, or perhaps as a result of, the report's exhaustive character, the commission's recommendations were curious in their lack of consistency and coherence. They seemed to mirror rather than resolve the contradictory "patchwork" of public laws, policies, and management practices that existed. As one BLM employee later explained, "it's a tremendously comprehensive document [but] . . . you end up . . . in utter frustration because it's so contradictory. You can find anything in it to satisfy your point of view. . . . The trouble always was, almost invariably you would find an opposing point of view within the document itself."[44] Or, as former Secretary Udall wrote in a *Newsday* column, the commission had produced a "goodies-for-all report that apparently pleases nobody."[45] It would seem that the commission followed Forest Service Chief McArdle's commitment to the contentious middle ground, for its report offered a careful cross section of American values and interests regarding the public lands.[46] Indeed, the report demonstrated the impossibility of crafting a truly comprehensive *and* fully representative public land policy rather than providing the guidelines necessary for such an enterprise.

In crafting a "goodies-for-all" report, the commission dealt quite consciously with the central problem of public lands planning and multiple-use management: representation. The commission developed a representational formula made up of six broad groups/interests: the national public, the regional public, the federal government as sovereign, the federal government as proprietor, state and local governments, and public land users. For each issue or resource use, the PLLRC weighed its preferred recommendation against the assumed interests held by the six groups, attempting to maximize the benefits of public lands and resources.

The six-group formula did not resolve the problems of representation that arise within each group, given their breadth, but it at least acknowledged that the public lands should not serve a single group. It was, at a congressional level, the kind of interest-group calculations that federal agencies already did routinely.

Indeed, part of what the BLM had been fighting for during the 1960s was the ability to give greater weight to the federal government's proprietary interests in the public lands in order to counter the dominance of commercial public lands users.[47]

Although the report offered diverse and conflicting recommendations that acknowledged the rise of new conservation interests, it also clearly bore the stamp of the PLLRC's chair, Wayne Aspinall, who wanted to make sure that traditional conservation was not drowned by the growing surge of environmental preservation.[48] Aspinall and the PLLRC majority were also staunchly opposed to the kind of administrative license that the BLM sought and the Forest Service enjoyed. For example, they "found that the actions of the Bureau of Land Management under the Classification and Multiple Use Act of 1964 have paralleled to a considerable extent the liberal use of the withdrawal power of public land agencies."[49] To check such liberal discretion, they called for an immediate congressional review of "existing withdrawals, set asides, and classifications of public domain lands that were effected by Executive action to determine the type of use that would provide the maximum benefit for the general public in accordance with standards set forth in this report."[50] In other words, the PLLRC insisted that Congress, and not executive agencies, should do the primary work of balancing competing interests in federal lands on an ongoing basis.

The PLLRC also embraced a particular interpretation of multiple-use management that echoed the utilitarian bent of traditional conservation. Multiple-use management, the commission argued, should maximize the number of compatible land and resource uses with deference given to the economic value of each use. To this end, it proposed a zoning system for the federal lands in which multiple use would "be subject to the qualification that where a unit, within an area managed for many uses, can contribute maximum benefit through one particular use, that use should be recognized as the dominant use, and the lands should be managed to avoid interference with fulfillment of such dominant use."[51] Furthermore, the commission recommended that economic efficiency be the guiding principle for commercial dominant-use areas. The commission also recommended a separate system of classification or zoning for environmental quality. This would serve as a planning layer that would establish separate criteria for management of the different dominant-use zones of public lands.[52]

Reactions to the report were as varied as the recommendations themselves, ranging from affirmations of the commission's work on such a difficult topic to fierce condemnations of the commission's alleged biases. Thus, rather than providing new national consensus on federal land policy, the report fueled the growing acrimony among the BLM's key constituency groups—the mining industry, the grazing industry, and environmentalists.[53]

The warmest response to *One Third of the Nation's Land* came undoubtedly from the mining industry. Articles published in mining trade journals were effusive in their praise of the commission's report. One author wrote in *Iron Age* that "the report couldn't have been more favorable to mining interests if they had written it themselves." Another author wrote in *Metals Week*, "The chapter . . . on mineral exploration will be well received in mining circles."[54] The mining industry had reason to celebrate the commission's recommendations.

The commission argued that due to the high percentage of critical minerals owned by the federal government and the value of these minerals to the national economy, federal mineral policy should be designed to promote mineral development. It was, the commission argued in what would become a refrain for subsequent congresses and presidents, a matter of overriding national security: "Our survival as a leading nation depends on our mineral supplies. . . . *Public land mineral policy should encourage exploration, development, and production of minerals on the public lands.*"[55] Consequently, the commission insisted, "*Mineral exploration and development should have a preference over some or all other uses on much of our public lands.*"[56]

The PLLRC did recommend changes in mining law that would give the secretary of the interior greater authority to impose environmental safeguards on mining activities and require rehabilitation after mining operations but made it clear that this new regulatory authority should not be used in a way that would impede mineral development: "*While an administrator should have no discretion to withhold a permit, he should have the authority to vary these restrictions to meet local conditions.*" If this sounded at all threatening to the mining industry, the commission pledged that the new regulatory authority would be "*exercised within the strict limits of congressional guidelines.*"[57]

The livestock industry was more cautious in its assessment of the report. The PLLRC recommended that grazing policy be designed to "support regional economic growth," that grazing be made the dominant use on lands valued chiefly for forage, and that grazing permittees be given compensation if their grazing permits were revoked. However, the commission also recommended that "fair market value, taking into consideration factors in each area of the lands involved, should be established by law as a basis for grazing fees."[58] Furthermore, the commission called for an end to or sharp reduction in predator control on public lands, which the livestock industry insisted was essential.[59]

The strongest criticism of the report came from environmental groups, which complained that the commission emphasized economic efficiency and production over all other social values. The Sierra Club president complained that the PLLRC was grossly biased toward commercial development: "The basic conclusion of the Report is that [federal lands] must be utilized to the full for production of commodities, and if necessary, sacrificed, to satisfy fires that glow in memory of the archaic Chamber of Commerce cliché that economic growth is necessarily always progress, necessarily always good, and necessarily always desirable." One author wrote in *Life Magazine* that "the report emits the unmistakable smell of commerce from almost every page."[60] Another later wrote, "After the expenditure of more than $7 million, after more than five years of study and research . . . the

Public Land Law Review Commission had produced a document that could have been scratched together in Aspinall's office by one of his administrative assistants without ever leaving Washington."[61]

In addition to popular articles and speeches, environmentalists mounted several detailed reviews of the report. The first came out of a project sponsored by the Natural Resources Defense Council (NRDC) to analyze and comment on commission study reports. The second major review, "*One-Third of the Nation's Land*: The Public Land Law Review Commission Report: A Summary Critique from the Environmental Perspective," was commissioned by Russell Train, director of the Environmental Protection Agency. These reviews denounced the commission's emphasis on economic considerations to the exclusion of broader social and noneconomic values.[62]

Officials in the BLM and Interior were also critical of the report, especially the recommended dominant-use zoning, which would limit rather than expand administrative autonomy and discretion. The BLM was just beginning to win greater control over livestock grazing, and the agency feared that dominant-use classifications would cause range politics to revert back to conditions of the 1930s and 1940s when the livestock industry controlled range management. The BLM was also trying to get mining law revised so that it or at least the Interior Department could control the location and rate of mineral development. The PLLRC's commitment to making mineral development the dominant use of public lands wherever minerals were discovered would undercut this effort. Finally, multiple use had been, rhetorically, the strongest argument for federal land retention and administrative discretion. Having just finished classifying 200 million acres of land for retention and multiple-use management, it is possible that BLM officials were concerned that dominant-use zoning would encourage more land disposal to miners and ranchers.

Just two and a half weeks after its release, the BLM sent a preliminary analysis of the report to Secretary Hickel, who submitted his own report to the White House at the end of July 1970.[63] Hickel asked the White House to oppose dominant-use zoning. He also asked the White House to oppose the PLLRC's bias for maximum economic return as the primary criterion in evaluating commercial public lands uses: "determination of maximum benefit for the general public," he argued, "must be based on social and biological as well as economic factors."[64] Finally, Hickel asked the White House to support a multiple-use bill that would give the Interior Department and the BLM broader discretionary authority than the PLLRC seemed to recommend: "administering agencies cannot be tied to tight legislative guidelines and ponderous legislative machinery. Adequate administrative discretion must be retained." BLM and Interior officials spent the next year working these recommendations into a multiple-use legislative proposal that the White House could submit to Congress. With the BLM's temporary multiple-use authority, the CMUA, set to expire on December 23, 1970, the stakes were high. The BLM was desperate to gain the kind of multiple-use authority the Forest

Service enjoyed under the MUSY rather than the qualified multiple-use scheme recommended in the PLLRC's report.[65]

In July 1971, the Interior Department submitted the BLM's legislative proposal, and Senator Henry Jackson introduced it as the National Resource Land Management Act of 1971.[66] The bill—developed in the BLM primarily by Irving Senzel, assistant director for legislation and plans; Michael Harvey, chief of legislation and regulatory management; and Robert Wolf, assistant to the director—reflected the BLM's conservative legislative strategy. Agency leaders understood that Congress was unlikely to pass a bill that made sweeping and controversial changes in range, minerals, and timber policy, so they focused instead on getting Congress to provide statutory authority for what the agency was already doing: land classification, planning, and multiple-use management. In addition, the bill repealed a host of outdated and largely unused land disposal laws, and it granted the BLM general right-of-way authority to access isolated lands. With this largely uncontroversial foundation in place, they planned to tackle controversial policy issues one at a time as political opportunity permitted.[67]

Yet the bill did include some language that was at least symbolically important to the BLM's bid for greater autonomy and discretion. As Mike Harvey, one of the bill's architects, wrote, "BLM's position was that there should be broad guidelines written in terms of goals and objectives, coupled with full authority to enable the public land administrators to reach those goals and objectives by appropriate means. We believed that specific guidelines in statutes which are not broadly goal-oriented circumscribe the authority of the administrator in such a way as to prevent him from achieving the objectives of the policy."[68] In addition, the bill would have given the public lands a new, proper name that conveyed national significance: the National Resource Lands. Although the basic provisions of the BLM's legislative request were well received in the Senate, the House, which was examining another more comprehensive bill introduced by Aspinall, was less impressed.[69] When the BLM's bill was introduced in the House, the House Subcommittee on Public Lands held a series of very negative western hearings. As Irving Senzel, another of the bill's drafters, recalls, "Each of these hearings started out with a statement that the bill was not acceptable to the Subcommittee [because it gave too] much authority without restrictions to the Interior Secretary."[70]

A public lands bill was introduced each year from 1971 until 1975 without success. Specific issues like grazing, mineral leasing, wilderness, and planning were all major points of contention throughout the debate. The BLM continued to press for broad, multiple-use authority to allocate resources on the basis of its own professional expertise, while congressmen sympathetic to either environmentalists or commercial interests fought over specific revision of the BLM's resource policies.

What became clear in the legislative debates was that no single statute or even series of statutes could establish a clear and comprehensive public lands policy; some governmental body would need to actively monitor and resolve multiple-use conflicts. The larger debate, then, was whether Congress or the BLM should control multiple-use decision making, and this debate extended beyond public lands legislation to the issue of administrative organization.

The PLLRC, led by Congressman Aspinall, had recommended consolidating responsibility and authority for all nonmilitary federal land use planning and management in a new Department of Natural Resources and creating a single congressional oversight committee for the new department. The commission argued, "Responsibility for public land policy and programs . . . in both the legislative and executive branches should be consolidated to the maximum practicable extent in order to eliminate, or at least reduce, differences in policies concerning the administration of similar public land programs."[71] Specifically, the PLLRC argued that the Forest Service should be merged with agencies in the Interior Department to form the new Department of Natural Resources, and congressional committees with responsibility for public land programs should be consolidated to provide one source of oversight and policy formation.[72] The commission's proposal, if enacted, would have given the chairman of the new congressional committee unprecedented power over natural resource policy and management.[73]

President Nixon, advised by his own council on executive organization (the Ash Council), supported the commission's call for a new Department of Natural Resources, but he emphasized the need for more systematic organization and oversight under *executive* control.[74] In addition to reducing the total number of agencies and departments in the executive branch, Nixon wanted to reorganize the lines of administrative authority around ten standard regions in the country matching those already in use by the military. A council of regional directors representing each department secretary would oversee the regions, and each region would also have its own supervisor who reported directly to the president, creating a kind of super-cabinet.[75] This, the president argued, would solve one of the most pressing problems in environmental and federal land planning, namely that "parts of the *interdependent* environment are still under the purview of highly *independent* Federal offices," which had a "hobbling effect . . . on elected leadership—and, therefore, on the basic principles of democratic government."[76] These proposals, like every other proposal to transfer the Forest Service back to the Interior Department, failed. Congressional committee members did not want to lose their turf; the Forest Service and the timber industry did not want to lose the agency's autonomy in Agriculture; and the existing cabinet members did not want to lose their authority to regional supervisors. The organizational and administrative precedents at that time were simply too well entrenched to overcome in a sweeping reorganization.

THROUGH THE LOOKING GLASS: THE DAWN OF THE ENVIRONMENTAL DECADE

While debates over multiple-use legislation, agency autonomy, and executive vs. congressional control continued throughout the Nixon administration, they were ultimately overshadowed by dramatic changes in federal environmental law and judicial review that reshaped public lands politics in the early 1970s. Calls for more comprehensive, ecological approaches to environmental protection had grown steadily throughout the 1960s. In 1963, for example, political scientist Lynton Caldwell wrote, "In brief, our national tendency is to deal with environmental problems segmentally, as specialists whose frequently conflicting judgments require compromise or arbitration," and by 1970 he argued that "to establish rapidly a land policy in which ecological principles predominated would require that the conventional matrix be unraveled and rewoven in a new pattern."[77] Through a long series of essays, Caldwell began to articulate what he called an ecosystems approach to federal land management: "An ecosystems approach is essentially a total systems approach. It therefore includes in its purview many things omitted in less comprehensive systems. And it would impose constraints upon single-purpose approaches to the environment and would arouse hostility among individuals whose single-purpose pursuits would thereby be constrained."[78] Caldwell's *eco*systems approach was new, reflecting the rising popularity of ecology, but it posed the same challenges as Ickes's earlier vision of a systems approach to federal lands management, namely the problems of representation and accountability in federal land policy and management.

Spurred on by Democratic environmental leaders such as Henry Jackson and Morris Udall, Congress responded in the late 1960s and early 1970s with a wave of environmental legislation that bore the clear stamp of a total-systems approach, including the Clean Air Act, Clean Water Act, the National Environmental Policy Act, and the Endangered Species Act. In retrospect it seems fairly clear that Congress and the president did not appreciate the impact that these statutes would have on traditional resource development activities, or they likely would not have passed with such broad support.

The power of the new legislation for environmental groups was augmented considerably by changes that occurred in the federal courts during the same period. Federal courts began to relax standing requirements for environmental litigation, making it much easier for environmental groups to challenge public lands planning and management decisions. Judicial review also became increasingly detailed, wading into the technical scientific data on which federal agencies based their decisions.[79]

These two developments—sweeping environmental laws and new levels of judicial review—were tremendously important for environmental groups. Since public lands oversight committees in Congress were still dominated largely by the livestock, mining, and timber interests, environmental groups had little power to influence statutory grazing, mining, and logging policy. With broad, new environmental legislation and new opportunities for detailed judicial review, however, environmentalists found a new entrance into public lands debate. Through the courts, they could attack public lands policy and management decisions during implementation.

In the early 1970s, the BLM was poorly prepared—legally and politically—for the kind of systems-oriented administration that environmentalists demanded. The agency's new planning process, for example, provided formal representation for established public lands user groups via specialists in each resource program. Since the BLM had neither staff nor a program dedicated to the environment or ecosystems, ecosystems considerations had no formal place at the center of the BLM's planning activity. It should be noted that field managers were asked to review their final management plans in light of the BLM's overall standards for "Environmental Protection and Enhancement," but this post-planning screening was a far cry from a systems approach to environmental protection.[80]

The BLM's planning program was built upon the assumptions of professional administration that favored professional autonomy and expertise, but it was completed at a time when public distrust of administrative expertise was growing exponentially and the most popular rhetoric in Washington was "*interest representation, cooperation, partnership, self-regulation, delegation of power, local option, creative federalism, community action, maximum feasible participation.*"[81] BLM field managers were encouraged to seek out formal and informal public participation *as needed*, but BLM field managers were too busy dealing with specific public lands users to pursue input from all interested citizens.[82] Here again, the BLM found itself defending its bid for professional autonomy and expertise not only against commercial clientele but against environmental groups as well.[83] As Marion Clawson writes, "Having been ignored earlier when they knocked politely at the door, the conservation groups were now able to hammer it down and force their way into the planning and decision-making process. The results were often traumatic to the federal agencies and to the historic users of the federal land."[84]

On January 1, 1970, President Nixon signed the National Environmental Policy Act (NEPA), and the next day, by executive order, he created the Environmental Protection Agency to coordinate environmental activities across the executive branch. In a signing ceremony designed to downplay the president's earlier opposition to the bill and its largely Democratic sponsorship, Nixon announced that he had become convinced that "the nineteen-seventies absolutely must be the years when America pays its debt to the past by reclaiming the purity of its air, its waters and our living environment . . . the decade of the seventies will be known as the time when this country regained a productive harmony between man and nature."[85] The bill itself contained an equally lofty declaration of the U.S. government's policy "to encourage productive and enjoyable harmony between man and his environment; to promote efforts which will prevent or eliminate damage to the environment and biosphere and stimulate the health and welfare of man; to enrich the understanding of the ecological systems and natural resources important to the Nation; and to establish a Council on Environmental Quality."[86] The popularity of this rhetoric was demonstrated just four months later during the first Earth Day celebration on April 22.

The gap between the rhetoric of NEPA and reality of public lands planning was substantial. Although a number of BLM employees, particularly specialists in planning and recreation, participated in Earth Day celebrations and developed programs for environmental education, these efforts remained peripheral to the BLM's central planning and management programs.[87] The tension was exacerbated by the Nixon Administration's dual commitments to environmental protection and resource development, particularly its quest for national energy independence.[88]

The tension between environmental protection and resource development was expressed most clearly on Earth Day by Interior Secretary Hickel. He called for a new "appreciation of man's place not *over* nature—but *in* nature,"[89] but amidst his rhetoric about humanity's place *in* nature, Secretary Hickel announced the issuance of a right-of-way permit for a utility road along the proposed Trans-Alaska Pipeline route, arguing that the pipeline itself would "prove that the environment *can* be protected; *must* be protected; and *will* be protected."[90] Hickel's argument that the human place "not *over* nature, but *in* nature" was best demonstrated by a massive oil pipeline had a hollow ring for environmentalists.

Clearly Secretary Hickel's view of environmental protection sounded more sympathetic with traditional conservation, for he described it on Earth Day as "wise use of our natural resources—without abuse."[91] This language may have pleased Progressive Era conservationists, but it was clearly out of step with the new conservationism (environmentalism) that had carried NEPA and other environmental statutes through Congress. Former secretary Udall lambasted what he called the pipeline fantasy, arguing with resource economist John Krutilla that the Interior Department had barely considered the pipeline's environmental impacts.[92] With the Nixon Administration angling toward traditional conservation, environmentalists used NEPA's very different language and procedural requirements to challenge public lands management.

In addition to broad statements about the federal government's commitment to environmental protection, NEPA contained an important procedural requirement that federal agencies prepare an environmental impact statement (EIS) for every "major Federal action significantly affecting the quality of the human environment." NEPA required that EISs contain, among other things, a detailed account of "(i) the environmental impact of the proposed action, (ii) any adverse environmental effects which cannot be avoided should the proposal be implemented, (iii) alternatives to the proposed action [and] (iv) the relationship between local short-term uses of man's environment and the maintenance and enhancement of long-term productivity.[93] The Council on Environmental Quality (CEQ), established by NEPA, held authority to direct the EIS process, and it delegated much of its procedural responsibility to the Environmental Protection Agency (EPA).

It is important to emphasize that NEPA itself did not establish any detailed guidelines for EIS preparation, leaving a number of important questions for CEQ, other federal agencies, and the courts to resolve: What constitutes a major federal action? What constitutes a significant effect on the environment? When should an

EIS be prepared? How should EISs be reviewed?[94] The initial CEQ guidelines, released in April 1971, did not answer these questions in any detailed sense. It is also important to recognize that EIS preparation under NEPA was, and is, purely a procedural mandate, because NEPA provides no legal authority for the CEQ or EPA to block a federal action that will harm the environment as long as the agency has fulfilled its obligation to disclose the action's potential environmental impacts and alternatives. What NEPA created, then, was a procedural opportunity for public debate over environmental trade-offs in resource development, yet this was enough to condemn the BLM's planning model to obsolescence.[95] Despite the BLM's emphasis on comprehensive planning, it proved very reluctant to produce EISs in the early 1970s, producing only two statements in 1970, two in 1971, four in 1972, five in 1973, and eight in 1974.[96] First, and foremost, EIS preparation challenged the BLM's decentralized organization and culture. The BLM director retained sole authority to initiate an EIS, so if field managers thought an EIS was necessary, they would have to pass that recommendation up the chain of command to Washington. However, field managers did have authority to decide that a project did not trigger NEPA's EIS requirements, thereby eliminating the need to involve the state and Washington offices.[97] In a highly decentralized agency, it is not at all surprising that field managers generally chose to avoid this centralized EIS process.

Furthermore, while the BLM director had the authority to initiate an EIS, even he did not have the authority to complete it and file it with the CEQ. Only the secretary of the interior could approve an EIS, and the secretary insisted that the agency coordinate its EIS preparation with the Interior Department's Office of Environmental Project Review. The secretary's refusal to delegate EIS filing authority to the BLM probably stemmed from the fact that many of the agency's early EISs were for sensitive energy development projects, which involved multiple agencies within the Interior Department and which the White House strongly supported. Whatever the reason, this meant that each time a BLM director identified something as a major federal action, the Office of Environmental Project Review would take control of the EIS process, adding time and cost to each EIS and limiting the agency's autonomy. No doubt the BLM's resentment of this oversight was fueled in part by the fact that the Forest Service and several other land and resource management agencies could file their own EISs.[98]

Second, like most other federal agencies, the BLM was not eager to implement a complex, time-consuming, and expensive layer of planning with its already limited staff and budget. The agency was struggling to get field managers to implement the new multiple-use planning system in a consistent and effective way, and the BLM received only modest appropriation increases for NEPA obligations.[99] Third, there was a broad sense among BLM leaders and field managers that they already complied with NEPA's basic exhortation to promote environmental protection and minimize environmental degradation. BLM specialists, particularly range conservationists and foresters, argued that by following the conservation standards of their profession they were already actively engaged in environmental protection. These specialists balked at the idea that the agency needed to prepare a comprehensive and multidisciplinary environmental impact statement on top of the specific program planning and multiple-use planning they already conducted. It is important to see that many BLM planners and specialists were slow to recognize or slow to admit that the traditional principles of conservation management embedded in professional range and forestry training did not meet the new demands for ecosystems-oriented planning found in NEPA or the environmental movement.[100]

This is not to say that the BLM ignored NEPA; it simply tried to avoid the EIS process. BLM leaders acknowledged, for example, that certain projects, such as Outer Continental Shelf (OCS) leases, the Trans-Alaska Pipeline, and possibly whole programs like livestock grazing, were major actions significantly affecting the environment and would therefore require EIS preparation.[101] From the agency's perspective, however, most routine management decisions either did not qualify as major actions or did not significantly affect the environment, and in the early 1970s NEPA compliance was sufficiently ambiguous that agencies had considerable latitude in making these judgments. Indeed, in January 1972, a U.S. district court in Maine summarized NEPA obligations this way: "NEPA and its implementing agency guidelines require all federal agencies to incorporate as an integral part of their planning process consideration of the environmental consequences of any proposed action, and whenever such consideration indicates that the action may significantly affect the quality of the human environment to prepare and file a detailed environmental impact statement pursuant to Section 102(2)(C) of the Act."[102]

In order to comply with NEPA while avoiding EIS preparation, BLM leaders worked in the early 1970s to build environmental analysis more thoroughly into the agency's planning and management operations. One June 1971 memorandum required that "all BLM actions receive environmental analysis" and that all BLM manuals be revised to provide for environmental analysis.[103] In response, the BLM began to prepare environmental assessments (EAs) for routine actions such as land classification, leases, permits, roads, and trails, producing what it called an environmental analysis record (EAR).[104] Today, CEQ guidelines require formal environmental assessments for all federal actions that do not automatically trigger an EIS. Federal agencies use information from the EA to either begin EIS preparation or issue a finding of no significant impact (FONSI) that essentially exempts the action from an EIS. The initial CEQ guidelines in 1971 did not include formal EAs or FONSIs, but this is essentially how the BLM used the EAR system in the early 1970s. Upon completing an EA, BLM field managers could decide that the action would not have a significant impact on the environment and therefore did not require an EIS, and with this motivation the BLM quickly became a leader in preparing EAs.[105]

By the mid 1970s, however, the BLM faced growing criticism for its failure to recommend environmental impact statements. In a 1975 evaluation prepared for the CEQ, consultants voiced numerous concerns with the BLM's approach: *"As the EAR* [environmental analysis record] *process has produced few recommendations calling for the preparation of the EIS, the analytical methodology inherent in the EAR process is a source of concern."*[106] The consultants went on to suggest there were five potential problems with the BLM's environmental assessment. First, BLM employees simply may not recognize or report potential environmental impacts. Second, BLM employees may be far too optimistic about the effectiveness of their proposed mitigation measures. Third, BLM employees may not adequately evaluate the results of applying mitigating measures to potential environmental impacts. Fourth, BLM employees may not ask the right questions about residual impacts. Fifth, and very important, the BLM's environmental assessment process precludes the kind of public participation occasioned by EIS preparation, so the BLM does not have the added benefit of formal public feedback.[107]

The BLM's efforts to integrate environmental analysis into its planning and management decisions while generally avoiding the preparation of EISs also exposed the agency to NEPA litigation, which clarified the act's requirements and challenged the agency's approach to comprehensive planning. Litigation over the department-led EISs for the Trans-Alaska Pipeline and OCS oil and gas leasing taught BLM leaders early lessons about the scope and detail required in an EIS to withstand judicial scrutiny. Indeed, the BLM had released initial procedures for EIS preparation on December 28, 1970, but it revised those procedures in May 1972 to reflect these lessons.[108] Nevertheless, the BLM maintained its position that the environmental assessment built into its planning and technical reports was sufficient to meet its NEPA obligations for most field-level decisions, and it reserved EIS preparation for high-profile actions like the oil pipeline and for its basic programs in grazing and mining. Environmental groups could therefore participate in decisions about the BLM's coal and grazing programs at the national level, but they still did not have access to decisions at the regional or local level. The second round of NEPA litigation forced the BLM to prepare local and regional EISs as well, giving environmental groups an invitation to participate in the agency's day-to-day decisions.

The first NEPA case involved the Trans-Alaska Pipeline, a hot-oil pipeline that would carry oil from Prudhoe Bay on Alaska's northern coast more than 800 miles to the southern port of Valdez. It was the first hot-oil pipeline built through areas of permafrost, where the warm pipeline threatened to melt the ground and render it unstable. It was also the most expensive privately financed project in the world, with a price tag of $8 billion, so the risks were substantial.[109]

Initially proposed in 1968, progress on the pipeline was slowed by legal disputes over land claims by the state of Alaska, Alaskan Natives, and the federal government. Secretary Udall had halted land classification and disposal later in 1968 to give Congress time to resolve the problems, but by late 1969, the Interior

Department and oil companies had agreed on stipulations for pipeline construction, and Secretary Hickel had assembled a BLM inspection team to provide surveillance and enforcement of those stipulations during pipeline construction. Appropriations and oversight committees in both the House and Senate reviewed the plan and voiced no objections. On January 1, 1970, the same day that President Nixon signed NEPA into law, the BLM published proposed Alaska land classifications in the *Federal Register*, classifying the pipeline route as a utility and transportation corridor, and a week later Secretary Hickel officially lifted Secretary Udall's land freeze for construction of a utility road along the pipeline corridor.[110]

Environmental groups met with President Nixon in late February and "'zinged' him hard on the Alaska pipeline," complaining that the federal government was negligent for approving the riskiest and most expensive oil pipeline in the country without any serious study of its environmental impacts. At the same time, Rogers Morton, then chairman of the Republican National Committee and soon to replace Secretary Hickel, urged the president to move forward with the project, because Alaskan oil development was essential to the Republican Party's control in Alaska, and he assured the president that the pipeline could be built without causing environmental damage.

In an attempt to mollify environmentalists and move forward with the project, Secretary Hickel proposed a master environmental plan for the North Slope.[111] For the initial road right-of-way along the path of the pipeline, however, Secretary Hickel issued a mere eight-page EIS, which concluded that the road posed no negative environmental impacts.. The Wilderness Society, Friends of the Earth, and the Environmental Defense Fund filed suit, arguing in part that the road could not be separated so neatly from the larger pipeline project it would eventually support.[112] The U.S. District Court for the District of Columbia found for the plaintiffs, and the judge enjoined the permit until the Interior Department completed a more comprehensive EIS. In his ruling, the judge found that the right-of-way permit not only violated NEPA, in failing to provide an EIS for the whole pipeline project, but also violated the Mineral Leasing Act of 1920, by exceeding the act's maximum right-of-way width. Secretary Hickel's hopes of pushing the right-of-way permits through vanished.[113]

The BLM worked furiously throughout 1970 under close departmental supervision to produce its first detailed EIS, and it worked under a clear departmental mandate to produce an EIS that would support the project. When BLM Director Rasmussen released the 246-page draft EIS in January 1971, however, it received a less-than-enthusiastic response. Environmentalists complained that the document failed to consider all of the potential environmental impacts and all of the relevant alternatives; former Secretary Udall testified that he was "deeply disturbed by its glaring omissions" and implied that the EIS was poorly prepared because the Interior Department began with predetermined conclusions.[114]

Complaints from environmentalists and members of the CEQ were strengthened after one BLM employee wrote a scathing review of the document. Environmentalists used this as an indication that the agency and the Interior Department were not engaged in a good-faith effort to consider environmental impacts of the pipeline.[115] Furthermore, the Interior Department's solicitor warned that the document was wholly inadequate as a final EIS, even if it went through minor revision. Citing recent NEPA cases, the solicitor warned that the current EIS document would not hold up under judicial review because it was not thorough, detailed, or complete. Specifically, the solicitor pointed out that the draft EIS failed to discuss the actual design of the pipeline to withstand seismic activity, the potential environmental impacts of marine transport once the oil reached Valdez, and all of the possible alternatives.[116] Secretary Morton, who had by this time replaced Hickel, concluded that submission of the draft EIS would be self-defeating: "It can only endanger, rather than insure the timely development of North Slope oil."[117]

This sent BLM and Interior Department officials back to the drawing board with marching orders in 1971–1972. They had to come up with an EIS that would justify the pipeline and would stand up in court. As one Nixon advisor wrote, "industry has decided they want a pipeline to Valdez. If we can say it's safe, then that is what we should do and Morton should put his troops to work to cover our biggest problem—the inadequacy of the present 102 statement on the tankers from Valdez to Seattle."[118] Morton was urged to finish the final EIS quickly so that construction could begin that year.

The BLM released its final EIS on March 20, 1972. The EIS itself was six volumes and came with an additional three volumes of supporting analysis. The project had cost a total of $9 million, and the revision from draft to final EIS had taken 175 man-years of work. Still, Secretary Morton was doubtful that the document would hold up in court, and he encouraged Nixon's advisors to consider alternatives. By this point, however, the president was too committed to the project, and the secretaries of State and Defense insisted that the pipeline was necessary for national security reasons.[119]

The District Court removed its injunction following the EIS, but the Wilderness Society quickly appealed the decision, leading to a second ruling against the project.[120] In desperation, the administration turned back to Congress, requesting revision of the Mineral Leasing Act and authority to develop the Alaska pipeline. Amidst the oil crisis of 1973 and growing pressure for energy independence, Congress responded by amending the Mineral Leasing Act to allow for the necessary pipeline right-of-way. Congress also exempted the project from any further NEPA requirements or review, clearing the way for the project to move forward.[121]

The Alaska Pipeline controversy was actually one of two simultaneous NEPA conflicts for the BLM in 1971–1972. On June 15, 1971, Secretary Morton announced a sale of oil and gas leases off the coast of Louisiana. As the agency responsible for oil and gas leasing, the BLM prepared a draft EIS. After the required public comment period and public hearings, BLM Director Burt Silcock released the final EIS on October 28, and the Interior Department opened bidding for the leases.

Environmental groups, led by the NRDC, immediately filed suit, challenging the adequacy of the BLM's EIS. The District Court granted a preliminary injunction, which the Circuit Court of Appeals upheld.[122] This time, the courts praised the BLM for its discussion of potential environmental impacts resulting from the leases, but they found that the BLM had not considered all of the alternatives to oil and gas leasing on the Outer Continental Shelf and therefore the potential environmental impacts of those alternatives. It did not matter, the courts stated, that the omitted alternatives lay beyond the BLM's authority to select; under their interpretation NEPA required that federal agencies consider *all* alternatives and impacts.

Litigation over the Trans-Alaska Pipeline and offshore oil and gas leases served as a warning to the BLM and the Interior Department. They could no longer simply assert, as Secretary Hickel and Secretary Morton had done, that in their professional judgment a project could be undertaken without undue risk to the environment. They would now have to prove in a court of law that they had considered *all* the possible environmental impacts of the project. Environmental groups had demonstrated that even if they could not stop resource development, they could slow it to a crawl through procedural litigation.[123] In these cases, the BLM was caught in the middle between environmental groups determined to use the courts to block BLM activities and a White House determined to push those activities forward.

In a third major NEPA controversy, the courts ruled that major planning efforts also required an EIS, even if they were not direct management decisions. Coal-leasing activity on the public lands had increased dramatically during the BLM's first twenty-five years, from approximately 80,000 leases in 1945 to approximately 778,000 leases in 1970, yet the total amount of coal taken from the public lands had dropped nearly 25 percent in that same period. In a 1970 study, the BLM found that 91.5 percent of federal coal leases were not producing any coal. BLM and Interior Department officials concluded that the department's coal-leasing policy was fundamentally flawed, since it seemed to encourage speculative lease holding rather than actual coal development. In May 1971, Secretary Morton placed a moratorium on federal coal permitting and leasing.[124]

The moratorium pleased environmentalists, who cited the environmental impacts of coal mining, particularly strip-mining operations. They wanted assurance that federal coal leases would only be issued once potential environmental impacts had been identified and mitigated, arguing that the secretary of the interior was required to reject any lease that posed significant environmental threats. The mining industry, on the other hand, argued that because NEPA had not replaced or amended existing law, the secretary was still required to issue leases wherever a valuable deposit was found. This debate went on both inside and outside the Interior Department.[125]

In 1973, Secretary Morton announced that the BLM would craft a new coal-leasing policy that would bring an end to speculative leases and give the federal government greater control over the rate of coal production on federal lands. For the BLM, this was a major opportunity to demonstrate its professional abilities, but one for which it had very limited staff and experience. The BLM was used to making decisions in a highly decentralized fashion, and this was reflected in its planning system as well as its regulations on EIS preparation.[126]

The BLM completed a draft of the Energy Minerals Allocation Recommendation System (EMARS I) and a draft programmatic EIS in May 1974, both of which met broad, scathing criticism. The BLM, despite the lessons of the previous two NEPA losses in court, had described the basic steps of allocation, tract selection, and leasing but offered very little specific policy guidance. As Robert Nelson writes, "The program it designed was described in only the barest terms. It was, in fact, a very easy target for the environmentalist torrent of technical and scientific criticism that was about to descend on federal coal-leasing efforts."[127]

Secretary Morton rejected the BLM's proposed program and ordered Interior officials to devise a second coal-leasing program, EMARS II. The new program was designed by economists and differed sharply from the BLM's proposal in that it shifted from the BLM's planning emphasis to a new market approach. As later secretary of the interior Thomas Kleppe stated, "The nub of the process . . . is the use of the marketplace itself, for the market will ultimately determine what coal, if any, will be leased and developed."[128] Rather than writing a new draft EIS for the program, the Interior Department simply updated the draft EIS it had prepared for EMARS I and issued it as a final EIS on EMARS II.

The following year, Congress passed the Federal Coal Leasing Amendments Act of 1976, which affirmed a number of basic principles written into EMARS II. Most important, the amendments required development of federal coal leases within ten years to avoid speculative leases, mandated competitive bidding for coal leases, required comprehensive land use plans before leases could be issued, and raised the federal royalty rate.[129]

Despite this congressional blessing of the EMARS II program, it was stopped in its tracks by yet another NEPA lawsuit by the Natural Resources Defense Council. In *Natural Resources Defense Council v. Hughes*, a federal district judge in Washington, D.C., found that the EMARS II EIS failed to meet NEPA requirements for two reasons: first, the Interior Department had changed the EMAR system significantly between EMARS I and EMARS II but chose not to write a new draft EIS; and second, it once again failed to carefully consider the full range of alternatives or justify the need for more coal leasing.[130] The court enjoined the Interior Department and BLM officials from all new coal-leasing activities until the EIS problems were resolved, requiring that the BLM conduct comprehensive land use planning to determine the need for and alternatives to coal leasing.[131]

The three energy-related NEPA cases highlighted broad conflicts between traditional conservation, based upon professional expertise, and the new demands of environmentalism for transparent environmental assessment. These were largely national debates over trade-offs between environmental protection and energy development and therefore had little effect on the BLM's field operations. The real impact of NEPA on the BLM's day-to-day planning and management decisions, therefore, came through NEPA litigation dealing with the agency's range program.

The BLM had decided very soon after the passage of NEPA that it would prepare a programmatic EIS for its grazing program, leaving more detailed environmental assessment of individual grazing districts and allotments to the general planning process. The agency released its first draft programmatic EIS in 1973, and environmental groups were quick to challenge the agency's approach. The NRDC demanded that the BLM prepare site-specific grazing EISs; when the BLM refused, the NRDC filed suit in October 1973.[132]

In court, the BLM argued that its programmatic EIS met NEPA requirements, since the agency would conduct environmental assessments and produce supplemental EIS statements whenever appropriate. In April 1974, however, the agency intentionally or unintentionally undermined its own defense when it released a report on Nevada range conditions that highlighted extensive overgrazing and environmental degradation: "uncontrolled, unregulated or unplanned livestock use is occurring in approximately 85 percent of the State and damage to wildlife habitat can be expressed only as extreme destruction."[133] BLM Director Curt Berklund was forthright in his admission that BLM range management was an abject failure: "Unfortunately, the attention given to the management of the Western public domain lands, in terms of money and manpower needed to reverse century-old declining trends, has taken a back seat to every other national priority."[134]

The BLM released the Nevada report to pressure Congress for more range improvement funds—"Now hopefully, with the increased impact of increased competition for public land uses and implementation of the National Environmental Policy Act, we will get the resources needed to provide adequate management and rehabilitation for public rangelands"[135]—but the report also heightened environmental skepticism that the BLM could adequately protect the public lands without close public scrutiny. The NRDC introduced the report in its case as evidence that a programmatic EIS was grossly insufficient to address the detailed, site-specific problems of public lands grazing.[136]

In 1974, the District Court judge found for the plaintiffs, referring to the Nevada report three times to support his decision.[137] Furthermore, the judge insisted that the agency's limited funding and manpower did not excuse it from this legal obligation. The Interior Department chose not to appeal the case and worked out a court-mandated agreement with the NRDC to prepare 212 site-specific EISs by 1988. The BLM could not deviate from this EIS schedule, neither the timeline for completion nor the actual planning boundaries for each EIS, without the court's permission.[138]

The BLM seems to have viewed the case and the court's decision with ambivalence, rather than outright resentment. On the one hand, field managers were frustrated by the decision. As a BLM associate director later explained, "the preparation of environmental statements was not the approach the Bureau wanted to take. Environmental statements, of themselves, solve no environmental problems, and the Bureau's range staff felt that they could achieve more with less cost and effort by working through the Bureau's planning system."[139] Furthermore, the judge enjoined implementation of all new allotment management plans (AMPs) prepared through the agency's multiple-use planning system, including new range improvement investments, until the EIS for that area was complete. Since the EIS process was scheduled to take thirteen years to complete, some areas would not receive range improvement funds for more than a decade.[140]

In other ways, however, BLM leaders seemed pleased with both the case and the outcome.[141] The BLM had, after all, been seeking greater control over the livestock industry, largely by leveraging scientific data and reports that highlighted poor range conditions. The court had basically ordered the BLM to take a hard look at livestock grazing on a case-by-case basis, to identify *all* of the environmental impacts of livestock grazing, and to consider alternative allocations of range resources to wildlife and other uses. It was an opportunity to publicize poor range conditions and build support for changes in livestock grazing that BLM range conservationists believed were necessary but politically impossible. Furthermore, BLM leaders could take the court's decision to Congress and demand higher appropriations and staffing levels for the range program, a demand that the agency had made in the past and rarely won. The BLM later found that the early EISs cost an average of $630,000 in direct costs, and one researcher estimated that when indirect costs are factored in, the price tag rises to $5 million per EIS.[142] This was a huge expenditure for the range program, which had a 1973 budget of $24 million. Although some of the EIS funding came out of existing appropriations, much of it came through budget increases, beginning in 1974.

If the NRDC was elated by the court's decision, and the BLM was ambivalent, ranchers who held grazing permits were furious. They were still in the midst of a bitter battle over grazing fees, which they appeared to be losing, and they viewed the NRDC lawsuit as a flanking maneuver to attack the informal rights they had acquired to the public lands range. Worse still, they saw the BLM as complicit or at least complacent in the suit: "while the permitees did not feel that the suit was collusive, it was apparent that it was nonadversarial in nature." Ranchers saw the BLM's response "as an attempt by an increasingly centralized bureaucracy to extend its powers over an industry struggling for survival."[143]

The grazing decision is important for a number of reasons. First, by ordering 212 range EISs, the courts effectively opened up the agency's entire range program to formal participation by environmental and other national groups. Whereas the BLM's planning system *encouraged* BLM field managers to involve the public, NEPA requirements made public participation a formal obligation. Furthermore, the BLM had enormous incentive to involve environmental groups in all of its EIS preparation, since it wanted to avoid NEPA litigation. Second, it raised important questions about the BLM's scientific capabilities in range management. Detailed EIS preparation would require detailed inventories of range conditions and other social, economic, and ecological factors. Yet the BLM's basic range science methodology was far from universally accepted, particularly its methodology for determining range conditions.[144]

CONCLUSION

Once again, it is difficult to overstate the important impact that NEPA had on the BLM and its planning process. By the end of the Nixon administration in 1974, the BLM's planning program was in crisis. The BLM's 1969 planning regulations created a formal system of interest-group bargaining. One critic has complained that this type of approach produced a system of "predatory pluralism," in which "coalitions of single-resource users and single-resource professional managers transform multiple use into an adversarial game of adjacent, single-resource, land allocations."[145] This multiple-use planning process was clearly in tension with the new demands of comprehensive environmental protection and open public participation.

The BLM had tried to shield its general planning process from the burden of EIS preparation, since EIS preparation required direct oversight from Washington. At first, this strategy seemed to work, and the BLM only prepared EISs for major programs like the Trans-Alaska Pipeline. When the courts ordered the BLM to prepare 212 site-specific grazing EISs, however, the BLM essentially had two competing planning programs. It was already producing Management Framework Plans through its regular planning process for all public lands, including the grazing districts. The court order required the agency to conduct a second round of environmental planning for grazing areas in the form of EISs. This overlapping planning created confusion for field managers. As Robert Jones, the principal architect of the 1969 planning regulations, recalls, "it was seriously damaging credibility of the multiple use planning process, since it was apparent that the [Management Framework Plan] was *not* the vehicle for analyzing and establishing resource allocation decisions. The EIS preparation process was."[146]

This is not to say that NEPA battles were entirely negative from the BLM's perspective. The court-ordered expansion of the BLM's NEPA program led to a significant expansion of both the agency's budget and staffing levels. Between 1971 and 1977, the BLM's workforce and budget nearly doubled, due in large measure to the agency's NEPA and energy responsibilities. To meet its NEPA requirements the agency had to hire entirely different types of specialists, such as sociologists and archeologists. These "ologists" brought greater depth to the agency's EIS analysis, began to serve in the agency's overall planning process, and began to transform BLM's administrative culture.[147] The forceful entrance of environmental groups into what had previously been the politics of a grazing, mining, and logging commons continued to erode the dominance that ranchers, miners, and loggers had enjoyed in the first half of the twentieth century. In short, during the environmental decade the BLM faced more controversy, yet through this it expanded its workforce expertise and culture, its budget and staffing levels, and its constituency groups.

The legislation of the late 1960s and early 1970s realigned the overarching political relationships of public lands politics. The old iron triangle that led to the livestock industry's "capture" of the BLM—the livestock industry, Congress, and the agency—gave way to what Mark Sagoff has recently called a four-sided triangle: special-interest groups, both commercial and environmental; members of Congress; the BLM; and the courts.[148] Mathematicians and political scientists both may be puzzled by Sagoff's geometry. Essentially, the BLM took, or was forced to take, a new interest in environmental protection; yet the system that emerged during this period was one of continued policy, planning, and management gridlock, because the number of groups holding veto power had increased substantially.

The conflicts of the early 1970s made the BLM's quest for organic legislation even more urgent and more challenging. The EIS process had brought a growing number of conflicting interests into public lands decision making, and BLM leaders desperately wanted augmented statutory authority to steer the decision-making process. Said another way, the new political and legal developments in the early 1970s demonstrated a growing federal interest in the public lands, and BLM leaders wanted Congress to provide a statutory link between federal ownership and agency control.

5

Political Inertia under a New Statutory Mandate

For its first thirty years, the BLM operated largely under the statutes it had inherited from the General Land Office and the U.S. Grazing Service, including but not limited to the Mining Law of 1872, the Mineral Leasing Act of 1920, the Taylor Grazing Act of 1934, and the Oregon and California Revested Lands Act of 1937.[1] On October 21, 1976, Congress passed the Federal Land Policy and Management Act (FLPMA), a comprehensive statute that served as a belated organic act for the BLM.[2]

In one sense, FLPMA gave the BLM a new start. It closed the statutory gap between the BLM and the Forest Service, giving the two agencies almost identical mandates for multiple-use management guided by a publicly transparent land use planning system. Yet the BLM's new statutory foundation was hardly a clean break from the past, because FLPMA did not repeal or amend a single one of the BLM's primary authorizing statutes noted above. By emphasizing multiple use without repealing the BLM's primary authorizing statutes, FLPMA essentially codified the ambiguities that had developed in the late 1960s and 1970s concerning the relationship between traditional resource programs and new demands for environmental protection, land use planning, and public participation.[3]

Because FLPMA did not chart a clear new course for the BLM and the public lands, the importance of the act came down to how it was implemented by the executive branch, funded and overseen by Congress, and interpreted by the courts. The Carter administration (1977–1981) used FLPMA to focus on environmental protection, particularly in the areas of range management and the expanding realm of energy development. This emphasis, more than the act itself, led to an antienvironmental, antiregulatory backlash expressed in the Sagebrush Rebellion, a movement among western states and interests to gain outright ownership or at least greater control of the public lands.[4] The Reagan administration (1981–1989) took Sagebrush Rebellion concerns to the White House. Led initially by Interior Secretary James Watt, the Reagan administration challenged the BLM's growing planning and regulatory programs, emphasizing private initiative and market control of resource development instead. The dramatic shift between the Carter administration and the Reagan administration illustrates the fact that the BLM's mission and identity continued to be driven by dynamic debates about public and private property rights, federalism in the American West, new environmental values, and the relationship between substantive ends and procedural means in public lands administration.

THE FEDERAL LAND POLICY AND MANAGEMENT ACT OF 1976 (FLPMA)

Organic legislation had been one of the BLM's top priorities during the 1960s and 1970s, going back to the initial work of the Public Land Law Review Commission (PLLRC). The temporary Classification and Multiple Use Act (CMUA) and Public Land Sales Act (PLSA) of 1964 had provided interim authority, and after they expired in 1970 the agency was desperate for a permanent replacement. Forerunners to FLPMA appeared in the 92nd and 93rd Congresses, but neither Congress succeeded in passing a final bill. The Senate bills emphasized environmental protection and gave broad administrative discretion to the secretary of the interior, presumably reflecting the dominance of eastern senators on the Senate Committee on Interior and Insular Affairs. The House bills were more deferential to commercial resource interests and emphasized congressional oversight, presumably reflecting the strength of western representatives on the House Committee on Interior and Insular Affairs.[5]

The 94th Congress took up the issue of a BLM organic act again in 1975 and 1976. On February 25, 1976, the Senate passed the National Resource Lands Management Act (S. 424) with strong support—78 to 11. On July 22, 1976, with only a month and a half left in session, the House passed the Federal Land Policy and Management Act (H.R. 1377) by a more narrow margin—169 to 155.[6] Once again, the Senate and House bills reflected very different priorities and approaches. The Senate version emphasized broad, national interests in the public lands, placed more restrictions on commercial land users, and received support from environmental groups. The House version continued to favor natural resource development and received greater support from commercial interests.[7] The House and Senate appointed a conference committee at the end of August, but with congressional election campaigns in full swing, committee staff worked alone for over two weeks before congressional conferees held their first working session on September 15. In retrospect, the two weeks of staff negotiations may have been instrumental in getting a compromise bill, because several of the key committee staff members on both sides were former BLM employees who had been involved in the BLM's classification and planning programs in the 1960s and early 1970s and who had common commitments to the agency.[8]

The conference committee dealt with a number of symbolic and substantive conflicts between the two bills, beginning with the title of the final bill. The Senate version gave the BLM lands a new title, the National Resource Lands, which the agency and the Interior Department supported. The title suggested at the very least that the BLM lands were a distinct and important system of federally owned lands. The House version, on the other hand, referred to the BLM lands simply as "the public lands," and bore the short title "Federal Land Policy and Management Act." Consistent with Congressman Aspinall's position throughout the 1960s and early 1970s, the House resisted efforts to give BLM lands greater national distinction.[9] In the end, the staff and the committee members agreed to adopt the House language, and the status quo prevailed.

Next, the committee had to agree on terms for granting the BLM law enforcement authority. After thirty years of public lands management, the BLM still did not have basic law enforcement authority to prevent trespass and other unlawful uses of the public lands. When BLM field managers discovered unlawful activities, they had to rely on state and local law enforcement authorities, which delayed law enforcement action considerably. As one author explains,

> If a Bureau field man spots a hundred minibikes wrecking the side of a mountain or catches someone walking off with a rock adorned with petroglyphs, his only recourse is to hop in his truck, drive to the nearest sheriff's office or police station, collar an officer of the law, and bring him back to the scene of the crime—by which time, of course, the dust of the minibikes would have settled and the rock be either gone or tossed on the ground.[10] Furthermore, BLM leaders complained that they could not always count on local officials to enforce the law fully when it hurt local economic interests. Many public lands users and western congressmen opposed broad BLM law enforcement authority, because it was an important symbol of the BLM's proprietary responsibility for the public lands and would increase federal control over local communities and interests. In the end, the committee agreed to give the BLM law enforcement authority similar to that held by the National Park Service and the Forest Service.[11]

With compromise on both sides, the committee faced more contentious issues related to grazing and mining on the public lands. In both cases, the House wanted to protect the privileges that ranchers and miners had enjoyed for decades, and the Senate wanted to circumscribe these privileges to give the BLM greater flexibility and control. With the 94th Congress nearing an end, the committee was deadlocked on the two issues that dealt most explicitly with the property rights regimes governing public lands: grazing fees and mining patents.

The grazing fee issue stalled because committee members could not agree on how the federal government should deal with the extralegal value that grazing permits held on the private market or on the exact formula for grazing fees. One faction favored a fee formula based on cattle prices and grazing-land lease rates, which would probably lead to consistent, moderate increases, and one faction favored a formula based on cattle prices and ranchers' operating costs. This would have limited the amount of fee increase substantially.[12]

The mining patent issue stalled because the committee members could not agree on how long a miner should be permitted to hold and develop a mining claim—that is essentially to treat the mining claim as private property—before applying for a mineral patent. This stalemate is revealing, because earlier Senate bills had included far more radical mining law reforms such as Senator Jackson's proposal to repeal the Mining Law of 1872 and institute a new leasing system for all federal minerals.[13]

With little hope of compromise, the committee agreed to drop both issues in order to get a final bill back to the House and Senate floors before the 94th Congress ended. Both sides had made significant compromises, although it appears that the Senate yielded more than the House in the final negotiations. After more than five years of debate, both sides decided that this was the best opportunity they had. The House approved the bill on September 30, and the Senate approved it on October 1, its final day in session. President Gerald Ford signed the act into law on October 21, 1976.[14]

FLPMA was undoubtedly a legislative victory for the BLM, for it codified a number of important changes in public lands politics that had occurred over the previous decades, and which the BLM already assumed in its operations. First and foremost, FLPMA declared that the federal government would retain ownership of the public lands, unless the secretary of the interior determined that specific parcels of land would serve a higher public purpose in state, city, or private ownership.[15] Permanent federal land ownership had been largely assumed in public lands politics for more than forty years, following President Hoover's failure to give the public lands away and the Taylor Grazing Act's range management provisions, even though western congressmen and ranchers had routinely cited statutory ambiguity over ownership to defend their control of public lands and resources. For BLM leaders, this provision was long overdue, and many of them saw it as vindication of their conservation management ambitions to link the fact of federal ownership with the exercise of administrative regulation.

Second, FLPMA declared that the public lands should be managed for multiple uses and values: "the public lands [should] be managed in a manner that will protect the quality of scientific, scenic, historical, ecological, environmental, air and atmospheric, water resource, and archeological values; that, where appropriate, will preserve and protect certain public lands in their natural condition; that will provide food and habitat for fish and wildlife and domestic animals; and that will provide for outdoor recreation and human occupancy and use."[16] Like the declaration of permanent federal ownership, this was an acknowledgement of the existing realities in public lands management rather than a radically new policy. By the time Congress passed FLPMA, the National Environmental Policy Act, the Endangered Species Act, the Clean Water Act, the Clean Air Act, the Recreation and Public Purposes Act, the Wild Horses and Burros Act, and growing recreational use on the public lands had already permitted or forced the BLM to embrace a broad multiple-use mission. Having validated this mission, the central question that FLPMA did not answer was how the BLM might reconcile the competing responsibilities it already had and which at that time were still being resolved largely in favor of commercial resource use.

Third, in recognition of permanent federal ownership and multiple-use management of the public lands, FLPMA repealed almost 2,000 anachronistic statutes that reflected nineteenth-century land disposal policies.[17] Most important, it repealed the Homesteading Act of 1864, acknowledging that the remaining public lands were ill suited for small agricultural enterprises and formally ending homesteading on the public lands in the lower forty-eight states. Still, this left the BLM with an estimated 1,000 to 3,000 public lands statutes and did nothing to amend or repeal the agency's two dozen or so primary authorizing statutes, such as the Taylor Grazing Act, the Mining Law of 1872, the Mineral Leasing Act, the Oregon and California Revested Lands Act, the Soil Conservation Act, the Recreation and Public Purposes Act, and so on.[18]

FLPMA also advanced a number of new policies that had a long-term impact on the BLM's mission and culture. First, FLPMA mandated a new, comprehensive planning system. As explained in the previous chapters, BLM leaders had developed a comprehensive planning system during the 1960s in order to standardize decision making and give the agency greater professional control over its clientele. However, the final planning system that the agency established in 1969 simply formalized existing patterns of interest-group politics that had been institutionalized in the BLM's resource programs. Furthermore, the final planning system was almost immediately overshadowed by NEPA requirements to consider environmental impacts of federal actions and to solicit broad public participation in important land use decisions. Title II of FLPMA, "Land Use Planning: Land Acquisitions and Disposition," acknowledged these growing tensions in public lands planning.

The planning system mandated by FLPMA was modeled more after EIS preparation than the agency's general Management Framework Plan (MFP) preparation. Like NEPA, FLPMA placed new priority on environmental protection in the planning process, particularly by encouraging the BLM to establish "areas of critical environmental concern," and it provided explicitly for judicial review of the agency's planning decisions.[19] Also like NEPA's EIS provisions, FLPMA's planning mandate made the agency's land use plans decision-making rather than background documents: "land use plans . . . provide by tracts or areas for the use of the public lands."[20] This was something that BLM planners in Washington were eager to implement, because they were frustrated both with the tension between

MFP and EIS preparation and by the inconsistent quality of MFPs coming from the field.[21]

Perhaps more important, however, the new planning system required the BLM to seek the kind of broad public participation mandated by NEPA for EIS preparation. For the last thirty years, the BLM had generally consulted only with those members of the public that had a direct stake in public lands and resources, such as ranchers, loggers, and local government officials. FLPMA, by contrast, directed the BLM to "give Federal, State, and local governments and the public, adequate notice and opportunity to comment upon and participate in the formulation of plans and programs relating to the management of the public lands."[22] FLPMA's planning requirements, then, reflected the ascendancy of participatory planning, which required federal agencies to "seek input from the general public, the mass public, the so-called man in the street. The mandate is no longer to provide an opportunity for those who will be affected by the decision to be heard. Under the new theory, the goal is to involve everybody."[23]

To aid in the BLM's new planning process, FLPMA directed the BLM to create and maintain an inventory of all public lands and resource values under its jurisdiction. The intention was to ensure that all land and resource values would be brought to light in a public form and considered in BLM management decisions. In theory, this would promote both rational decision making and informed public participation. The BLM, like other federal agencies, had long used inventories and other formal data sets to advance particular agendas, since technical information enhanced the agency's political power. For example, the BLM had used new recreation inventories in the 1960s as its justification for the first natural areas and other special scenic and scientific designations. More important, it amassed range condition data and frail watershed inventories to pressure Congress and the livestock industry for reduced grazing. However, FLPMA's inventory mandate created two problems for the agency: first, the BLM lacked anything like sufficient appropriations for such an endeavor, and second, comprehensive inventories had the potential to threaten rather than advance the agency's agendas when opened to public scrutiny.[24]

Fourth, although Congress did not establish a new grazing fee in FLPMA, it did make important changes to the BLM's range program. FLPMA mandated a new study of grazing fees on national forest lands and the public lands to establish whether a fee is "equitable to the United States and to the holders of grazing permits and leases."[25] This provision validated one of the underlying assumptions of the 1969 grazing fee schedule, namely that the BLM and the Forest Service should have a uniform grazing fee. FLPMA also standardized policies on permit tenure and regulation. It established a ten-year permit period with virtually guaranteed permit renewal for ranchers who were not in violation of their permits, and it reaffirmed the secretary's authority to set permit terms and conditions in keeping with good range management practices and to suspend a permit if those terms are violated.[26]

In order to ensure accountability in range management, FLPMA required the BLM to prepare an Allotment Management Plan (AMP) for each grazing allotment and to incorporate the AMP into the grazing permit unless the secretary specifically determines that this step is not necessary. In keeping with FLPMA's overall emphasis on land use planning, the AMP provisions were intended to link range conditions and capacity to range management decisions and grazing levels. To balance these regulatory provisions with a carrot, Congress granted the BLM greater funding for range improvements. FLPMA provided that 50 percent of the grazing fee receipts would go toward range improvement, with half of this amount dedicated to range improvements in the district where the fees had been collected and the other half used wherever the secretary of the interior deemed necessary.[27]

FLPMA also revised provisions for grazing advisory boards established under the Taylor Grazing Act amendments of 1939 and 1949. FLPMA provided for optional grazing advisory boards until 1985, and it restricted their role to advising the BLM in the development of AMPs and the distribution of range improvement funds.[28] Elsewhere in the act, Congress affirmed the practice that had begun in the early 1960s of establishing multiple-use advisory councils. The new advisory councils of ten to fifteen people were to reflect the major citizen interests concerning each land area and were required to include at least one local elected official. FLPMA marked the statutory end of home-rule on the range that had defined Grazing Service and early BLM range administration.

Fifth, as with range policy, FLPMA did make a number of changes to the BLM's minerals management program despite the fact that Congress chose not to include a specific timetable for mineral patenting. For the first time ever, FLPMA required hard rock miners to file copies of their mining claims with the BLM and to file an annual report on their development of the claim, and failure to fulfill these two requirements would negate the claim.[29] The mining industry had strongly supported this provision not because it favored bureaucratic oversight but because this measure would allow mining companies a much more efficient way of determining which public lands were open to new mineral claims.[30] The BLM also supported the provision, since, after thirty years of frustration, the agency would finally be able to prepare land use plans with complete information about the location and activities of hard rock miners on the public lands.

FLPMA also mandated that the secretary of the interior "take any action necessary to prevent unnecessary or undue degradation of the land."[31] So, despite the clause that FLPMA "shall not in any way amend the Mining Law . . . or impair the rights of any locator or claims under that Act, including, but not limited to, rights of ingress and egress,"[32] FLPMA granted the secretary of the interior broad discretion to restrict the actual development of a mining claim or mineral lease in order to protect land and other resources. The secretary's regulatory authority was strengthened a year later by the Surface Mining Control and Reclamation Act of 1977 (SMCRA), which authorized the interior secretary to designate certain federal lands unsuitable for mining operations. The act focused primarily on coal mining, but it applied to all surface mining activities.[33]

Finally, FLPMA mandated new forms of preservation and protection. The most dramatic and controversial mandate in this area was undoubtedly extending provisions of the Wilderness Act of 1964 to the public lands. The original Wilderness Act of 1964 had excluded the public lands, and the BLM had made only a modest number of special designations under the CMUA to protect wilderness values. The agency's limited interest in wilderness preservation reflected both direct pressure from the livestock and mining industries and the BLM's professional orientation and culture. BLM field employees, mostly range and mineral specialists, were committed to resource use, and like Forest Service employees before them, they believed that congressional wilderness designations unduly hampered their management discretion.[34]

The contentious nature of this wilderness provision is clearly demonstrated in FLPMA's legislative history prior to the final conference committee negotiations in 1976. The Senate committee supported a BLM wilderness provision in most of the organic act bills introduced between 1971 and 1975, but the House committee was resistant to the idea. Congressman Aspinall's initial bill in 1971 made no provision for BLM wilderness, and later House bills that did include a wilderness provision did so with carefully drawn limitations.[35] Western congressmen shared the BLM's concern that wilderness designations would hamper grazing and mining activities.

As FLPMA drafts moved through the legislative process, however, environmental groups made it clear that they would not support a BLM organic act unless it had a wilderness provision. This placed BLM leaders who opposed the wilderness provision, particularly Director Curt Berklund, in a difficult position, and in the end they gave in to environmental pressure and accepted wilderness in the final version of FLPMA.[36] BLM and Interior officials did try to place additional restrictions on the criteria for wilderness review. For example, Assistant Secretary Jack Horton wrote to the House committee complaining that review of all roadless areas greater than 5,000 acres would include 89.5 million acres of the public lands, and he requested an amendment to raise the minimum size to 50,000 acres. In the end, however, both the House and the Senate agreed to require review of all roadless areas greater than 5,000 acres.[37]

The more serious congressional debate focused on interim management provisions for BLM wilderness study areas. Both the House and the Senate agreed that in general existing uses of wilderness study areas should continue, but they disagreed on how to protect wilderness study areas from undue degradation from these uses. The Senate bill gave full discretion to the secretary of the interior to prohibit existing uses inconsistent with wilderness protection or new uses. The House bill, on the other hand, prohibited the secretary from withdrawing wilderness study areas from mining, but it required the secretary to ensure that existing uses would not impair the suitability of wilderness study areas for full wilderness designation. In the end, the House bill's language prevailed, and it is perhaps ironic that the House committee's insistence on limiting the secretary's discretion led to more restrictions on mining and grazing in BLM wilderness study areas than existed under Forest Service or Park Service administration.[38]

In addition to the wilderness provisions, FLPMA also directed the BLM to expand its system of special conservation and environmental protection areas by, among other things, establishing areas of critical environmental concern (ACECs). FLPMA defined these as areas "where special management attention is required . . . to protect and prevent irreparable damage to important historic, cultural, or scenic values, fish and wildlife resources or other natural systems or processes, or to protect life and safety from natural hazards."[39] The BLM had requested this authority in its initial legislative request in 1971 in order to support the agency's existing efforts to protect scientific natural areas and resource conservation areas.[40] As the agency interpreted FLPMA, the new ACEC provision was intended to protect fairly limited areas of "'special significance' with 'notable' or 'outstandingly superior' characteristics."[41] As one author explains, "the concept of ACEC's appears to fit in a niche, probably a limited one, between areas worthy of national attention and perhaps legislative action on the one side and, on the other, lands whose environmental values can be adequately protected through normal management practices."[42]

FLPMA also included provisions to protect the California Desert Conservation Area, including the 12.5 million acres managed by the BLM. The California desert had been one of the most significant areas in the BLM's struggle to regulate off-road vehicles and to gain law enforcement authority from 1967 until the passage of FLPMA. By the mid-1970s, the BLM had already prepared a series of studies detailing the damage done to the fragile desert by uncontrolled recreation.[43] As Congress explains in FLPMA, it "is a total ecosystem that is extremely fragile, easily scarred, and slowly healed."[44] To protect the desert, FLPMA supported multiple use and sustained yield as the BLM's operating management philosophy, but it directed the agency to manage the desert with sensitivity to its unique and fragile ecology. Among other things, the BLM was directed to prepare a special land use plan for the desert by September 30, 1980, and even more important, FLPMA authorized appropriations of $40 million to produce the plan.[45]

Viewed in its entirety, then, FLPMA certainly validated the expanding multiple-use mission that the BLM had either pursued or been forced to pursue in its first thirty years. Senator Jackson, who had championed the BLM's initial legislative proposal in 1971, argued, "The Federal Land Policy and Management Act of 1976 represents a landmark achievement in the management of the public lands of the United States. For the first time in the long history of the public lands, one law provides comprehensive authority and guidelines for [their] administration."[46] Nonetheless, to win passage in Congress, the final version of FLPMA was stripped of substantive provisions that might have genuinely reshaped the property rights regimes and the goals of public lands management, so that it ended up looking much like the PLLRC report: a comprehensive document that reflected rather than resolved the complexity of public lands management.[47] As one author complains, "The political coalition required for passage of the Act ensured a document that in many ways broke little new ground in existing public lands management or in formal public land policy."[48] When boiled down, FLPMA is essentially a mandate for the BLM to resolve multiple-use conflicts through a more comprehensive and inclusive planning process. So rather than marking a new beginning for the BLM, FLPMA should be viewed as a congressional acknowledgement and endorsement of the new pluralism in public lands management.[49]

The most significant long-term impact of FLPMA on the BLM may in fact be cultural rather than legal. FLPMA accelerated the diversification of the BLM's staff that had begun in response to NEPA. To meet its expanding planning responsibilities under the two acts, the BLM hired an entirely new set of professionals with backgrounds in recreation, planning, wildlife biology, and archeology instead of range conservation and forestry. This chipped away at the BLM's traditional culture, which was decidedly western and oriented toward resource development, opening up the possibility that the agency's implementation of public lands policy might shift toward environmental interests.[50]

THE CARTER ADMINISTRATION: ENVIRONMENTAL VALUES GAIN PRIORITY

President Carter took office just months after President Ford signed FLPMA into law, so FLPMA's implementation was filtered through the Carter administration's complex domestic priorities: cutting federal spending; increasing oil, gas, and coal development; and strengthening environmental protection. Public lands issues were complicated politically by the facts that President Carter had no public lands record and had not won a single western, public lands state in the 1976 election.[51]

To head the administration's oversight of public lands management, President Carter selected a western conservationist as interior secretary: Cecil Andrus. As governor of Idaho, Andrus had supported land use planning during the 1970s, had opposed a power plant near Boise, and had helped create the Hells Canyons National Recreation Area. Andrus assumed his new cabinet position in 1977, determined to strengthen federal conservation efforts, including federal land use planning.[52] As he told the National Wildlife Federation in 1977, "The initials BLM no longer stand for Bureau of Livestock and Mining. . . . The days when economic interest exercised control over decisions on the public domain are past."[53] Or, as he said in an interview on April 6, 1977, "people . . . have basically for the last 8 years looked upon this department as the keeper of the natural resources for the purpose of development, whereas my philosophy would be the keeper of the natural resources of America for the future."[54]

Despite the administration's tough rhetoric regarding the public lands, the BLM was not its top priority among the Interior agencies, particularly after President Carter tried to eliminate western water projects that couldn't be justified economically.[55] For example, FLPMA had made the BLM director a political appointee, and it took the Carter administration more than a year to nominate Frank Gregg for the position. This and other delays during the Carter administration's first eighteen months slowed the BLM's progress implementing FLPMA.[56]

Frank Gregg, like Secretary Andrus, was a westerner with strong conservation credentials, including his most recent position as director of the New England River Basins Commission.[57] Gregg shared the administration's commitment to professional management, but he also understood the BLM's political history. Consequently, he worked at one and the same time to centralize the BLM's policy formation and coordination in the Washington office in order to increase professional accountability within the agency and to reaffirm decentralized management built upon collaboration with local clientele. This, for Gregg, was the first step in nationalizing the BLM's operations and hopefully building a national constituency for the agency.

Many of the Carter administration's other appointees came with conservation credentials as well, including service with the same conservation organizations that had effectively challenged the BLM's environmental planning operations in court.[58] These appointees, like Andrus and Gregg, were deeply committed to professional regulatory management and deeply suspicious of the livestock and mining industries. As Secretary Andrus explained, the Carter administration was making fundamental changes in Interior "to end what I see as the domination of the department by mining, oil, and other special interests. . . . Policy-making," he promised, "will be centralized and it will be responsive to my philosophy and the philosophy of President Carter."[59] Decisions, they argued, should be made on the basis of objective data and analysis and should favor conservation; they should not be made on the basis of clientele or market pressure. This attitude was reflected first and foremost in the Carter administration's reorganization plans and in the BLM's comprehensive planning efforts, which reached their zenith in the final years of the 1970s, but it also appeared to a certain extent in the administration's treatment of the BLM's range and coal programs.[60]

Secretary Andrus's rhetoric suggested the development of a comprehensive and coherent approach to federal conservation. Congress had clearly not provided such an approach in its recent legislation governing the public lands, the national forests, reclamation, and other important areas, so President Carter tried first to consolidate administrative discretion for federal conservation. Carter had promised substantial government reorganization during his campaign, and after taking office, he set in motion a massive review of the federal bureaucracy. The administration proposed a new Department of Natural Resources that would combine existing Interior Department agencies with the U.S. Forest Service and the National Oceanic and Atmospheric Administration, complaining that the "present Federal organization for managing our natural resources is scattered, cumbersome, and wasteful. It is no longer suited to the complex role of the Government in the wise development of our natural resources—development that insures conservation of the resource themselves and protection of their environmental values."[61]

The new Department of Natural Resources, the Carter administration argued, would place integrated responsibility for all natural resources under one Cabinet member, produce clearer accountability, facilitate comprehensive and long-range planning, save money, and protect the overall public interest: "a comprehensive overview of all resource areas within a single department will aid in dealing objectively with the many conflicts inherent in resource decisions."[62] The administration's argument echoed a long line of reorganization proposals going back to Secretary Ickes's proposed Department of Conservation back in 1938, and the president cited reorganization proposals by the Hoover Commissions, the PLLRC, the Ash Council, the Stratton Commission on Oceans, and the National Commission on Supplies and Shortages.[63] President Carter might well have paraphrased Ickes, saying, "[since the lines of our general land policy are still unclear after two centuries of congressional oversight] there should be close association and cooperation between all the principal agencies involved in the formulation of public land policies and in the administration of public land use. The objective should be a balanced administration of the resources so that each can be given its proper place."[64]

Like the past proposals that President Carter cited, the reorganization proposal was rejected by Congress. Nevertheless, the philosophy that had guided the reorganization plan had an impact on the BLM. When Frank Gregg became director in 1978, he centralized coordination and control of public lands policy by reorganizing the BLM's Washington office, explaining that the main goal of this reorganization was to "provide clear policy guidance to the field [so that the Washington office could] delegate the widest range of decision authority to the field within the framework of that policy."[65] To ensure better communication with the field, Gregg instituted more frequent and lengthier meetings with state directors in Washington. Closer coordination of BLM policy and field management operations, Gregg hoped, would allow the Washington office to infuse the agency with a stronger sense of professional authority and power: "It is important that the Bureau move quickly to recognize that it has won its battle for final legitimacy and to build a different set of expectations on the part of public land users, and a different set of expectations on the part of our Bureau field people."[66]

While the reorganization increased communication and accountability between the BLM director and that agency's state offices, it did little to increase coordination and accountability at the district level. For this, BLM leaders in Washington turned to the agency's planning system, which was being revised in light of FLPMA's planning requirements. In the early months of the Carter administration, BLM planners had argued that the agency's existing planning system would meet the basic requirements of FLPMA, and they had begun working on draft planning regulations that kept the existing system largely intact. While this might have met the agency's strict FLPMA requirements, it aggravated the growing tension between the agency's multiple-use planning process and its EIS preparation process.

For the BLM, multiple-use planning—that is the preparation of Management Framework Plans (MFPs)—was largely a local process focused on resource use. MFPs were prepared entirely by field specialists and approved by district and state managers, most of whom were attendant primarily to local and regional interests. BLM field managers were encouraged to solicit public participation and feedback, and this came invariably from local sources that had a direct interest in the public lands. BLM managers would print summaries of major MFP issues and distribute them locally, they would hold public hearings that were advertised locally, and they would rely on formal and informal local advisory boards. The final MFP documents were available for public review in the local BLM offices.[67]

By contrast, EIS preparation in the early 1970s was a national process focused on environmental protection. As noted in chapter four, early EIS preparation was handled primarily by the Washington office under close departmental supervision, in part because the BLM's field offices lacked the necessary specialists to complete an EIS. NEPA required not only that the BLM consult with those directly affected by the EIS but with the public at large. Consequently, draft EISs were announced in the *Federal Register*, printed in Washington, and made available for national distribution. Through this process, the BLM solicited comments from national conservation and environmental organizations.[68]

This disparity between local multiple-use planning and national EIS preparation led to lawsuits like *NRDC vs. Morton*, because the BLM had chosen not to prepare EISs on local decisions to which environmental groups wanted access. As the BLM began to prepare the court-ordered, site-specific grazing EISs, it became clear that these statements functioned as multiple-use planning documents, for they raised and answered many of the questions that the BLM had to address in the preparation of an MFP. What is more, with the threat of judicial review and guidance lurking in the NEPA process, EISs began to overshadow MFPs as the BLM's primary decision-making documents. This created important political problems for the BLM's field managers, because it meant that the EIS decisions approved by the Washington office in consultation with input from national organizations superseded conclusions that field managers had reached in MFPs that were approved by district managers with input from local interests.

Gregg encouraged BLM planners to rethink their commitment to the MFP system in light of the new political realities of public lands administration. As Robert Jones, the BLM's chief planner in the 1960s and 1970s, writes, the agency's first planning system "had been developed for a Bureau with . . . no capability or history of multiple use land use planning, no legislative requirement for multiple use planning and little national environmental legislation which required specific compliance steps."[69] Gregg directed BLM planners to resolve some of the growing tensions between MFP and EIS preparation by integrating them.[70]

Their first step was to acknowledge that MFPs, renamed Resource Management Plans (RMPs), were major federal actions under NEPA and required EISs. Next, BLM leaders convinced the secretary of the interior to delegate EIS filing authority to the BLM director so that the agency would have greater freedom in producing the new wave of combined RMPs/final EISs. As new draft regulations took shape, BLM leaders sought significant guidance from the Forest Service on how to integrate the RMP/EIS processes, since the Forest Service had long ago combined its multiple-use planning system with EIS preparation. They also sought input from other federal agencies, national user groups, and environmentalists. The final planning regulations were published in 1979 and included provisions for announcement, publication, and distribution of planning documents to solicit broad public participation.[71]

The new regulations effectively nationalized the BLM's multiple-use planning. By implementing FLPMA's provisions for public participation and by combining RMP preparation with EIS preparation, the BLM opened up its entire planning system to national organizations and the general public. As a result of this and EIS litigation, national environmental organizations began to focus considerably greater attention on the agency. They began to educate their members in the east and in urban centers about public lands issues, and they interacted more significantly with BLM planners and managers.

Just as NEPA shaped the BLM's multiple-use planning operations, it significantly altered the BLM's approach to range planning and management. The *NRDC v. Morton* decision in 1974, which challenged the BLM's decision to prepare a single programmatic EIS for all range management activities, rendered the BLM's traditional grazing AMP process obsolete. Under court order, the BLM had reached an agreement with the NRDC in April 1975 to prepare 212—later cut back to 144—individual EISs covering roughly 150 million acres of rangeland by 1988, regardless of funding or staffing shortages. Although each EIS covered numerous grazing allotments, it still required the BLM to dig below the general information contained in its programmatic EIS and address detailed range conditions, grazing patterns, and environmental impacts at the allotment level.[72]

The court chose a site near Challis, Idaho, for the BLM's first site-specific EIS, in large part because of recent conflicts there between livestock and wildlife grazing. Under court order and intense pressure from the NRDC, the stakes for this EIS were high. This was the BLM's chance to demonstrate its professional and scientific understanding of range conditions, broader environmental conditions, and range management alternatives for the Challis area, and this EIS would serve as the template for the remaining 143 range EISs. In the spring of 1976, just as Congress was debating the FLPMA, the BLM released the Challis draft EIS. It provided extensive details about the range and environmental conditions, and it recommended a careful system of rest-rotation grazing as the primary means of protecting range quality and increasing available forage for both livestock and wildlife.[73]

The draft EIS received a blistering review, most prominently from the NRDC and a leading independent agricultural organization, the Council for Agricultural Science and Technology (CAST). The agency could shrug off the NRDC complaint perhaps as ideologically driven, but it was more difficult for the agency to ignore CAST's professional criticism. Furthermore, both groups focused their criticism on the BLM's commitment to rest-rotation grazing as a panacea for range deterioration, arguing that the agency lacked sufficient scientific data to predict its success in the Challis area.[74] After two extensions, the BLM finally released its final Challis EIS in January 1977, but the agency had taken such a beating over the quality of its science that the Idaho state director promised to prepare entirely new draft and final EISs for the Challis area.

The Idaho state director's promise to prepare a new EIS came just after FLPMA's passage and President Carter's inauguration, so the Idaho BLM found itself working in a different statutory and political context. FLPMA mandated that the BLM maintain a complete inventory of the public lands and that it prepare AMPs for each grazing allotment based upon the data and alternatives listed in the BLM's site-specific EISs. The Carter administration took office pledging to enforce rigorous standards for data collection and analysis. The new context highlighted several basic problems with the BLM's range management program.

First, the BLM was still struggling to defend its assessment of range conditions after more than forty years of public lands range management. The U.S. Grazing Service had faced this problem acutely in the 1930s and 1940s before range conservation existed as an organized profession. The livestock industry had argued that the Grazing Service's negative assessment of range conditions was based on visual surveys taken during a severe drought, and it had argued that range conditions would improve naturally "if and when it rains."[75] Even in the 1970s, when range science and conservation were well established academically and professionally, the BLM could not produce a current inventory of range conditions that could withstand critical scrutiny.[76] For example, the range condition report that the BLM published for the Senate Appropriations Committee in 1975 concluded that "range conditions are deteriorating at an alarming rate," yet much of the data used to reach this conclusion were more than a decade old. At the same time, a report for the Council on Environmental Quality in 1976 found that public rangelands had improved between 1936 and 1966 in response to federal management.[77] What the BLM needed, then, was a system of range inventory and monitoring that the livestock industry, agency professionals, and environmentalists could all trust as an accurate measure of range conditions and trends, but creating this was a nearly impossible task.[78]

Second, the BLM was engaged in overlapping and conflicting range planning activities that emphasized very different range values. The AMPs focused primarily on the availability of livestock forage, whereas EIS preparation involved the broadest possible assessment of range values. Furthermore, since the BLM needed to complete the prerequisite EIS before preparing the attending AMPs, the dual planning process was remarkably time-consuming with the agency's existing budget, staff, and priorities. A 1977 report by the General Accounting Office (GAO) found that the BLM had prepared land management plans for only about 26 million acres of public rangeland, mainly because it had halted new AMP preparation until it could complete the prerequisite, site-specific EISs. Many of the plans the agency did have were obsolete or could not be implemented because of insufficient funding. In the face of these planning and funding problems, BLM leaders estimated that uncontrolled, destructive grazing continued on about 49 million acres of public rangeland.[79]

The third problem, which grew out of the BLM's inventory and planning dilemmas as well as its political weakness, was the agency's commitment to range improvement rather than grazing reductions in the face of serious range degradation. The agency had made some successful grazing reductions in the 1950s and 1960s on a tough, case-by-case basis, but the next round of cuts proved too challenging. The BLM then turned to rest-rotation grazing and range improvements to improve range conditions and increase the available forage without reducing grazing levels further.[80] This was evident in the BLM's first Challis EIS, and environmental groups, such as the NRDC, complained that this ignored both wildlife needs and broader environmental conditions. If the basic problem was overgrazing, environmentalists argued, then the agency simply needed to find the gumption to make substantial grazing cuts.

With new statutory and political direction, the BLM began preparing a supplemental Challis EIS in May 1977. The assistant secretary for Land and Water Resources announced that the BLM would broaden the focus of its grazing EISs to address the total carrying capacity of the range to support all forage uses. He rejected the BLM's traditional emphasis on meeting existing grazing levels through intensive management and suggested that the agency would instead focus on reducing grazing levels to fit the range's carrying capacity.[81] As the BLM's site-specific EISs went to press, it became clear that the process would lead to significant grazing reductions on the public lands range.

The BLM released a supplemental EIS for the Challis area in 1978, which reflected the agency's new approach. In the original EIS, the BLM had proposed no change in the existing grazing levels, focusing instead on increasing forage production through rest-rotation grazing. In the supplemental EIS, by contrast, the BLM proposed reducing the livestock grazing levels by 40 percent, from 17,444 animal unit months (AUMs) to 10,439 AUMs. This was the management path that environmental groups had demanded for years. The NRDC wrote, "The proposed 40 percent reduction in grazing . . . reflects the first serious commitment by the Bureau to deal with serious overgrazing evident in the unit. . . . Every effort should be made . . . to insure that the Bureau has adequately explained the justification for this desperately needed reduction."[82] The BLM was at that time engaged in precisely this type of effort, as it submitted appropriations requests for a massive expansion of its range inventory budget. As one author explains, "The objective of the vastly increased inventory effort was to assemble an arsenal of scientific evidence strong enough to stand up in expected court fights and other battlegrounds."[83]

In the late 1970s, many of the BLM's grazing EISs followed the pattern set by the Challis supplemental EIS. By 1980 the BLM had released twenty-two final grazing EISs, and many of them recommended significant grazing reductions. A survey of ten EISs showed that the BLM proposed reductions on roughly half of the grazing units, totaling an overall reduction of 15 percent. Several of them proposed cuts comparable to the Challis reductions, with some ranchers facing reductions of 30 to 40 percent.[84]

This does not mean that the BLM abandoned its promise to improve range conditions through intensive management and range improvement investments. The agency hoped to achieve significant increases in forage through a combination of grazing reductions and range improvements, and to do this it needed more money to invest in the range. The agency had developed an unsuccessful legislative proposal during the Ford administration for nearly $2 billion in range improvement funds, and when Frank Gregg became the BLM director in 1978, he revived the BLM's range improvement proposal and sent it to Congress to dampen some of the livestock industry's resentment at the agency's recent grazing reduction proposals.[85]

What emerged was the Public Rangelands Improvement Act (PRIA), which reflected significant compromises by the Carter administration. The act confirmed the interior secretary's authority to reduce grazing levels during PRIA's implementation period to ensure adequate range protection, but the real thrust of the act was range improvement to increase the available forage. While PRIA fell short of the BLM's initial $2 billion proposal, it authorized $345 million for range improvements over the next twenty years. The BLM was required to allocate these funds through its sluggish AMP process. The BLM had roughly 1,200 AMPs in place in the late 1970s, and under the agency's FLPMA and PRIA regulations, it was scheduled to prepare another 7,000 plans beginning in 1980.[86] PRIA also established a new temporary fee formula for BLM and Forest Service grazing permits for the years 1979–1985. The new formula was weighted to the price that ranchers received for cattle, which kept it well below most estimates of market value.[87]

Bolstered by PRIA's increased authority and funding, BLM EISs evinced an optimism about the trend in range conditions and grazing levels. In 1979, for example, the BLM released its final EIS for the Caliente area in southeastern Nevada. There the BLM proposed grazing reductions from 78,235 AUMs to 74,293 AUMs, but it projected that by 2015 the area would support 146,001 AUMs.[88]

At the end of the 1970s, then, the BLM had a new set of planning, funding, and management processes for public lands range management. With ten- and twenty-year time frames, however, EIS preparation, AMP preparation, and PRIA range improvements did not promise a swift response. Instead, they were slow and costly processes that promised a hard look at grazing practices, and ranchers, environmentalists, and the BLM dug in for a new battle in the public lands range war.

BLM leaders in the Carter administration had to deal with the other major fallout from early EIS litigation that had crippled the BLM's coal-leasing program. Coal leasing had been suspended since 1971 while the Interior Department developed a new leasing program. As noted in the previous chapter, the BLM's initial proposal in 1974 followed the agency's budding conservation professionalism and emphasized a planned approach to coal leasing. The agency would establish regional targets for coal production and then offer leases to meet those goals. After rejecting the BLM's proposal, the Interior Department prepared a second proposal, which shifted from a system of central planning to a planned-market approach. The interior secretary at the time explained that "the nub of the process is the use of the marketplace itself, for the market will ultimately determine what coal, if any, will be leased and developed."[89]

When President Carter took office, he promised to reform federal coal leasing yet again in order to ensure that "it can respond to reasonable production goals by leasing only those areas where mining is environmentally acceptable and compatible with other uses."[90] He instructed Secretary Andrus to make a full review of federal coal leasing. In September 1977, the D.C. District Court added additional guidance, rejecting the coal-leasing EIS that the Department of the Interior had prepared and instructing Secretary Andrus to "personally reevaluate federal coal-leasing policy . . . [and] make a new decision as to whether a new leasing program shall be instituted and, if so, what kind of program it should be."[91]

With these marching orders, Secretary Andrus and several task forces drew up a new coal-leasing system that returned substantially to a central planning approach that had long been the hallmark of federal conservation. The new system was announced in June 1979 and consisted of three distinct phases. First, the BLM would tie leasing levels to the Department of Energy's coal production targets, which were based on computerized forecasts of coal demand.

Second, the BLM would use the revised comprehensive planning system that it developed under FLPMA to zone federal lands for coal production so as to balance coal production with environmental protection.[92] Specifically, the BLM would use several screens in its planning process to weed out lands that were unsuitable for coal production. Lands would be eliminated if (1) they did not have a high to moderate potential for coal development based on existing government data; (2) they fit the department's existing unsuitability criteria; (3) they were more valuable for other multiple uses; (4) they were judged unsuitable based on consultation with private land owners who controlled the surface land above federal coal; (5) coal development on those lands would exceed impact thresholds established in the BLM's RMPs; or (6) they were part of an ACEC and coal development would jeopardize environmental values in that area.[93]

Third, within these government-established boundaries, mining companies were free to identify specific tracts of public lands for leasing, and the BLM would review each site-specific application. This was the Interior Department's one concession to a market approach, although Secretary Andrus was quick to emphasize that input from mining companies would come only after the agency had made its final suitability determinations. As Robert Nelson explains, "The central theme is the great importance of fully retaining the basic decisions in the hands of the federal government, which hold industry influence to a minimum."[94]

The new coal leasing program demonstrated the Carter administration's commitments to government-led conservation, and it supported the goals of BLM leaders to achieve greater autonomy from the mining industry. The leasing program also elevated the agency's developing planning program by giving it significant decision-making responsibility for future coal development on BLM lands. Within the new program, BLM managers had more power to make balancing and trade-off decisions in their land use plans.

What the coal leasing program and the range planning programs illustrate is the overall rise in the BLM's inventory and planning programs that occurred as a result of congressional, executive, and judicial forces during the Carter administration. Indeed, between these developments and the planning system that Congress authorized in FLPMA, the agency's inventory and planning activities probably reached their twentieth-century peak in 1980 and early 1981. The agency's workforce had risen to almost 10,000, and its budget had swollen to more than half a billion dollars.[95] At the end of the Carter administration, the BLM enjoyed a larger workforce, a larger budget, broader discretionary authority, a stronger planning mandate, and more important symbols of bureaucratic success in professional conservation management than at any earlier point in its history. Nevertheless, at the end of the Carter administration, public lands conflicts were far from being resolved, and it was in part the BLM's professional success that sparked a powerful backlash from the West.

BACKLASH: THE SAGEBRUSH REBELLION

The Sagebrush Rebellion of 1978–1982 was a movement among western states to claim ownership of the public lands and, more broadly, to challenge the federal government's growing regulatory role in public lands management. This was by many accounts the fourth such rebellion in the history of federal land and resource management, and it was the second rebellion directed primarily at the Bureau of Land Management.[96] Sagebrush rebels articulated their basic complaint against federal control in a number of ways: the East unduly controlling the West, bureaucracy unduly controlling individuals, in absentia environmental groups unduly controlling local communities, and so on. Led by the state of Nevada, in which the federal government was the majority landowner, the rebels argued that the sheer scale of federal ownership and land use control in the West violated the Northwest Ordinance of 1787, which declared that new states carved out of the public domain "shall be admitted . . . on equal footing with the said original states."[97] The issue was framed, in other words, as a matter of political and social justice. Even Arizona governor Bruce Babbitt, who vetoed Sagebrush Rebellion legislation in his state, argued that "management of the public domain in the West is not fairly shared."[98]

Despite the rhetorical focus on public lands ownership, it became clear over the course of the movement that ownership was not the central issue. Complaints about ownership were really complaints about the structures of control. Governor Babbitt wrote in 1982: "What angers most westerners is not the fact of federal ownership, but the federal government's insistence that it is entitled to exercise power 'without limitation.' When this sovereign power is wielded by a continually changing parade of federal administrators, each with a different agenda, the situation becomes intolerable."[99] In one form or another, the sagebrush rebels argued that western public lands communities and users had a right to greater self-determination, and this required that the federal government give them a stronger voice in public lands planning and management decisions.[100]

By focusing on challenges to federal control, particularly the federal government's growing regulatory role in public lands management, rather than federal ownership, it is possible to see how events during President Carter's first years in office and President Carter himself helped to spark the Sagebrush Rebellion. The Sagebrush Rebellion was not simply a reaction to statutory developments of the 1970s, although these are important pieces of the story; it was a reaction to the way that the Carter administration used these developments.[101]

The Carter administration strained political relationships with western states by its approach to a broad range of issues. President Carter triggered western hostility immediately after taking office, when he announced that he would cut funding for eighteen major water projects, amounting to a budget cut of $289 million. This "hit-list" attacked one of the most prominent forms of federal patronage in the West, and President Carter paid a significant political price for it. Hostility grew in response to several other initiatives. In his energy policy, President Carter called for greater energy conservation, increased oil and gas development on the Outer Continental Shelf (OCS), and increased coal, oil, gas, and oil shale development in the western states. Many western states objected, not to increased energy development, but to the limited control they had over the process. Finally, President Carter announced that he would deploy hundreds of MX Missile silos on federal lands in the West, virtually ignoring the protests of many western governments.[102]

If these issues aroused suspicion and anger in western states, the issues that ultimately sparked the Sagebrush Rebellion probably stemmed from the way that leaders in the Carter administration implemented FLPMA. Western states were frustrated by the zeal with which the Carter administration had pursued increased range regulation. When Carter took office, grazing fees were on the rise, having gone from $.32 per AUM in 1970 to $1.50 in 1976. Furthermore, FLPMA had affirmed the trend toward uniform grazing fees and regulations on BLM and Forest Service land, it had placed the last nail in the coffin of the old grazing advisory board system, and it had mandated more careful grazing allotment plans. More important, FLPMA reflected the growing reality that grazing was just one of many uses on the public lands and ranchers just one of many BLM clientele.[103]

The Carter administration pushed these developments even further, pressing for a much tougher stance against overgrazing and advocating sharp grazing reductions wherever grazing levels exceeded the BLM-calculated range carrying capacity. Indeed, one author argues, "One can trace much of the initiative, emotionalism, and dynamism of the Sagebrush Rebellion directly to the rangeland management practices of the Carter administration as it implemented the Federal Land Policy and Management Act (FLPMA) in the West."[104]

On top of growing tension over range management, FLPMA thrust the BLM into the political fray of wilderness review. When President Carter took office in 1977, he immediately sought to expand the national wilderness preservation system by endorsing all existing wilderness proposals and requesting more wilderness recommendations from federal land management agencies. He appointed people to the Interior Department who supported wilderness expansion, and these appointees guided the BLM through its first wilderness review process in a way that alarmed many western commodity interests.[105]

Western states were alarmed in particular with the way that the Carter administration interpreted FLPMA's conflicting mandates in Section 603, which directed the BLM to manage all wilderness review areas in a manner that would prevent degradation of their wilderness qualities *and* to continue allowing existing uses in wilderness review areas. In September 1978, the interior solicitor issued an opinion on the meaning of these conflicting clauses for the BLM's wilderness review process. The solicitor concluded that Section 603 required the secretary of the interior to prevent activities that would degrade wilderness qualities on all public lands until the BLM completed its wilderness review. In other words, rather than seeing the nonimpairment clause of Section 603 lands as applicable to areas that the BLM identified for wilderness study, the solicitor argued that the clause applied to all public lands until they were specifically released from wilderness study.[106] This broad interpretation of Section 603 only confirmed western suspicions that the Carter administration was using FLPMA to restrict commercial use of the public lands in general.

Perhaps because of the restrictions implied by the solicitor's opinion, the growing western resentment of the BLM's wilderness review, and ambivalence toward wilderness designation among field managers, the BLM moved very swiftly on its preliminary inventory, completing the process in November 1980. Out of roughly 174 million acres in the lower forty-eight states, the BLM designated 919 wilderness study areas totaling almost 24 million acres. The agency pledged to complete full wilderness studies of the areas by the 1991 deadline that FLPMA imposed.[107]

While the BLM handled wilderness review in the lower forty-eight states, the Carter administration was engaged in its own, massive wilderness review in Alaska that included millions of acres of public lands. A detailed account of the Alaska story lies beyond the scope of this project, since public lands in Alaska have a unique political history in federal law and in BLM management. Nevertheless, it is important to briefly note the dramatic action that the Carter administration took to preserve Alaska lands, since this played into the rancorous debate of the late 1970s.

The Alaska Native Claims Settlement Act of 1971 (ANCSA) included a provision in Section 17(d)(2) that directed the secretary of the interior to withdraw up to 80 million acres of public lands for study as new national parks, wilderness areas, and so on. Secretary Morton had presented his final recommendations for the withdrawal of 83 million acres in December 1973, and according to Section 17(d)(2), Congress had to approve or reject the withdrawals by December 1978. In 1977, Secretary Andrus offered an even more ambitious proposal to protect almost 92 million acres. As the deadline approached for congressional action, it became clear that Congress was deadlocked on the issue. On December 1, 1978, President Carter took unilateral action and created seventeen new national monuments in Alaska that totaled 56 million acres of land. This dramatic action, together with Ronald Reagan's election in November 1980, broke the congressional deadlock, and in December 1980 Congress passed the Alaska National Interest Lands Act, which set aside 104.1 million acres as national parks, wildlife refuges, recreation areas, and national conservation areas.[108]

The Carter administration's emphasis on planning and scientific management, its tough stance on range management, and its strong endorsement of wilderness preservation ignited and then fanned the flames of the Sagebrush Rebellion. Frank Gregg and other leaders responded to the Sagebrush Rebellion in a variety of ways. The Office of Public Affairs produced a briefing package entitled *The Nation's Public Lands* for field managers to use in their interactions with the press and public lands users. Agency leaders insisted that much of the Sagebrush Rebellion rested on misleading clichés such as development vs. environment, federal vs. state, and East vs. West, and they encouraged field managers to move beyond these clichés to emphasize BLM partnership with state and local officials and interested members of the public.[109] Agency leaders reached out to the National Governors Association and other associations of state and local officials to build greater trust in the agency, but in the heat of the 1980 election these efforts seem to have done little to improve the overall tenor of public lands debate.

THE REAGAN ADMINISTRATION: A SAGEBRUSH REBEL IN THE WHITEHOUSE

Ronald Reagan's election signaled a change in the structures and processes of public lands control. For President Reagan, bureaucracy was itself the primary obstacle to good government: "In this present crisis, government is not the solution to our problem; government is the problem. . . . It is time to check and reverse the growth of government, which shows signs of having grown beyond the consent of the governed."[110] The Reagan administration, political scientist Robert Durant argues, believed that markets are the most effective methods of resource allocation, that government spending was causing inflation, and that "government rather than market failures increasingly spawned social ills."[111] When President Reagan took office in 1981, he was committed to an all-out war on the burgeoning federal bureaucracy, and his appointees were meticulously screened to ensure that they shared his agenda. Unlike President Carter's appointees, many of whom came from environmental organizations, President Reagan's appointees came primarily from private-sector and regulated industries, "reflecting Reagan's determination to shift the balance of representation in executive agencies toward the business community."[112]

To carry out his agenda in the Interior Department, President Reagan selected James Watt as secretary of the interior. Watt had extensive credentials, both in federal service and the Republican Party, and he was fully committed to Reagan's agenda. Watt had been deputy assistant secretary for Water and Power and chief of the Bureau of Outdoor Recreation under President Nixon, and he had served on the Federal Power Commission under President Ford. During the Carter administration, however, Watt had left federal service to become president of the Mountain States Legal Foundation, an organization dedicated to protecting private property rights, resource development industries, and western state interests. Indeed, it was Watt who took the BLM to court on behalf of New Mexico ranchers to challenge grazing reductions that the BLM proposed in a 1977 EIS.[113]

Secretary Watt took office pledging to restore balance to the Department of the Interior. Whereas balance for the Carter administration had meant balancing existing resource development activities with environmental protection through scientific management, balance for Watt meant pushing back "extremist" environmentalists, who, in his view, were locking up the national natural wealth on the basis of a flimsy ideology. As he told the Outdoor Writers Association of America in June 1981, "narrow special interest groups [environmentalists] have lost their privileged access and their control of high government officials from the White House on down."[114] Watt's hostility toward environmental groups was reciprocated in full.[115]

Watt referred to his first year in office as "A Year of Change: To Restore America's Greatness."[116] In this, he was committed to President Reagan's agenda of "making America move" by eliminating the tangles of bureaucratic red tape.

Watt advocated a "common sense" approach to natural resource decision making, which meant that he supported decision making based on practical resource knowledge gained by public lands users over elaborate systems of scientific inventory, analysis, and planning. For Watt, the professional land manager, who sought "objective" data and decisions in isolation from public lands users, posed the greatest threat to good management.

In many respects, then, Watt's nomination and first year in office may have caused a sigh of relief for BLM field managers, who were struggling to implement the complex planning systems mandated by NEPA and the BLM's new FLPMA regulations. Watt seemed to be calling on BLM managers to return to the days of face-to-face deliberations with ranchers, miners, and loggers about the practical problems of resource development on the public lands. One critic writes, "Mr. Watt evinced a reactionary desire to return to an earlier age,"[117] and it is certainly the case that Secretary Watt fought the trend of the Carter administration toward broad, systematic inventories and data analysis.

Secretary Watt's 1981 agenda for the public lands emphasized three goals: "Enhance America's ability to meet our energy and minerals needs with *domestic* resources [,] improve State and local relationships with the federal government through a 'good neighbor' policy [, and] bring better government through good management and decisive leadership."[118] Within the broader framework of the Reagan administration, these goals might be translated this way: increase domestic resource production by removing regulatory barriers, reach out to Sagebrush Rebels in western states, and provide more decisive leadership by eliminating lengthy procedural obligations.

Secretary Watt appointed Robert Burford as BLM director, and together Watt and Burford set out to reshape the agency's mission. Burford had a background in mining and ranching, and he had been a vigorous participant in the Sagebrush Rebellion at the end of his three terms in the Colorado House of Representatives, 1974–1980. Like Secretary Watt, Burford promised to restore balance to public lands management by tipping the scales toward resource developers to offset the upper hand that environmentalists enjoyed during the Carter administration.[119] As Burford later explained, "When I first came to Washington, our public lands were being managed . . . along the lines of private playgrounds for a number of special interests. The primary concern was the preservation of those playgrounds."[120]

Secretary Watt and Director Burford did not attempt any major revisions of the BLM's authorizing legislation, since they both argued that that legislation already mandated greater resource development than the Carter administration had permitted. Indeed, they argued, the real problem lay not in the law but in the "dictatorial, uncompromising attitudes of bureaucrats during the Carter years."[121] They attacked this perceived arrogance through a number of key initiatives, including major budget cuts, reorganization and staffing changes, and resource policy changes, and they achieved a remarkable amount during their first year in office.

Perhaps the most dramatic attack on the BLM's existing patterns came through changes in the agency's appropriations. President Reagan was committed to a massive reduction in federal spending to reduce the overall scope and control of federal bureaucracy, but for a number of legal and political reasons, he focused particular attention on regulatory and environmental budgets administered by the EPA and Interior Department. Whereas agency and department heads in past administrations might have objected to deep cuts in their budgets, Watt, Burford, and EPA Director Anne Gorsuch fully supported the changes that these cuts produced.[122] As Secretary Watt declared, "We will use the budget system to be the excuse to make major policy decisions."[123] Whereas the Carter administration had projected an increase in natural resource and environmental spending from $13 billion in 1980 to $16 billion in 1984, the Reagan administration planned to cut spending down to $9 billion in that same period.[124]

For the BLM, these cuts attacked the agency's noncommercial, inventory, and environmental planning programs that had expanded during the Carter administration: recreation and wilderness were cut by 24.4 percent, cultural programs by 40.3 percent, enforcement by 17 percent, and wildlife by 14 percent. The oil and gas leasing program was cut by only 1.9 percent, and while grazing was cut by 15 percent and coal leasing by 30 percent, these cuts came primarily in technical, monitory, or regulatory areas and would not limit resource development.[125] Given the BLM's growing emphasis on planning over the past twenty years, the most significant cuts were probably those made in the agency's formal planning budget, which dropped by 45 percent between 1981 and 1982, implying a 52 percent reduction in planning field personnel. In keeping with Secretary Watt's promise to use the budget as an excuse for policy decisions, Director Burford took further actions to reduce the role of BLM planners in the agency's state offices. In October 1981, for example, he announced cuts in pay and civil service grade for planners in the state office, demoting them so that they no longer answered directly to the state directors.[126]

Burford continued the Reagan administration's assault on the BLM's planning edifice in a number of ways, all designed to reduce the agency's planning burden and make resource development decisions faster and easier. In the fall of 1981, Burford removed Robert Jones, who had guided the BLM's planning program for almost eighteen years and was strongly committed to making the BLM's planning system the focal point for agency decisions.[127] Jones's replacement, David Williams, was directed to revise the agency's new planning regulations, which had been issued just two years earlier, and the BLM released new draft planning regulations in November 1981.

The new regulations were substantially shorter than the 1979 regulations and were intended to speed up the planning process, reduce planning costs, and give field managers greater freedom. The new regulations were, among other things, an attack on the ideals of scientific management, and they basically eliminated requirements that the BLM conduct extensive land and resource inventories prior to planning: they reduced the number of alternatives that planners needed to consider; they reduced the number of new plans that the agency had to prepare by retaining older plans the agency viewed as adequate; and they further decentralized planning responsibility.[128] In other words, the new planning regulations moved away from the idea that managers should assemble all relevant scientific data, consider all possible options, and then make resource allocations under state office supervision, all with extensive public input. Instead, BLM field managers were encouraged to make decisions in the field, based on available information and working most closely with public lands users.

Reactions to Secretary Watt and Director Burford, while uniformly negative among conservation and environmental groups, were mixed within the agency. Many field managers applauded the administration's emphasis on decentralized management and streamlined decision making. These field managers had objected to efforts by the Washington office to centralize agency policy and decision making, and they appreciated the renewed flexibility that the Reagan administration promised them at the local level. Nevertheless, employees who sympathized with environmental interests often felt besieged by the Reagan administration. Their marching orders to increase energy production and not to cut grazing levels flew in the face of the environmental emphasis of the 1970s, and new BLM employees who had been hired after FLPMA to help with wilderness inventory, cultural resources, and recreation found that their role in the BLM was greatly diminished.[129]

Burford's top policy priorities when he took office were range management, mineral leasing, wilderness review, and past administrative land withdrawals.[130] In each of these areas, Burford focused on streamlining regulatory and environmental procedures that delayed or limited resource development. While it would be an exaggeration to say that Burford called for a return to the home-rule days of the 1930s, his leadership in range policy was clearly intended to roll back the BLM's regulatory hand.

Watt and Burford took office at a time when the BLM's grazing EIS program was beginning to show that forage allocations made through grazing permits exceeded forage production on the public lands. Both the secretary and the director took a dim view of the elaborate range inventory process used to establish this claim, arguing that a onetime inventory, no matter how intensive, could not capture the dynamic conditions of the western range.[131] In response they ordered several key changes in range planning and management.

First, just months after taking office, Burford ordered a revision of the rangeland planning regulations. The BLM was slated under its new FLPMA regulations and its *NRDC v. Morton* agreement to conduct a full inventory of all public rangelands as the foundation for planning, but the new range regulations cut these requirements substantially through "selective management." Under the new regulations the BLM would only collect baseline soil and ecological data and categorize its rangeland in order of management priority. The agency would then complete a full inventory only for those areas that required immediate action. In this way, "the level of data being gathered would be commensurate with the decisions being made."[132]

Second, Secretary Watt issued a moratorium on all grazing reductions proposed through the BLM's EIS process, essentially requiring BLM planners to select the "no action alternative" in their EIS conclusion. Congress had already passed an appropriations rider on the FY 1981 budget, limiting grazing reductions to a maximum of 10 percent in any given two-year period, but this cut grazing reductions down to nothing.[133]

Third, arguing that grazing cut proposals had been based on shoddy science in the intensive inventory process, Watt and Burford shifted the BLM's focus from range inventory to range monitoring. They argued that after five years of continuous monitoring the BLM would finally have reliable data on range trends, rather than just snapshots of range conditions, on which to base future grazing reductions.[134]

Finally, in 1983 the BLM issued new proposed regulations that would have created Cooperative Management Agreements with grazing permittees. Under the new regulations, permittees who signed these agreements would be given far greater autonomy in range management decisions; they would be given greater deference in permit renewal; and the agency would reduce its enforcement activities for permit violations.[135]

Although the courts ultimately rejected the Cooperative Management Agreement regulations as an abdication of federal responsibility, they upheld the BLM's decision to halt all grazing reductions. In reviewing a plan from Reno, Nevada, the Ninth Circuit court found that even if the plan made little management or ecological sense, the court's job was only to determine whether or not it was clearly irrational under the law.[136]

If the key issue in range management was control, issues in BLM minerals management under Watt and Burford were about both control and production levels. Presidents Nixon, Ford, and Carter had all emphasized increased domestic energy production in light of various energy crises, which had been difficult for them to juggle with their environmental commitments. For the Reagan administration, however, energy production was more than a practical goal: it was something closer to a moral goal, because the administration placed much greater emphasis on the national security value of energy independence. In the area of minerals management, then, extensive planning and regulation of energy minerals development were seen as a threat to national security, and Watt pursued increased domestic energy production with fervor.[137]

Director Burford took office with a mineral mandate: "One of our primary objectives," he declared, "is to increase the availability of federal lands and resources for energy and mineral exploration and development."[138] In the summer of 1981, Burford reorganized the BLM's Washington office to reflect the administration's new emphasis on energy production: "I have established the position of Deputy Director for Energy and Minerals," Burford explained, "to elevate the role of energy and minerals decisionmaking and to emphasize the importance of energy and minerals issues in multiple-use management."[139]

Secretary Watt followed this up in February 1982 with a departmental reorganization that eliminated the Conservation Division of the U.S. Geological Survey (USGS) and created the Minerals Management Service (MMS). The new agency was responsible for mineral royalties and development. Later that year, however, Watt moved all onshore mineral permitting and development responsibilities out of MMS to the BLM. Thus, while MMS still handled all royalty management and all off-shore mineral development, the BLM now enjoyed greater responsibility for onshore minerals management. In addition to permitting, which the agency had always done, it was now responsible for monitoring actual mining activities, which the USGS used to do.[140] This meant that Secretary Watt's controversial plan to lease a huge area of the OCS for oil and gas no longer implicated the BLM.

The most controversial mineral policy changes for the BLM, then, were probably those affecting coal leasing. The Interior Department's new program was a compromise that incorporated elements of centralized planning and market approaches, but when Watt took office he viewed these as burdensome, placing too much responsibility and control with the federal bureaucracy. The Interior Department issued new coal-leasing regulations in July 1982 in what it called a system of "leasing to meet the demand for reserves." The administration's basic idea was to craft regulations that would create a competitive coal market and allow that market to determine coal production rates. As the administration explained, "In order to achieve this objective, the coal supply under lease must exceed the amount that will be dedicated to development in the near term. By no means should this be considered to be an 'over supply' situation. Such a coal supply is necessary for the efficient development and for the proper pricing of the coal which is dedicated to development."[141]

At the same time, the Interior Department relaxed its requirements of diligent development of coal leases, sustaining older leases that companies had not yet developed; it invited coal companies to identify lands they wanted for lease earlier in the land use planning process, before the department had determined which lands were suitable or unsuitable for coal development; and the department changed regulations dealing with regional coal teams and consultation with western state governments, which generated significant protest from western governors. These shifts were all intended to place more coal under lease, thus giving coal companies greater freedom to determine when and how much coal to develop.[142]

Watt released the new regulations just two months after offering one of the largest coal leases in history—1.6 billion tons—in the Powder River area of Montana and Wyoming. As with Watt's proposal to lease vast areas of the OCS, the scale of the Powder River lease aroused significant opposition. Opponents charged that Watt had given the coal away at "fire sale prices," and the House Appropriations Committee launched an investigation. The GAO reviewed the sale and concluded that the Interior Department had accepted bids at something close to $100 million short of the coal's fair market value. Watt then engaged in a battle with Congress over coal leasing in the Fort Union area of Montana and North Dakota. There he offered a lease despite a congressional appropriations rider that withdrew the area from leasing, and a federal judge enjoined the sale. After Watt resigned from office in 1983, a congressional commission released a scathing review of his leasing policies, and his successor promised to return to the drawing board and prepare yet another coal-leasing system.[143]

In connection with mineral leasing, Secretary Watt and Director Burford focused significant energy on the BLM's wilderness inventory required under FLPMA. Since the Wilderness Act was passed in 1964, secretaries of the interior had generally upheld an informal policy of denying mineral leases in wilderness areas. The Mountain States Legal Foundation, the organization that Watt directed before assuming his cabinet position, had successfully sued the Interior Department over this policy in 1980. With Watt in office, the Interior Department began to aggressively pursue mineral leases within wilderness areas, something that was legal but politically volatile. This initiative set Watt at odds with Congress in interesting ways. For example, the Forest Service was processing an oil and gas lease application for the Bob Marshall Wilderness Area in 1981 when the House Interior Committee ordered Watt to withdraw it from mineral leasing. Watt protested but complied and was, in turn, sued by the Mountain States Legal Foundation. Ultimately, the courts upheld the withdrawal, and Congress passed a series of appropriations riders temporarily blocking mineral leasing in wilderness areas.[144]

Beyond the question of leasing *within* wilderness areas, Watt emphasized the need to release mineral lands from wilderness study and designation to accelerate federal mineral production. Watt first announced that the BLM would not consider areas of less than 5,000 acres for wilderness study or designation, arguing that under FLPMA, "the Bureau may create a wilderness from an area with fewer than 5,000 acres only if it has some outstanding or unique feature."[145] He also placed all split estate areas—areas where the BLM controlled the surface area but not the mineral rights—off-limits to wilderness review. Here again, Watt's policies aroused substantial resistance among environmentalists and in Congress, placing the BLM in a difficult position between its commercial and environmental constituencies.[146]

James Watt resigned in 1983, and President Regan replaced him with William P. Clark (1983–1985). What became clear through the remainder of Reagan's tenure, however, was that Watt had indeed been following the president's directives. The Reagan administration continued to challenge the growth of federal land use and environmental planning and to look for ways to encourage market control of natural resources on the federal lands. The administration's sympathy with the Sagebrush Rebellion and its opposition to the kind of scientific management that environmental groups demanded in the 1960s and 1970s turned into an attack on the BLM's budding professionalism. At the same time, the extreme policy positions that the administration pursued coupled with Watt's open hostility to environmentalism created a kind of counterrebellion. Membership in environmental organizations rose substantially during the 1980s, reflecting a growing commitment to environmental protection and noncommercial resource values on the public lands. The BLM was once again trapped between powerful political forces without a clear sense of mission.

CONCLUSION

Although FLPMA was a significant victory for the BLM and offered the agency more secure statutory footing, it did not resolve the basic tensions of public lands politics and management. The ambiguity of FLPMA's multiple-use mandate played out in the late 1970s and early 1980s during the administrations of President Carter and President Reagan. President Carter's appointees used FLPMA authority to bolster the BLM's planning and environmental programs and to exert greater professional control over the agency's clientele. President Reagan's appointees were openly hostile to federal bureaucracy and to decisions based upon bureaucratic processes. They tried to streamline the BLM's management programs to turn resource development decisions over to public lands users and to economic markets.

Unfortunately for the BLM, which was caught in the middle, the whiplash between the Carter administration and the Reagan administration only confirmed the agency's ambiguous role in federal land management, symbolized by the controversies over wilderness vs. energy. The whiplash reflected not only the BLM's conflicting statutory responsibilities, but also the conflicting commitments that were emerging within the agency's staff and culture.

The political rancor of the period also stopped the agency from achieving some of its basic and long-standing goals for clearer boundaries and responsibilities. For example, one of Secretary Watt's proposals that failed is one that, in principle, all parties agree is important for the BLM and public lands management: land exchanges. Secretary Watt argued that through outright land sales and land exchanges the Interior Department should rearrange the public lands pattern in the West. He initiated a land exchange program that if carried out fully would have blocked up areas of the public lands by eliminating private, state, and other federal inholdings. Watt's reasons for the exchange program were mainly that well-blocked lands would allow for more efficient administration and would limit the degree to which federal land management agencies impinge on private and state landowners.[147] Many advocates of strong federal regulation and professional scientific management had proposed land exchange programs for quite different reasons. In fact, President Carter's BLM director, Frank Gregg, published a proposal to do just that in 1982: *Federal Land Transfers: The Case for a Westwide Program Based on the Federal Land Policy and Management Act*.[148] The advocates' reasons had mainly to do with limiting private and state control of federal land management decisions.

It would seem, then, that there was general consensus that the boundaries of public lands management, both the boundaries of the public lands themselves and the structures of public lands control, needed to be clarified and simplified. Armed with FLPMA, both the Carter and the Reagan administrations sought to do just that at a broad level, but they found that these boundaries were too well established to move in any permanent, comprehensive sense.

6

BLM in the 1990s: Bureau of Landscapes and Monuments?

After twelve years of Republican control in the White House, the Clinton administration returned once again to the idea that the BLM should have a comprehensive conservation mission that would subordinate individual resource development programs to a larger vision of environmental protection. Secretary of the Interior Bruce Babbitt pressed the BLM to shore up the besieged multiple-use management framework with a new framework called ecosystem management. As will be discussed in detail below, it called for a new type of scientific management aimed not principally at *efficiency* in resource development, but at *ecosystem protection and restoration*.

In many ways, the Clinton administration's efforts to reshape the BLM harkened back to the Kennedy and Johnson administrations, when the idea of ecosystems-oriented management first gained public currency. All three administrations argued for an end to fragmented policy and the institution of a systems approach to management. One important difference, however, is that while the Kennedy and Johnson administrations followed a Republican administration that was openly hostile to a systems approach, the Clinton administration was able to build on the foundation set by the George H. W. Bush administration, particularly the efforts of BLM Director Cy Jamison.

The Clinton administration's main conservation contributions in the BLM came through brokering the Northwest Forest Plan, which fundamentally altered the BLM's timber program in the Pacific Northwest; rewriting the agency's grazing and hard rock mining regulations to raise ecosystem protection and restoration standards; building the agency's environmental and preservation programs; and establishing new focal points for ecosystem protection in the National Landscape Conservation System. The Clinton administration also shook up the BLM's career ladder and culture, but there is not enough data to assess whether this instilled a new sense of mission or merely increased frustrations within the agency.

At the end of the Clinton administration, the BLM was struggling once again with the basic question of identity, both of the public lands and of the agency itself. On the one hand, Secretary Babbitt had focused public attention on a new mission for the BLM within the context of the new American West. New BLM national monuments appeared on roadmaps, drawing increasing numbers of tourists. BLM employees with backgrounds in noncommercial programs, like recreation and cultural resources, had moved to top positions in the agency, and new regulations emphasized greater environmental protection and regulation. At the same time, the BLM continued to manage scattered tracts of land that were more embedded in the surrounding private and state land use patterns than in any grand system of landscape conservation. It also continued to administer subsidized grazing on marginal rangelands, and it continued to implement the most enduring symbol of nineteenth-century federal land policy, the Mining Law of 1872.[1] At the end of the twentieth century, then, the BLM continued to be torn between two very different interpretations of its mission and identity: the "Bureau of Livestock and Mines" and the "Bureau of Landscapes and Monuments."

THE BUSH ADMINISTRATION

The seeds of environmental reform that the Clinton administration nurtured were sown during the George H. W. Bush administration with support from swelling ranks in environmental organizations. During President Reagan's eight years in office, environmentalists complained that the administration was trying to roll public lands management back to the nineteenth century, when the public lands were open to unregulated and unrestricted economic development. Secretary Watt, who claimed that the Department of the Interior had been engaged in a "war on the West" and had drifted politically to "far left field," helped forge this perception. He emphasized energy production, refused to involve environmental groups in policy negotiations, and openly attacked environmental regulation and planning. While President Reagan's next two secretaries took a more conciliatory approach with environmental groups, they continued to emphasize the need to streamline environmental regulations and reduce bureaucracy, and the BLM director during this period, Robert Burford, was careful to keep the BLM's budget for environmental programs down.[2]

By the end of Reagan's second term, however, an environmental backlash was sweeping through Washington. Membership in environmental groups had swelled dramatically, Democrats were gaining strength in Congress on environmental issues, and by 1988, environmental issues were important in the presidential campaign. Vice President Bush pledged his loyalty to the conservation tradition of Teddy Roosevelt and promised to be an "environmental president."

Specifically, he pledged a "no net loss" wetland policy, strict enforcement of toxic waste regulations, and a new program to address global warming.[3]

When President Bush took office in 1989, three important things changed. First, he worked directly with environmental groups and appointed several environmental leaders to key positions in his administration. Second, he worked more collaboratively with Democrats in Congress on federal land and environmental issues. Third, he ended President Reagan's all-out war on the federal bureaucracy. Like all presidents in the late twentieth century, President Bush promised to control the federal budget and bureaucracy, but he gave far more freedom to bureaucratic leaders to act according to their professional judgment.[4] These changes created a very different atmosphere for the BLM, which slowly began to rebuild the environmental planning, monitoring, and enforcement capabilities that had declined during the Reagan administration.

Interior Secretary Manuel Lujan and BLM Director Cy Jamison faced the challenging task of maintaining commodity production on the public lands while rebuilding the BLM's environmental programs and winning greater public trust. The transition document prepared for Jamison by senior BLM managers laid out some of the key challenges. After eight years of budget cuts and red tape reduction, they argued that the BLM needed to rethink some of its primary commitments mandated by the Federal Land Policy and Management Act (FLPMA), the Public Rangelands Improvement Act, and the National Environmental Policy Act (NEPA). For example, they argued that the BLM needed to adopt more vigorous recreation and fish and wildlife programs in order to demonstrate that they were as important as the agency's commercial programs; the agency needed to create a more comprehensive range management strategy; and it needed to deal with hard rock mining regulations. In addition, they argued that the BLM needed a much more vigorous public relations program and a new name for the public lands in order to build public awareness and support, and they argued that the agency needed to create a program to formalize a shared decision-making process, so that BLM field managers were better equipped to serve as policy brokers among competing interests at the local level.[5]

Senior BLM managers were not the only ones pressing for change. The General Accounting Office (GAO) echoed many of these criticisms in its own 1988 transition report and in a series of reports requested by leading Democrats like Morris K. Udall, chairman of the House Committee on Interior and Insular Affairs, and Bruce F. Vento, chairman of the House Subcommittee on National Parks and Public Lands. The GAO focused particularly on livestock grazing, wildlife protection, mining reclamation, and planning, and in each case found the agency's efforts woefully inadequate.[6]

The GAO found, for example, that the BLM remained seriously understaffed and underfunded to carry out its basic responsibilities, pointing to the fact that from 1981 to 1990 the BLM's range staff decreased by 25 percent, and other specialists had decreased by an even higher percentage. The GAO found that the

BLM was not enforcing its own regulations regarding grazing trespass, that it was not adequately monitoring the public lands range, that it was not taking necessary steps to reduce overgrazing, that it was not protecting wildlife habitat and forage, that it was not requiring necessary bonds from miners or ensuring adequate mine reclamation, and that it was not completing or implementing resource management plans.[7]

Many of these reports were requested as part of Congress's ongoing battle over BLM reauthorization, which the FLPMA required every four years. Congress had reauthorized the BLM in 1982, but all subsequent efforts in the 1980s and early 1990s failed because Congress was deadlocked over provisions to raise grazing fees, broaden BLM authority, expand the system of national conservation areas, set deadlines for counties to file for RS 2477 rights-of-way over BLM land, and so on.[8] Stalemate over the BLM's reauthorization was perhaps the best indicator of the difficulty in bringing major change to public lands policy and BLM management. Congress had been able to pass the FLPMA in 1976 largely because it did not overhaul the BLM's key commercial resource programs; as noted in the previous chapter, the most significant changes under FLPMA were the inclusion of BLM land in the wilderness preservation system and procedural changes in public lands planning.[9] This illustrates the fact that at the national level environmental groups had achieved sufficient power to add responsibilities to the BLM's mandate but not to eliminate existing commercial responsibilities.

BLM Director Cy Jamison (1989–1993) looked for opportunities to build the BLM's noncommercial programs and professional capabilities without challenging the agency's commitment to resource use and extraction. Jamison had worked for the BLM from 1971 to 1981 in a variety of positions, ending in the agency's public affairs office. He had then worked for Representative Ron Marlenee (R-MT) on the House Committee on Interior and Insular Affairs. In that capacity, he had worked on considerable public lands legislation; he had served briefly as a congressional liaison between the House Committee and Secretary Watt; and he had become close friends with President Reagan's BLM director, Robert Burford (1981–1989).[10]

Unlike Watt, Burford, and Marlenee, Jamison did not express an open hostility toward environmentalists and environmental planning, reflecting President Bush's cautious attempts to embrace an environmental agenda. As BLM director, Jamison was a reconciler who tried to serve the interests of agency professionals, commercial land users, and environmentalists: "I saw that the BLM needed to broaden its base because it was getting too much over into the commodities side. It was losing a lot of its broad support on the Hill."[11] What Jamison and the Bush administration clearly understood was that since the interests of commercial public lands users and environmentalists were both well established in legislation, court decisions, and the BLM's mix of professional staff, the administration could not openly cater to a narrow interest group or coalition as the Reagan administration had done. As a result, they sought to maintain commercial resource outputs at existing levels while paying greater attention rhetorically and substantively to environmental interests.[12]

Jamison set out to garner broader public awareness of the public lands and stronger public support for BLM management by emphasizing the agency's non-commercial programs that had received fairly limited appropriations and attention from the Reagan administration. Jamison hired a career scientist from the Forest Service, Mike Dombeck, and asked him to push the plans forward. As Dombeck recalls, Jamison told him, "I want a fifty million dollar fish and wildlife program. I want a fifty million dollar recreation program. I want a fifty million dollar range program. Do whatever you have to do, whatever you can."[13] Under Jamison the BLM released *Fish and Wildlife 2000* followed shortly by the revised *Recreation 2000*, and these plans served as the basis for significant appropriations increases during the Bush administration. By the time Jamison left office, the BLM was close to its $50 million goal for these programs.[14]

Jamison used the strategic planning process as an entrance into the BLM's more controversial programs as well. Under his direction, the BLM developed a strategic plan for range management entitled *Range of Our Vision*, which articulated broad principles that the BLM would follow in range management. As with most strategic plans, this one was largely a general, consensus document designed to avoid confrontation, but Jamison then asked members of the agency's National Public Lands Advisory Council to form a blue ribbon panel and make specific recommendations on how to translate these principles into concrete action.[15]

The panel, made up primarily of academics and BLM employees, released its report in March 1992, drawing attention to fundamental problems that had plagued the public lands grazing program for half a century. Essentially, the panel highlighted the fact that the BLM lacked a clearly articulated plan for setting, achieving, and monitoring range management goals, and it called for the BLM to develop "a National Rangeland Management Plan that clearly defines program goals, objectives and opportunities."[16] The panel also recommended that the BLM develop "a broad-based and ecologically sound rangeland management program," noting that after almost fifty years of management the BLM had yet to develop a rigorous, scientific, and broadly accepted method of determining range conditions and trends that could be used authoritatively in management decisions.[17]

Jamison chose not to implement the panel's recommendations directly, since it would undoubtedly lead to a pitched battle over range management. Instead, he emphasized specific steps that were important to both environmentalists and ranchers. For example, he pledged full support for riparian area protection. He also emphasized the need for a stronger science program in the BLM that would eventually put the BLM's range program on stronger professional footing. In his final two years (1991–1993), Jamison, with Dombeck, actively sought funding and a location for a BLM research station. Although science would not resolve public lands disputes directly, they argued that it would give BLM managers more detailed, technical knowledge to use in management debates and decisions.[18]

During the same period, Jamison addressed the BLM's administration of the contentious Mining Law of 1872. By the early 1990s there was growing support in Congress for reform of the Mining Law, especially the establishment of a royalty system and tougher environmental regulations. While Congress debated larger reform measures, Jamison proposed new rules that would have given the BLM more control over mining operations and cleanup. He pledged to enforce existing mining regulations promulgated under FLPMA and issued a new policy requiring all miners disturbing more than five acres to post a bond for mine reclamation.[19]

In 1991–1993, Jamison also oversaw a comprehensive strategic planning initiative intended to articulate goals and management principles for the agency's overall multiple-use mission.[20] To symbolize progress toward a clearer BLM mission and to garner broader public support, Jamison asked the president to give the public lands a new name, such as the national resource lands, the national trust lands, the national heritage lands, or the national wildlands. President Bush came very close to changing the title by presidential proclamation, but he backed down over opposition from western governors and others who opposed the BLM's bid for a stronger national constituency.[21]

Overall, then, Jamison sought ways to build BLM professionalism, build the BLM's noncommercial resource programs, and gently shift range and mining regulations to achieve greater agency control. There was, however, one significant exception to this overall story of incremental and largely uncontroversial change that had a profound effect on the BLM: the spotted owl crisis in the Pacific Northwest. The spotted owl controversy changed the context of federal multiple-use management in the Pacific Northwest for both the BLM and the Forest Service and gave new meaning and urgency to calls for planning and management focused primarily on ecological protection.

The BLM and the Forest Service had been working on protecting the northern spotted owl for more than a decade when, in 1988, the states of Oregon and Washington listed the spotted owl as threatened and endangered under state laws. This placed new pressure on the Fish and Wildlife Service to do the same under the Endangered Species Act (ESA) of 1973. An interagency committee reviewed the spotted owl situation, releasing its report in the spring of 1990. The report called not only for protecting the owl and its nesting sites but also for protecting landscapes and ecosystems that would support the owl. Since these landscapes included the richest timber in the Pacific Northwest, it threatened to cut the federal timber flow substantially.[22]

In June 1990, the Fish and Wildlife Service listed the spotted owl as threatened, which required the BLM and the Forest Service to manage their lands in ways that would protect the owl and its habitat. The Forest Service pledged to follow the basic guidelines of the committee's report, but Jamison argued that the BLM would deal with the spotted owl issue through its existing planning system. Jamison hoped that the agency could mitigate the problem without immediate reductions in timber harvesting.[23]

In 1991 and 1992, federal district courts enjoined the Forest Service and the BLM from timber harvesting in spotted owl habitat.[24] In response, Jamison invoked a provision of the ESA that permitted a federal committee, often called "the God squad," to exempt certain projects from ESA requirements. In May 1992 the committee exempted thirteen of the BLM's forty-four proposed timber sales from the provisions of the ESA, but it also directed the BLM to implement the draft "Northern Spotted Owl Recovery Plan" immediately.[25]

The injunctions and the God squad's decision had clearly altered the BLM's priorities in the Oregon and California Revested Lands (O & C lands) dramatically and altered the distribution of power in the spotted owl debate. The BLM and the Forest Service had lost their opportunity to resolve the crisis administratively, and they now had to answer primarily to the courts.[26] These decisions were even more dramatic than the *NRDC v. Morton* decision that enjoined the distribution of range improvement funds until the BLM produced site-specific EISs for its grazing allotments. First, the decision halted the use of timber resources, effectively shutting down a large segment of the timber industry in the Pacific Northwest. Second, the two agencies faced not simply a procedural planning requirement but a substantive requirement to protect the spotted owl based on the best available biology and ecology research.

By the fall of 1992, then, the BLM had regained some of its inventory and planning momentum and was building its noncommercial resource programs. Jamison had guided the BLM through a series of symbolic and incremental changes. This kept opposition from the BLM's commercial users down, frustrated rather than angered environmentalists, and bolstered the BLM's professional morale. Nevertheless, debates over the agency's basic range, minerals, and timber programs still raged in Congress, in the courts, and in the press, and the spotted owl controversy challenged much of the BLM's progress in building public credibility and trust. BLM Director Cy Jamison saw himself as "more environmental than any Bureau Director [had] been before,"[27] yet his commitment to the timber industry helped lead to the 1991 and 1992 injunctions that shut down BLM and Forest Service timber harvesting in the Pacific Northwest.[28] Furthermore, President Bush had promised to be "the environmental president" but had grown increasingly frustrated with environmental issues over the course of his presidency.

THE CLINTON ADMINISTRATION AND THE PUBLIC LANDS

The spotted owl crisis made the ESA and timber harvesting key issues in the 1992 presidential race in the Pacific Northwest.[29] President Bush emphasized his commitment to protecting timber jobs and called the ESA "a sword aimed at the jobs, families and communities of entire regions."[30] Governor Clinton, on the other hand, promised to return to the Pacific Northwest if elected and resolve the spotted owl conflict in a way that would protect *both* jobs and the spotted owl. This helped ensure Clinton's victories in California, Oregon, and Washington.[31]

When the Clinton administration came to Washington in January 1993, environmental groups had high hopes for sweeping reforms of federal land policy and management. As John Leshy, Department of the Interior solicitor during the Clinton administration, recalls, "the general assumption among organized interest groups was that the activist, pro-regulation stance that had marked the early days of the modern environmental movement would be restored."[32] If President Clinton himself did not inspire this confidence, since he "was better known as a friend to small business and the poultry industry than as an environmental champion," his selection of Al Gore as his running mate and his early environmental appointments suggested that he was serious about fulfilling his environmental promises. For example, President Clinton appointed Kathleen McGinty, one of the vice president's former environmental aides, to lead the new White House Office of Environmental Policy, and he appointed Carol Browner, another former Gore protégée, to head the EPA.[33]

Clinton's cabinet and agency appointments further encouraged environmentalists. Secretary of the Interior Bruce Babbitt had served nearly three terms as governor of Arizona, where he had dealt extensively with federal land issues, and he had served more recently as president of the League of Conservation Voters, where he had conveyed an even stronger commitment to environmental reform.[34] As governor, Babbitt had earned a reputation as a pragmatist and a problem solver, describing his approach as a matter of "getting everyone together and rolling around in the dirt."[35] In this way, Babbitt followed President Clinton's approach, which "favored freewheeling competition of ideas from many advisers to allow him to deliberate on policy options before making final decisions," but he was for the most part very careful in selecting and framing the issues he worked on so as to control the overarching goals and boundaries of debate.[36] As Babbitt later explained, "the best way to work this, first of all, is to understand that you have to have a legislative stick to get anywhere. You have to come from a position with some power to cause a result that will inflict pain."[37] In other words, Babbitt looked for issues where he could force negotiations and push conflicting groups to reach consensus. It is what one critic has called "coercive harmony."[38]

Babbitt argued that public lands policy and the old image of the BLM as the bureau of livestock and mines were out of touch with the current economic, social, and political realities of the American West and that the New West, with an increasingly urban demographic and increasing demands for environmental protection and restoration, would support a major overhaul of public lands policy and management.[39] For many environmentalists, then, Babbitt promised to be the next Stewart Udall, a western politician who could speak to traditional resource users but could also articulate a national environmental ethic that transcended particular economic interests. Indeed, environmentalists supported Babbitt so strongly that when President Clinton considered him for a Supreme Court nomination in the early months of his presidency environmental groups gathered emergency petitions to block his selection and keep him in the Department of the Interior.[40]

Clinton's first BLM director, Jim Baca, also raised expectations for environmental reform. As the New Mexico state land commissioner, Baca had raised higher state royalties and fees for hard rock miners and ranchers, created financial incentives for good range practices on state land, and opposed federal predator control on state school lands. As one reporter described him, Baca was "a maverick reformer known as much for his fiscal conservatism as his environmental advocacy."[41] Baca was also quite outspoken, explaining after the 1992 election that ranchers were "in for the biggest reaming they've ever seen in the next Congress."[42]

Furthermore, environmental groups expected strong support for environmental reform in Congress. Democrats controlled both the House and the Senate, and the 123 freshmen in Congress generally favored stronger environmental protection. It appeared, then, that President Clinton and the 103rd Congress were poised to break the stalemate over key public lands issues that the 101st and 102nd Congresses had not been able to resolve—grazing and mining fees, environmental regulations and enforcement for mining operations, reauthorization of the ESA, new wilderness areas throughout the West and Alaska, and wetlands protection under the Clean Water Act.[43]

Support and optimism from environmental groups, however, were quickly challenged in the early days of the Clinton administration. On his first day at the Interior Department, Secretary Babbitt found that the administration's Office of Management and Budget (OMB) had already attacked grazing and mining policy in the president's budget proposals. The president was committed to increasing federal spending within a balanced budget. In addition to tax increases and selective budget cuts, the president's strategy called for an end to virtually all subsidies for federal land grazing, mining, logging, and recreation. Under the president's budget, federal land users would pay for increased federal conservation efforts.[44]

Under the Mining Law of 1872, miners paid no royalty on the minerals they extracted, and the president's plan called for a 12.5 percent royalty. Under the Public Rangelands Improvement Act, ranchers paid $1.86 per animal unit month (AUM), and the president's plan called for an immediate increase in the fee to something approximating fair market value, which one recent House bill had set at $8.70 per AUM. In the president's plan the exact fee was left to the secretaries of Interior and Agriculture, but the increase needed to generate an additional $76 million by FY 1997.[45]

The president's proposal seemed to fit Jim Baca's confident rhetoric that ranchers were in for a beating, but instead the proposal led to a stunning defeat for the administration and an enormous loss of political capital.[46] In March 1993, several western Democrats met with the president and threatened to thwart his overall budget strategy unless grazing fees and hard rock mineral royalties were dropped from the plan. The president quickly cut those proposals from the budget and asked Secretary Babbitt to find another way to raise fees.[47]

The president's retraction made environmental organizations furious, because they too had hoped for a swift victory on grazing and mining fees, and their early support for Secretary Babbitt and the Clinton administration cooled considerably.[48] Babbitt would later explain that "the environmentalists' job is to move the goal post. When you get near the goal post, they celebrate briefly and then they say you haven't done enough. It's part of the job."[49] At the same time, Babbitt expressed his own frustration with the OMB's immediate emphasis on grazing and mining fees, which he said "distorted important values" and took attention away from the real issue, which was rangeland and mineral land conditions.[50]

If the prospects of legislative reform looked grim in 1993, they grew exponentially worse for the administration after Republicans won control of Congress in 1994. Newt Gingrich, the new Republican Speaker of the House, promised to restore the Republican agenda that dominated the 1980s and to thwart the Clinton administration's goals for environmental reform. Thus, Secretary Babbitt essentially abandoned all hope of reform through congressional action and focused almost exclusively on administrative action.

In fact, Babbitt later explained that he had accepted President Clinton's appointment to Interior in large part because he saw the recent spotted owl controversy as an opportunity to push endangered species protection forward. He saw the endangered species debate as an opportunity to forge a new approach to scientific management, termed *ecosystem management*, which combined the science and ethics of conservation biology and applied ecology with extensive public participation, negotiation, and collaboration. This approach, he argued, would allow federal debate to move beyond the economy versus environment debate that had characterized the spotted owl controversy.[51]

Ecosystem management was hardly a new idea in 1993, but Secretary Babbitt made the concept a central part of his rhetoric and strategy. Ecosystem management, like the concepts of conservation and multiple use, permits a wide range of definitions.[52] The important aspects that Babbitt emphasized were organizing planning and management activities around ecosystems rather than around property ownership and restoring natural systems. As the Interagency Ecosystem Task Force explained, ecosystem management was about "sustaining or restoring natural systems and their functions and values."[53] Ecosystem management thus favored administrative discretion over binding statutory direction, because it required complex negotiations at a variety of scales simultaneously.

For Babbitt and the Clinton administration, ecosystem management was an opportunity to resurrect scientific, rational management tempered by the emphasis on citizen participation that had characterized the last thirty years of American politics. As with Gifford Pinchot's use of the language of conservation, Secretary Babbitt used the idea of ecosystem management in all of its ambiguity to bring together a number of goals and to build broader public support for stronger federal land protection.[54]

Secretary Babbitt's emphasis on ecosystem management brought new energy to two debates, both within agencies like the BLM and the Forest Service and in Congress: the adequacy of the basic multiple-use, sustained yield management framework and the role of science in federal land management. In 1992, after court injunctions against BLM and Forest Service timber sales, the Congressional Research Service held a workshop to discuss the viability of the multiple-use, sustained yield framework that had ostensibly guided federal land management for decades. Presenters offered mixed reviews, but there was general consensus that the multiple-use, sustained yield framework, or at least its current application, was not effective in meeting the increasingly complex demands placed on federal land, resources, and management. As John Leshy pointed out, the framework began as a justification for enormous executive agency discretion in federal land management, particularly for the U.S. Forest Service. In the 1960s and 1970s, however, Congress began to rein in that discretion through environmental statutes like NEPA and ESA and by special land designations like wilderness areas and national parks. Federal agencies continued to cling to MUSY, but the spotted owl crisis and many other cases illustrated that its application was no longer adequate.[55] Some presenters were even more critical of the framework itself, because of its fundamental orientation toward resource *uses* rather than the resources themselves. Policy scholar Richard Behan, for example, complained that "multiple use is seen primarily as a *policy*; both national forest and BLM lands will be harvested or used (and have been) for anything deemed to be of value."[56] These detractors supported calls for a new approach.

Ecosystem management, as it was articulated in the early 1990s, was the new iteration of scientific management updated to meet the basic and often competing emphases of federal land management: scientific rationality, professional discretion, and public participation/collaboration. One researcher explained to the House Committee on Natural Resources in 1994, "ecosystem management means that decisions about the use and management of natural resources will be based on science, not politics, to the maximum extent possible."[57] At the same time, the Interagency Ecosystem Management Task Force argued that ecosystem management "is goal driven, and it is based on a collaboratively developed vision of desired future conditions that integrates ecological, economic, and social factors."[58]

For Babbitt, ecosystem management was promising despite its inherent ambiguity and tension. First, it changed the nature and politics of land use planning by shifting the scale and boundaries of planning debates. By tackling land use planning on a broader, ecosystem scale, Babbitt could increase competition among conflicting interest groups and political subsystems. Forcing interest groups and public lands users into a different political arena could break iron triangles that had developed over particular resources or particular geographic areas.[59] Mike

Dombeck, who served as acting director of the BLM (1994–1997) and then chief of the Forest Service (1997–2001), argues that many intractable local problems can be resolved if they are understood from a broader ecosystem or landscape perspective: "If the goal is systemwide—such as restoring the overall health of the watershed—then the proper solution becomes more obvious."[60]

Second, ecosystem management changed the nature and politics of land use planning by elevating ecological sciences in the planning process. In the wake of the spotted owl crisis, for example, the Forest Service and the BLM needed wildlife biologists, ecologists, and conservation biologists rather than foresters to meet the demands of ecosystem protection and restoration. This was reflected in the make-up of the Interagency Scientific Committee that studied spotted owl protection in 1990 and the Interagency Ecosystem Management Task Force that Katie McGinty of the Council on Environmental Quality chaired during the Clinton administration. It was also reflected in Babbitt's efforts to establish the National Biological Survey to handle biological and ecological sciences for federal agencies.

Almost immediately after taking office, Secretary Babbitt made the Pacific Northwest a laboratory for ecosystem management, in no small part because the courts had effectively mandated an ecosystem approach. In April 1993, President Clinton kept his campaign pledge to address the spotted owl controversy when the White House convened the Northwest Forest Summit. The summit was a show of executive force, including the president, vice president, and the secretaries of Interior, Agriculture, and Commerce. At the end of the event, the president mandated that the departments of Interior and Agriculture develop an ecologically, economically, and legally sustainable plan for protecting the spotted owl.[61]

One week later, Babbitt returned to the Pacific Northwest for a meeting with federal and state scientists. The Interagency Scientific Committee that had studied spotted owl protection during the Bush administration had recommended broad habitat protection measures throughout the region, and many of these scientists were placed on a new Forest Ecosystem Management Assessment Team. Secretary Babbitt stood with a map of the entire Pacific coastline from Seattle to San Francisco behind him and instructed the scientists to address the spotted owl habitat as a single unit or ecosystem, working to make trade-offs for owl protection within these broad boundaries. Babbitt encouraged the scientists specifically to look beyond jurisdictional boundaries of national forests and public lands and beyond the narrow requirements of the spotted owl. This, he argued, was an opportunity to develop a plan to sustain all threatened and endangered species in the Northwest forest ecosystem, and he instructed them to "create a scientifically driven ecosystem plan based on the viability analysis of 200 species and produce a result."[62]

The Forest Ecosystem Management Assessment Team released its report in July 1993, calling for numerous habitat conservation areas, late-successional forest reserves, riparian reserves, and new watershed analysis procedures. This report was later revised and released as the Northwest Forest Plan in 1994. The plan called for an annual timber harvest within the Northwest Forest Plan area—both BLM and Forest Service lands—of 1.1 billion board feet. This was an 80 percent reduction from the peak harvest of the late 1980s, yet it was almost double the harvest that occurred under the 1991 and 1992 injunctions.[63]

On the face of it, the Northwest Forest Plan did not produce a win-win situation in terms of protecting owls and protecting timber jobs in the Pacific Northwest. The emphasis, stemming from the court decision and the ESA, was first and foremost on protecting the forest ecosystem, and the planners worked to protect jobs within those parameters. However, the plan called for significant job retraining and other transition funding to ensure that those who lost logging jobs would not be unemployed, and Congress allocated millions for this purpose.[64]

The shift in focus was a shock to both the Forest Service and the BLM, which had both focused, to that point, more on achieving a sustained yield of merchantable timber and sustaining local communities and economies. The agencies had to completely retool their management and planning process in order to achieve the kind of habitat protection mandated by the plan. In the Pacific Northwest forests, the two agencies were given a concrete goal of protecting spotted owl habitat and fairly clear parameters for what this entailed, subordinating virtually all other uses and interests. Compromises were made, but they were made within the broader limits of ecosystem protection. In other areas, where ecosystem management was not mandated and enforced by the courts, Babbitt ran into more obstacles.

In August 1993, Babbitt announced a proposed administrative rule making called Rangeland Reform '94. The proposed range regulations, which took an ecosystem approach, included a substantial grazing fee increase from $1.86 per AUM to $4.28 per AUM over three years, and Babbitt argued that this reflected a very conservative estimate of fair market value. In addition to the fee increase, the proposed regulations would make other substantial changes: (1) ranchers would no longer be able to claim new water rights or title to range improvements; (2) grazing advisory boards would be replaced with "resource advisory councils" made up of representatives of diverse interests; (3) the department would set a national rangeland standard that emphasized ecosystem protection, particularly of riparian zones; and (4) the tenure of grazing permits would be tied to each rancher's "stewardship record."[65]

The proposed regulations were in fact farther reaching than OMB's initial proposal, because they involved changes on virtually every contentious issue in public lands grazing policy: grazing fees, permit tenure, property rights, rancher influence in BLM decision making, and grazing levels based on range standards and carrying capacity. The implications of the proposed regulations were clear: Secretary Babbitt aimed to eliminate any sense that ranchers held property rights to the public lands and to concentrate greater management power in the Department of the Interior.

Secretary Babbitt faced withering criticism, particularly from western Republicans who called Babbitt's actions a war on the West. They argued that the new regulations violated the most basic principles of political and social justice. As one senator from Montana complained: "The Babbitt proposal turns the management of our nation's rangeland over to a bunch of inside-the-Beltway bureaucrats who don't know a good stand of grass from a manicured lawn."[66] In September, Senator Pete Domenici (R-NM) tried to block the new regulations in the appropriations process, placing a moratorium on all funding used to implement the fee increase and new regulations. The moratorium amendment led to a three-week filibuster of the Interior appropriations bill. Senator Harry Reid (D-NV) tried to broker a compromise, but by then opposition to Interior's basic reform goals was simply too well entrenched. Babbitt finally announced that he would seek a new and more inclusive round of administrative rule making, and on November 9, the Senate dropped grazing language from the appropriations bill.[67]

A week later Secretary Babbitt left Washington and began a three-month tour of the western states, essentially making an end run around western congressmen by taking his case directly to ranchers and other westerners. As he traveled, Babbitt continued to emphasize the need for stronger conservation measures on the public rangelands, a stronger assertion of the federal government's proprietary interest in the public lands, and a more significant role for science in management decisions. At the invitation of Colorado governor Roy Romer, however, Babbitt joined a group of ranchers and environmentalists called the Colorado Working Group in direct negotiations over these goals. Here, Babbitt was in his element, guiding and mediating a contentious debate among those directly affected by range policy while holding the authority to issue his own regulations if the group failed to reach consensus. Babbitt hoped that regulations based on consensus agreements from western ranchers and environmentalists would silence congressional opposition.[68]

In March 1994, Secretary Babbitt released new draft regulations entitled Rangeland Reform '94. The new regulations, which drew heavily on the Colorado Working Group, reflected some significant changes from the proposed rule making released in 1993, but they maintained Babbitt's basic reform goals. Under the new regulations, public lands grazing fees would rise to $3.96 per AUM instead of the original proposal of $4.28, and ranchers who met certain environmental standards would receive up to a 30 percent discount. The new regulations would also abolish grazing advisory boards and replace them with "resource advisory councils" made up of representatives of diverse commercial, environmental, and local governmental interests. They maintained a surcharge for subleasing grazing permits but would waive the fee for subleasing to family members. Under the new regulations ranchers would retain existing water rights and title to range improvements, but the federal government would not grant any future rights or titles. Finally, and perhaps most important, under the new regulations Babbitt dropped his original proposal to establish a national standard for rangeland quality, opting instead for standards set through a collaborative process in each state. However, if states failed to establish rangeland standards within eighteen months, the BLM would revert to a national standard.[69]

The compromise regulations placed Babbitt and the BLM squarely in the middle of the larger national debate. Many western members of Congress were still furious over Babbitt's basic attack on the status quo, and environmentalists were furious that Babbitt had compromised on important issues. Just before the new regulations became public, for example, four Democratic congressmen sent Babbitt a scathing letter complaining that he had abandoned the basic spirit of reform that they had supported in 1993. They opposed the new regulations for several reasons: (1) they gave greater control to local groups in the form of re-source advisory councils rather than national representatives; (2) they failed to provide national standards for rangeland health; and (3) they set a lower target for grazing fees.[70]

The Senate held hearings on the new regulations in April and May, and in those hearings Babbitt appeared contrite yet determined. The proposed regula-tions from 1993, Babbitt explained, were "way, way too prescriptive," and he had sought a far greater role for local interests and voices in preparing the new draft regulations.[71] The new regulations, he argued, were based on western con-sensus, not on eastern or bureaucratic prescriptions, but senators still claimed that any sharp increase in grazing fees or changes in permit tenure and regulation were an attack on the West and on a struggling industry. Frank Murkowski (R-AK) warned, "As ranchers lose their financing, and operations go out of business, ranch property values will fall. Banks will lose even more money, property taxes will decrease, local governments will lose their bonding capacities. Important community health and safety facilities will not be built."[72]

After almost a year of bruising congressional hearings, debates, and threats, the Department of the Interior published final grazing regulations as "Final Rule, 43 CFR Parts 1780 and 4100." In the final regulations, Babbitt and other Interior officials decided not to repeat the disaster of OMB's initial budget proposal. In or-der to advance the most dramatic changes in decades concerning range standards and regulation, they agreed to drop the issue of grazing fees and leave it instead to congressional prerogative.

Administrative reform of mining policy followed a very similar path as graz-ing policy. When President Clinton took office in 1993, there was significant con-gressional support for reforming the Mining Law of 1872, which governs the lo-cation, development, and patenting of hard rock minerals on federal land.[73] Even the mining industry agreed to some modifications in the law in order to reduce fraudulent mining claims and agreed that the time may have come for a token royalty. This law, more than any other major BLM statute, reflected the charac-ter of nineteenth-century public lands policy.[74] It offered hard rock minerals and the lands above them as an outright gift to miners, who had to pay only $2.50 to $5.00 an acre for title to their mining claims. Furthermore, it allowed most miners, especially those impacting less than five acres, to develop their claims with almost no federal oversight. They could treat their mining claims as private property, even before they patented their claims. The law defied the basic thrusts of twentieth-century public lands policy: permanent federal ownership and con-servation through land use planning.[75]

President Clinton's first budget proposal to impose a 12.5 percent royalty on hard rock minerals, however, undermined the reform momentum considerably. The mining industry, which still held enormous lobbying power in Congress, had been open to a token royalty, but it was not about to accept a royalty roughly equal to that imposed on federal oil and gas. The political situation was further compli-cated by ill will among western congressmen over the grazing fee controversy.[76]

Without much hope of legislative reform, Babbitt protested the mining law by refusing to sign mineral patents until ordered to do so by the courts. He also used the forced signings as occasions to protest the law. In one public appearance he signed a patent with a large check hanging behind him emphasizing that he was about to sign over an estimated $10 billion in federal land and minerals for $10,000. In another appearance Babbitt used a pen that had belonged to President Ulysses S. Grant to sign a patent worth $1 billion that granted 110 acres in Idaho to a Danish mining company for just $275.[77]

Compared to rangeland reform, Babbitt was far more deferential to the 103rd and 104th Congresses, which remained deadlocked on mining law revisions. In 1993, both the Senate and the House passed legislation reforming the Mining Law, but the two bills died at the end of the session. The Senate's bill, S. 775, was strongly influenced and supported by the mining industry, which argued that the basic structure of the law was still essential to ongoing hard rock mineral develop-ment in the United States. The bill would impose a 2 percent royalty on all new mining claims after mining companies deducted all of the costs of exploration, development, and processing, and it would impose modest location and annual maintenance fees. In terms of environmental regulations, the Senate bill required only that mining companies adhere to state reclamation standards.[78]

The House bill, H.R. 322, reflected the Clinton administration's call for more serious reform. Under H.R. 322, the federal government would retain ownership of mineral lands and impose an 8 percent royalty on the gross value of all federal minerals, minus the cost of smelting. The House bill also went much further on environmental regulation and reclamation. It directed the Interior Department to deposit all royalties in a fund for abandoned mine reclamation, required min-ers to file detailed operation and reclamation plans and adhere to strict federal reclamation standards, and gave the secretary broad authority to declare areas of federal land "unsuitable" for hard rock mining.[79] Like the Senate bill, the House bill would impose modest location and annual maintenance fees.

The Senate and the House never got to conference negotiations over the two bills, however. House Natural Resources Committee chairman George Miller (D-CA) refused to appoint House conferees until the grazing issue was resolved, arguing that he wanted the two issues to be resolved separately on their own terms. Nevertheless, in the absence of new legislation, Congress placed a one-year moratorium on mineral patents through an appropriations rider, and for the rest of the Clinton administration Congress continued to renew the moratorium.[80]

In 1995, the Republican-controlled Congress finally passed a mining reform bill, which looked a great deal like the original Senate bill. Denouncing it as a sham, President Clinton vetoed the bill. Stalemate once again ensued, because Democrats lacked the strength to push a stronger reform bill through Congress, and the president pledged to veto mining bills that did not make more substantial reform.[81]

As with rangeland reform, then, Babbitt made greater headway through administrative action, beginning in 1997. He and Interior Solicitor John Leshy created a new review process for mining patents that provided more centralized control over patent decisions; they stopped the practice of allowing mining companies to pay for mineral reports upon which patenting decisions were made, a practice that the Reagan and Bush administrations had allowed; and they looked for ways to enforce existing environmental regulations more stringently.[82]

To justify the new regulations, Babbitt pointed to the FLPMA of 1976 and its provision authorizing the interior secretary to, "by regulation or otherwise, take any action necessary to prevent unnecessary or undue degradation of the [public] land."[83] Under this authority, Secretary Andrus had promulgated regulations in 1980, known as Part 3809 regulations, which placed a number of new requirements on mining companies. The regulations required all miners to notify the BLM before beginning operations, and they required all miners disturbing more than five acres to have a plan of operation approved by the BLM. There had been growing consensus, however, that these regulations were inadequate, because the five-acre limit exempted the vast majority of mining operations from NEPA review, the regulations did not require any financial bond to cover mining reclamation, and they did not provide penalties for violations.[84]

Secretary Babbitt ordered a comprehensive review of the Part 3809 regulations led by Interior Solicitor John Leshy, an expert on federal mining law. The process took a full four years, in large part because of congressional involvement. Congress took an active interest in the rule-making process and passed numerous appropriations riders that constrained and directed Secretary Babbitt's actions. Riders required active consultation with state governments, created the National Research Council to review hard rock mining policy, and required that the new regulations be consistent with the recommendations of the council.[85]

Secretary Babbitt issued new final regulations in 2000, which strengthened environmental regulation of hard rock mining activities. The new regulations required financial assurance for mining reclamation of all mines, regardless of their size; they required approved mining plans for all mines, regardless of their size; and they strengthened the BLM's administrative power to levy penalties for mining violations.[86] In addition, John Leshy issued an opinion in 1999 that affirmed the secretary's authority to refuse any mining operation that would cause "significant irreparable harm to outstanding resources that could not be mitigated."[87] Together the new regulations, the solicitor's opinion, and the congressional moratorium on mineral patents altered the policy and management landscape of hard rock mining substantially. They made hard rock mining a multiple use that BLM field managers could balance alongside other legitimate uses, rather than the de facto dominant use of the public lands.

For all that Secretary Babbitt and BLM leaders attacked the Mining Law of 1872, it is important to emphasize that they were not antimining. The framework that Secretary Babbitt and BLM leaders brought to mining law reform pervaded the oil, gas, and coal programs, though these sparked less controversy. During the Clinton administration, offshore oil and gas production increased substantially. The administration's approach to oil and gas production was perhaps best illustrated by its position on oil development in Alaska. Secretary Babbitt opened a substantial portion of the National Petroleum Reserve–Alaska while opposing oil drilling in the Arctic National Wildlife Refuge. Coal production also increased by 30 percent during the Clinton administration, yet Secretary Babbitt eliminated coal mining in key land areas like the BLM's first national monument.[88] Compared to the Reagan administration's approach, which was to accelerate leasing and let the market decide where and when to mine, Secretary Babbitt and BLM leaders took a more active role in regulating mining operations.

BLM NATIONAL MONUMENTS AND THE CLINTON LEGACY

As Secretary Babbitt traveled throughout the West, on the run from a Republican Congress, he found a new opportunity to reshape some public lands management around the ecosystem management approach: the designation and planning of BLM national monuments created largely for ecosystem or landscape protection.[89] Babbitt had started his tenure with an attack on the most powerful symbols of the BLM's nineteenth-century legacy, grazing and mining fees, with mixed results; he ended with national monument designations that symbolized what he saw as the BLM's twenty-first-century mission.

Under the Antiquities Act of 1906, the president is authorized to designate federal lands as national monuments and to place new land use restrictions on the monuments in order to protect "objects of historic or scientific interest."[90] Although Congress most likely passed the act to protect small archeological sites, it contains no acreage limitations or clear definition of what qualifies as an object of scientific or historical interest. What is more, national monument designations require no public notice or participation and no congressional approval. President Theodore Roosevelt demonstrated the act's expansive power in 1908, when he created the more than 800,000-acre Grand Canyon National Monument in order to stop development on the canyon's rim. He argued that the entire canyon was an object of scientific interest. The record in terms of size goes to President Carter, who, as noted in the previous chapter, designated roughly a dozen national monuments in Alaska totaling 54 million acres.[91] Most other presidents have used the act to help build the national park system, to stop specific types of development, and to break congressional gridlock.

Prior to the Clinton administration, the BLM had never managed a national monument, although many National Park Service monuments had been created from the public lands. BLM employees had often lobbied against national monument designations in order to keep lands under BLM management and had lobbied against a number of other special land designations, like wilderness, in order to maintain maximum management flexibility in the field. For many people in the BLM this pattern reinforced the idea that the BLM lands were the leftovers suited largely for commercial use.[92]

The idea of a BLM national monument, then, certainly did not come from within the agency, nor did it come through a carefully crafted plan from the Interior Department. Instead, according to Secretary Babbitt, the idea came from one of President Clinton's campaign strategists, who noticed that environmental issues were beginning to poll higher in 1995 and 1996 and argued that the president needed a dramatic environmental gesture that would grab news headlines just before the election.[93] Since the administration wanted to keep it a secret, the Antiquities Act was a perfect tool for a dramatic land conservation gesture without prior congressional debate or public notice.

According to Secretary Babbitt, the Grand Staircase–Escalante National Monument idea rose to the top of the list immediately.[94] It is a vast, remote, and rugged area in southern Utah that is ringed by national parks and other national monuments. More important, it was at that time the subject of heated debate over coal mining, wilderness protection, road rights-of-way, and grazing, leading to a bitter political standoff.[95] Secretary Babbitt selected a small group of people to draw up the monument boundaries and proclamation in complete secrecy during the summer of 1996. No one from the Utah state government, the Utah congressional delegation, or the county governments, and almost no one in the BLM knew about the monument designation in advance. In fact, the BLM district manager who was responsible for most of the BLM land in the new national monument, Jerry Meredith, did not find out about the monument designation until it happened.[96]

On September 18, 1996, President Clinton, Vice President Gore, and Secretary Babbitt traveled to the rim of the Grand Canyon in Arizona, where President Clinton announced the new monument:

This high, rugged, and remote region, where bold plateaus and multi-hued cliffs run for distances that defy human perspective, was the last place in the continental United States to be mapped. Even today, this unspoiled natural area remains a frontier, a quality that greatly enhances the monument's value for scientific study. The monument has a long and dignified human history: it is a place where one can see how nature shapes human endeavors in the American West, where distance and aridity have been pitted against our dreams and courage.[97]

With this sweeping rhetoric he walked to a desk that was perched on the rim of the Grand Canyon and signed the proclamation into law. As one author put it, President Clinton had learned "the art of audacity."[98]

Secretary Babbitt has complained that much of public lands politics is like Kabuki drama: "we tend to argue the future by simply adopting the costumes, the masks and the rhetoric of the past."[99] By this, he means that commodity producers in the range, mineral, and timber industries play the part of nineteenth-century settlers and explorers, treating the public lands as an inexhaustible commons. Yet President Clinton and Secretary Babbitt clearly knew how to stage dramas of their own that reenacted the past. The Grand Staircase–Escalante National Monument designation was a reenactment of President Theodore Roosevelt's dramatic federal land reservations.

The Grand Staircase–Escalante National Monument was the first BLM national monument, and as a result of the proclamation and the BLM's legislative mandates it was the first official multiple-use national monument. Secretary Babbitt had asked the president to leave it under BLM management to give the BLM a chance to prove its conservation capabilities. He saw the monument as an opportunity to create a new focal point for the BLM, a place where the BLM could continue to honor most existing uses but subordinate them to ecosystem and landscape protection.[100]

Reaction to the monument was predictable. Environmentalists cheered and at least initially congratulated the president for his conservation concern. The Utah governor and legislature, western members of congress, local county commissioners, and livestock and mining representatives virtually all denounced the monument proclamation, arguing that it was probably illegal and certainly unjust for the president to make such a dramatic change unilaterally. Clinton, Babbitt, and the BLM were castigated in the local press, county commissioners continued to hire bulldozers to improve roads within the monument to try to block wilderness designations, and Congress held a series of hearings with titles like "Behind Closed Doors: The Abuse of Trust and Discretion in the Establishment of the Grand Staircase–Escalante National Monument."[101] As Babbitt recalls, "we paid a terrible political price for [planning the monument in secret] and understandably."[102]

Nonetheless, what the Grand Staircase–Escalante National Monument provided was an opportunity to restart or reframe management debate about 1.8 million acres of BLM land in southern Utah, where future grazing, mining, road construction, wilderness protection, and recreation were all at stake. The monument proclamation made resource protection the BLM's top management priority without altering any of the existing rights or uses, and it shifted the debate from a regional issue to a national issue. Monument designation put the Grand Staircase–Escalante region on the map, literally and figuratively: it both appeared on standard road atlases and received national attention. This meant that the BLM's planning process received much broader national attention and much closer scrutiny from the Utah state and county governments, from interest groups, and from Secretary Babbitt and the Interior Department.[103]

The monument proclamation's ecosystem protection language and the increased attention led to many important changes in BLM planning and management. Since Secretary Babbitt cited coal mining as one of the greatest threats to the monument, it received considerable attention in the following years. The monument proclamation closed Grand Staircase to future mineral entry but did not revoke any valid existing mineral rights within the monument. Furthermore, the state of Utah held mineral lands within the monument boundaries, which the BLM had no authority to manage. Secretary Babbitt negotiated the purchase of all federal coal leases within the monument, and he negotiated one of the largest federal/state land exchanges in history to eliminate state inholdings from the monument.[104] In Babbitt's interpretation, then, mining was one activity that was incompatible with landscape preservation in the monument.

One of the most innovative and interesting results of the BLM's first monument management plan was the agency's treatment of visitor services and tourism. Virtually everyone who participated in the planning process, from ranchers to wilderness advocates, agreed that developing a better road system and visitor centers within the monument would degrade the area's frontier quality, a quality that was tied to the monument's remoteness and isolation. It was clear, however, that the monument designation would draw more tourists and recreational users. To meet this growing demand, the BLM developed five visitor centers in towns around the monument. The new visitor centers provided economic development in local communities and gave those communities a greater role in interpreting the monument for visitors. The centers also established new working relationships between the monument land and local communities.[105]

At the same time, the monument designation intensified some of the longstanding conflicts in BLM range management.[106] The BLM made grazing allotments in the monument a priority as they implemented Secretary Babbitt's new range regulations, including the Utah range standards that had only recently been established. This scrutiny brought to light a number of cases of overgrazing within the monument, and the BLM looked for creative ways to reduce overgrazing without an all-out battle with ranchers. One such approach was to allow ranchers and environmental groups to reach private agreements to effectively eliminate grazing on about 10 percent of the monument.[107]

BLM managers ran into trouble, however, when they tried to take more aggressive approaches to grazing reductions. In 2000, after a prolonged drought, the BLM ordered permit holders to remove their cattle from an extremely remote area of the monument. After permittees failed to remove all of their livestock, Kate Cannon, the second monument manager, authorized a helicopter roundup of almost 200 cattle, which were taken to auction in Arizona. The livestock owners retrieved their cattle and protested the heavy-handed management posture that BLM had taken. The conflict led to Kate Cannon's dismissal at the beginning of the George W. Bush administration and her replacement by Dave Hunsaker, who assumed a more conciliatory and collaborative posture.[108]

As Secretary Babbitt oversaw the Grand Staircase–Escalante National Monument's initial planning and management, he began to see the Antiquities Act as a key tool with which to redefine the BLM, and he pressed President Clinton to consider additional designations. After the response that President Clinton received for his campaign stunt at the Grand Staircase–Escalante, this was not an easy task. One evening at a White House reception, Babbitt handed the president a conservation scorecard he had drawn up comparing the conservation acreage designated by President Teddy Roosevelt and President Clinton. As Babbitt tells the story, "That was the moment. It wasn't the environment, it was legacy. That's the moment that I had his mandate to use at my discretion."[109]

Secretary Babbitt took a very different approach in identifying additional national monuments than he had for the BLM's first monument. Rather than working in secret, Babbitt engaged in very public debates over potential areas. His later monument recommendations were backed by strong and demonstrable public support, in large measure because he selected areas that had a long history of grassroots conservation interest. Many of the new monument areas were among those designated as scientific natural areas or primitive areas in the 1960s;[110] BLM managers knew about them;[111] and recreational users often sought them out. Many of the monuments also encompassed smaller areas of special designation, such as wilderness study areas or late successional reserves, which previously had not received much national attention for a number of reasons, including the fact that BLM managers often did not want to promote them for fear of losing them to the National Park Service.

In all, Secretary Babbitt recommended and President Clinton designated fourteen national monuments, totaling approximately 5 million acres of BLM land and ranging in size from the 51-acre Pompey's Pillar National Monument in Montana to the 1.8-million-acre Grand Staircase–Escalante National Monument (Appendix C). These monuments were, in a very important sense, an effort to nationalize the BLM by giving it high-profile management responsibilities that would draw national attention and would receive special attention from the BLM's upper management. These monuments were to become a showpiece for the kind of planning and management that Babbitt wanted to promote in the BLM. In addition to the new monuments, Secretary Babbitt used the threat of monument designations to break planning and management gridlocks in places like the Steen Mountain area of Oregon. The threat of a unilateral monument designation was enough to send disgruntled interest groups back into negotiations, although Babbitt produced his share of resentment for the tactic.[112]

Babbitt worked to institutionalize the new monuments within the BLM's mission, organization, and culture. First and foremost, he arranged for the new monuments to have their own appropriations, ensuring that they would receive direct funding for planning and management. Second, he arranged for most of the monuments to have full-time staff, even if the number of staff was small, ensuring that the monuments received special attention. To further institutionalize the monuments within the BLM's mission and culture, Babbitt unveiled a new program called the National Landscape Conservation System (NLCS) in June 2000. The system did not involve any new land designations or regulations; rather it elevated what Babbitt described as the "crown jewels" of the public lands in BLM management. The system included virtually every special conservation and preservation area under BLM administration, including national monuments, wild and scenic rivers, national scenic and historic trails, wilderness areas, wilderness study areas, national conservation areas, national recreation areas, cooperative management and protection areas, forest reserves, and outstanding natural areas (see Appendix D).[113]

The NLCS served several important functions for the BLM. First, it was a strategic advertising and public relations tool intended to weaken the public perception of the BLM as a bureau of livestock and mines and to strengthen public perception of the BLM as a broad conservation agency, or bureau of landscapes and monuments. Second, and equally important, the NLCS was a strategic tool intended to make at least a modest change in the BLM's internal culture and identity. Having hired monument managers with backgrounds and commitments to ecosystem management and protection and having emphasized through rhetoric and budgets the importance of national monuments and other conservation and preservation areas, Secretary Babbitt wanted NLCS areas to become the flagships of BLM management and to slowly change the management standards and practices on other public lands areas. As Babbitt said when he explained the new system to BLM employees:

> In the twenty-first century, the BLM faces a choice. It can become the greatest modern American land management agency, the one that sets the standard for protecting landscapes, applying evolving knowledge and social standards, and bringing people together to live in harmony with the land. . . . Or it can become a relic, a historical artifact, its most desirable lands carved up and parceled out to other land management agencies, with the remainder destined for the auction block of divestiture.[114]

In an important sense, then, the NLCS was a political challenge and a threat to the BLM: Babbitt told the BLM to manage the NLCS units to the highest ecosystem protection standards or they would be stripped away and given to another agency.[115]

It will be a number of years before the impact of the national monument designations and the NLCS is clear. On the one hand, they shifted the terms of public lands debate for these areas. The Grand Staircase–Escalante National Monument is undoubtedly the clearest example of this, because it is the oldest BLM national monument and because Secretary Babbitt spent four years actively involved in the monument's planning and management.

On the other hand, the new designations clearly did not lead to a paradigm shift in BLM management toward ecosystem management. Many national monument managers and staff saw ecosystem management as either the latest name for traditional multiple-use management or as a lofty and overly intellectual concept that could not take root in the agency's existing statutes, regulations, and appropriations, and Kate Canon's experience as manager of the Grand Staircase–Escalante National Monument made it clear that the BLM did not necessarily have the political power or will to unilaterally dictate the terms of resource use on the new monuments. What is more, some BLM managers were frustrated that they did not enjoy the same appropriations increases as the Grand Staircase–Escalante National Monument, confirming fragmented rather than systems-oriented management in the BLM as a whole.[116]

In the end, then, the national monuments fulfilled Babbitt's intention of challenging the BLM but not his hope that they would lead to a paradigm shift in the agency's management framework. There are several reasons for this, including the obvious fact that the agency's authorizing legislation and congressional oversight did not change. An equally important reason is that the other monuments, particularly those designated during President Clinton's final month in office, never received the same high-level support, appropriations, or staffing that the Grand Staircase enjoyed. Planning for these later monuments was carried out under the Bush administration, which took office openly critical of President Clinton's monument designations.[117]

BLM ORGANIZATION AND CULTURE DURING THE CLINTON ADMINISTRATION

Transitions in presidential administration always have an impact on federal agencies, although some transitions are more jarring than others, and some agencies are affected more than others.[118] Prior to the Clinton administration, the two most significant presidential transitions for the BLM were from Eisenhower to Kennedy and from Carter to Reagan. In each case, new leadership worked swiftly to change the BLM's appropriations, planning, and management priorities. The Kennedy administration marked the beginning of comprehensive planning and a substantial expansion of BLM responsibilities, and the Reagan administration attempted with some success to check this development by slashing the BLM's planning and environmental assessment budgets and by pressing for increased commodity production and increased deference to commercial land users.

For the BLM, the transition from the Bush administration to the Clinton administration was significant in many ways. From the BLM's perspective, Secretary Babbitt appeared to take office with a fairly dim view of the agency and its commercial clientele. For many BLM employees, this was reflected in Babbitt's strong support for the California Desert Protection Act of 1994, which transferred millions of acres of BLM land to the National Park Service.[119] From the very start of the Clinton administration, Babbitt challenged the BLM's existing range, mining, and logging policy. When he failed to get major reform initiatives through Congress, he turned to administrative initiatives to reshape both the BLM's resource policies and the BLM's organization and culture.[120] Indeed, not since the Kennedy administration had there been such a concerted effort to alter the BLM's mission and identity toward a more centralized and ecosystems-oriented approach.

Organizational changes in the BLM were driven during the Clinton administration by two broad initiatives: Secretary Babbitt's push for ecosystem management—discussed above—and the White House's program to "reinvent" the federal bureaucracy. Secretary Babbitt used the ideas of ecosystem management to advance new goals for BLM management and new decision-making arrangements that cut across resource programs and agency jurisdictions. Ecosystem management worked for Babbitt the way the multiple-use framework had worked for Secretary Udall during the Kennedy administration. It was used to challenge the political subsystems that had controlled or at least strongly influenced range, minerals, and timber management for half a century, forcing these programs to compete in a more diverse political arena.

The White House was not involved to any great extent in the push for ecosystem management, but it had a strong influence on the BLM's organization and workflow through its attempts to reshape the executive branch. Through the National Partnership for Reinventing Government (NPR), Vice President Gore worked directly with federal agencies on issues of organization, procedure, and regulations in order to improve the efficiency and quality of their customer service. The reinvention campaign was an attempt to apply many trends in business organization and theory to the federal bureaucracy, and it dovetailed with some of Secretary Babbitt's efforts to push the BLM in a new direction. However, the reinvention campaign also led to a new emphasis on outsourcing a wide range of planning and management activities in both the BLM and the Forest Service.[121]

During President Clinton's first term, the NPR emphasis was on reducing the size and scope of federal bureaucracy—measured primarily in terms of staff and budget numbers—and creating new performance goals, standards, and measurements for each federal agency, designed to make them more responsive to their "customers." During President Clinton's second term, the focus of the NPR shifted more to revamping each agency's organization, regulations, and culture to better institutionalize these goals.[122]

The BLM received significant attention in the NPR initiative because of its size and the level of day-to-day interaction it had with the public, and it was among the thirty-two "high-impact agencies" that Vice President Gore worked with most closely. There were, in other words, very high expectations and pressures on the BLM to make substantive changes in the way that it set goals, linked resources to those goals, measured outcomes, and rewarded success. This led to very visible organizational changes, described below, but it also led to more subtle changes. For example, under pressure from the NPR and the Government Performance and Results Act of 1993, the BLM revised its regulations, particularly those regulations that governed the agency's procedures and workflow, reducing the complexity of BLM regulations substantially.[123]

Any major attempt to reshape a federal bureaucracy is both a destructive and constructive process, involving the elimination of organizational patterns, key staff, and processes that maintain the status quo and replacing them strategically to institutionalize new priorities. Efforts to reinvent the BLM during the Clinton administration were no exception. While working on rangeland reform, asking for hard rock mining reform, and forcing coordination of timber management in the Pacific Northwest, Secretary Babbitt and his first two BLM directors, Jim Baca (1993–1994) and Mike Dombeck (acting director, 1994–1997), tried to unify the BLM organizationally and culturally.

Jim Baca came into the BLM with an aggressive reform agenda, which fit Secretary Babbitt's initial foray into range reform. As Babbitt went to work on major BLM policy initiatives, Baca focused on reorienting the BLM's staff and planning to the new ecosystem management framework. Taking control of and redirecting the BLM was no easy task, as past directors had found. BLM decision making was still highly decentralized. The BLM still operated as a closely-knit federation of state offices, and BLM state directors held enormous power within the agency.[124]

Baca announced that many of the BLM's state directors and other leaders would likely leave during his tenure and would be replaced with people who had a fresh perspective on public lands management. Although it is not uncommon for BLM state directors to change at the start of a new administration, the number of these changes at the start of the Clinton administration was significant. When Secretary Babbitt removed Baca from the BLM early in 1994, largely because of Baca's confrontational style and the need for a more conciliatory approach to range reform, five state director positions were vacant along with numerous other high-level management positions. In total, eight out of twelve BLM state directors were replaced in 1993 and 1994, and by 1995, only one BLM state director who had served during the Bush administration remained.[125]

The new BLM state directors brought decidedly different backgrounds into the state offices, including backgrounds in recreation, planning, or some other noncommercial area. On the one hand, this reflected the steady workforce diversi-fication that had followed the NEPA, the ESA, and the FLPMA. New specialists in wilderness and recreation, wildlife, planning, archeology and cultural resources, and so on, had simply worked their way up through the agency during the 1970s and 1980s and were poised to take top leadership positions by the 1990s. On the other hand, Babbitt, Baca, and Dombeck passed over a number of career range conservationists and foresters to hand-select new state directors who had stronger environmental credentials, and in several cases they recruited people from outside the agency. Furthermore, before the Clinton administration, only one woman had ever held a state director position, and after promoting her to associate director in 1993, Babbitt, Baca, and Dombeck selected three women to fill state director positions.[126]

The overall impact of these leadership changes on BLM culture is difficult to assess, but it did shake up the traditional career ladders in the agency. Through key staff changes Babbitt, Baca, and Dombeck were trying to break what many saw as the "good old boy" network in the BLM, which reflected and reinforced the dominance of range, minerals, and timber in BLM management.

Changes in leadership were part of a much broader effort to reshape the BLM's culture and sense of mission. As one report explains, the new framework "suggested a change in focus from program or commodity specific goals to more resource or landscape based objectives. This approach suggested the need for a more thorough integration of economic, social, and environmental considerations in land use decision-making."[127] In April 1994, the BLM held a meeting near Lake Tahoe entitled "The Bureau of Land Management Summit." It was by far the larg-est meeting of BLM employees ever held, bringing BLM directors and managers from the Washington office, state offices, and district and area offices, along with guest speakers from the academy and members of the press. The purpose of the summit was to try to do interpersonally what the agency had not been able to ac-complish in its legislation, budget, or planning process: namely, articulate a unify-ing vision and mission for public lands management. One reporter explained that "Babbitt . . . wants to turn the $1 billion per year agency into a single outfit fol-lowing a national program rather than a series of mining, grazing and oil and gas programs dictated by Western industries, Western governors and the individual congressional delegations."[128]

Secretary Babbitt addressed the summit, calling on BLM employees to em-brace ecosystem management. In Babbitt's rhetoric ecosystem protection, mean-ing the protection of ecosystem health and biological diversity, was the highest good that the BLM could pursue. It was, to borrow from the Forest Service's mythology, "the greatest good to the greatest number for the longest time."[129] The framework that Babbitt articulated, like multiple-use management before it, did not resolve resource conflicts; rather it emphasized the need for better scientific and professional attention to the public lands in order to set new goals that put the land rather than land users first:

Properly done, your reward will be that no decision will ever be entirely pleasing to anybody, and none of your good deeds will go unpunished at any time. You'll be vilified from every single quarter. And that indeed, in case you think that's an abstract observation, has been exactly my experience as your Secretary of the Interior. And when those dark moments come, when they're flailing you bloody in the local press and the local establishment is sort of turning its back and nobody will talk to your kids in the classroom, let me just console you by saying that is almost inevitable. . . . And we have to recognize that we're doing it in the public interest and if the decisions are rendered through process and they're sound, then someone, some day, not in any sort of near term, will look back and say, "You know that guy really done a hell of a good job. That was a real public servant."[130]

Babbitt acknowledged that ecosystem management did not provide an immediate solution to every public lands dispute, but he argued that the basic approach was sound and that the BLM needed to identify areas where ecosystem management could work: "It has worked in some places. I believe the models are sound. I believe we can spread them. There will be places where it doesn't work. If it doesn't work, fine. We're just right back where we started."[131] He pointed to the Northwest Forest Plan and in the Colorado Working Group as examples of success, where broader ecosystem goals, scientific data, and public participation all came together to resolve public lands controversy.

Most of the other conference speakers addressed the issue of change for the public lands and the BLM, either the history of change that had led to current conflicts and demands or the prospect of change in the near future. Academic speakers like Patricia Limerick talked about the changing character of the American West and the BLM's role in this new arena. Agency and department speakers talked about changes within the BLM. BLM managers were most concerned with the prospect of agency reorganization and changes in agency planning and management, an issue that was still very much in flux at the time of the summit. Assistant Secretary Bob Armstrong and Dombeck simply explained that the BLM would be reorganized to meet the challenge of ecosystem management, which did little to assure field managers that the changes would help them.[132]

In September 1994, Dombeck issued the BLM's new strategic plan, entitled "Blueprint for the Future."[133] Influenced both by the new emphasis on ecosystem management and Vice President Gore's NPR, the plan stated five themes or goals:

1. Maintain healthy ecosystems
2. Serve current and future publics
3. Promote collaborative leadership
4. Improve business practices
5. Improve human resource management practices.

The plan was broad and the goals were uncontroversial in themselves. As BLM leaders began interpreting these goals and applying them to specific organizational and management decisions, however, they challenged the BLM's existing culture and mission.

Reorganization efforts that followed the strategic plan were aimed at reducing middle management in the BLM to improve the service that field management delivered on the ground and increase the level of accountability and control for agency leaders.[134] Cy Jamison had unveiled an ambitious plan in 1991 to transfer nearly 15 percent of the Washington office staff to state and field offices for similar reasons, but the plan ended up being too costly to implement. Baca and Dombeck returned to this plan, and between 1994 and 1996, the Washington office staff was reduced from 515 to about 320.[135] Critics of the plan complained that this would strengthen the already powerful state offices, which was clearly a concern for Secretary Babbitt in trying to unify the BLM. At the BLM Summit, Babbitt had joked that California State Director Ed Hastey, the only state director not replaced during Clinton's first term, "is known in Washington as the Viceroy of California [and] occasionally deigns to call me up and inform me about what he's doing."[136] It appears, however, that Babbitt planned to deal with this issue by appointing new state directors who shared his vision for ecosystem management.

In 1994, Dombeck also reorganized the Washington office, eliminating top positions for the individual resource programs and placing those programs directly under assistant directors with broader responsibility. This was intended to reduce the autonomy of individual resource programs and ensure that at the national level decisions, were made by staff that took a comprehensive view of public lands resources. The agency then conducted numerous field reorganization studies to determine the best way to improve the key ratios targeted by the administration.[137] Dombeck wanted to accomplish this partly by shifting the field organization from a three-tier structure—with state, district, and resource area offices—to a two-tier structure—with state and area offices. Over the next several years a number of states complied, while other states simply streamlined their three-tiered structure. By 1997, when the BLM underwent a performance review under the Government Performance Results Act of 1993, eight of the BLM state offices had moved toward a two-tiered organization, while the other four retained a three-tiered organization. Although this reflected to some extent the diverse responsibilities of each state, it also disrupted the BLM's existing career ladder and created a certain amount of organizational confusion.

It is difficult to measure the extent to which staffing, strategic planning, and reorganization changes pushed the BLM toward a more unified, ecosystem management approach. What was clearly measured during this period, however, was agency morale. In 1995 and again in 1998, the BLM conducted staff surveys designed to assess staff satisfaction. Roughly half of the BLM's staff participated in the surveys, and the results were not encouraging for agency leaders.[138] It appeared that the attempts to dramatically reshape the BLM's identify and organization, coupled with the heated battles over range regulations, had effectively challenged the BLM's existing organization and culture without providing an alternative that BLM employees would embrace. Field managers most likely felt that in the absence of dramatic changes in clientele/interest group pressure, congressional statutes, and appropriations—which Babbitt had struggled unsuccessfully to achieve—they were trapped between powerful political forces.

The problems were most likely compounded by the instability of BLM leadership during the Clinton administration. In the eight years of the Clinton administration, the BLM went through five directors and acting directors, and the agency had an acting director for more time than it had a confirmed director.[139] Secretary Babbitt and Assistant Secretary Armstrong filled this gap to some extent, but they could not provide stable leadership at the agency level and in some ways increased tension between Washington and the field offices. Many older BLM employees and retirees were frustrated by Babbitt's attack on the BLM's traditional resource programs and clientele and his focus on national monuments and special conservation areas. As George Lea, a BLM retiree and president of the Public Lands Foundation explained to Secretary Gale Norton soon after she took office in January 2001, "under the leadership of strong Directors like Robert Burford and Cy Jamison, the BLM became a leader in developing programs for using and conserving public lands resources. In contrast, the Clinton administration chose to emphasize the non-commercial uses and the protection of 'special places' on the BLM lands."[140] It would seem, then, that many BLM employees preferred the cautious path that Jamison had taken by building *both* commercial and noncommercial programs to Babbitt's frontal assault on public lands policy and BLM culture.

CONCLUSION

The Clinton administration was a time of considerable turmoil for the BLM. The agency was caught between the powerful forces of environmentalists armed with the ESA, grazing and mining interests with strong support in Congress, and an administration intent upon breaking down the traditional jurisdictional boundaries in federal land management. Under the rhetoric of ecosystem management, Secretary Babbitt pushed the BLM toward a new comprehensive mission for the public lands, but the agency stopped far short of achieving this goal. Instead, ecosystem management, like many other environmental initiatives in the past, was ensconced in particular BLM programs and among certain BLM staff, ensuring that it would survive as one competing paradigm within public lands management. The BLM's national monuments, wilderness areas, and other special conservation areas remain as important opportunities for the agency.

It is tempting to speculate what might have happened if Vice President Gore had won the 2000 election instead of Governor Bush, because there would have been greater continuity in the administration and greater support for some of the BLM's new initiatives. Instead, the Bush administration brought a renewed emphasis on energy production and greater self-regulation by public lands ranchers. It is a reminder that the BLM's traditional commitments to commercial resource use and self-regulation by commercial resource users still enjoy considerable support in Congress and in the Republican Party. At the end of the twentieth century, the BLM is still searching for a stable and unifying mission. It can no longer be described accurately as a bureau of livestock and mines, but neither can it be described as the bureau of landscapes and monuments. Its responsibilities have simply expanded to embrace livestock, mines, landscapes, and monuments. These responsibilities are prioritized differently, depending upon the specific area of public lands and the particular leaders who control Congress and the White House.

7

Neosagebrush Politics

In its final days, the Clinton administration rushed to secure a conservation legacy. The most visible actions included the creation of five new national monuments totaling more than 1 million acres of BLM land and publication of a final "Roadless Rule" protecting 58.5 million acres of inventoried roadless area within the national forest system.[1] These and other last-minute decisions helped to fill more than 26,000 pages in the *Federal Register* during the administration's final three months, surpassing the previous record of 24,000 pages held by the outgoing Carter administration. This flurry of activity was both an attempt to wrap up long-term initiatives before handing them over to a Republican administration and a last-minute effort to shape the incoming administration's policy options.[2]

The Clinton administration's activities did not go unnoticed by the incoming Republican administration. Throughout his presidential campaign, George W. Bush decried these initiatives, complaining that the Clinton administration had "virtually shut down the ability of a lot of people to use lands."[3] The incoming vice president, Dick Cheney, likewise complained that President Clinton had run "willy-nilly all over the West."[4] In response, Bush insisted that "*proper* balance with the environment and with [the American] way of life" could not be achieved through federal regulation, and he took office in 2001 committed to reducing regulatory hurdles to federal land and resource development.[5]

The extensive last-minute actions by the Clinton administration and the antiregulatory posture of the incoming Bush administration looked in many ways like a replay of the 1981 transition from the Carter administration to the Reagan administration. In both cases, the outgoing Democratic administration struggled to solidify environmental regulations, and the incoming Republican administration rushed to dismantle them in order to promote resource development. Indeed, the Bush administration brought a new kind of sagebrush rebellion to the White House, advancing an agenda very similar to that of the Reagan administration through a very different political strategy. For the BLM, transitioning from the Clinton administration to the George W. Bush administration was jarring, highlighting yet again the BLM's lack of a clear mission, constituency, and political support.

POLITICAL STRATEGY AND ENVIRONMENTAL POLICY

When President George W. Bush took office in 2001, he sounded more like his father, President George H. W. Bush (1989–1993), than like President Reagan. President Bush (I) ran for office as "the environmental president," and President Bush (II) ran for office pledging, "when I leave office, the air will be cleaner, the water will be cleaner and the environment will be better."[6] Yet it quickly became clear that despite using his father's rhetoric, George W. Bush intended to follow in the aggressive antiregulatory path laid out by the Reagan administration.

For a number of reasons, the Bush administration succeeded more than the Reagan administration in reducing environmental regulation and increasing resource development during the president's first term. First, the Republican Party controlled both houses of Congress when President Bush took office, providing greater legislative cooperation than President Reagan had enjoyed. Second, the Bush administration advanced its policy goals against the backdrop of terrorism and catastrophic wildfires, which weakened opposition to changes in energy and forest policy.[7]

Third, and just as important, the president and his staff had learned an important lesson from the Reagan administration about the political cost of overt attacks on environmentalism. Here, the administration's rhetoric was shaped significantly by political consultant Frank Luntz, who warned that "the environment is probably the single issue on which Republicans in general—and President Bush in particular—are most vulnerable."[8] Luntz, in a 2002 report to the president, is worth quoting at length:

> I don't have to remind you how often Republicans are depicted as cold, uncaring, ruthless, even downright anti-social. . . . Therefore, *any discussion of the environment has to be grounded in an effort to reassure a skeptical public that you care about the environment for its own sake*—that your intentions are strictly honorable. Otherwise, all the rational arguments in the world won't be enough for you to prevail. The good news, amidst all the doom and gloom, is that once you *are* able to establish your environmental *bona fides*, once you show people that your heart is in the right place and make them comfortable listening to what you have to say, then the conservative, free market approach to the environment actually has the potential to be quite popular.[9]

The strategy was essentially to convince Americans that the president simply offered a more efficient approach to environmental protection and that the Democratic reliance on regulation was overreaching and unnecessarily costly. Following Luntz's recommendations, the Bush administration advanced its antiregulatory agenda *as an environmental agenda*. It avoided phrases such as "cost-benefit analysis," "risk assessment," and "rolling back environmental regulations," choosing instead to emphasize the importance of "environmental federalism," "balance," and "common sense."

The administration's approach was reflected well by top political appointees.[10] Interior Secretary Gale Norton, for example, shared many conservation convictions with President Reagan's first interior secretary, James Watt, but none of his penchant for open, verbal assaults on the environmental movement. Indeed, Norton had worked for Watt's Mountain States' Legal Foundation, but she had proven far less controversial than Watt in her work as a member of George H. W. Bush's Western Water Policy Commission and as the associate solicitor for the Interior Department.[11]

Norton embraced the Bush strategy of arguing that the administration offered a more efficient and effective program for environmental protection. As she explained on April 19, 2002:

> This Earth Day, more than ever, Americans are ready to take action as *self-motivated stewards* of the environment we hand down to future generations. . . . To accomplish this, we need a new environmentalism, based on the Four C's—Communication, Consultation, and Cooperation, all in the service of Conservation. At the heart of the Four C's is the fact that successful conservation calls for involving the people who live on, work on, and love the land.[12]

Although the rhetoric is almost indistinguishable from that of the Clinton administration, it reflected the Bush administration's traditional Republican faith that economic motivations provide the best possibility of maximizing both economic development and environmental protection. One way to interpret the subtext of the administration's rhetoric is through the bumper sticker slogan, "Are You an Environmentalist, or Do You Work for a Living?"[13] The people necessary for good, collaborative decision making, Secretary Norton admonished, are those "who live on, *work on,* and love the land."[14] Those who simply recreate on the land or care about it from afar but do not have an economic interest in it, Secretary Norton implied, do not know how to achieve a proper balance in land management, because they are not forced by necessity to weigh both economic and environmental trade-offs.

Accordingly, the Bush administration blamed environmental groups for energy shortages and wildland fires. Rolling blackouts in California and soaring energy prices nationwide, President Bush insisted, were caused by the excessive environmental regulation championed by environmental groups, and catastrophic wildfires were increasing because environmental groups held up critical fuel reduction projects that the Bush administration supported.[15] In both cases, the president suggested, environmental groups had been misguided because of their distance from the real trade-offs involved in environmental protection, and policy correction required greater input from those with an economic stake in the land and resource questions.

Privileging economic stakeholders in public lands decisions consistently was a difficult task in the face of environmental lobbying and congressionally mandated citizen participation in federal decision making, but it was also difficult because even in the early twenty-first century the BLM remained highly decentralized. The Bush administration worked to overcome this problem in two interrelated ways. First, the administration exercised the tightest control over information flow since the Reagan administration, limiting administrative transparency. This can be seen most clearly in the White House's tendency to claim executive privilege to withhold documents from public view, even when the issues in question were of limited political importance. For Vice President Cheney at least, this was a matter of principle as much as it was an attempt to avoid political embarrassment, and his attitude was passed down the chain of command into the Interior Department and the BLM.

Second, the Bush administration developed the most centralized administration since President Reagan, routing both high-profile and routine decisions through Washington. One BLM manager interviewed in 2003, for example, explained that it took two and a half years to assemble a Resource Advisory Council because nominations were rejected or held up by officials in Washington.[16] While the Clinton administration was equally controlling on a number of specific and high-profile land use issues, the Bush administration made centralized decision making its default mode of operations.

Information control and centralized decision making reached far down the BLM's chain of command, ensuring that the number of oil and gas wells on public lands increased while the overall number of endangered species listings, wilderness inventory determinations, and other restrictive designations dropped precipitously.[17] Martha Hahn, a BLM state director in Idaho in the first year of the Bush administration, puts it this way: "People at the very local level are getting phone calls from these political people within the (Interior) department, saying what to do."[18]

The administration's emphasis on centralized control also created opportunities for a number of embarrassing scandals that implicated the BLM. The most prominent scandal involved Deputy Secretary J. Steven Griles, who was accused of violating government ethics standards and his own recusal agreements by steering BLM technology contracts and by involving himself in a coalbed methane case that would benefit companies with whom he had previous ties. In March 2004, the Interior Department's inspector general issued a 145-page investigative report on Griles's conduct, identifying twenty-five potential ethics violations.[19]

In his letter of transmittal to Secretary Norton, the investigator general asked her to review the potential violations closely. Nonetheless, within hours of receiving the report, Secretary Norton concluded that Secretary Griles had been cleared of all wrongdoing. She explained that he had acknowledged a lapse in judgment and had taken steps to ensure that it wouldn't happen again: "This closes the issue."[20] Several years later, however, the issue of Griles's ethical conduct was reopened, when a federal court convicted him of lying to the Senate Committee on Indian Affairs about his relationship with the lobbyist Jack Abramoff. He told the committee in 2005 that he had no special relationship with Abramoff but later admitted to having frequent contact with the lobbyist.

A second scandal involved Julie MacDonald, deputy assistant secretary for Fish, Wildlife, and Parks, who oversaw the Endangered Species Program of the U.S. Fish and Wildlife Service (FWS). She reviewed and edited major reports about endangered species candidates, demonstrating a clear effort to keep new species from the list. What makes her work so striking was not just her willingness to alter reports in order to fit the administration's agenda, but her willingness to bypass the normal chain of command and challenge individual biologists and ecologists doing the primary scientific investigation. According to several sources interviewed by the Interior Department's investigator general, MacDonald regularly clashed with the FWS over her role in reviewing and editing the agency's scientific reports.[21]

To some extent, MacDonald was simply doing her job to ensure the accuracy and quality of the FWS's reports. The agency's reports are often rushed because it tends to work under court-ordered deadlines, and as a result, one assistant regional solicitor commented, they "are not particularly good."[22] Nonetheless, Deputy Assistant Secretary MacDonald's editing appears to have gone far beyond checking the documents for quality and rigor. For example, when the FWS was ordered to conduct a periodic review of the southwestern willow flycatcher, a small bird whose habitat range lies in New Mexico, Arizona, Nevada, and Southern California, the agency's biologists determined that flycatcher has a range of 2.1 miles from its nesting site. According to Dale Hall, who was the FWS regional director in that area, MacDonald insisted that the biologists change the range to 1.8 miles so that the bird's critical habitat would not extend into California.[23]

More commonly, MacDonald would either require scientists to remove data or select a specific number at the high or low end of an established range. The case most important for the BLM was the potential endangered species listing of the sage grouse, first the greater sage grouse and then the Gunnison sage grouse, because such a listing would place significant restrictions on the BLM's range management and minerals management programs in the West. The FWS began a formal review of the greater sage grouse in April 2004. Deputy Assistant Secretary MacDonald received the FWS report in October of that year and made extensive changes to the document, removing information, interpretations, and citations that suggested the greater sage grouse was threatened or endangered.

MacDonald deleted citations, and text based on those citations, because they were to secondary sources, because they did not include countervailing sources, because they involved some amount of interpretation, inference, or speculation, or because they weren't peer-reviewed in a way that she approved. MacDonald's approach was reminiscent of the posture taken by the U.S. Forest Service when it adopted the "purity doctrine" with regard to wilderness inventories in the 1960s. On one level, insisting that wilderness areas meet the highest standards of purity would encourage strong protection for the areas included in the wilderness system. Clearly, however, the U.S. Forest Service was also using the purity doctrine to limit the number of wilderness areas Congress would designate.[24]

Many environmental groups and scientific organizations pointed to this and other cases involving scientific research as evidence that the Bush administration was overtly hostile to science itself, but this simplifies the administration's approach. It is more appropriate to say that the Bush administration's antipathy toward environmental regulation made it exceedingly discriminating and selective in its use of science. Whereas the Clinton administration at times interpreted scientific uncertainty as cause for precautionary regulation, the Bush administration generally refused to regulate in cases that involved any significant scientific uncertainty.

The Bush administration's overall posture was reflected in its appointees. The Clinton administration appointed advanced scientists to a number of important land management positions. For example, Secretary Babbitt holds an M.S. in geophysics; Mike Dombeck, who served as the acting director of the BLM and then chief of the U.S. Forest Service, holds a Ph.D. in fisheries biology; and Jack Ward Thomas, who served as Forest Service chief before Dombeck, holds a Ph.D. in forestry. The administration also encouraged peer review and collaboration with academic scientists, as was evident in development of the Northwest Forest Plan. Thus, the Clinton administration relied on the language of science in building its policy position. The Bush administration's appointees came more often from law and business. For example, Mark Rey, undersecretary for Natural Resources and Environment, and James Connaughton, chairman of the Council on Environmental Quality, were both lobbyists prior to their appointments. Interior Secretary Gale Norton, Assistant Secretary for Land and Minerals Management Rebecca Watson, and Bennett Raley, assistant secretary for Water and Science, are all lawyers. This does not mean that President Bush's appointees lacked scientific knowledge, but it does mean that they tended to privilege economic and legal information over information from the natural sciences.

A third scandal during the Bush administration involving a Wyoming rancher and the BLM's Worland Field Office in Wyoming was perhaps the most unnerving for BLM employees. In 1994, the Worland Field Office began issuing notices of grazing and trespass violations to Harvey Frank Robbins, a significant contributor to the Republican Party who had recently purchased a ranch with attached grazing permits. In 1996, after continued grazing and trespass violations, the BLM began to issue decisions to suspend some of Robbins's grazing privileges, and Robbins responded by restricting the BLM's access to public lands near his ranch and filing administrative appeals and lawsuits. By 2002, Robbins and the BLM were joined in sixteen administrative appeals and numerous cases in Federal District Court.

In addition to appeals and lawsuits against the BLM, Robbins also filed a civil complaint in Federal District Court that accused eight specific BLM employees from the Worland field office of extortion and blackmail—under the Racketeer Influenced and Corrupt Organization Act—in their efforts to obtain rights-of-way easements to reach public lands. Since the complaint named these employees in both their personal and professional capacities, it exposed them to personal liability amounting to Robbins's request for $12 million in economic, emotional, and punitive damages.[25]

In the face of escalating conflict, Washington BLM officials arranged for Robbins to meet with BLM, Interior, and congressional staff on February 8, 2002. Following the meeting, the BLM conducted an internal review that exonerated the Worland Field Office and the eight BLM employees named in the civil complaint, at least of all formal charges. The review team sent their report to the Wyoming state director for BLM, the Department of Justice, and the Interior's solicitor, which asserted that "Robbins had demonstrated a complete disregard for BLM's authority to manage public lands and failed to abide by the terms and conditions of the BLM permits he was issued."[26] The review found further that the BLM's Worland Field Office had done everything possible to work with Robbins without effect. The review team then met with BLM Director Kathleen Clarke and the associate solicitor for the Division of Land and Water, Robert Comer, to brief them on the case. According to one participant in the meeting, Director Clarke directed Comer to produce a settlement agreement with Robbins, although Clarke stated that the settlement agreement was Comer's idea.[27] In either case, Clarke delegated the settlement agreement to Comer and her deputy director, Fran Cherry.

Comer took the lead on the settlement agreement and instructed a staff attorney to draft the document. Comer sent the draft settlement agreement to the assistant U.S. attorney in Wyoming who was defending the eight BLM employees in Robbins's civil suit. The attorney recalled expressing concern that the settlement agreement established a unique process by which Robbins could appeal future cases directly to the BLM director and concern that "this process clearly involves the Office of the Director of the BLM in Washington, D.C., in micromanaging the Wyoming Bureau of Land Management with regard to one permitee."[28] The attorney's complaint was corroborated by other statements indicating that Comer handled all negotiations with Robbins's attorney directly and without consultation.

Upon review of the revised draft settlement, the assistant U.S. attorney wrote to Comer expressing his concern that the settlement would inhibit the U.S. Attorney's Office in future efforts to represent the BLM in criminal or civil matters related to Robbins and that it would greatly inhibit the BLM Worland Field

Office staff in the exercise of their duties, since they would have to get permission from the BLM director before taking any future action against Robbins. According to one BLM employee, who reviewed drafts, and Deputy Director Fran Cherry, who signed the final settlement, Comer never shared the assistant U.S. attorney's concerns with them. Furthermore, according to the staff attorney who drafted the settlement document, Comer directed him not to share it or information about it with BLM staff in Wyoming or even with his direct supervisor.[29]

The settlement reached between the BLM and Robbins in January 2003, which the Wyoming acting state director and the Worland Field Office manager both opposed, required the BLM to suspend sixteen grazing and trespass adjudications and required Robbins to suspend his administrative appeals and all but one of his lawsuits against the BLM. Despite the favorable terms of the settlement, Robbins continued to violate the terms of his grazing permits. In January 2004, a manager from the Wyoming state office and the Worland Field Office manager met with Robbins to discuss the violations and reported that Robbins simply insisted that they drop the issues. Later that month the Worland Field Office notified Robbins that the settlement agreement was void because of his continued violations.[30]

The most troubling part of the settlement agreement for BLM employees while it was in effect during 2003, however, was that it did not require Robbins to drop his action against the eight named BLM employees, thus leaving them exposed to civil penalties if Robbins prevailed in the case. What became apparent in the investigator general's report on the issue was that Comer disregarded concerns expressed by the Department of Justice, by the assistant U.S. attorney in Wyoming, and by BLM employees in his efforts to reach a settlement agreement that was acceptable to Robbins.[31]

In light of all three scandals, it is not surprising that when Inspector General Earl Devaney later testified before the House Subcommittee on Energy and Resources in September 2006, he gave the Interior Department a scathing review: "Simply stated, short of a crime, anything goes at the highest levels of the Department of the Interior. Ethics failures on the part of senior Department officials— taking the form of appearances of impropriety, favoritism, and bias—have been routinely dismissed."[32] Further, he lamented, "Numerous OIG reports, which have chronicled such things as complex efforts to hide the true nature of agreements with outside parties; intricate deviations from statutory, regulatory, and policy requirements to reach a predetermined end; palpable procurement irregularities; massive project collapses; bonuses awarded to the very people whose programs fail; and indefensible failures to correct deplorable conditions in Indian Country, have been met with vehement challenges to the quality of our audits, evaluations, and investigations."[33]

These and other scandals, along with micromanagement by the Washington office, did nothing to boost the BLM's already sagging morale. The agency's staff satisfaction surveys in 1995 and again in 1998 had revealed frustration among employees across the entire spectrum of the agency's program areas. While no comparable data emerged during the Bush administration, there were other indications of low agency morale. In a 2007 assessment by the Partnership for Public Service and American University's Institute for the Study of Public Policy Implementation, the BLM received low employee satisfaction scores, ranking 157 out of 222 agency scores. Furthermore, employee satisfaction had dropped since 2005.[34]

Just as significantly, the Interior Department's inspector general evaluated the department's conduct and discipline in a 2004 report, raising serious concerns about the department's work environment. He summarized twenty-two group interviews this way:

> Participants in our group meetings revealed that they felt trapped—afraid to complain about the workplace environment or expose poor administration and employee misconduct. According to one participant, "If you tell management what they don't want to hear, you're punished. There's little or no confidentiality." Others were so discouraged and bitter that they openly expressed suspicion and skepticism about our intentions for meeting with them and about the evaluation overall. One meeting participant explained, "We live in a culture of fear." Many participants stated that they feared retaliation by management and the possibility of working in a hostile environment if they shared their perceptions with us. Comments such as "The 'hatchet people' can't wait to get rid of someone" were not atypical.[35]

The Bush administration certainly did not create these working conditions within the Interior Department, but the administration's close supervision of career employees and its forceful direction of field management decisions did increase the fear among BLM employees that they would face retaliation if they opposed their supervisors.

THE BUREAU OF LIVESTOCK AND MINES REVISITED

The Bush administration's ambivalence about scientific data, and its antipathy toward environmental regulation, reflected its underlying commitment to principles of free-market environmentalism implemented within the nonmarket context of federal land and resource policy. This paradox translated first and foremost into an emphasis on solidifying private rights and privileges to public resources.

In this context, the Clinton administration's grazing and mining regulations may have been the most substantive issues for the Bush administration to tackle, but President Clinton's national monument designations and the BLM's new National Landscape Conservation System were perhaps more important symbolic issues for the Bush administration to challenge. Indeed, for the Bush administration, President Clinton's national monument designations and Forest Service "roadless rule" represented the most audacious and damaging exercises of executive power, locking up federal lands and, it suggested, undermining private property rights.[36]

The Bush administration's refrain in criticizing the monuments was that the Clinton administration had acted unilaterally without considering the needs of local people. In contrast, Vice President Cheney argued, "We need an opportunity for all to be heard."[37] Tom Fulton, deputy assistant secretary for land and minerals management in the Interior Department, echoed Cheney's pledge in testimony before Congress in July 2001, encouraging Congress to pass a bill that would limit presidential use of the Antiquities Act to designate national monuments. The Interior Department, he argued, "is committed to bringing common sense and balance to the decision process by listening to the people most affected by these decisions."[38] The Bush administration's refrain is curious in that it accurately describes the BLM's first national monument designation, Grand Staircase–Escalante National Monument, which President Clinton planned in secret as a political maneuver in the 1996 presidential election. Yet Secretary Babbitt recommended all subsequent national monuments only after soliciting extended public input.[39]

After concluding that President Bush did not have the authority to overturn President Clinton's national monuments, Interior Secretary Gale Norton turned to the monument planning processes as a means to protect resource development activities. She explained in February 2001, "The monument designations were more show than substance. We now have to provide the substance," and she pledged to work with local officials, property owners, and business executives to shape monument management plans.[40] After all, she insisted, "farmers and ranchers are often the best stewards of wild places. Those who own property are the ones who often understand the habitat on the property and the uses of the property."[41]

In March 2001, Secretary Norton sent over 200 letters to local officials in areas around President Clinton's national monuments, requesting their input on monument planning and management. "The Interior Department is opening up lines of communication with local people that were not always properly fostered in the past," she explained. "Local people have intimate knowledge of their land and can offer first hand insight and perspective to promote stewardship in these cherished areas."[42] In the letter, Norton asked for input on specific issues:

Are there boundary adjustments that the Department should consider recommending [to Congress]? Are there existing uses inside these Monuments that we should accommodate? I would like to know your views on vehicle use, access to private inholdings, rights-of-way, grazing, and water rights, as well as the wide spectrum of other traditional multiple uses that might be appropriately applied to these lands. I also want to learn from you which areas within these Monuments are truly special and should be reserved for their unique environmental or historic characteristics. If you believe the Monument would benefit tourism or recreation, please advise me of that as well.[43]

The subtext of the letter appears to be a request for local officials to complain about any ways that national monument status had restricted land use and a promise to work with local officials to eliminate such restrictions in the planning process.

Secretary Norton's letter outraged not only environmental groups but also local citizens who supported the monuments. Speaking on their behalf, Oregon Governor John A. Kitzhaber expressed concern about Norton's perceived intent:

> I am concerned that your letter appears to focus on activities that could potentially be incompatible with the [Cascade-Siskiyou National Monument in southern Oregon], rather than soliciting input from Oregonians about the most appropriate way to meet the goals and objectives contained in the Monument declaration. . . . By focusing on the most divisive and controversial issues rather than on how best to achieve the purposes for which the Monument was created, I am afraid your letter will only serve to create conflict and engender false expectations in the local community.[44]

Nonetheless, the Bush administration moved forward with its efforts to maintain existing resource development activities in and road access to the BLM's national monuments.

Two examples of the Bush administration's approach come from Utah, where President Clinton designated his first national monument. First, as explained in the previous chapter, wilderness debates in Utah had been among the most contentious in the nation, and the Grand Staircase–Escalante National Monument designation was in part a challenge to the wilderness stalemate in Utah that grew during the 1980s and 1990s. The BLM had finished its official wilderness inventory in Utah by 1991, as required by the Federal Land Policy and Management Act (FLPMA) of 1976. Wilderness advocates challenged the inventory, arguing that the BLM ignored millions of acres of potential wilderness area in its inventory, and in 1996 Secretary Babbitt ordered a team of BLM wilderness specialists to review lands with wilderness potential. The team identified 5.8 million acres of land with wilderness characteristics, a full 2.6 million acres more than the BLM's original inventory.[45] Secretary Babbitt issued an order giving those 2.6 million acres interim wilderness protection and a second, less restrictive order, protecting another 3.3 million acres with wilderness potential.[46]

The state of Utah sued Secretary Babbitt, arguing that the inventory was illegal, but their case was ultimately rejected because the plaintiffs lacked standing to sue.[47] On March 31, 2003, the state of Utah once again sued the secretary of the interior, Gale Norton. On April 10, 2003, environmental groups sought to intervene in the case, but on April 11 the state of Utah and the Interior Department filed a settlement agreement, which the court accepted on April 14, closing the case. With the settlement Secretary Norton announced that she was revoking the *Wilderness Inventory and Study Procedures Handbook*, which the BLM had released during the final days of the Clinton Administration,[48] including Secretary

Babbitt's orders to protect additional land with wilderness potential. "Only Congress can create a wilderness area," Norton explained, "We are making that clear by settling the lawsuit."[49] Secretary Norton's basic argument was that identifying lands with wilderness characteristics and protecting those characteristics was essentially creating de facto wilderness areas contrary to law and in violation of the BLM's overall multiple-use mission. Eliminating these areas would allow the BLM to consider the full range of multiple uses, including oil, gas, and coal development, in its management plans.

Second, the Interior Department settled a dispute with the state of Utah over road rights-of-way on federal lands. In 1866, Congress added a provision to the Mining Law, known as R.S. 2477, which permitted rights-of-way and highway construction across public lands. Although Congress later repealed the provision in 1976, it grandfathered in all existing R.S. 2477 claims. The BLM's dilemma, similar to the one it had long faced with hard rock mining claims, was that the R.S. 2477 provision required no federal permission or documentation, so most R.S. 2477 claims were invisible to the agency. By 1993, the BLM had acknowledged some 1,453 R.S. 2477 rights-of-way and identified another 5,600 outstanding claims, mainly in Utah. At the same time, the state of Utah claimed roughly 10,000 rights-of-way across public lands, including many areas of the Grand Staircase–Escalante National Monument. In 1994, the Interior Department issued a formal rule to resolve the R.S. 2477 disputes, but Congress placed a moratorium on all administrative R.S. 2477 activity.[50]

Beginning in 2000, the state of Utah threatened to sue over its R.S. 2477 claims, a threat that it continued to make to the Bush administration. On January 6, 2003, however, the BLM issued a revised rule, "Final Rule on Conveyances, Disclaimers, and Correction Documents," implementing its FLPMA authority to issue disclaimers of interest in certain lands. The BLM indicated that it might use the new rule to settle R.S. 2477 claims. Then, on April 9, 2003, Secretary Norton and Utah Governor Mike Leavitt announced that they had signed a Memorandum of Understanding designed to speed up R.S. 2477 settlements. In the MOU, Utah agreed to give up all claims to unimproved dirt roads in what might be called dominant-use federal land areas: national parks, fish and wildlife refuges, and wilderness areas. In exchange, Secretary Norton established a "State and County Road Acknowledgment Process" to settle remaining R.S. 2477 claims, which were located primarily on public lands. The Interior Department would settle these claims, despite the congressional moratorium on specific R.S. 2477 rules, by working through its new FLPMA disclaimer regulations. The MOU opened the Grand Staircase–Escalante National Monument and many other public lands areas to the state's 10,000 claims.[51] The new process went forward, despite a General Accounting Office (GAO) assessment that it expressly violated the congressional moratorium, but the process proved time-consuming and costly and did not lead to rapid disclaimers during Secretary Norton's tenure.[52]

The wilderness and R.S. 2477 conflicts are just two examples of the Bush administration's antipathy toward Clinton-era obstacles to resource development on the public lands. The Bush administration chafed at Secretary Babbitt's characterization of the BLM as the Bureau of Landscapes and Monuments, arguing through its policy initiatives that this mistook the BLM for the National Park Service and violated the agency's multiple-use mission. With Secretary Norton and BLM Director Kathleen Clarke as the spokespersons, the Bush administration rejected the Bureau of Landscapes and Monuments and advanced new rhetoric intended to convey an environmentally responsible Bureau of Livestock and Mines.

Secretary Norton and Director Clarke advanced a new rhetorical model for the BLM's range program that maintained Secretary Babbitt's landscape language and situated livestock grazing within the larger sustainability vocabulary used by environmental organizations: "Sustaining Working Landscapes" or the "Working Landscapes Initiative." Nonetheless, the new model was clearly a departure from ecosystem management, defined as the "integration of ecological, economic, and social principles to manage biological and physical systems in a manner that safeguards the long-term ecological sustainability, natural diversity, and productivity of the landscapes."[53] As with the Bush administration's environmental policy more broadly, the Working Landscapes Initiative did not challenge ecosystem protection, per se; rather, it simply rejected the priorities of ecosystem management, which rhetorically and operationally subordinated economic sustainability to ecological sustainability.

Allan Fitzsimmons, the Interior Department's fuel coordinator for the Healthy Forest Initiative, expressed in radical form the Bush administration's objections to ecosystem management: "While the ecosystem concept may be helpful as a tool for researchers to better grasp the world around us, it is far too ambiguous to serve as an organizing principle for the application of federal law and policy."[54] To justify overturning ecosystem management rather than refining it, Fitzsimmons argued that advocates of ecosystem management were ultimately trying to advance private religious convictions through public law: "A revolution is upon us. Its backers want to make protection of ecosystems the number one goal of federal environmental and land management policies. . . . There is a strong element of nature worship here that advocates of this view often cloak in secular definitions."[55] Thus, he implied, ecosystem management raises constitutional questions about the relationship between church and state.

Fitzsimmon's ,rhetoric, particularly that about religious confrontation, was extreme, but Secretary Norton and Director Clarke certainly shared his view that their duty was to restore balance to public lands management by prioritizing human use over a set of ecological and biodiversity goals. Whereas Secretary Babbitt had directed ecologists to use the spotted owl and other vulnerable species as indicators of ecosystem health, the Bush administration appeared to use ranching viability as a proxy measurement for rangeland health.

As noted in the previous chapter, the BLM implemented major revisions to its grazing regulations in August 1995, called Rangeland Reform '94, in order to bring range management more into line with the principles of ecosystem management. Among other things, the 1995 regulations expanded opportunities for public participation in grazing decisions, eliminated the earlier requirement that a person be "actively engaged in the livestock business" to qualify for grazing use, made permit renewal contingent on the permittee's performance record, asserted that the federal government owns full title to all new permanent range improvements, and established a new process for assessing and protecting rangeland health.[56]

In March 2003 the BLM announced that it would revise its Clinton-era range regulations to promote working landscapes, which it defined as landscapes "on the public lands that are both economically productive and environmentally healthy."[57] After a scoping and public comment period the BLM published a proposed rule amending grazing regulations, explaining that the changes would "improve working relationships with permittees and lessees, enhance administrative efficiency, and cost effectiveness, clarify the regulations, and protect the health of rangelands."[58]

The Rangeland Reform '94 regulations had been designed to subordinate livestock grazing more fully to rangeland health, to reassert the federal government's full authority to regulate livestock grazing, and to open range management decision making at all levels to the general public. The BLM designed its new proposed regulations, by contrast, to shield grazing permittees from rapid changes to their grazing privileges and give them more flexibility to work collaboratively with the BLM to manage their grazing allotments.[59]

As the BLM worked through public comments on eighteen major revisions to the existing grazing regulations, some of the critical differences between the 1995 regulations and the 2003 proposed regulations became increasingly clear. First, whereas in 1995 the BLM had explicitly expanded opportunities for public involvement in range management decision making, the 2003 proposal limited those opportunities in significant ways. For BLM leaders, the public participation change was motivated by frustration with environmental groups who participated sporadically in management decision making, sometimes joining very late in the process and thwarting compromises that existing parties had worked out over time. But as the agency explained in response to public comments, the change was also principled: "BLM believes that in-depth involvement of the public in day-to-day management decisions is neither warranted nor administratively efficient and can in fact delay BLM remedial response actions necessitated by resource conditions. . . . Cooperation with permittees and lessees, on the other hand, usually results in more expeditious steps to address resource conditions and can help avoid lengthy administrative appeals."[60] Essentially, the BLM argued that public participation at all levels was inefficient and unfair to those most directly and economically affected by federal land management.

Second, whereas the 1995 regulations provided that the federal government would hold full title to all permanent range improvements, the 2003 regulations allowed permittees to "share title to range improvements of public lands proportionate to the value of their contributed labor, material, or equipment to make on-the-ground structural improvements."[61] The difference reflected, in part, partisan tendencies in the long-standing debate over the degree to which ranchers *owned* their permits. Democratic administrations have tended to emphasize the fact that grazing permits do not convey any legal rights to the range but are revocable privileges; Republican administrations have tended to bypass the question of legal rights but insist that the federal government has a political obligation to protect grazing privileges, treating them in some sense as political property rights. Sharing title to range improvements factored into this partisan debate because while it would not grant grazing permittees any legal rights to the underlying rangeland, it clearly helped permittees put down roots in their grazing allotments that made it more difficult politically for the BLM to revoke grazing privileges.[62]

Third, whereas the 1995 regulations provided strict timetables for enforcement of rangeland health standards, the new regulations removed timetables requiring agency enforcement and added a new timetable requiring the agency to phase in grazing reductions of greater than 10 percent over a five-year period. The difference between the two regulations is essentially about the burden of proof necessary to modify grazing management practices. The 1995 regulations placed a greater burden of proof on the side of resource use, serving both as a way to support range managers who saw the need for grazing modifications and as a way to force reluctant range managers to modify grazing management. The 2003 regulations, by contrast, emphasized the economic impact that grazing modifications would have on permittees, placing a greater burden of proof on the side of grazing modification. They essentially encouraged, but did not require, longer periods of range study before the BLM could make any grazing modifications and provided permittees with greater opportunity to challenge the adequacy of range determinations. Thus, the 2003 regulations both supported grazing permittees who opposed grazing modification and encouraged range managers to act slowly and carefully in their range health determinations.

It would be difficult to determine the overall assessment of the proposed regulations by BLM field managers. Certainly many field managers were frustrated that so many of their decisions were open to public review and scrutiny, slowing the decision-making process down considerably. On the other hand, field managers were no less frustrated by the difficulties they had trying to implement grazing modifications, particularly those that reduced grazing activities, without significant political support. This later frustration was highlighted in the Harvey Frank Robbins scandal mentioned above, because it clearly raised concerns among range managers about their ability to enforce range regulations and permit conditions and potential retaliation by grazing permittees if they did exercise their full legal authority.[63]

The most widely representative voice for BLM managers during this debate was most likely the Public Lands Foundation, a nonprofit organization composed primarily of BLM retirees who had extensive experience in range management and who were free to speak critically without fear of administrative reprisal. George Lea, the Public Lands Foundation president, presented comments on the proposed regulations at a BLM hearing, explaining at the outset that he saw no need for new regulations so soon after the 1995 regulations had taken effect. Furthermore, he argued, the new regulations represent "an effort by the administration to undo what has been done and to return to the past rather than to propose progressive improvements [and] to provide the livestock industry with more control on the management of the lands."[64]

Debate over the proposed regulations was lengthy and heated. Among other things, critics accused the BLM of editing its draft environmental impact statement to hide potential environmental impacts of the changes.[65] In June 2005, the *Los Angeles Times* reported that the agency had removed or altered critical statements by BLM scientists. In one case, BLM leaders replaced a warning that the new regulations would have a "significant adverse impact" on wildlife with the conclusion that they would be "beneficial to animals." In another case BLM leaders simply removed the conclusion that the new regulations would have "a slow, long-term adverse impact on wildlife and biological diversity in general."[66] The BLM responded to these charges in an addendum to the final environmental impact statement on March 31, 2006, although it explained that the addendum's primary purpose was to address comments from the U.S. FWS received after the comment period deadline. The BLM insisted that it had not subverted the NEPA process in any way, but had instead "corrected misstatements about the proposed rule."[67]

The BLM published the final rule amending grazing regulations on July 12, 2006, more than three years after its initial advance notice of proposed rule making. The final regulations, which included only minor clarifying changes since the proposed regulations, were slated to take effect on August 11, 2006, but the BLM faced a barrage of litigation. On August 11, a federal district judge enjoined the BLM's revisions dealing with public participation: "Public participation is, by nature, messy. . . . At the same time, the agency's management of public input cannot defeat NEPA's purpose of 'ensuring that the agency will have . . . detailed information concerning significant environmental impacts, and . . . that the public can . . . contribute to that body of information.'"[68]

Even more significant, the same judge enjoined the BLM's revised regulations dealing with the fundamentals of rangeland health and split ownership of range improvements on September 25, 2006. Judge Winmill cited the redacted environmental impact statement and argued that there were serious doubts as to whether or not the agency had fulfilled its NEPA responsibilities to "insure the professional integrity, including scientific integrity, of the discussions and analyses in environmental impact statements."[69] Specifically, he noted that the BLM published its proposed regulations just ten days after the deadline for receiving internal comments on the draft EIS, suggesting that the agency had not taken a close look at comments from its internal experts.[70] Judge Winmill issued an even more scathing injunction on June 8, 2007:

> The parties seek a ruling on the legality of the BLM's revisions to nationwide grazing regulations. Past BLM regulations imposed restrictions on grazing and increased the opportunities for public input to reverse decades of grazing damage to public lands. Without any showing of improvement, the new BLM regulations loosen restrictions on grazing. They limit public input from the non-ranching public, offer ranchers more rights on BLM land, restrict the BLM's monitoring of grazing damage, extend the deadlines for corrective action, and dilute the BLM's authority to sanction ranchers for grazing violations.[71]

Thus, more than a year after publishing the final grazing regulations, the BLM was forced to implement an amended set of regulations that eliminated the three most controversial changes.

The importance of the national grazing regulation debate for local grazing management was underscored in September 2007, when an administrative law judge issued an opinion against the BLM's grazing management on the Nickel Creek and the Nickel Creek Fenced Federal Range (FFR) grazing allotments in the Idaho BLM's Owyhee Resource Area. Judge Pearlstein found that in issuing a final grazing decision in November 2003, the BLM had violated both the fundamentals of rangeland health and NEPA.

Judge Pearlstein consolidated two cases, bringing claims made by the Glenns Ferry Grazing Association (GFGA), the Western Watersheds Project (WWP), and the BLM together in one opinion: "Beauty is in the eye of the beholder," he explained. "For the ranchers of the GFGA, beauty is seen in a healthy, fat cow that will sell at a high price. For the environmentalists of WWP, beauty is seen in a natural pristine range, free of cattle and other non-native animals and plants. For the bureaucrats of BLM, beauty is probably seen in not being sued by either or both the ranchers and environmentalists."[72] Not surprisingly, he notes, the three groups had very different interpretations of the BLM's 2003 grazing decision. The GFGA argued that the BLM had erred in determining that the Nickel Creek and FFR grazing allotments failed to meet rangeland health standards, WWP argued that the allotments failed to meet the standards and that the BLM's final decision would illegally perpetuate the conditions, and the BLM argued that the allotments failed to meet the standards but that the final decision would improve range conditions.[73]

As the case moved forward, a number of key findings of fact not only supported WWP's position but also raised significant questions about the integrity of grazing management under the Bush administration. First, in April 2002, the BLM Washington office directed the local BLM office to contract with Ranges West to assist in communication with ranchers and members of the interested public. The lead from Ranges West was a former range science professor, who was a member of the Idaho Cattle Association and who had filed affidavits for ranching interveners in previous litigation. Environmentalists had objected to his involvement in the process, and Judge Pearlstein found that while he had had extensive contact with the GFGA and the BLM, he had "personally never met with representatives of WWP or communicated with them concerning the Allotments although he was hired by BLM to facilitate communication among BLM, the permittees, and the interested public groups."[74] Second, Judge Pearlstein found that the supervisory range management specialist, Bill Reimers, who had supported changes to grazing management in earlier litigation, was transferred against his will out of the Owyhee Field Office during the Nickel Creek and FFR allotment decision-making process.[75] Reimers filed an internal administrative action challenging his transfer. Both findings point to the Washington office's direct involvement in and control over field management decisions.

In his written opinion, Judge Pearlstein decided that (1) the BLM had properly determined that ecological conditions on the Nickel Creek and FFR allotments failed to meet rangeland health standards, (2) the BLM's decision "unreasonably relied upon inadequate data and unsupported assumptions to perpetuate a stocking rate that exceeds the carrying capacity of the Allotments," (3) the BLM's decision will not lead to progress toward meeting rangeland health standards, and (4) the BLM's decision violated NEPA because the agency had not adequately considered a light grazing alternative proposed by WWP.[76]

Judge Pearlstein's decision underscores the complexity and difficulty of grazing management decisions at the allotment level. In the case of the Nickel Creek and FFR allotments, the differences between the 1995 and the 2006 grazing regulations would have been significant. The 1995 regulations gave the WWP opportunity to participate in determinations about grazing permit renewal, and they required that the BLM take action to improve range conditions within a fixed period of time. The 2006 regulations, by contrast, would have reduced WWP's involvement and given the BLM additional time not to act. As of this writing, the 1995 regulations prevail.

Although the Bush administration changed the BLM's priorities and regulations in a number of management programs, President Bush and Vice President Cheney made it clear that energy development trumped all other discretionary priorities. As with the Reagan administration in the 1980s, the Bush administration treated energy development rhetorically as far more than an economic issue. For Presidents Reagan and Bush, accelerated energy development was a moral issue of the highest national order because it was essential for national security and independence. Both administrations therefore spoke of energy development as the highest and best use of the public lands, although the Bush administration was more successful in following through on that rhetoric.

On January 29, 2001, just days after taking office, President Bush created the National Energy Policy Development Group (NEPDG) made up of Vice President

Cheney, nine cabinet-level officials, and four additional administrative officials. The president requested two reports from the NEPDG: a report on the obstacles to energy supply and a report containing recommendations for a national energy policy.

The NEPDG released its first report on March 19, 2001, which outlined problems with the current system of energy production and distribution. President Bush and members of the NEPDG interpreted the results as a clear indication that the United States faced an energy crisis.[77] For example, Energy Secretary Spencer Abraham explained the report's findings this way: "America faces a major energy-supply crisis over the next two decades. The failure to meet this challenge will threaten our nation's economic prosperity, compromise our national security and literally alter the way we live our lives."[78] In subsequent weeks, members of the NEPDG made it reasonably clear that their final recommendations would emphasize energy production. Indeed, unlike President Carter, who had emphasized the need for energy conservation and efficiency, Vice President Cheney explained in April 2001: "Conservation may be a sign of personal virtue, but it is not a sufficient basis for a sound comprehensive energy policy."[79] Furthermore, even before the NEPDG released its final report, the Bush administration made its commitment to a supply-side approach clear in its FY 2002 budget proposal, which called for research on "clean coal" technology and accelerated energy production on public lands while making substantial spending cuts across virtually all conservation, energy efficiency, and renewable energy programs.[80]

It was therefore no surprise that the NEPDG's final report on May 16, 2001—despite forty-two recommendations to promote conservation, energy efficiency, and renewable energy—made expanded energy production the primary goal of the national energy policy.[81] As a *New York Times* journalist put it, "The Bush administration's national energy policy is a glossy, picture-filled and comprehensive look at nearly every energy issue facing the United States today, but buried in the text is a single stark conclusion: Excessive regulation has produced the worst energy crisis in decades."[82] The fundamental causes of the nation's energy crisis, the report explains, are that energy production has not kept pace with consumption, and "our current, outdated network of electric generators, transmission lines, pipelines, and refineries that convert raw materials into usable fuel has been allowed to deteriorate."[83]

According to the report the federal government bears an enormous burden of guilt for "the most serious energy shortage since the oil embargoes of the 1970s" and explained that "one reason for [the crisis] is government regulation, often excessive and redundant. Regulation is needed in such a complex field, but it has become overly burdensome. Regulatory hurdles, delays in issuing permits, and economic uncertainty are limiting investment in new facilities, making our energy markets more vulnerable to transmission bottlenecks, price spikes and supply disruptions."[84] To break the bottlenecks and price spikes, the report argues, the federal government needs to cut red tape and reduce regulatory barriers to energy development.

The similarity between this national energy policy and that of the Reagan administration is clear in both rhetoric and substance. In fact, in an interview with the *Denver Post* in 2001, President Reagan's first interior secretary, James Watt, emphasized this continuity:

> Everything Cheney's saying, everything the president's saying—they're saying exactly what we were saying 20 years ago, precisely. . . . Any reasonable, halfway intelligent person is going to come to the same conclusion: You've got to have more oil, you've got to have more coal, you've got to have more of everything. . . . You've got to have more conservation too, but conservation and solar energy and wind energy—they're just teeny infant portions. You're not going to run the world with solar energy by the year 2001 or 2002 or 2010.[85]

Thus, the NEPDG report suggested that the only way to reach the goal of "a steady supply of affordable energy"[86] was to take energy development decisions away from federal regulators and place them in the hands of the energy market.

As noted above, the primary difference between the Reagan and Bush administrations in the energy arena was not in their agenda but in their success meeting that agenda. President Reagan had faced a Democratic Congress that was less willing to support his agenda, and the Reagan administration made some significant mistakes in its initial years by overstepping its administrative authority.[87] President Bush, on the other hand, enjoyed support from a Republican Congress and made more effective tactical decisions.

The NEPDG report sparked two heated debates that captured public and media attention, giving the Bush administration space to act quietly and administratively on other issues. The first debate raged over the process by which the NEPDG crafted its report. Environmental groups charged that Vice President Cheney had gotten much of the group's information and advice from energy executives and lobbyists, thereby leading to a report that was grossly skewed to benefit the energy industry. Environmental groups and members of Congress demanded to see records of the NEPDG's meetings, but Vice President Cheney, true to his staunch defense of executive privilege, refused to turn over the documents. This only fueled public suspicion. The GAO began a formal review of the NEPDG process in May 2001 and received the same rebuff when it pressed the vice president for documents. It was forced to conclude that while the NEPDG solicited and received advice from petroleum, coal, nuclear, natural gas, and electricity industry representatives and lobbyists, it was unclear from the available information how much of a role these participants played.[88]

A second and more important debate raged in Congress over recommendations to open the Arctic National Wildlife Refuge (ANWR) to oil and gas drilling.

The ANWR debate is curious, in part because it isn't at all clear how much oil and gas ANWR contains. Although the NEPDG report calls ANWR "the single most promising prospect in the United States," capable of producing the equivalent of forty-six years' worth of current oil imports from Iraq, subsequent estimates from various sources have contradicted this assessment.[89] Some have speculated that ANWR oil is not the real prize for oil companies but would be used as a land base for offshore exploration and development.[90]

Whatever the real prize is for oil companies, for the Bush administration ANWR was a critical symbolic battle in the war over government regulation. Since energy development was such a clear moral priority for the Bush administration, particularly after the September 11, 2001, attacks on the World Trade Towers and Washington, energy needed to be developed wherever it was found. ANWR was, for the Bush administration, a symbol of excessive and obstructive federal regulation that needed to give way in the face of a national energy crisis. The Bush administration echoed the testimony of Mark Rubin, general manager for the American Petroleum Institute, who told Congress that "to ensure reliable and secure sources of oil . . . we must remove the barriers that currently impede the U.S. oil and natural gas industry's ability to compete both domestically and abroad."[91] Rubin indicated that the oil and gas industry would not drill in parklands or designated wilderness areas, but he insisted that Congress needed to open up other restricted lands in Alaska and the American West.

With media and public attention focused on the NEPDG and ANWR, the Bush administration found other, more effective, ways to reduce regulatory and administrative obstacles to oil and gas development. On May 18, just two days after receiving the NEPDG's report, "National Energy Policy: Reliable, Affordable, and Environmentally Sound Energy for America's Future," President Bush issued a pair of executive orders to accelerate energy development on federal lands. The first order, "Actions to Expedite Energy-Related Projects," directed federal agencies "to expedite projects that will increase the production, transmission, or conservation of energy."[92] The second order, "Actions Concerning Regulations That Significantly Affect Energy Supply, Distribution, or Use," directed federal agencies to prepare a Statement of Energy Effects for any "significant energy action," as determined by the Office of Management and Budget. In each statement, the agency was required to detail all potential negative effects on energy supply, distribution, or use and detail all reasonable alternatives to the action.[93]

The BLM was already engaged in a review of key energy reserve areas of public lands in accordance with the Energy Policy and Conservation Act (EPCA) amendments that President Clinton had signed into law in 2000. The act directed the BLM to produce a scientific estimate of oil and gas reserves and identify any impediments to energy development in those areas. Of the land the BLM inventoried, 36 percent was off-limits to oil and gas development, but these lands contained only 15 percent of the recoverable oil and 12 percent of the recoverable gas.[94] Furthermore, of the 40 million acres of land under oil and gas leases by 2004, only about one quarter was producing any oil or gas. These statistics suggest that oil and gas exploration could expand without opening restricted areas, highlighting the fact that the Bush administration's emphasis on exploration grew out of an a priori commitment to place all mineral lands in the energy market so that the industry could determine the pace of development. This was particularly true of lands within the most productive basins identified in the BLM's EPCA phase I report: Paradox–San Juan Basin, Uinta–Piceance Basin, Greater Green River Basin, Powder River Basin, and Montana Thrust Belt, which stretch along the Rocky Mountains from New Mexico to Montana.[95]

The president's message to the BLM was clear: energy development was the agency's top priority, and field managers would have difficulty justifying any action that inhibited energy development on the public lands. As BLM supervisors wrote early in 2002 to field managers in Utah, the BLM "needs to ensure that existing staff understand that when an oil and gas lease parcel or when an application for permission to drill comes in the door, that this work is their No.1 priority."[96] Just two months later, BLM Assistant Director for Minerals and Resource Protection Peter Culp explained that energy companies could expect faster permit reviews, more open access to minerals, and fewer environmental regulations in the coming years.[97]

Culp's prediction was far from an empty promise. In 1999 the BLM approved 1,803 drilling permits; in 2004 the agency approved 6,399.[98] The rapid increase in drilling permits, as with leasing activity, was concentrated along the Rocky Mountains and focused even more specifically in the five major basins identified in the BLM's EPCA report. The BLM's field office in Wyoming's Powder River Basin earned the "Unit Award for Excellence of Service" in 2002 for approving more drilling permits than almost all other field offices combined. In 2004, the office broke its previous record by approving 2,720 of the agency's 6,399 drilling permits that year.[99]

Even with this remarkable growth in permits, however, the BLM lagged behind demand from energy companies, which were encouraged by the Bush administration and driven by rising oil and gas prices. Faced with growing backlogs of permit applications without a corresponding growth in staff, several of the busiest field offices began to use outside consultants paid by the oil and gas industry to process permit applications. BLM offices in Nevada accepted a similar arrangement, using industry-paid consultants to do the environment analysis for hard rock mining operations.[100]

Even more important for environmental groups, the accelerated drilling activity created a dramatic backlog on environmental monitoring. In 2005, the GAO found that the increased activity had "lessened the BLM's ability to meet its environmental protection responsibilities."[101] The GAO report noted that the BLM's Buffalo, WY, and Vernal, UT, field offices, which saw the greatest increase in drilling permits, had failed to meet their environmental inspection targets five out of the last six years, and in 2004 the Buffalo, WY, field office met only 27 percent of its inspection goals.[102]

As drilling increased and environmental review decreased, the BLM and the Bush administration received an increasingly cool reception in the West. Their insistence that the BLM open up all available lands containing oil and gas for development outraged many westerners, both Democrats and Republicans. For example, in 2003 and 2004, Utah governor Mike Leavitt (R), New Mexico governor Bill Richardson (D), and Wyoming governor Dave Freudenthal (D) all challenged BLM leasing or permitting activities in areas of unique recreational, wildlife, or scenic value. Governor Bill Richardson insisted, "We have sufficient areas in the West to drill. We don't have to go into sensitive ecological areas."[103]

What is more, the accelerated drilling revealed schisms in the Republican base in some western states, where oil and gas companies were pitted against property owners and grazing permittees. One of the most publicized detractors was Tweeti Blancett, who had run Senator Pete Domenici's (R-NM) campaign in 1996 and coordinated President Bush's 2000 campaign in part of New Mexico. She and her husband owned a ranch that included grazing permits for tens of thousands of acres of federal lands. The drilling on their grazing lands left polluted settling ponds that poisoned their cattle and otherwise disrupted livestock operations, slowly forcing the couple toward selling the ranch. "Here's what I once believed," Blancett wrote. "If the president knew about the damage done to our land by the energy industry, the damage would cease," but not even a personal meeting with BLM director Kathleen Clarke changed drilling operations on her land.[104] To Blancett, the sudden rush of drilling amounts to federal negligence: "Why would we consider opening new areas when we haven't made companies comply with existing regulations?"[105]

Blancett's attorney, herself a prominent Republican who got her start with the Mountain States Legal Foundation, which once housed James Watt and Gale Norton, explained that this was not an isolated case: "I'm amazed at the number of calls we're getting from landowners who are really frustrated with what's going on." Essentially, the pressure for energy development was fracturing the traditionally Republican bond between property rights and energy development. For some, in fact, drilling was damaging their privately owned property. These cases involved the vast areas of split estate throughout the West, where one party owns the surface land and the other party owns the subsurface mineral rights. Although in many cases the subsurface owner will essentially lease the land from the surface owner, the subsurface owner has a legal right to access the minerals whether or not the surface owner approves. This is contentious enough when the disputes are between two private parties, but it is particularly problematic when the surface is privately owned and the subsurface is federally owned. Here, leasing the subsurface rights is a political decision.[106] In early 2005, the Interior Department came under particularly strong criticism when it put new gas leases up for auction without informing the surface land owners.[107]

Elsewhere, unlikely coalitions of ranchers, environmentalists, businesspeople, and hunters were forming to oppose drilling in roadless or otherwise remote areas. From the Roan Plateau in Colorado and the Otero Mesa in New Mexico to Wyoming's Red Desert, oil and gas drilling drew truly bipartisan, grassroots opposition.[108] At hearings the BLM held in 2003 over the Roan Plateau, for example, over 90 percent of the public comments opposed drilling.[109]

While the majority of the BLM's attention went to energy development, the Bush administration also worked to remove regulatory barriers to hard rock mining. Just two months after President Bush took office, the BLM published a proposed rule to suspend provisions of the Clinton administration's new hard rock mining regulations.[110] The proposed rule came in response to complaints and lawsuits by the mining industry and the state of Nevada, which claimed that the Clinton regulations would damage the industry irreparably. In February 2001, for example, the governor of Nevada wrote to Secretary Norton:

These new regulations will, if not overturned, impose significant new and unnecessary regulatory burdens on Western States and will preclude mining companies from engaging in operations they might otherwise pursue, thereby leading to a dramatic decrease in employment and revenue in the mining sector and a corresponding decrease in tax revenue and other economic benefits to Western states. BLM's own Final Environmental Impact statement concludes that the new rules will result in a loss of up to 6,050 jobs, up to $396 million in total income and up to $877 million in total industry output.[111]

The BLM's final regulations, published on October 30, 2001, retained many features of the Clinton regulations, including a feature endorsed by the National Research Council that required mining companies to post bonds that could pay for environmental cleanup costs. However, in the final regulations the BLM eliminated the interior secretary's authority to veto mines that would cause irreparable environmental damage, arguing that it was unnecessary for public lands protection and would cause irreparable damage to the mining industry.[112]

The Clinton and Bush administration regulations reflect different interpretations of the FLPMA, which requires that the interior secretary, "by regulation or otherwise, take any action necessary to prevent unnecessary or undue degradation of the public lands."[113] Secretary Babbitt had interpreted this more literally to offer veto power over mining projects, and he had used that power to deny a permit for the Glamis gold mine in California, which was sited on lands that held religious significance for the Quechan Indian Nation.[114] The Bush administration interpreted the FLPMA provisions more narrowly as a requirement to enforce clean air and water standards and to ensure adequate cleanup after mining operations. As one *New York Times* reporter relayed, the BLM spokesman argued that "it was not fair to force a mining company to go through the lengthy permit process and then deny a permit on the basis of . . . a subjective standard."[115]

CONCLUSION: WHAT HAPPENED TO
ECOSYSTEM MANAGEMENT?

The BLM has had considerable experience dealing with the political whiplash that a change in presidential administration can bring.[116] Indeed, there is good evidence that during the second half of the twentieth century these transitions have affected the BLM's priorities more than those of any other federal land agency, contributing to ongoing confusion over the agency's primary mission and increasingly low agency morale. The Clinton administration, for example, pursued a particularly intentional and aggressive program to reshape the BLM's culture for the conceptually, legally, and politically complex task of ecosystem management. George W. Bush took office in January 2001 with a very different set of priorities for the federal lands that harkened back to the Sagebrush Rebellion days of the Reagan administration, and he was ultimately far more effective in advancing resource development than the Reagan administration.

Like the Reagan administration before, the Bush administration denounced growing environmental regulation and planning, complaining that they had led to national energy and wildfire crises. At a deeper level, the Bush administration evinced the contemporary Republican contempt for federal bureaucracy and a deep suspicion of any systems-oriented approach to public lands management, particularly ecosystems management. Given the administration's complex commitments, this translated into an attack on administrative discretion in the BLM and an emphasis on executive discretion and authority. For example, in October 2003, BLM Director Kathleen Clarke told the Interstate Oil and Gas Compact Commission that she was "dealing with an agency that I think lost some discipline, lost some accountability, did a lot of freelancing. . . . Individual priorities were pursued. Individual agendas maybe were allowed to take hold and personal interpretation of how things should be done became an issue. . . . Frankly, the hardest thing in Washington is to get the word down from the top."[117]

This placed the BLM in a difficult position. On the one hand, many BLM employees may have shared Allan Fitzsimmons's criticism of the Clinton administration's efforts to establish ecosystem management: "It turns out that the high-sounding notions [of] population ecosystem ecology are long on style and short on substance."[118] For those employees it may have been a relief to transition to an administration that emphasized action and had no interest in building a comprehensive approach to ecosystem management. On the other hand, the Bush administration's intense focus on energy development did not eliminate the agency's legal mandates for environmental regulation and planning or its mandate to serve a broad range of disparate interests. Although Director Clarke later apologized to the BLM for her criticism about the agency's lack of discipline and its field discretion, she reflected the Bush administration's insistence that the White House would set multiple-use priorities, thus limiting the room that BLM field managers had to fulfill other parts of the agency's complex mission. As a result, President

Bush and the BLM found themselves not only in the middle of disputes between environmentalists and natural resource industries but also between mining industries with strong White House support and grazing permittees whose allotments were affected by energy development.

Thus, as with past efforts by both Democratic and Republican administrations to exert greater centralized control over the agency, the Bush administration highlighted the difficulty of balancing the flexibility necessary for site-specific land management with centralized accountability. The transition from the Clinton administration to the Bush administration also highlighted the fact that the BLM's mandates are diverse enough and its political support weak enough that future administrations will be able to push the agency in very different directions.

Conclusion

Bruce Babbitt recently published a series of reflections on the lessons that he learned as secretary of the interior from 1993 to 2001, called *Cities in the Wilderness: A New Vision of Land Use in America*. The purpose of *Cities in the Wilderness*, Babbitt explains, "is to show how we can prevent the loss of natural and cultural landscapes and watersheds through stronger federal leadership in land use planning."[1] He points out that land use is often treated as a local matter in the United States, "obscuring the historical reality that the national government has been involved in land use planning since the early days of the republic."[2] This role has always raised important questions about the authority and scale of federal land policy and management that go to the heart of debate about federalism and democracy in the United States.

One of the most revealing sections of the book comes at the end of the first chapter, where Babbitt contrasts the success of watershed planning in Florida and California with the failure of planning in the Mississippi-Missouri watershed. In these three cases, Babbitt had radically different experiences with the Army Corps of Engineers, which is responsible for a great deal of river basin planning. In Florida and California the Corps supported Secretary Babbitt's proposals for ecological restoration, while in the Mississippi-Missouri watershed they helped thwart his efforts.

The problem, Babbitt argues, is that "Corps projects do not flow from policy set by the executive branch in Washington; they reflect the priorities of individual members of Congress carried out through the classic log-rolling process within appropriations committees. . . . The budget of the Corps reflects, not a national policy, but the aggregate sum of what individual members of Congress want."[3] The problem, in other words, is the lack of a systematic, rational approach to national land and watershed use planning. Babbitt recounts flying over the Missouri River at 30,000 feet in 2002. From that altitude, he writes,

> it was not difficult to imagine the bottomland forests that once wrapped an emerald ribbon all the way across Missouri, sheltering and feeding vast flocks of ducks, geese, sand hill cranes, plovers, and songbirds. And it was easy to visualize restoring the forests by simply removing the levees and allowing the river to reclaim its floodplain, letting it meander back and forth between the natural levees of the surrounding hilly uplands.[4]

Babbitt explained to the passenger sitting next to him, "The entire river corridor from St. Louis to Kansas City should be a national park. Imagine re-creating the river that Lewis and Clark saw when they set out from St. Louis to discover and lay claim to the continent."[5]

Babbitt's comments are revealing because what he saw from 30,000 feet was a land free of the politics, political precedent, and federal bureaucratic cultures that he had struggled against during his eight years in Washington. Federal land use planning, he argues, "must begin with a consideration of exactly what the national interest consists of," because this is a conversation that "with few exceptions we have not engaged."[6] The national interest for Babbitt seems to have referred to a scale or scope of perspective. It is, metaphorically, the view from 30,000 feet rather than from a particular ranch, sawmill, or mine. Yet this view is difficult to maintain, because to implement it one must return again to the complex details of resource allocation.[7]

In many ways, this reflects the central struggle, largely but not exclusively by Democratic administrations and environmental groups, to redefine and reform public lands policy and the BLM. It has been a struggle to redraw the physical and discursive boundaries of the public lands in order to reshape them as a comprehensive and cohesive *system* of *national lands* that is managed in service of the *national interest*. This struggle has existed since Secretary Ickes began fighting with Farrington Carpenter over proper implementation of the Taylor Grazing Act in the 1930s, and it has been at the center of BLM politics since the agency's formation in 1946. This struggle is the centripetal force that has pushed the BLM toward a more systems-oriented approach to public lands management. The BLM's primary means to achieving this has been through the growth of inventory data, comprehensive planning, agency professionalization, and noncommercial programs that appeal to a broader national constituency.

Looking back through BLM history, gradual success in systematizing public lands management can be seen in both symbolic and substantive steps. It began as soon as the BLM's budget started to recover from the drastic cuts of 1947 and the agency started to build a professional range program. It appeared in a number of simple, symbolic steps in the 1960s—the BLM's first comprehensive plan in 1960, "Project 2012," the agency's new emblem in 1964, the first state and national maps of the public lands produced in the mid-1960s—and more substantive steps like the agency's classification and planning programs, the growth of its recreation and wildlife programs, and new multiple-use legislation. This trend continued with a rapid burst in the 1970s through the BLM's responsibility for National Environmental Policy Act (NEPA) implementation, endangered species and wild horses and burros protection, and planning under the Federal Land Policy and Management Act (FLPMA) of 1976.

As a result, the BLM's workforce and culture have shifted from that of a bureau of livestock and mines to something far more complex. Beginning especially in the 1970s after NEPA and FLPMA, the agency hired an entirely new cadre of professional "ologists" to focus on wildlife, ecology, archeology, recreation, and so on in the planning process. As these employees moved up through BLM ranks, arriving in top leadership positions during the Clinton administration, they began to change the agency's priorities and culture from the inside to match the statutory and clientele shifts that had occurred on the outside since the 1960s.

This is not to say that the BLM's systematic planning and noncommercial programs replaced the agency's traditional commitments to commercial resource development and commercial resource users, nor did they replace the fierce independence and decentralized decision making of BLM field managers. Instead the new programs and emphases grew alongside the agency's commercial resource programs, sometimes complementing them and sometimes challenging them. In *Cities in the Wilderness*, Babbitt describes his encounters in Florida, California, and the Midwest with the "enormous political obstacles inherent in multistate river restoration planning."[8] In the case of the BLM, Babbitt struggled even more generally against the power of political and institutional precedent in public lands patronage. Indeed, his failure to achieve overarching rangeland or mining reform in 1993 and 1994 is a testament to the tremendous durability of certain property rights regimes embedded in public lands law, politics, and administration. It is a reminder that no president, secretary, BLM director, or congressional leader will ever be able to wipe the public lands slate clean. Public lands policy and management have an inertia built upon the long history of public lands patronage, the deep resistance that many members of Congress have to federal regulation of the public lands, and entrenched elements of the BLM's culture that are resistant to centralized coordination and accountability. These factors serve as centrifugal forces that maintain the fragmented character of public lands policy and management.

Resistance to visions of comprehensive public lands planning and regulation has been clearly visible in the history of the public lands and the BLM, bubbling into a full-blown Sagebrush Rebellion twice during the agency's short history— once in the 1940s and once again in the late 1970s and early 1980s.[9] Resistance is based upon property rights regimes that Congress in particular has sustained over the years, as members of Congress have chosen to view the public lands from the perspective of their constituents rather than from 30,000 feet. Ranchers, for example, have long insisted that they hold something like a common law property right to the public range. Even though the federal courts have consistently repudiated this claim, Congress has often encouraged it by its treatment of grazing fees, permit tenure, and grazing levels.[10] Mining companies have insisted that the very future of mineral development depends upon an extremely liberal patronage system for federal minerals, and their supporters in Congress and the White House defended the existing system as a matter of national security.

These forces are part of the reason why, as Secretary Babbitt laments, we have not been able to articulate a clear national interest in the public lands. For many years members of Congress argued that the national interest would be best met by fulfilling the economic interests of particular land users. Efforts to replace this articulation of the national interest with something more "national" were slow to take hold. These are, after all, the lands that the federal government tried to give to the western states; they are the lands that even in the 1970s were still open to homesteading; they are the lands that were only recently declared "permanent" federal lands in 1976; and they are the lands that have not generally been identified on road atlases or other general maps. All of this is to say that against the claims that ranchers, miners, loggers, and a few recreational users staked on the public lands in the first two thirds of the twentieth century, the BLM has struggled to articulate the public lands' national value, to build a national constituency, and to think of itself as a national agency.

At the beginning of the twenty-first century, then, the BLM is still an agency in search of a mission. Other agencies like the Forest Service may also lack a unifying mission today, but the Forest Service is now in search of a different mission from the one that guided it through the first half of the twentieth century. The BLM, by contrast, has always been looking.

Secretary Babbitt never succeeded in bringing a new perspective to the public lands as a whole, which is why he packed his bags after the 1994 elections and spent much of his eight years traveling and working in the West. There he found opportunities to bring a new perspective to specific areas of public lands through national monument designation and planning, habitat conservation plans, the Northwest Forest Plan, and so on. In these specific cases he had the power to force at least temporary consensus among competing interests, because they knew that Babbitt or the courts would act unilaterally if they failed to agree. Beyond these specific efforts, Babbitt was forced to approach public lands policy and the BLM itself with what BLM consultants in the 1960s had called a strategy of becoming. He worked to plant a vision of comprehensive, systematic, ecosystems-oriented management within the agency's organization, culture, and management priorities. He could only provide the seed of that vision, and the way that it has taken root and grown in the twenty-first century reflects a host of other influences.

THE PUBLIC LANDS PUZZLE

At the beginning of the twenty-first century, public lands policy and management remain an interesting puzzle that can be explained primarily through their complex history. Laws governing the public lands, from the Mining Law of 1872 to the California Desert Protection Act of 1994, have accumulated over more than a century, reflecting shifting national and regional concerns for resource development and environmental protection. The fact that these laws give the BLM overlapping and conflicting mandates should come as no surprise, because Congress passed these laws in response to the overlapping and often conflicting interests that Americans have in the public lands.

On the one hand, the conflicts and ambiguity of public lands law is a symptom of the law's sheer size and complexity, a problem that is common to any bureaucracy or system. Programmers at Microsoft, for example, are finding it more and more challenging to write new versions of the popular operating system Windows. Because Microsoft promises to make new versions compatible with older versions, programmers can never start with a clean slate. They must add functions and correct problems by inserting new code into the literally tens of millions of lines of code that already exist. In this process, new functions that programmers test often conflict with existing commands in the program, causing it to malfunction or crash.[11] The same basic principle is at work in public land law, for Congress is continually adding new functions and responsibilities to a complex mix of public lands laws. Sometimes, as was the case with NEPA, Congress does not anticipate what impact the new law will have on the BLM's existing responsibilities and practices.

On the other hand, however, conflict over the public lands is not simply about complexity. Conflicts and contradictions in public lands law and management are a reflection of the ambiguous place that the public lands have always had in American history. They are at one and the same time the vast frontier of opportunity, the desolate wasteland unfit for settlement, the recreational wilderness, and so on. They are legally federal, and therefore national, lands, but politically and geographically they are very clearly western lands.

This ambiguity is reflected in the BLM as well, as it searches for a mission and an identity that will build stronger national support. The BLM's staff, like the public lands laws themselves, reflect the accretion of responsibilities over the years. From a collection of range, mineral, forestry, and lands and realty staff, the BLM has expanded to become a relatively diverse agency. Since NEPA and FLPMA, the BLM has hired a host of new staff for what might be called amenity or environmental programs: wildlife biologists, environmental specialists, archeologists, wilderness and recreation specialists, and others. At times the new staff has supported the agency's traditional programs and culture; at other times they have provided a clear challenge. As these employees have moved to top leadership positions, they have elevated the concerns of their professions within the agency.

In a similar sense, the profile of public lands users has changed dramatically over the last sixty years. The West is no longer predominately rural, nor is its economy based primarily on natural resource development. BLM field staff must now manage the full spectrum of public lands users and interests, from traditional commercial clientele to new recreational and environmental clientele. Furthermore, many BLM field staff now work with a decidedly urban clientele from Las Vegas, Salt Lake City, Phoenix, Denver, and other cities. Public lands policy and management will continue to change in response to these evolving physical pressures on the public lands and political pressures on the BLM.

KEY ISSUES FOR THE TWENTY-FIRST CENTURY

This project is a historical account of the BLM and is not intended to offer prescriptive solutions to the complex public lands policy and management problems that confront the agency. Indeed, the contingencies and particularities traced above in the agency's history demonstrate that no final solution to public lands policy and management is possible. Nonetheless, as the BLM turns sixty this year, it may be time for new reflection and debate about the direction in which public lands policy and the BLM are headed. In particular, it may be time for Congress and the president to convene a new public land commission to review the overall policies and administration of federal land.

There have been four principal public land commissions in U.S. history, and each of them has marked major transitions in federal land policy:[12] the Public Land Commission of 1879–1883,[13] the Public Lands Commission of 1903–1905,[14] the Committee on the Conservation and Administration of the Public Domain of 1929–1931,[15] and the Public Land Law Review Commission of 1964–1970.[16] Between 1879 and 1970, the federal government undertook a massive review of federal land policy and management every twenty to thirty years.

The Public Land Law Review Commission (PLLRC) of 1964–1970 completed the most comprehensive study of federal land policy and management to date. Still, it has now been nearly forty years since that commission released its report in 1970, and there have been a number of important changes in federal land policy, politics, and management that warrant review. Indeed, the PLLRC began its work just at the moment when ecosystems-oriented policy and citizen participation were beginning to take hold in federal law and management, as evidenced by the NEPA of 1969 and the Endangered Species Act (ESA) of 1973. Consequently, the PLLRC's report and recommendations are anachronistic, for they reflect the tensions in federal land management from the 1960s rather than in the 1970s and beyond.

Since the late 1960s, the goals of federal land management have changed, and the procedural requirements for administrative decision making have expanded. As noted in the introduction, the goals and the decision-making processes of federal land policy and management are closely linked, for interest groups demand decision-making processes that will favor their goals. Commercial land users have generally favored limited federal regulation and decentralized management to promote resource development. Environmental groups have generally favored federal regulation and public participation on a national level to give their constituents in the East and in western urban centers greater leverage. A new land review commission will need to deal with the relationship between the statutory goals and procedures that Congress has established for federal land agencies, recognizing that at times the two sets of mandates work in harmony, but at other times they work against one another.

If Congress or the president convenes another public land commission in the twenty-first century, then, there are a number of key issues that would need to be on the table. First, the commission would need to address new ecological and environmental interests in the public lands. These are represented by the rise of ecosystem management during the 1990s and the federal government's commitment to habitat and ecosystem *restoration*. These goals are radically different from those that guided federal land policy in the nineteenth century and most of the twentieth century, which dealt generally with *preserving* particular land areas — parks, monuments, and so on — and *conserving* natural resources.[17] Laws such as the ESA, as interpreted by the courts, require something farther reaching, including the preservation and *restoration* of endangered species habitat. The scope of these commitments, as evidenced by the Northwest Forest Plan, the California Desert Protection Act, restoration of the Everglades, and others, is enormous.

Second, the commission would need to address the question of collaboration in public lands management, for questions about decision-making processes are as contentious as questions about policy and management goals. If federal land agencies are to look beyond their jurisdictional boundaries in order to focus on protecting whole ecosystems, they will need additional tools and incentives to achieve interagency cooperation while meeting their own primary responsibilities. This type of cooperation has worked to a limited extent in some areas, such as in the greater Yellowstone ecosystem, but interagency cooperation will always remain a challenge. Likewise, federal land agencies need clearer guidelines for collaborating with private groups, both commercial groups and environmental groups, and state governments in land management projects. With tight budgets, federal land agencies are seeking ways to share the cost of land management initiatives with outside groups, raising questions about agencies being co-opted by interests that run counter to their congressionally mandated responsibilities. More generally, collaboration gives certain government officials, groups, and individuals greater influence over policy and management decisions, raising important questions of political justice.

More specifically, the commission would need to review the impact of outsourcing on the BLM and the Forest Service. The outsourcing trend started in earnest during the Clinton administration, and the George W. Bush administration increased outsourcing exponentially.[18] Increased fiscal efficiency is certainly a worthy goal for the federal government, but it is not and has never been *the criterion* for federal lands. Indeed, one of the primary justifications for federal land ownership is to shield the federal lands from the vicissitudes of market efficiency.

Third, the commission would need to address the role of scientific research and data in ecosystem management and the relationship of these data to public participation and deliberation. Secretary Babbitt tried to establish a U.S. Biological Survey to bolster public trust in the quality of federal science, an initiative that ultimately failed. Academic science relies on a peer review process to weed out bad science and faulty assumptions. There is room in the academy for extensive trial and error. In federal land management, science takes on even higher stakes, because management decisions based on this science often impose immediate restrictions on land and resource use. Good science is indispensable to federal land management, both in setting management priorities and in measuring management success or failure. Good science, however, is not sufficient to guide the values and goals of land management; these need to be established through the political process.

Fourth, the commission should return to a host of questions about the basic property rights regimes that govern the public lands, particularly rangelands. Commitments to habitat and ecosystem restoration, along with growing public lands recreation, challenge the property rights regimes that have governed public lands range for half a century. The commission should examine very closely the legal and political limitations that the BLM faces in adjudicating these challenges. In particular, the commission should address whether the BLM may issue *nonuse* leases and permits for range to the highest bidder, allowing private markets to determine whether or not public lands are grazed. In many cases today, for example, environmental groups are prepared to buy out and retire grazing permits from willing ranchers, reducing the overall grazing levels on the public lands, yet there has been ongoing controversy over these initiatives.[19]

Likewise, a new commission would need to address the growing importance of mineral development—specifically energy development—on federal lands, and the property rights regimes that give preference to mineral development over other land uses. The PLLRC argued that in many cases mining should be the dominant use of federal lands, and a new commission would have to return to this question. In particular, what are the circumstances under which federal land agencies or the secretaries of Interior should close an area of federal land to mineral development? The Arctic National Wildlife Refuge is an excellent case that illustrates this problem. The commission would also need to revisit the Mining Law of 1872, the most archaic and outdated public lands law on the books that governs hard rock minerals such as gold and silver. Congress has placed a moratorium on patenting mining claims, suggesting that there is support for revision of the law.

The first four issues deal with broad questions of national priorities for both public lands goals and decision-making processes. In addition, the commission should return to some more specific questions that have haunted the BLM for sixty years. A new commission should examine the possibility of significant land exchanges and sales, with both private landowners and state governments, that would simplify federal land boundaries. This is particularly important in the case of the public lands, which are scattered among state and private lands and include many small and isolated tracts. The last attempt at a systemwide adjustment of land jurisdiction and boundaries took place during the Reagan administration, and it failed to a considerable extent. Congress and the Clinton administration made some progress on land exchanges in Utah, Nevada, the California Desert, and Oregon, and the new commission should look for ways to encourage these activities on a broader scale. In particular, the commission should look for ways to eliminate private and state inholdings in special designation areas of public lands like national monuments and national conservation areas. It addition, it may be time to revisit the possibility of exchanging land between the Forest Service and the BLM or merging the two agencies to reduce at least one layer of confusion and tension in federal land administration. In reviewing land exchange possibilities, the commission would need to look closely at land appraisal methods, which have caused enormous controversy during the last two administrations.

A new public land commission should reexamine the land use planning systems employed by the BLM and the Forest Service. These planning systems have grown increasingly expensive and cumbersome without commensurate benefits, and there are still some legitimate concerns that these planning systems are not the locus of decision making for the agencies. As Roger Sedjo has recently argued, if the systems do not resolve land use conflicts in any clear way they should at least be streamlined so that they will work more quickly and less expensively.[20]

At the end of the commission's review of federal land policy and management, it may or may not be able to articulate a clear mission for the BLM in the twenty-first century. To the extent that it succeeds, it should consider giving the public lands a new name that will reflect this. Even if the commission cannot articulate a clear mission for the BLM, it should encourage Congress to provide permanent statutory authority for the name "National System of Public Lands," which Interior Secretary Dirk Kempthorne authorized administratively in December 2008. This would convey their status alongside the national forest, national park, and national wildlife refuge systems.

There should be no illusion that a new commission will resolve public lands conflicts any more than past commissions did. Public lands law will remain complex, and it is highly unlikely that Congress will provide any comprehensive overhaul of public lands law in the near future. Rather, Congress will continue to pass specific new laws and amendments that push specific BLM programs or land management areas in one direction or another. Nonetheless, a new commission can make an important contribution by reframing political debate and restructuring congressional priorities.

Whatever Congress does or does not accomplish in the near future, public lands policy and management will remain dynamic, particularly because of likely changes within the agency. Turnover through retirement has already gained momentum in the BLM, and some 40 percent of all BLM employees were eligible for retirement in 2008.[21] The BLM faces an incredible loss of institutional memory from this turnover, and it has taken only the most modest steps to try to capture some of this asset. The BLM's internal culture will depend largely on how quickly these employees choose to retire and with whom the BLM chooses to replace its retiring staff. Today the BLM is a bureau of livestock, mines, landscapes, monuments, and so forth. What the BLM will be in another sixty years, assuming that it continues to survive in a fairly hostile political environment, remains an open-ended question.

APPENDIX A

Public Lands by State

State	Total Land Area (Million Acres)	BLM Surface Land (Million Acres)	BLM Subsurface Mineral Estate (Million Acres)	BLM Mineral Operations On Tribal Lands (Million Acres)
Alaska	365.5	81.1	237	1.2
Arizona	72.7	12.2	35.8	20.7
California	100.2	15.2	47.5	.6
Colorado	66.5	8.3	29	.8
Idaho	52.9	11.6	36.5	.6
Montana	93.3	7.9	37.8	5.5
Nevada	70.3	47.8	58.7	1.2
New Mexico	77.8	13.3	36	8.4
Oregon	61.6	16.1	33.9	.8
Utah	52.7	22.8	35.2	2.3
Washington	42.7	.4	12.5	2.6
Wyoming	62.3	18.3	41.6	1.9
Eastern States		1	40	2.3

Source: Figures taken from "Public Land Statistics 2007" (Washington, DC: Bureau of Land Management, 2008).
Note: The BLM's eastern states office has jurisdiction over lands and resources in 31 states located along and east of the Mississippi River.

APPENDIX B

Significant Public Lands Laws and Administrative Policies

1780–1934		Congress passed thousands of land and resource disposal laws designed to encourage the transfer of land and natural resources from federal to private ownership. Laws included: Homestead Law of 1862, Morrill Law of 1862, Lode Mining Law of 1866, Placer Mining Law of 1870, General Mining Law of 1872, Coal Lands Law of 1873, Timber Cultural Law of 1873, Desert Land Law of 1877, Timber and Stone Law of 1878, General Public Lands Reform Law of 1891, Carey Land Law of 1894, Homestead Law extended to Alaska in 1898, Coal Lands Law extended to Alaska in 1900, Reclamation Law of 1902, Enlarged Homestead Law of 1909, Three-Year Homestead Law of 1912, Stockraising Homestead Law of 1916, Mineral Leasing Law of 1920, and the Recreation Law of 1926. Several of these laws, which are included in the list below, continued to guide public lands management through much of the twentieth century.
1872	General Mining Law	30 U.S.C. §§21–54, 19 Stat. 91. The law was designed to consolidate and reshape existing hard rock mining laws. Its opening line reads, "All valuable mineral deposits in lands belonging to the United States . . . are hereby declared to be free and open to exploration, and purchase, and the lands in which they are found to occupation and purchase, by citizens of the United States."[1]

1920	Mineral Leasing Law	30 U.S.C. §181 *et seq.* Ended mineral land patenting for certain minerals, such as oil and gas. The new law made mineral lands available for lease on a discretionary basis and charged a royalty on all minerals extracted.
1926	Recreation Act	44 Stat. 741. Allowed sale or lease of public lands to state and local governments for recreational purposes.
1934	Taylor Grazing Act	43 U.S.C. §§315–3160, P.L. 73-482. Established the Grazing Division to regulate grazing on 80 million acres (quickly expanded to 142 million acres) of public lands. Law was intended to improve the range and stabilize the western livestock industry.
1937	Oregon and California Revested Lands Sustained Yield Management Act	P.L. 75-405. Instituted sustained yield management for the timber-rich Oregon and California Revested Lands (O & C Lands). Responsibility for this act was placed in the General Land Office.
1938	Small Tract Act	52 Stat. 609, as amended in 1954 by 68 Stat. 239. Permitted the sale or lease of tracts of 5 acres or less primarily for homesites.
1946	President Truman's Reorganization Plan No. 3	President Truman created the BLM in 1946 by merging the General Land Office and the U.S. Grazing Service into a single agency. To block the reorganization, the Congress had to pass concurrent resolutions against it. The House passed such a resolution, but the Senate did not, and the plan became law on July 16.
1947	Acquired Minerals Leasing Act	43 U.S.C. §§351–3600, 61 Stat. 913, 915. Extended minerals leasing to lands acquired by the federal government.
1947	Materials Act	P.L. 80-291. Authorized the BLM to dispose of timber, sand, gravel, and several other common minerals.
1948	O & C Mining	P.L. 80-477. Opened the O & C lands to entry under the Mining Law of 1872, with the exception that the timber resources would remain in federal ownership.

1952	Halogeton Glomeratus Control Act	7 U.S.C. §§1651–1656, P.L. 82-529. Authorized a program to eradicate *Halogeton glomeratus*, a poisonous weed. This bill greatly advanced the BLM's range appropriations, which had been slashed in 1946.
1953	Submerged Lands Act	P.L. 83-31. Granted submerged "tidelands" to the states out to between 3 and 10.5 miles from shore. This settled an important dispute between the states and the federal government over mineral leasing and royalties.
1953	Outer Continental Shelf Lands Act	43 U.S.C. §§1331 *et seq.*, P.L. 83-212. Established federal control and mineral leasing for lands beyond state-owned submerged lands out to the edge of the continental shelf. Lessees were required to pay a royalty rate of not less than 12.5 percent.
1954	Recreation and Public Purposes Act	43 U.S.C. §§869 *et seq.*, P.L. 83-387. Allowed sale or lease of public lands to state and local governments for recreational purposes.
1954	Taylor Act Acreage	P.L. 83-375. Abolished the 142-million-acre limit on the grazing districts.
1954	Multiple Mineral Development Act	30 U.S.C. §§521–531, P.L. 83-585. Permitted multiple mineral development activities on a single piece of land.
1955	Multiple Surface Use Mining Act	30 U.S.C. §§611–615, P.L. 84-167. Provided for the development of multiple minerals on the same tract of public lands.
1955	Grazing Fee Increase	New grazing fee formula for the grazing districts raised fees from $.12 to $.15 per animal unit month (AUM). The National Advisory Board Council approved the new formula.
1958	Grazing Fee Increase	Fees rose again from $.15 to $.22 per AUM.
1958	Alaska Statehood Act	P.L. 85-508. Permitted the state of Alaska to select 102,950,000 acres of public lands within 25 years.
1958	Recreation Policy Statement	Secretary of the interior approved a formal statement that directed the BLM to identify areas of high recreational value.

1959	Recreation Law Amendments	P.L. 86-66. Raised the limit under the Recreation and Public Purposes Act from 640 to 6,400 acres.
1960	Public Lands Administration Act	P.L. 86-649. Gave the BLM broader administrative authority.
1960	Mineral Leasing Amendments	P.L. 86-705. Amended the mineral leasing act of 1920 to encourage more mineral prospecting.
1961	Land Application Moratorium	Secretary of the Interior Stewart Udall ordered an 18-month moratorium on nonmineral land applications—2/14/61–9/4/62—to allow the BLM to reduce its backlog of almost 45,000 such applications.
1962	Recreational Facilities Appropriations	BLM received its first appropriations for recreational facilities construction through the Accelerated Public Works Act of 1962 (P.L. 87-658).
1963	Grazing Fee Increase	Following a 2-year study of grazing fees, the secretary of the interior implemented a new fee formula that set grazing fees at 150 percent of the average price of beef per pound. Under the new formula the BLM's grazing fee rose from $0.19 to $0.30 per AUM.
1963	Resource Conservation Areas	Secretary Udall created 85 resource conservation areas to emphasize conservation priorities.[2]
1963	The Vale Project	The BLM received additional funding for range conservation in the Vale district. The project was intended to showcase the possibilities of strong conservation management.
1964	First Regular Appropriations for Recreation	P.L. 88-356. Congress authorized the BLM's first regular appropriations for recreation, providing $700,000 for sanitation and recreational facilities.
1964	Public Land Law Review Commission	P.L. 88-606. Established the Public Land Law Review Commission (PLLRC), which conducted the most comprehensive review of federal land law to date. The PLLRC was given until December 31, 1968, to submit its report to Congress, and it received a budget of $4,000,000. P.L. 90-213, 81 Stat. 660, extended the deadline until June 30, 1970, and increased the budget to $7,390,000.

1964	Classification and Multiple Use Act	P.L. 88-607. Gave the BLM temporary authority to classify the public lands as suitable for retention and multiple-use management or disposal under existing law. This authority expired with the release of the PLLRC's report.
1964	Public Land Sales Act	P.L. 88-608. Gave the BLM broader temporary authority to sell public lands that were suitable for disposal or which the agency did not need. This authority also expired with the release of the PLLRC's report.
1964	The Wilderness Act	16 U.S.C. §§1131–1136, P.L. 88-577. Established the National Wilderness Preservation System, composed of federal lands congressionally designated as wilderness areas. The secretaries of Agriculture and Interior were charged with reviewing federal lands and recommending areas suitable for wilderness. *The act excluded the public lands from wilderness review.*
1965	Scientific Natural Areas	Secretary Udall designated 16 scientific natural areas to highlight the natural wonders and value of the public lands.
1967	Red Rocks Recreation Lands	BLM designated its first recreation area under the Classification and Multiple Use Act.
1968	Wild and Scenic Rivers Act	16 U.S.C. §§1271–1287, P.L. 90-542. Authorizes preservation of designated free-flowing rivers. As of 2004, the BLM managed 38 wild and scenic rivers, totaling 2,061 miles.[3]
1968	National Trails System Act	16 U.S.C. §§1241–1251, PL 90-543. Authorized the establishment of a national trails system made up of recreation and scenic trails. As of 2004 the BLM managed portions of 2 trails—the Continental Divide National Scenic Trail and the Pacific Crest National Scenic Trail—totaling 640 miles.
1968	Johnny Horizon	BLM created a public lands icon, named Johnny Horizon, to raise awareness of the public lands.
1968	Primitive Areas	BLM established its first primitive area in Arizona and Utah under the Classification and Multiple Use Act.

1968	Pryor Mountains Wild Horse Range	Secretary Udall created the BLM's first wild horse range on the Montana-Wyoming border.
1969	Grazing Fee Formula	Secretary of the Interior Stewart Udall published a new grazing fee schedule that would raise the fees to $1.23 per AUM over a 10-year period.
1969	Comprehensive Planning	The BLM published final regulations for its first comprehensive multiple-use planning system.
1970	National Environmental Policy Act of 1969 (NEPA)	42 U.S.C. §§4321–4347, PL 91-109. Established a federal policy on environmental protection and required agencies to prepare environmental impact statements (EISs) for each major federal action.
1970	Geothermal Steam Act	30 U.S.C. §§1001–1027, as amended 1977, 1988, and 1993. Authorized the leasing of geothermal energy on the public lands.
1970	King Range National Conservation Area	Congress established the BLM's first national conservation area in the King Range of California. As of 2004 the BLM managed 17 national conservation areas totaling 15.4 million acres.[4]
1970	*One Third of the Nation's Land*	The Public Land Law Review Commission released its report, sparking congressional debate about passing an organic act for the BLM.
1971	Alaska Native Claims Settlement Act	43 U.S.C. §§1601–1624, P.L. 92-203. Authorized Alaska Natives to select 44 million acres of public lands in Alaska and granted them $962 million to relinquish other outstanding land claims.
1971	Wild and Free-Roaming Horse and Burro Act	16 U.S.C. §§1331–1340, P.L. 92-195. Protects wild and free-roaming horses and burros on federal land from capture, harassment, and hunting.
1971	Snake River Birds of Prey Area	Protects raptor nesting areas.
1972	Federal Advisory Committee Act	P.L. 92-463. Placed new limits on and procedures for advisory boards, task forces, and committees that advise the federal government.

1973	*NRDC v. Morton*	388 F.Supp. 829, 1974. The Natural Resources Defense Council (NRDC) sued the BLM to require it to prepare an environmental impact statement (EIS) for each grazing district and won.
1973	Endangered Species Act (NEPA)	16 U.S.C. §§1531–1544. Provides protection for plants and animals that are deemed threatened or endangered by extinction.
1973	The Trans-Alaska Pipeline Act	30 U.S.C. §185. Authorizes the secretary of the interior to determine the suitability of public lands for oil and gas pipeline rights-of-way and to issue rights-of-way permits for construction of the Trans-Alaska pipeline.
1976	Federal Land Policy and Management Act (FLPMA)	43 U.S.C. §§1701–1782, P.L. 94-579. Commonly referred to as the BLM's organic act, FLPMA provides the BLM with comprehensive, multiple-use authority.
1977	Surface Mining Control and Reclamation Act	30 U.S.C. §§1201–1328, P.L. 95-87. Provides the secretary of the interior with greater authority to regulate surface coal mining and reclamation activities.
1978	Public Rangelands Improvement Act	43 U.S.C. §§1901–1908, P.L. 95-514. Reaffirmed the national policy of protecting and improving the public lands range.
1980	Alaska National Interest Lands Conservation Act	43 U.S.C. §§1602–1784, P.L. 96-487. Established millions of acres of national parks, forests, wilderness areas, and wildlife refuges in Alaska.
1980	Jurisdictional Transfer Program (BLM/FS Interchange)	This was a failed attempt to consolidate BLM and Forest Service lands to reduce overlapping jurisdictions and administrative redundancy.
1980	The Paperwork Reduction Act	44 U.S.C. §§3501–3520. Requires federal agencies to use automated technologies to reduce the information processing burden for the federal government and the general public.
1981	Interior and Related Agencies Appropriations Act	42 U.S.C. 6508. Authorizes competitive oil and gas leasing in the National Petroleum Reserve.
1982	Federal Oil and Gas Royalty Management Act	30 U.S.C. §§1701–1757, P.L. 97-451. Increased regulation, inspection, and enforcement of onshore oil and gas activity.

1987	Federal Onshore Oil and Gas Leasing Reform Act	30 U.S.C. §§226, *et seq.*, P.L. 100-203. Made all onshore oil and gas leasing subject to competitive bid.
1987	Clean Water Act (Amendments)	33 U.S.C. §1251 *et seq.* Provides the BLM with objectives for protecting the nation's water.
1987	Federal Land Exchange Facilitation Act	43 U.S.C. §1716, 102 Stat. 1086. Amends FLPMA to streamline federal land exchange procedures.
1990	Clean Air Act (Amendments)	42 U.S.C. §§7401 *et seq.*, P.L. 101-549. Directs the BLM to protect air quality and meet designated federal air quality standards.
1993	The Government Performance and Results Act of 1993	P.L. 103-62. Required 10 federal agencies, including the BLM, to launch a 3-year pilot project to develop annual performance plans that ties management activities to performance goals.
1994	The California Desert Protection Act of 1994	16 U.S.C. §410, P.L. 103-433. Established boundaries and management goals for areas in the California Desert, including 69 new wilderness areas.
1996	The Electronic FOIA Act	P.L. 104-231. Requires that federal agencies make more information available in electronic format to the public.
1996	The Information Technology Management Reform Act	P.L. 104-106. Requires federal agencies to use information technologies to improve service and performance.
1996	Establishment of the Grand Staircase–Escalante National Monument	Proclamation No. 6920, September 18, 1996.
1998	Utah School Lands Act	P.L. 103-93. Permitted the secretary of the interior to exchange public lands in Utah. Secretary Babbitt used this act to acquire Utah state lands within the Grand Staircase–Escalante National Monument.
1998	Southern Nevada Public Land Management Act	P.L. 105-263. Authorizes the disposal of public lands in Clark County, Nevada (primarily for the expansion of Las Vegas) and acquisition of environmentally sensitive lands in Nevada.

2000	National Landscape Conservation System (NLCS)	Established by order of the secretary of the interior, the NLCS serves as an administrative category for the BLM's special conservation and preservation areas.
2000	Energy Policy/ Conservation Act Amendment	P.L. 106-469. Directs the interior secretary to inventory all onshore oil and gas reserves and to identify obstacles to energy development.
2003	Healthy Forests Restoration Act	P.L. 108-148. Authorizes the BLM to expedite hazardous fuel reduction projects, particularly in wildland/urban interface areas.
2005	Energy Policy Act	P.L. 109-58. Directs the BLM to ensure reliable energy production.
1970– 2009	In addition, Congress passed a number of acts authorizing specific lands exchanges and establishing a number of National Conservation Areas and Wilderness Areas on public lands that are now part of the National Landscape Conservation System.	

Sources: This table is drawn substantially from "Digest of Federal Resource Laws of Interest to the U.S. Fish and Wildlife Service" (Washington, DC: U.S. Fish and Wildlife Service, 1992); "Public Land Statistics, 2003"; Dana and Fairfax, *Forest and Range Policy*; Muhn and Stuart, *Opportunity and Challenge*; Thomas Schroth, ed., *Congress and the Nation, 1945–1964: A Review of Government and Politics in the Postwar Years*, 1st ed. (Washington, DC: Congressional Quarterly Service,1965).

1. Mayer and George, *Public Domain, Private Domain*, 44.

2. *Our Public Lands* 13, no. 3 (January 1964).

3. "The Bureau of Land Management's National Landscape Conservation System" (Washington, DC: Bureau of Land Management, 2004).

4. Ibid.

APPENDIX C

BLM National Monuments

State	Name	Date	Designation	BLM Acres
Arizona	Agua Fria	01/00	Proclamation 7263	71,100
	Grand Canyon–Parashant	01/00	Proclamation 7265	808,724
	Ironwood Forest	06/00	Proclamation 7330	129,022
	Sonoran Desert	01/01	Proclamation 7397	486,603
	Vermillion Cliffs	11/00	Proclamation 7374	279,558
California	California Coastal	01/00	Proclamation 7264	883
	Carrizo Plain	01/01	Proclamation 7393	204,107
	Santa Rosa–San Jacinto	10/00	PL 106-351	86,400
Colorado	Canyons of the Ancients	06/00	Proclamation 7317	163,892
Idaho	Craters of the Moon	11/00	Proclamation 7373	273,847
Montana	Pompeys Pillar	01/01	Proclamation 7396	51
	Upper Missouri Breaks	01/01	Proclamation 7398	374,976
New Mexico	Kasha-Katuwe Tent Rocks	01/01	Proclamation 7394	4,124
Oregon	Cascade-Siskiyou	06/00	Proclamation 7318	52,947
Utah	Grand Staircase–Escalante	09/96	Proclamation 6920	1,870,800

Source: Taken from "The National Landscape Conservation Summary Tables," updated April 2007 (Washington, DC: Bureau of Land Management).

APPENDIX D

Areas in the National Landscape Conservation System

Unit Title	Number of Units	BLM Acres	BLM Miles
National Monuments	15	4,807,977	
National Conservation Areas	13	14,101,234	
Wilderness Areas	190	7,732,769	
Wilderness Study Areas	591	13,753,370	
Wild and Scenic Rivers	38	1,002,756	2,052
National Historic Trails	10		4,877
National Recreation Trails	3		610
Cooperative Protection and Management Areas	1	428,156	
National Recreation Areas	1	998,702	
Outstanding Natural Areas	1	100	
Forest Reserves	1	7,472	
Total	864	42,832,536 (17% of the public lands)	7,539

Source: Taken from "The National Landscape Conservation Summary Tables," updated April 2007 (Washington, DC: Bureau of Land Management).

APPENDIX E

Developmental Differences: The U.S. Forest Service and the BLM

The U.S. Forest Service and the BLM have almost identical missions, as articulated in the National Forest Management Act of 1976 and the Federal Land Policy and Management Act of 1976, respectively. Both agencies embrace what is called the multiple-use, sustained yield management framework, which emphasizes maximizing diverse benefits without impairing future use. Despite these similarities, the two agencies have long functioned very differently in terms of their organization, culture, political power, and management. The Forest Service was, for most of the twentieth century, a powerful and relatively autonomous agency that exercised considerable control over national forest policy and over national forest users. For at least the first half of the twentieth century, it set the standard for professional, scientific management. The BLM, by comparison, has been a weak agency politically and has had far more limited control of public lands policy and public lands users. While environmental laws like the National Environmental Policy Act and the Endangered Species Act have closed the gap between the two agencies to some extent—particularly after the spotted owl crisis in the Pacific Northwest in the 1980s and 1990s—the differences are still visible. There are a number of reasons for these enduring differences, but the most important are:

U.S. FOREST SERVICE

1.   Established in 1905 during the Progressive Era, a period of high public trust in the federal government.
2.   Established shortly before *U.S. v. Grimaud* (220 U.S. 506), in which the Supreme Court validated broad delegations of power from Congress to the executive branch.

3. Established with a relatively clear mission to protect a valuable national resource (primarily timber).
4. Established with a charismatic and politically elite leader, Gifford Pinchot, who enjoyed a close relationship with the president.
5. In its early years the Forest Service enjoyed a near monopoly on forestry expertise.
6. Foresters were united by a common set of professional values inculcated in their forestry training and sustained by professional associations.
7. Early national forests were largely uninhabited by European Americans, so the Forest Service started with a blank slate.
8. The Forest Service's political success was reflected in its appropriations and staffing levels.

BLM

1. Established in 1946, well past the Progressive Era.
2. Established shortly after the Franklin D. Roosevelt administration, when the Supreme Court was restricting the delegation of authority.
3. Established without a clear mission and with overlapping and conflicting responsibilities.
4. Established without a charismatic or politically influential leader.
5. Initially the BLM depended on the practical expertise of grazing permit holders.
6. BLM employees lacked any unifying set of professional values or culture. The cleavage between its two predecessor agencies remained clearly visible for years.
7. By the time the BLM was formed, the public lands had had more than a century of unregulated or loosely regulated private use, and these private users had established claims to the public lands that functioned politically like common law rights.
8. The BLM was formed just as Congress slashed appropriations for range management. Throughout its history the BLM has lagged well behind the Forest Service in its appropriations and staffing levels.

Sources: This comparison is drawn substantially from the work of Sally Fairfax, Jeanne Nienaber Clarke, and Daniel C. McCool: Clarke and McCool, *Staking Out the Terrain: Power and Performance among Natural Resource Agencies*; Dana and Fairfax, *Forest and Range Policy: Its Development in the United States;* Fairfax, "Coming of Age in the Bureau of Land Management: Range Management in Search of a Gospel"; Fairfax, "The Difference between BLM and the Forest Service," in *Opportunity and Challenge: The Story of BLM*, ed. James Muhn and Hanson R. Stuart.

Notes

ABBREVIATIONS

BLML   Bureau of Land Management Library (Denver, CO)
BSL   Boise State University Library (Boise, ID)
FHS   Forest History Society (Durham, NC)
JFKL   John F. Kennedy Library (Boston, MA)
MHS   Minnesota Historical Society (St. Paul, MN)
NAB   National Archives Building
NAII   National Archives Building II
NSTC   National Science and Technology Center, renamed the National Operations
        Center, Division of Resource Services in 2007
PLFA   Public Lands Foundation Archive (Phoenix, AZ)
SMOF   Staff Member and Office Files
WHCF   White House Central Files

PREFACE

1. For some BLM employees, this political weakness is a source of deep frustration, but for others it helps to maintain the agency's decentralized culture.

2. Leslie Allen, *Wildlands of the West: The Story of the Bureau of Land Management* (Washington, DC: The National Geographic Society, 2002); Marion Clawson, *The Bureau of Land Management* (New York: Praeger Publishers, 1971); James Muhn and Hanson R. Stuart, *Opportunity and Challenge: The Story of the BLM* (Washington, DC: U.S. Government Printing Office, 1988).

3. Sally K. Fairfax, "Coming of Age in the Bureau of Land Management: Range Management in Search of a Gospel," in *Developing Strategies for Rangeland Management: A Report Prepared by the Committee on Developing Strategies for Rangeland Management* (Boulder, CO: Westview Press, 1984), 1725.

4. Samuel P. Hays, "Public Values and Management Response," in *Developing Strategies for Rangeland Management: A Report Prepared by the Committee on Developing Strategies for Rangeland Management* (Boulder, CO: Westview Press, 1984), 1819.

5. Sally Fairfax describes the BLM as "a scrappy and creative survivor of a uniquely hostile political environment." Fairfax, "Coming of Age in the Bureau of Land Management," 1716.

CHAPTER ONE. ENDURING TENSIONS OF PUBLIC LANDS MANAGEMENT

1. The BLM's initial land base included 190 million acres in the western United States and 330 million acres in the Alaska Territory. U.S. Congress, Senate, Committee on Interior and Insular Affairs, *National Resource Policy*, 1st sess., January 31, February 1–4, 7, 1949, 293; "Public Land Statistics, 2007" (Washington, DC: Bureau of Land Management, 2008).

2. "Public Land Statistics, 2003" (Washington, DC: Bureau of Land Management, 2004).

3. See the Federal Land Policy and Management Act of 1976, 43 U.S.C. §§1701–1785, P.L. 94-579.

4. In fiscal year (FY) 2002, for example, the BLM collected a total of $1.6 billion in fees and royalties and gave $1 billion of this directly to western states as directed by law. "Public Land Statistics, 2003."

5. In FY 2006, the BLM had an annual operating budget of $1.8 billion and 12,000 full-time employees. This amounts to $6.87 per acre and one employee per 21,833 acres. By contrast, in FY 2006, the U.S. Forest Service proposed a budget of $4.9 billion and had 36,000 full-time employees. This amounts to $25.38 per acre and one employee per 5,361 acres. Comparisons with the National Park Service are even more dramatic. The National Park Service's FY 2006 budget was $2.5 billion, or $31.65 per acre, and it had 20,680 employees, or one employee per 3,820 acres. "Budget Justifications and Performance Information: Fiscal Year 2006: National Park Service" (Washington, DC: Department of the Interior, 2005); "Bureau of Land Management: 2006 Budget Justification" (Washington, DC: Bureau of Land Management, 2005); "U.S. Forest Service: 2006 Budget Justification" (Washington, DC: U.S. Forest Service, 2005).

6. Samuel P. Hays, "Public Values and Management Response," in *Developing Strategies for Rangeland Management: A Report Prepared by the Committee on Developing Strategies for Rangeland Management* (Boulder, CO: Westview Press, 1984), 1819.

7. If federal agencies are neutral or instrumental institutions that execute the will of Congress, then democratic representation should remain confined to Congress. If federal agencies are constitutive institutions that shape and even make policy through implementation of congressional statutes, then there is reason to think that they should be responsive to public input and allow for democratic representation. Brian J. Cook, *Bureaucracy and Self-Government: Reconsidering the Role of Public Administration in American Politics* (Baltimore: Johns Hopkins University Press, 1996).

8. The Federal Land Policy and Management Act of 1976 permanently reserved all remaining public lands in federal ownership, although it permits the continued sale of public lands for certain public purposes.

9. Article IV, §3 of the U.S. Constitution states, "The Congress shall have Power to dispose of and make all needful Rules and Regulations respecting the Territory or other Property belonging to the United States." In 1890, the Supreme Court explained, "The whole system of the control of the public lands of the United States as it had been conducted by the government, under acts of Congress, shows a liberality in regard to their use which has been uniform and remarkable." Indeed, the Court concluded, "there is an implied license, growing out of the custom of nearly a hundred years, that the public lands of the United States, especially those in which the native grasses are adapted to the growth and fattening of domestic animals, shall be free to the people who seek to use them where they are left open and unenclosed, and no act of government forbids this use." *Buford v. Houtz,* 133 U.S. 320, 326–327 (1890). In 1911, the Supreme Court reaffirmed its position that ranchers held a common-law right to use the public lands *until* Congress chose to prohibit it. The court argued that the government's failure to object to public lands use "did not confer any vested right . . . nor did it deprive the United States of the power of recalling any implied license under which the land had been used for private purposes." *Light v. United States* 220 U.S. 523, 535 (1911).

10. Paul W. Gates, *History of Public Land Law Development* (Washington, DC: Government Printing Office, 1968), 524.

11. Charles E. Winter, *Four Hundred Million Acres: The Public Lands and Resources* (New York: Arno Press, 1979), 187.

12. Karen R Merrill, *Public Lands and Political Meaning: Ranchers, the Government, and the Property between Them* (Berkeley: University of California Press, 2002), 106.

13. Gates, *History of Public Land Law Development,* 525.

14. "Report of the Committee on the Conservation and Administration of the Public Domain to the President of the United States" (Washington, DC: Government Printing Office, 1931), 2.

15. Ibid.

16. Ibid., 2–3. It is interesting that the committee seems to have intended that both federal and state ownership be temporary. The committee argued that "as to agricultural and grazing lands, private ownership, except as to such areas as may be advisable or necessary for public use, should be the objective in the final use and disposition of the public domain" (8).

17. For example, the committee commended the Forest Service, writing that it had achieved "conservation of the range, its betterment, and the checking of overgrazing and erosion." Ibid., 14–15.

18. Ibid., 15.

19. S. 17, S. 2272, and S. 4060.

20. U.S. Congress, Senate, Committee on Public Lands and Surveys, *Granting Remaining Unreserved Public Lands to States,* 72d Cong., 1st sess., March 15, 16, 19, 24, 29, 31, and April 1, 5, 1932, 99 (emphasis added).

21. 167 U.S. 524 (1897).

22. 220 U.S. 523, 536 (1911).

23. Gifford Pinchot, the governor of Pennsylvania and former chief of the U.S. Forest Service, argued that "before any final disposition is made of these public lands their value for these various purposes should be studied by the Geological Survey, and we should know what we are giving away accurately, what the value is of this land, before we do give it away." In other words, they weren't opposed to large-scale disposal, only suspicious that

the federal government would give land and resources away indiscriminately. U.S. Congress, Senate, Committee on Public Lands and Surveys, *Granting Remaining Unreserved Public Lands to States*, 303.

24. Merrill, *Public Lands and Political Meaning*, 107.

25. Phillip O. Foss, *Politics and Grass: The Administration of the Public Domain* (Seattle: University of Washington Press, 1960), 48.

26. U.S. Congress, Senate, Committee on Public Lands and Surveys, *Granting Remaining Unreserved Public Lands to States*, 39.

27. George Cameron Coggins and Margaret Lindberg-Johnson, "The Law of Public Rangeland Management II: The Commons and the Taylor Act," *Environmental Law* 13 (Fall 1982).

28. Lynton K. Caldwell, *Environment as a Focus for Public Policy*, ed. Robert V. Bartlett and James N. Gladden (College Station: Texas A&M University Press, 1995); James R. Skillen, "Closing the Public Lands Frontier: The Bureau of Land Management, 1961–1969," *Journal of Policy History* 20, no. 3 (2008).

29. The shift in BLM hiring began in the 1960s with the agency's first comprehensive classification and multiple-use planning programs, but it occurred even more dramatically after the National Environmental Policy Act of 1969 and the Federal Land Policy and Management Act of 1976. For a comparative look at how new conservation values have reshaped Forest Service culture, see James J. Kennedy and Thomas M. Quigley, "Evolution of USDA Forest Service Organizational Culture and Adaptation Issues in Embracing an Ecosystem Management Paradigm," *Landscape and Urban Planning* 40, no. 1 (1998).

30. The Federal Land Policy and Management Act of 1976 (FLPMA) states that the public lands should (1) "be managed in a manner that will protect the quality of scientific, scenic, historical, ecological, environmental, air and atmospheric, water resource, and archeological values; that, where appropriate, will preserve and protect certain public lands in their natural condition; that will provide food and habitat for fish and wildlife and domestic animals; and that will provide for outdoor recreation and human occupancy and use . . . [and (2)] be managed in a manner which recognizes the Nation's need for domestic sources of minerals, food, timber, and fiber from the public lands." 43 U.S.C. §1701.

31. This struggle appears in all of the BLM's basic resource programs, but it has intensified the most in debates over environmental protection and energy development, particularly in wilderness areas. Richard N. L. Andrews, "Environment and Energy: Implications of Overloaded Agendas," *Natural Resources Journal* 19, no. 3 (1979).

32. For full discussions of this development, see Wesley Calef, *Private Grazing and Public Lands: Studies of the Local Management of the Taylor Grazing Act* (Chicago: University of Chicago Press, 1960), especially 49–92; Foss, *Politics and Grass*, especially 117–39; Merrill, *Public Lands and Political Meaning*.

33. Karen Merrill argues that Ickes chose to swallow the livestock industry's power in order to avoid giving the western states any more control over public lands ownership. Merrill, *Public Lands and Political Meaning*, 144–45.

34. Quoted in ibid., 169.

35. Quoted in ibid., 180.

36. Jeanne Nienaber Clarke, *Roosevelt's Warrior: Harold Ickes and the New Deal* (Baltimore: Johns Hopkins University Press, 1996); Harold L. Ickes, *The Secret Diary of Harold L. Ickes*, 3 vols., vol. 1 (New York: Simon and Schuster, 1954); T. H. Watkins,

Righteous Pilgrim: The Life and Times of Harold L. Ickes, 1874–1952 (New York: H. Holt, 1990).

37. Harold L. Ickes, "Why a Department of Conservation" (Washington, DC: Government Printing Office, 1938).

38. Oscar Chapman, Undersecretary of the Interior, "Address to Be Given before the American Forestry Congress," 10/11/46, Folder: Speeches General, Box 9, Joel T. Wolfsohn's files, Records of the Bureau of Land Management: Record Group 49 (RG 49), National Archives Building (NAB), Washington, DC

39. Ickes, "Why a Department of Conservation," 11.

40. Ibid., 12.

41. Memorandum, Vernon D. Northrop to Acting Secretary of the Interior, 3/5/46, Folder: Reorganization, Box 2566, Administration General, Records of the Office of the Secretary of the Interior: Record Group 48 (RG 48), National Archives Building II (NA II), College Park, MD.

42. U.S. Congress, House, Subcommittee on Public Lands of the Committee on Public Lands, *Public Lands Policy: Hearings Pursuant to H. Res. 93, Committee Hearing No. 30*, 80th Cong., 1st sess., April 21 and May 10, 1947; Foss, *Politics and Grass*, 176.

43. BLM leaders have generally drawn on the language of multiple-use management, arguing that professional managers are in the best position to allocate resources fairly and achieve the maximum, sustainable output of resources. Sally K. Fairfax, "Beyond the Sagebrush Rebellion: The BLM as Neighbor and Manager in the Western States," in *Western Public Lands: The Management of Natural Resources in the Time of Declining Federalism*, ed. John G. Francis and Richard Ganzel (Totowa, NJ: Rowman & Allanheld, 1984); Samuel P. Hays, *Beauty, Health and Permanence: Environmental Politics in the United States, 1955–1985* (New York: Cambridge University Press, 1987); Samuel P. Hays, *Conservation and the Gospel of Efficiency: The Progressive Conservation Movement, 1890–1920* (Cambridge, MA: Harvard University Press, 1959).

44. Fairfax, "Coming of Age in the Bureau of Land Management," 1740.

45. Consider, for example, the prominent column that Bernard DeVoto wrote for *Harper's* at the time, entitled "The Easy Chair." See "The West against Itself," *Harper's* 194 (1947), as well as the larger collection of DeVoto's essays in Bernard DeVoto, *The Western Paradox: A Conservation Reader*, ed. Douglas Brinkley and Patricia Nelson Limerick (New Haven, CT: Yale University Press, 2000).

46. Robert B. Keiter, "Change Comes to the Public Lands: New Forces, Directions, and Policies," *Rocky Mountain Mineral Law Institute* 46, no. 3-1 (2000); Gundars Rudzitis, *Wilderness and the Changing American West* (New York: John Wiley & Sons, 1996); Joseph Sax, "Perspectives Lecture: Public Land Law in the 21st Century," *Rocky Mountain Mineral Law Institute* 45, no. 1-1 (1999).

47. For one recent example of ranchers and environmentalists teaming up to fight oil and gas drilling, see Gail Binkly, "The BLM Stabs at a Tired Land," *High Country News* 34, no. 17 (2002); Charles Davis and Sandra Davis, "Analyzing Change in Public Lands Policymaking: From Subsystems to Advocacy Coalitions," *Policy Studies Journal* 17, no. 1 (1988).

48. Daniel Press, *Democratic Dilemmas in the Age of Ecology: Trees and Toxics in the American West* (Durham, NC: Duke University Press, 1994), 61–78.

49. Craig W. Thomas, *Bureaucratic Landscapes: Interagency Cooperation and the Preservation of Biodiversity* (Cambridge, MA: MIT Press, 2003).

50. Charles E. Lindblom, "The Science of Muddling Through," *Public Administration Review* 19, no. 2 (1959).

51. Foss, *Politics and Grass*; Grant McConnell, *Private Power and American Democracy* (New York: Vintage Books, 1966), 196–245.

52. Much has been written on the ideals of rational, scientific management that dominated the Forest Service and much of public administration in the first half of the twentieth century. For an overview of progressive era conservation, see Hays, *Conservation and the Gospel of Efficiency*. For a pointed critique of the rational, scientific approach to federal land management, see Robert H. Nelson, *Public Lands and Private Rights: The Failure of Scientific Management* (Lanham, MD: Rowman & Littlefield Publishers, 1995).

53. Hugh Heclo, "The Issue-Network and the Executive Establishment," in *The New American Political System*, ed. Anthony King (Washington, DC: American Enterprise Institute for Public Policy Research, 1978); Paul A. Sabatier, ed. *Policy Change and Learning: An Advocacy Coalition Approach* (Boulder, CO: Westview Press, 1993).

54. Mark Sagoff, *Price, Principle, and the Environment* (New York: Cambridge University Press, 2004).

55. Christopher McGrory Klyza and David Sousa, *American Environmental Policy, 1990–2006: Beyond Gridlock* (Cambridge, MA: MIT Press, 2008).

56. G. Brown and C. C. Harris, "The US Forest Service: Whither the New Resource Management Paradigm?" *Journal of Environmental Management* 58 (2000); Kennedy and Quigley, "Evolution of USDA-Forest Service Organizational Culture"; Laura Paskus, "Up in Smoke: Obama Administration Will Inherit a Beleaguered Forest Service," *High Country News* 40, no. 23 (2008).

CHAPTER TWO. BORN INTO CONTROVERSY

1. 60 Stat. 1097.

2. U.S. Congress, Senate, Committee on Interior and Insular Affairs, *National Resource Policy*, 293.

3. U.S. Congress, Senate, Committee on the Judiciary, *President's Plan for Reorganization of Executive Departments: Hearings on S. Con. Res. 64, 65, and 66 Concurrent Resolutions Disapproving Reorganization Plans 1, 2, and 3*, 79th Cong., 2nd sess., June 14, 15, 18, 19, 20, 21, 25, 26, 27, 1946; U.S. Congress, House, Committee on Expenditures in the Executive Departments, *Reorganization Plans Nos. 1, 2, and 3 of 1946: Hearings on H. Con. Res. 151, H. Con. Res. 154, H. Con. Res. 155*, 79th Cong., 2nd sess., June 4, 5, 6, 7, 11, 12, 13, 1946. Political scientist Sally Fairfax writes, "The GLO/Grazing Service union was apparently not a widely discussed or well-documented undertaking. In virtually every source, the BLM simply emerges without comment from the billows of dust surrounding the grazing service fee controversy." Fairfax, "Coming of Age in the Bureau of Land Management," 1725.

4. As illustration, trade magazines like the *American Cattle Producer* and the *National Wool Grower* continued to refer to the BLM's grazing branch as the "Grazing Service."

5. Fairfax, "Coming of Age in the Bureau of Land Management," 1726.

6. See Luther Gulick and Lyndall Urwick, eds., *Papers on the Science of Administration* (New York: Columbia University, Institute of Public Administration, 1937); Hays, *Conservation and the Gospel of Efficiency*; Nelson, *Public Lands and Private Rights*.

7. Fairfax describes the BLM "as a scrappy and creative survivor of a uniquely hostile political environment." Fairfax, "Coming of Age in the Bureau of Land Management," 1716.

8. The first professional society and journal for range management did not appear until 1948. Marion Clawson, interviewed by James Muhn, transcript, undated (BLM Library, Denver, CO); Fairfax, "Coming of Age in the Bureau of Land Management," 1729; Christopher James Klyza, "Patterns in Public Lands Policy: The Consequences of Ideas and the State" (Ph.D. diss., University of Minnesota, 1990), 258; William D. Rowley, "Historical Considerations in the Development of Range Science," in *Forest and Wildlife Science in America: A History*, ed. Harold K. Steen (Durham, NC: Forest History Society, 1999).

9. William Voight, Jr., *Public Grazing Lands: Use and Misuse by Industry and Government* (New Brunswick, NJ: Rutgers University Press, 1976), 278–89.

10. Merrill, *Public Lands and Political Meaning*.

11. U.S. Congress, Senate, Committee on Public Lands and Surveys, *Hearings Pursuant to S. Res. 241: Resolutions Authorizing the Committee on Public Lands to Make a Full and Complete Investigation with Respect to the Administration and Use of the Public Lands*, 79th Cong., 1st sess., January 22–23, 1945, 5–6.

12. Representative Frank Barrett of Wyoming articulated this position best in a 1945 hearing of the Senate Public Lands Committee: "It seems to me the Department, Mr. Forsling, has taken the wrong approach to the whole thing. . . . It seems to me that the rule of the law was under the common law of England which was adopted by my State of Wyoming and many of the States in the West and by this country as the law of the land and under the common law of England they had a right to use that public domain. There were restrictions which have been written into the Taylor Act that they had to preserve the public domain, they could not destroy it. Consequently, these users of the public domain have a certain right. Now, the Department says that it is by sufferance and they can be thrown off at any time. That is not true. Under the law they had a right. The common law of England was adopted and amended by the Taylor Act. They adopted those old customs and restricted the right of use. But it comes back to the fundamental question of having a semivested right to use the public domain. It was not intended that they would pay the full value for the use of it. That is my position." Ibid.

13. Coggins and Lindberg-Johnson, "Law of Public Rangeland Management II"; Foss, *Politics and Grass*, 83–84.

14. In addition, banks recognized these permits as part of a ranch's property value in issuing mortgages. Battles over grazing fees have always included debate over this "permit value," which the federal government has been unwilling to recognize. U.S. Congress, Senate, Committee on Interior and Insular Affairs, *Grazing Fees on Public Lands*, 91st Cong., 1st sess., February 27–28, 1969, 118; American National Cattlemen's Association, "The Livestock Grazing Permit—Its Economic Importance" (Denver: American National Cattlemen's Association, 1968); Foss, *Politics and Grass*, 73–98.

15. U.S. Congress, Senate, Committee on Public Lands and Surveys, *Administration and Use of Public Lands*, 79th Cong., 1st sess., 1945, 5010.

16. Memorandum, Forsling to Assistant Secretary Chapman, May 28, 1945, Folder: Grazing, Box 11, Chapman 1933–1953, Record Group 48 (RG 48), National Archives Building II (NAII), College Park, MD.

17. Ibid.; Memorandum, Dale Doty to Secretary Chapman, January 25, 1944, Folder: Grazing, Box 11, Chapman, RG 48, NAII

18. McCarran introduced a bill in 1945 (S. 1402) to make this a legally binding requirement.

19. Confidential letter, Forsling to Assistant Secretary Chapman, October 29, 1945, Folder: Grazing, Box 11, Chapman, RG 48, NAII; Confidential memorandum to Assistant Secretary Chapman, September 26, 1945, Folder: Documents Relating to Establishment of Bureau of Land Management, Papers Compiled by James Muhn, BLM Library, NSTC (National Science and Technology Center, renamed the National Operations Center, Division of Resource Services in 2007). Memorandum, Dale Doty to Assistant Secretary Chapman, July 13, 1944, Folder: Grazing, Box 11, Chapman, RG 48, NAII.

20. Confidential letter, Forsling to Assistant Secretary Chapman, October 29, 1945.

21. Confidential memorandum to Assistant Secretary Chapman, September 26, 1945.

22. 59 Stat. 613.

23. Memorandum, Assistant Secretary Chapman to Secretary Ickes, January 10, 1946, Folder: Documents Relating to Establishment of Bureau of Land Management, BLM Library, NSTC; President Truman to Harold D. Smith, Director, Bureau of the Budget, December 20, 1945, Folder: Documents Relating to Establishment of Bureau of Land Management, BLM Library, NSTC.

24. Memorandum, Forsling to Secretary Ickes, January 16, 1946, Folder: Grazing Service Fees, Box 10, Chapman, RG 48, NAII; Secretary Ickes to Harold D. Smith, Director, Bureau of the Budget, January 24, 1946, Folder: Documents Relating to Establishment of Bureau of Land Management, BLM Library, NSTC.

25. Secretary Ickes to Harold D. Smith, Director, Bureau of the Budget, January 24, 1946.

26. "Grazing Service Work Program" and "General Land Office Work Program," 4/3/46, Box 2566, Administration General, RG 48, NAII; "Oral History Interview," Oscar L. Chapman, interviewed by Jerry N. Ness, April 21, 1972, Truman Library, Independence, MO.

27. E. Louise Peffer, *The Closing of the Public Domain: Disposal and Reservation Policies 1900–50* (Stanford, CA: Stanford University Press, 1951), 267–72.

28. 11 F.R. 7875, 60 Stat. 1097.

29. U.S. Congress, Senate, Committee on the Judiciary, *President's Plan for Reorganization of Executive Departments*, 25, 317.

30. Merrill, *Public Lands and Political Meaning*, 191.

31. U.S. Congress, Senate, Committee on Expenditures in the Executive Departments, *Reestablishing Registers of Land Offices*, 80th Cong., 1st sess., March 10, 1947, 12.

32. Ibid.

33. Memorandum, Joel Wolfsohn to Secretary Krug, June 24, 1946, Folder: Secretary, Box 3, Wolfsohn's Files, RG 49, NAB.

34. U.S. Congress, House, Subcommittee on Public Lands of the Committee on Public Lands, *Public Lands Policy: Hearings Pursuant to H. Res. 93*, Committee Hearing No. 30, 80.

35. Voight, *Public Grazing Lands*, 278–89.

36. Kenneth Reid to Oscar Chapman, 9/26/47, Grazing Controversy and National Advisory Meeting, Box 11, Chapman, RG 48, NAII.

37. "Public Land Meeting," *American Cattle Producer* 28, no. 4 (1946).

38. Rex L. Nicholson, "Reorganization Plan No. 3 as Proposed to J. A. Krug Secretary of the Interior" (Washington, DC: Bureau of Land Management, 1946), 1, 18.

39. Foss, *Politics and Grass*, 173; Nicholson, "Reorganization Plan No. 3," 27.

40. Nicholson, "Reorganization Plan No. 3," 26.

41. Ibid., 49.

42. Press Release, 11/22/46, Folder: Reorganization Plan No. 3, Box 3, Wolfsohn's Files, RG 49, NAB.

43. Memorandum, "Contributions for Named Grazing District Employees," Acting BLM Director Fred Johnson to BLM Chief, Branch of Operations, 10/21/46, File: BLM 1946–1947, Chapman, RG 48, NAII; Peffer, *Closing of the Public Domain*, 277.

44. Interior Appropriations for FY 1947. See Muhn and Stuart, *Opportunity and Challenge*, 56.

45. Peffer, *Closing of the Public Domain*, 287.

46. U.S. Congress, House, Subcommittee on Public Lands of the Committee on Public Lands, *Public Lands Policy: Hearings Pursuant to H. Res. 93*, Committee Hearing No. 30, 4.

47. Ibid., 3.

48. Ibid., 76–77.

49. Ibid., 80.

50. Minutes from a meeting of BLM regional administrators, 8/10/47, Folder: BLM 1946–1947, Box 16, Chapman, RG 48, NAII.

51. "Minutes of a Meeting of Livestock Representatives from Eleven Western States with Secretary Krug," 9/3/47, Folder: Grazing Controversy and National Advisory Meeting, Box 11, Chapman, RG 48, NAII, 23.

52. Marion Clawson, *From Sagebrush to Sage* (Washington, DC: Ana Publications, 1987), 206.

53. Marion Clawson, *The Western Range Livestock Industry* (New York: McGraw-Hill, 1950).

54. "Minutes of a Meeting of Livestock Representatives"; Muhn and Stuart, *Opportunity and Challenge*, 58. There has generally been some confusion in the public lands literature over whether or not the BLM director is a political appointee, and this confusion has been reinforced by the routine changes of BLM directors following party changes in the White House. Although Senator McCarran introduced legislation to make the BLM director a political appointee in 1947 (*Reestablishing Registers of Land Offices*), the BLM directorship remained a civil service position from 1946 until the Federal Land Policy and Management Act of 1976. This meant that BLM directors could assume their official duties immediately upon secretarial appointment and were not subjected to Senate confirmation.

55. Clawson, *From Sagebrush to Sage*.

56. Clawson, *Bureau of Land Management*, 38.

57. Ibid.

58. Muhn and Stuart, *Opportunity and Challenge*, 58–61.

59. Samuel Trask Dana and Sally K. Fairfax, *Forest and Range Policy: Its Development in the United States*, 2nd ed. (New York: McGraw-Hill, 1980), 180.

60. Marion Clawson, interviewed by James Muhn.

61. Clawson, *From Sagebrush to Sage*, 247.

62. Ibid., 246.

63. The Supreme Court had restricted delegation of authority in the 1930s in decisions such as *Panama Refining Co. v. Ryan* (293 U.S. 388, 1935) and *Schechter Poultry Corp. v. United States* (295 U.S. 495, 1935), but it relaxed restrictions in the 1940s in decisions

such as *American Power and Light Co. v. Securities and Exchange Commission* (325 U.S. 385, 1945) and *Yakus v. United States* (321 U.S. 414, 1944). In the twenty years leading up to the BLM's formation, the federal government had grown from roughly 500,000 to 2 million civil servants and its budget had grown by a factor of thirteen, from $3 to $39 billion. William L. Dawson, "Summary of the Objectives, Operations, and Results of the Commissions on Organization of the Executive Branch of the Government" (Washington, DC: House Committee on Government Operations, 88th Congress, 1st Session, 1963), 4.

64. Ibid.

65. Leslie A. Miller, Horace M. Albright, John Dempsey, Ralph Carr, Donald H. McLaughlin, Isaiah Bowman, Gilbert White, Samuel T. Dana, and Ernest S. Griffith, "Organization and Policy in the Field of Natural Resources: A Report with Recommendations Prepared for the Commission on Organization of the Executive Branch of the Government" (Washington, DC: Commission on Organization of the Executive Branch of the Government, 1949), 9.

66. While the committee on natural resources did recommend that forest, range, fish, and wildlife responsibilities for public and private lands reside in a single department, this was based upon expertise and knowledge and did not erase the distinction between the government's responsibilities for publicly and privately owned land. Ibid., 8.

67. Ibid., 11.

68. Ibid., 12.

69. Ibid., 13–14.

70. Herbert Hoover, Dean Acheson, Arthur S. Flemming, James Forrestal, George H. Mead, George D. Aiken, Joseph P. Kennedy, John L. McClellan, James K. Pollock, Clarence J. Brown, Carter Manasco, and James H. Rowe, Jr., "Reorganization of the Department of the Interior: A Report to the Congress by the Commission on Organization of the Executive Branch of the Government" (Washington, DC: Commission on Organization of the Executive Branch of the Government, 1949).

71. Ibid., 79

72. Ibid., 65, 80.

73. *Light v. United States*, 220 U.S. 523, 536 (1911).

74. Merrill, *Public Lands and Political Meaning*, 68.

75. Oscar Chapman, "Comments of the Department of the Interior on the Recommendations of the Commission on Organization of the Executive Branch of the Government Concerning the Department of the Interior" (Washington, DC: Department of the Interior, 1949).

76. Memorandum, Clawson to Assistant Secretary Davidson, 10/19/49, Box 2563, Administration General, RG 48, NAII; Fred Strosnider, Irving H. Cowles, Walter M. Gilmer, Gordon Griswold, Ernest H. Gubler, E. R. Marvel, R. T. Marvel, J. A. Wadsworth, and R. A. Yelland, "A Study of the Hoover Commission's Recommendation for a New Forest and Range Service in the Department of Agriculture" (Reno, NV: Central Committee of Nevada State Grazing Boards, 1949), 10.

77. Strosnider et al., "A Study of the Hoover Commission's Recommendation," 14.

78. Ibid.

79. U.S. Congress, Senate, Committee on Expenditures in the Executive Departments, *Hearings on S. 1149: A Bill to Provide for the Reorganization of the Department of Agriculture in Accordance with the Recommendations of the Commission on Organization of*

the Executive Branch of the Government, 82nd Cong., 1st sess., August 28–29; September 5–7, 10–12, 18, 1951, 176.

80. Strosnider et al., "Study of the Hoover Commission's Recommendation."

81. Clawson, *Bureau of Land Management*, 91; Dana and Fairfax, *Forest and Range Policy*, 166; Elmo Richardson, *BLM's Billion-Dollar Checkerboard: Managing the O&C Lands* (Santa Cruz, CA: Forest History Society, 1980), 19–57.

82. P.L. 75-405.

83. Richardson, *BLM's Billion-Dollar Checkerboard*, 95–111.

84. Ibid., 99.

85. Muhn and Stuart, *Opportunity and Challenge*, 66.

86. Clawson, *Bureau of Land Management*, 94; Muhn and Stuart, *Opportunity and Challenge*, 82.

87. Muhn and Stuart, *Opportunity and Challenge*, 66; Richardson, *BLM's Billion-Dollar Checkerboard*, 113–24.

88. Clawson, *Bureau of Land Management*, 107.

89. Foss, *Politics and Grass*.

90. Fairfax, "Coming of Age in the Bureau of Land Management."

91. Marion Clawson, interviewed by James Muhn, 38.

92. For further reading, see George Cameron Coggins, "The Law of Public Rangeland Management III: A Survey of Creeping Regulation at the Periphery, 1934–1982," *Environmental Law* 13 (Winter 1983); Coggins and Lindberg-Johnson, "Law of Public Rangeland Management II"; Dana and Fairfax, *Forest and Range Policy*; Foss, *Politics and Grass*.

93. Quoted in Rowley, "Historical Considerations in the Development of Range Science," 254.

94. Ibid.

95. Ibid.

96. Marion Clawson, interviewed by James Muhn, 8.

97. Fairfax, "Coming of Age in the Bureau of Land Management," 1729.

98. U.S. Congress, Senate, Committee on Interior and Insular Affairs, *Grazing Fees on Public Lands*, 7.

99. Marion Clawson, *Rebuilding the Federal Range* (Washington, DC: U.S. Government Printing Office, 1951), 69–88; Muhn and Stuart, *Opportunity and Challenge*, 63–64.

100. Clawson, *Bureau of Land Management*, 131.

101. John D. Leshy, *The Mining Law: A Study in Perpetual Motion* (Washington, DC: Resources for the Future, 1987).

102. Clawson, *Bureau of Land Management*, 124.

103. Ibid.

104. Ibid., 126–35.

105. Ibid., 134.

106. Ibid., 132.

107. 43 USC 315.

108. Quoted in Phillip O. Foss, ed., *Public Land Policy: Proceedings of the Western Resources Conference* (Boulder: Colorado Associated University Press, 1970), 87.

109. Robert A. Jones, interviewed by Hans Stuart and James Muhn, transcript, 1988 (BLM Library, Denver, CO), 19–20.

110. Dana and Fairfax, *Forest and Range Policy*, 186.

111. See, for example, Bernard DeVoto, "Sacred Cows and Public Lands," in *The Western Paradox: A Conservation Reader*, ed. Douglas Brinkley and Patricia Nelson Limerick (New Haven, CT: Yale University Press, 2001).

112. U.S. Congress, House, Subcommittee on Public Lands of the Committee on Public Lands, *Public Lands Policy: Hearings Pursuant to H. Res. 93*, Committee Hearing No. 30.

113. Jeanne Nienaber Clarke and Daniel C. McCool, *Staking Out the Terrain: Power and Performance among Natural Resource Agencies* (Albany: State University of New York Press, 1996), 157–78; Muhn and Stuart, *Opportunity and Challenge*, 99.

CHAPTER THREE. THE NEW BLM

1. Muhn and Stuart, *Opportunity and Challenge*, 104.

2. As noted in Chapter 2, President Hoover's effort to transfer the public lands to state ownership was probably the last real opportunity for a full-scale disposal of the public lands.

3. Muhn and Stuart, *Opportunity and Challenge*, 154.

4. Irving Senzel, interviewed by Hans Stuart and James Muhn, transcript, March 3, 1988 (BLM Library, Denver, CO), 55, 41. Woozley's orientation to commercial users was supported by the BLM's basic statutory authority, which focused almost exclusively on commodity development to the near exclusion of recreation or amenity resources. Multiple-use management was defined for the BLM by statutes such as the 1955 Multiple Surface Use Mining Act, which permitted multiple mineral production activities if they were compatible and permitted mineral activities on grazing land. The law was designed to permit the maximum economic development of the public lands. 30 U.S.C. §§611–615, P.L. 84–167.

5. Charles H. Stoddard, "Administration of Federal Lands," in *America's Public Lands: Politics, Economics & Administration*, ed. Harriet Nathan (Berkeley: University of California, Institute of Governmental Studies, 1972), 243.

6. Scott W. Hardt, "Federal Land Management in the Twenty-First Century: From Wise Use to Wise Stewardship," *Public Land and Resources Law Digest* 32, no. 1 (1995): 54.

7. Many of these new range conservationists were veterans who returned from World War II and went to college on the GI Bill. Fairfax, "Coming of Age in the Bureau of Land Management," 1728–29.

8. Paul Culhane describes this adjudication process, begun under Marion Clawson but not finished until 1967, as "the most important local level manifestation of the professional maturation of the BLM in the 1950s and 1960s." Paul J. Culhane, *Public Lands Politics: Interest Group Influence on the Forest Service and the Bureau of Land Management* (Baltimore: Johns Hopkins University Press, 1981), 92.

9. William Lerner, ed., *Historical Statistics of the United States, Colonial Times to 1970* (Washington, DC: U.S. Bureau of the Census, 1975), 432.

10. Fairfax, "Coming of Age in the Bureau of Land Management," 1728.

11. P.L. 86-66.

12. Cyril L. Jensen, "A Preliminary Study and Report on Frail Watershed Lands," August 26, 1964, Clarence Luther Forsling Papers, Library and Archives, Forest History Society, Durham, NC; *Our Public Lands* 7, no. 4 (1958) and 12, no. 4 (1963); "Report and Summary of Actions in the Bureau of Land Management during the Directorship of Charles H.

Stoddard—June '63 to June '66," Uncatalogued Papers (UP), compiled by James Muhn (Muhn), Bureau of Land Management Library (BLML), 13.

13. Luther Gulick, *Administrative Reflections from World War II* (Birmingham: University of Alabama Press, 1948); Gulick and Urwick, eds., *Papers on the Science of Administration*; Herbert Kaufman, "Emerging Conflicts in the Doctrines of Public Administration," *American Political Science Review* 50, no. 4 (1956).

14. Herbert Simon, *Administrative Behavior: A Study of Decision-Making Processes in Administrative Behavior*, 4th ed. (New York: Free Press, 1997).

15. James G. March and Herbert Simon, *Organizations* (New York: Wiley, 1958), 141.

16. Philip Selznick, *TVA and the Grass Roots* (Berkeley: University of California Press, 1949), 260.

17. See, for example, Chris Argyris, *Organization of a Bank* (New Haven, CT: Yale University Labor and Management Center, 1954); *Personality and Organization* (New York: Harper & Brothers, 1957); *Understanding Organizational Behavior* (Homewood, IL: Dorsey Press, 1960). Argyris's work provided the theoretical foundation for BLM consultants George Shipman and David Paulsen, who are discussed below.

18. Foss, *Politics and Grass.*

19. McConnell, *Private Power and American Democracy.*

20. "On the whole," one scholar had written in 1951, "the Forest Service's achievements are distinguished . . . [while the] BLM has virtually lost control of the range. . . . Continued impotence of the Bureau of Land Management not only prevents effective conservation of Taylor Act land but jeopardizes the independence of the Forest Service as well." Robert L. L. McCormick, "Management of Public Land Resources," *Yale Law Journal* 61 (1951): 64–66.

21. Pinchot writes, "The administration of the public-land laws by the General Land Office of the Interior Department is one of the great scandals of American history"; and, "The management of the Forest Reserves under the Land Office had been as full of abuses as an egg is full of meat." Gifford Pinchot, *Breaking New Ground* (Washington, DC: Island Press, 1998), 243, 299.

22. H. A. Wallace, "The Western Range" (Washington, DC: Government Printing Office, 1936).

23. Herbert Kaufman, *The Forest Ranger: A Study in Administrative Behavior* (Baltimore: Johns Hopkins University Press, 1960).

24. P.L. 86-649.

25. P.L. 86-517.

26. John Carver, Speech before the Washington Section of the Society of American Foresters, Washington, DC, November 30, 1961, 3, File: Speeches: Assistant Secretary of the Interior for Public Lands Management, Series 1, Personal Papers of John A. Carver, John F. Kennedy Library (JFKL), Boston, MA.

27. Culhane, *Public Lands Politics*, 218; Ann Marie Poyner, "Fighting over Forgotten Lands: The Evolution of Recreation Provision on the United States Public Domain" (PhD diss., University of Bristol, 1999); Hal Rothman, "'A Regular Ding-Dong Fight': The Dynamics of Park Service–Forest Service Controversy during the 1920s and 1930s," in *American Forests*, ed. Char Miller (Lawrence: University Press of Kansas, 1997).

28. Marion Clawson and Carlton S. Van Doren, eds., *Statistics on Outdoor Recreation* (Washington, DC: Resources for the Future,1984), 23, 42, 177, 197.

29. Act of June 28, 1958 (72 Stat. 238).

30. Marion Clawson, "The Crisis in Outdoor Recreation," *American Forests* 65, no. 3 (1959); Marion Clawson, "The Crisis in Outdoor Recreation, Part II," *American Forests* 65, no. 4 (1959).

31. Marion Clawson, R. Burnell Held, and Charles H. Stoddard, *Land for the Future* (Baltimore: Johns Hopkins University Press, 1960), 464.

32. "But, in general, the public domain does not have the qualities which attract large-scale use and, by and large, it is no more conveniently located with respect to most users than are national forest areas which are deemed more attractive. For all of these reasons, recreational use of the public domain in the States is probably low and likely to remain so." Marion Clawson and Burnell Held, *The Federal Lands* (Baltimore: Johns Hopkins University Press, 1957), 93.

33. Dana and Fairfax, *Forest and Range Policy*, 194. In 1960, the BLM had one recreation specialist and an estimated 11 million recreational visits and by 1965 the number of recreational visits more than doubled. Clawson and Van Doren, eds., *Statistics on Outdoor Recreation*, 226; E. K. Peterson, "Recreation on the National Land Reserve," *Our Public Lands* 11, no. 3 (1962): 5.

34. Robert G. Healy and William E. Shands, "A Conversation with Marion Clawson: How Times (and Foresters) Have Changed," *Journal of Forestry* 87, no. 5 (1989): 20.

35. Royale K. Pierson, "Cooperative Agreement on Recreation," *Our Public Lands* 3, no. 2 (1953): 3.

36. Irving Senzel, interviewed by Hans Stuart and James Muhn, 42–43.

37. Muhn and Stuart, *Opportunity and Challenge*, 69–72, 128. See also Gene Peterson, *Pioneering Outdoor Recreation* (McLean, VA: Public Lands Foundation, 1996), 18–44.

38. Quoted in Peterson, "Recreation on the National Land Reserve," 6; Poyner, "Fighting over Forgotten Lands," 123.

39. "Public Land Statistics 1961" (Washington, DC: Bureau of Land Management, 1962), 66; "Public Land Statistics 1962" (Washington, DC: Bureau of Land Management, 1963), 64.

40. "Report and Summary of Actions in the Bureau of Land Management during the Directorship of Charles H. Stoddard."

41. U.S. Congress, House, Committee on Interior and Insular Affairs, *Policies, Programs, and Activities of the Department of the Interior*, 88th Cong., 1st sess., February 5, 1963, 89–90.

42. 78 Stat 986; "Legislative Analysis Public Law 88-607: The Classification and Multiple Use Act 78 Stat. 986," P1099:1, Charles H. Stoddard Papers, Minnesota Historical Society (MHS), St. Paul, MN.

43. Muhn and Stuart, *Opportunity and Challenge,* 111–15, 128–32.

44. Wayne N. Aspinall, interviewed by Charles T. Morrisey, transcript, November 10, 1965 (Oral History Interviews, JFK Library, Boston, MA); Thomas G. Smith, "John Kennedy, Stewart Udall, and New Frontier Conservation," *Pacific Historical Review* 67, no. 3 (1995).

45. Wayne N. Aspinall, interviewed by Charles T. Morrisey; John F. Kennedy, speech delivered at the Shrine Auditorium, Billings, MT, September 22, 1960.

46. Kennedy pledged in a campaign speech in Billings, MT, "I propose a nine-point program for resource development to be initiated promptly in January of 1961. First, we will reverse the policy of no new starts. I hope that in the United States in the sixties, when we are going to have to move again, that no slogan is ever put forward which says no new

starts, no movement forward, let us stand still. . . . And we are going to move ahead under that program on comprehensive plans for multi-purpose river development." John F. Kennedy, speech delivered at Shrine Auditorium, Billings, Montana.

47. Stewart L. Udall, interviewed by William W. Moss, transcript, April 7, 1970 (Oral History Interviews, JFK Library, Boston, MA), 88. Udall often complained in his journal when Kennedy fell short of his conservation heroes such as the Roosevelts, Gifford Pinchot, and Harold Ickes: "I can hardly, with fairness," he wrote," complain that my man does not have a streak of Thoreau or Robert Frost in his New England makeup, but I long for a flicker of emotion, a response to the out of doors and overwhelming majesty of the land"; Kennedy "had good environmental instincts 'whether it be parks or wildlife or pollution— but he doesn't feel the indignation that two truly great conservation presidents felt for the despoilers, and he doesn't respond to the land with their warmth or excited interest'"; and "there is such a thing as having a poetic feeling about the land. Even a politician can have it (though most only feign it). The chief lacks it, I'm sorry to say. Imagine a conservation trip where the leader never gets out of his suit or steps off the asphalt. How TR would have hooted at us—he who slept out in the snow with Muir and had the time of his life at 45. Either you love nature or you don't, I guess it's that simple." Quoted from Smith, "John Kennedy, Stewart Udall, and New Frontier Conservation," 355–56.

48. "Report to the President, June 20, 1961 from Secretary Udall," Box 20, Personal Papers of Orren Beaty, JFKL.

49. Stewart L. Udall, "Resources for Tomorrow: 1961 Annual Report of the Secretary of the Interior" (Washington, DC: Department of the Interior, 1961), 17–18.

50. Stewart L. Udall, *The Quiet Crisis* (Salt Lake City: Peregrine Smith Books, 1988); Norman Wengert, "The Ideological Basis of Conservation and Natural Resources Policies and Programs," *Annals of the American Academy of Political and Social Sciences* 344 (1962): 68.

51. Smith, "John Kennedy, Stewart Udall, and New Frontier Conservation," 357.

52. John Carver, interviewed by William W. Moss, transcript, October 21, 1969 (Oral History Interviews, JFK Library, Boston, MA), 59; Barbara Laverne Blythe Leunes, "The Conservation Philosophy of Stewart L. Udall, 1961–1968" (Ph.D. diss., Texas A&M University, 1977); Smith, "John Kennedy, Stewart Udall, and New Frontier Conservation," 361; Stewart L. Udall, *The Third Wave . . . America's New Conservation*, vol. 3, Conservation Yearbook (Washington, DC: Department of the Interior, 1966).

53. John F. Kennedy, "Special Message to Congress on Natural Resources," in *Public Papers of the President of the United States: John F. Kennedy, 1961* (Washington, DC: Government Printing Office, 1962), 114, 119.

54. John F. Kennedy, speech delivered at the White House Conference on Conservation, Washington, DC, May 24–25, 1962, 100; Kennedy, "Special Message to Congress on Natural Resources."

55. Lyndon B. Johnson, "Special Message to Congress on Conservation and Restoration of Natural Beauty," February 8, 1965, in *Public Papers of the Presidents of the United States: Lyndon B. Johnson, 1965* (Washington, DC: Government Printing Office, 1966), 155–65; White House Conference on Natural Beauty, May 25–26, 1965 (Washington, DC, 1965).

56. Robert Wolf, interviewed by Claire Rhein, transcript, November 15, 1989 (Robert Wolf Oral History Project, Maureen and Mike Mansfield Library and K. Ross Toole Archives, Missoula, MT), 224.

57. See, for example, U.S. Congress, House, Committee on Interior and Insular Affairs,

Policies, Programs, and Activities of the Department of the Interior, 87th Cong., 1st sess., February 15, 21, 27, 1961, 8.

58. Panel on Conservation and the Congress, White House Conference on Conservation, May 24–25, 1962 (Washington, DC: Government Printing Office, 1962), 62.

59. Ibid.

60. Aspinall to Kennedy, October 15, 1962, Box 489, White House Central Files, JFKL.

61. Kennedy to Aspinall, Draft Letter, January 12, 1963, Box 489, White House Central Files, JFKL.

62. PLLRCA, PL 88-606; the Wilderness Act, P.L. 88-577; CMUA, P.L. 88-607; and PLSA, PL 88-608.

63. Steven C. Schulte, *Wayne Aspinall and the Shaping of the American West* (Boulder: University Press of Colorado, 2002), 241. As Schulte writes, Aspinall viewed the PLLRC as an opportunity to "counteract the dangerous trend wherein Congress had been shunning its constitutional obligation to make laws and policies for federal land management . . . [which had allowed] the executive branch free control to exert its capricious political will upon federal land management" (239).

64. Dana and Fairfax, *Forest and Range Policy*, 232.

65. Schulte, *Wayne Aspinall and the Shaping of the American West*, 241.

66. Richard A. Baker, "The Conservation Congress of Anderson and Aspinall, 1963–64," *Journal of Forest History* 29, no. 3 (1985): 107; Wolf, interviewed by Claire Rhein, 4.

67. CMUA, P.L. 88-607; PLSA, P.L. 86-517; MUSY, P.L. 88-608.

68. Muhn and Stuart, *Opportunity and Challenge*, 113.

69. Clawson, *Bureau of Land Management*, 50.

70. See House Report No. 1243, 88th Cong., 2nd sess.

71. Karl S. Landstrom, interviewed by Hans Stuart and James Muhn, transcript, May 23, 1988 (BLM Library, Denver, CO), 4; Smith, "John Kennedy, Stewart Udall, and New Frontier Conservation"; "Report and Summary of Actions in the Bureau of Land Management during the Directorship of Charles H. Stoddard," 1.

72. "Report to the President," February 3, 1961, File: White House Reports, 1961, Box 20, Personal Papers of Orren Beaty, JFKL. Quoted in Leunes, "Conservation Philosophy of Stewart L. Udall, 1961–1968," 113.

73. John Carver, "Remarks at the American Mining Congress Convention," Seattle, WA, September 12, 1961, Folder: Speeches: Assistant Secretary of the Interior for Public Lands Management, Personal Papers of John A. Carver, JFKL.

74. David Frederick Paulsen, "An Approach to Organizational Analysis: A Case Study of the Bureau of Land Management" (Ph.D. diss., University of Washington, 1966), 258.

75. Muhn and Stuart, *Opportunity and Challenge*, 116–17.

76. *Our Public Lands* 3, no. 2 (April, 1953).

77. Charles H. Stoddard, "Public Land Management: 1963–1968" (Washington, DC: Bureau of Land Management, 1968), 4.

78. It is also interesting that the seal depicts land features that were fairly rare on public lands, since BLM lands were generally low in elevation and arid or semiarid.

79. Kennedy, "Special Message to Congress on Natural Resources," 119.

80. Executive Order 6910, 11/26/1934, and Executive Order 6964, 2/5/35, BLM Press Release, January 26, 1961, UP, Muhn, BLML.

81. BLM Press Release, January 26, 1961.

82. Ibid.

83. Mike Harvey, interviewed by Hans Stuart and James Muhn, transcript, May 26, 1988 (BLM Library, Denver, CO); Landstrom, interviewed by Hans Stuart and James Muhn, 25; Schulte, *Wayne Aspinall and the Shaping of the American West*, 241. As Schulte writes, Aspinall wanted to "counteract the dangerous trend wherein Congress had been shunning its constitutional obligation to make laws and policies for federal land management . . . [which had allowed] the executive branch free control to exert its capricious political will upon federal land management" (239).

84. First announced on October 28, 1963. *Our Public Lands* 13, no. 3 (1964); *Our Public Lands* 14, nos. 3–4 (Winter and Spring 1965).

85. Instruction Memo. No. RM-55, July 1, 1963. Cited in Curtis V. McVee, "Discussion of Resource Conservation Areas," District Managers Conference, April 20, 1964, UP, Muhn, BLML.

86. Ibid, 2.

87. Director's Office Instruction Memorandum No. 64–80, September 24, 1964. Charles H. Stoddard Papers, P1099:1, MHS; see also Memorandum, BLM Director to the Secretary of the Interior, "Background Material for BLM Briefing," September 30, 1964. Charles H. Stoddard Papers, P1099:1, MHS.

88. *Our Public Lands* 14, nos. 3–4 (1965).

89. U.S. Congress, House, Committee on Interior and Insular Affairs, *Policies, Programs, and Activities of the Department of the Interior*, 87th Cong., 1st sess., February 15, 21, 27, 1961, 49; John Carver, interviewed by John F. Stewart, transcript, October 7, 1969, 47; Landstrom, interviewed by Hans Stuart and James Muhn, 4.

90. U.S. Congress, House, Committee on Interior and Insular Affairs, *Policies, Programs, and Activities of the Department of the Interior*, 87th Cong., 1st sess., February 15, 21, 27, 1961, 55, 68.

91. Ibid., 8–9.

92. Kennedy, "Special Message to Congress on Natural Resources," 119.

93. Landstrom, interviewed by Hans Stuart and James Muhn, 17; Charles H. Stoddard, interviewed by Helen McCann White, transcript, November 29, 1967 (Charles H. Stoddard Papers, Minnesota Historical Society, St. Paul, MN), 2.

94. "Bureau of Land Management: Significant Changes in Programs under Budget Estimates Proposed by President Kennedy for Fiscal Year 1962," File: Estimated Appropriations 1961–1962, Box 15, Beaty, JFKL; Charles H. Stoddard, interviewed by Helen McCann White, 6.

95. Jones wrote that the new system was essential, since the present land disposal functions of the BLM were chaotic and uncoordinated: "In this day of space exploration, automatic data processing, and urban planning, our original national heritage, the public domain, is often still considered in 'horse and buggy' terms [;] the classification job has been proceeding, but largely on an uncontrolled, irregular, and unsystematic basis." Robert A. Jones, "Master Unit Classification," *Our Public Lands* 11, no. 3 (1962): 8.

96. Ibid., 9–17.

97. There was some support for extending multiple-use principles to the BLM. Congressional committees working on the MUSY of 1960 considered extending the bill to the BLM but chose not to because they believed it would delay passage of the bill. And in congressional debate, Congressman Aspinall lamented that the multiple-use bill had not

been extended to the BLM. Karl S. Landstrom, Speech before the Western Governor's Conference, Portland, OR, June 11, 1965, UP, Muhn, BLML.

98. Ibid., 5.

99. U.S. Congress, House, Committee on Interior and Insular Affairs, Policies, Programs, and Activities of the Department of the Interior, 88th Cong., 1st sess., February 5, 1963, 90–91.

100. "Interior Announces New Multiple Use Advisory Boards," U.S. Department of the Interior, December 13, 1961.

101. Executive Order 11007, February 26, 1962.

102. Culhane, *Public Lands Politics*, 218ff.

103. John Carver, Address at the 65th Annual Convention of the American National Cattleman's Association, Tampa, FL, January 26, 1962, File: Speeches: Assistant Secretary of the Interior for Public Lands Management 1962, Carver, JFKL.

104. Stewart L. Udall, *Annual Report of the Secretary of the Interior* (Washington, DC: U.S. Government Printing Office, 1963), 66.

105. Phillip O. Foss, *The Battle of Soldier Creek, Inter-University Case Program* (Tuscaloosa: University of Alabama Press, 1961); Foss, *Politics and Grass*, 140–70.

106. Wolf, interviewed by Claire Rhein, 2.

107. Karl Landstrom, "Remarks to the National Advisory Board Council for Public Lands," Las Vegas, NV, November 15, 1962, UP, Muhn, BLML.

108. "The brochure is handsome, the proposals vague—a perfect copy of Mission '66, Operation Outdoors, and Operation Multiple Use—and nothing was accomplished. Its existence does indicate, however, that the bureau was on its feet, ambitious, and attempting to become a land managing rather than a temporary land holding and disposal agency." Dana and Fairfax, Forest and Range Policy, 230–31.

109. Landstrom, interviewed by Hans Stuart and James Muhn, 17; Karl S. Landstrom, "Program for the Public Lands and Resources" (Washington, DC: U.S. Department of the Interior, Bureau of Land Management, 1962), 7.

110. Landstrom, "Program for the Public Lands and Resources," 21.

111. "I have always felt that this multiple use slogan is just that. It's a good idea, but it doesn't help you make any decisions when you've got to choose between uses which are not compatible one with the other. You can talk all you want about having multiple uses, but there comes a time when, if you're going to have a campground, you can't have any grazing or if you're going to have a dam there and cover it with water you can't do something else with it." John Carver, interviewed by William W. Moss, September 11, 1969, 38.

112. Orren Beaty, interviewed by William W. Moss, transcript, October 10, 24, 31, 1969, November 7, 14, 21, 1969, December 19, 1969, January 9, 16, 1970, February 13, 20, 27, 1970 (Oral History Interviews, JFK Library, Boston, MA), 71. Beaty explains that Landstrom "had an unfortunate personality; he couldn't disagree with a senator without becoming disagreeable. And while he was doing exactly what the administration wanted him to do, what we wanted him to do, what the Bureau of the Budget wanted us to do on the grazing fees, he became almost persona non grata on the Senate Interior Committee." John Carver, interviewed by John F. Stewart, September 20, 1968, 20–21. Carver argues that Landstrom was "an unmitigated disaster . . . [he was an] absolutely outstanding staff man but totally unqualified to be a bureau head"; John Carver, interviewed by William W. Moss, October 7, 1969, 53. See also Landstrom, interviewed by Hans Stuart and James Muhn, 28–29, and *Our Public Lands* 12, no. 4 (1963).

113. John Carver, interviewed by John F. Stewart, 13.

114. Initially called the Technical Review Staff.

115. Memorandum from Stoddard to Udall, "Unfinished Matters Needing Attention," May 1963, UP, Muhn, BLML (emphasis added).

116. This was reflected in the 1963 publication of *The Quiet Crisis*, where Udall concluded, "Only an ever-widening concept and higher ideal of conservation will enlist our finest impulses and move us to make the earth a better home both for ourselves and for those as yet unborn" (202).

117. "Report and Summary of Actions in the Bureau of Land Management During the Directorship of Charles H. Stoddard," 17.

118. Paulsen, "Approach to Organizational Analysis," 2.

119. "Report and Summary of Actions in the Bureau of Land Management during the Directorship of Charles H. Stoddard," 2. Shipman viewed bureaucracies as essentially organic entities. He reflected the new theories of administrative behavior advanced by Herbert Simon and utilized in Kaufman's study of the Forest Service, which focused considerable attention on the internal goals and social systems. Shipman encouraged Stoddard to set goals around which the BLM could be reorganized. With a new focus and direction, Shipman and Stoddard believed that the BLM could begin to take charge of its mission and begin to develop a comprehensive conservation program for the public lands.

120. George A. Shipman and David F. Paulsen, "The Bureau of Land Management: United States Department of the Interior: The Organization of the Washington Office" (Seattle: University of Washington, Institute for Administrative Research, 1963), 2.

121. Ibid., 3.

122. Ibid., 9.

123. George A. Shipman and David F. Paulsen, "The Bureau of Land Management: United States Department of the Interior: The Program Action System" (Seattle: University of Washington, Institute for Administrative Research, 1964), 2.

124. Ibid., 3.

125. Paulsen, "Approach to Organizational Analysis," 259.

126. Ibid., 263–64, 233, 265.

127. Ibid., 260.

128. Ibid., 265.

129. Jones, "Master Unit Classification," 6.

130. Instructional Memo No. 64-222, May 6, 1964, UP, Muhn, BLML.

131. "Report and Summary of Actions in the Bureau of Land Management during the Directorship of Charles H. Stoddard," 4–5, 18; Wolf, interviewed by Claire Rhein, 223.

132. "Report and Summary of Actions in the Bureau of Land Management during the Directorship of Charles H. Stoddard," 4–5.

133. Instruction Memo No. 64-195, "Problems Faced in Administering Bureau Programs," April 17, 1964, UP, Muhn, BLML.

134. Charles Stoddard, Introductory remarks: "Multiple Resources Planning for the Future," Denver, April 20, 1964, UP, Muhn, BLML, 1.

135. Robert Jones, "The New Look in Public Lands Management" (paper presented at the District Managers Conference, Denver, April 20, 1964), 3.

136. Ibid., 7–9.

137. Charles H. Stoddard, "Public Participation in Public Land Decisions," in *Public Land Policy: Proceedings of the Western Resources Conference*, ed. Phillip O. Foss

(Boulder: Colorado Associated University Press, 1968), 77. This was unlike anything that the Forest Service or the National Park Service practiced, since both agencies acted as proprietary landowners. The National Park Service in particular developed a reputation for ignoring local interests in pursuit of its national ideals. Darwin Lambert, *The Undying Past of Shenandoah National Park* (Boulder, CO: Roberts Rinehart, 1989); Joseph Sax, "Do Communities Have Rights? The National Parks as a Laboratory of New Ideas," *University of Pittsburgh Law Review* 45, no. 3 (1984); Joseph Sax, "The Trampas File," *Michigan Law Review* 84, no. 7 (1986).

138. Stoddard, "Public Participation in Public Land Decisions," 78–79.

139. Director's Office Instruction Memorandum No. 64-80, September 24, 1964, Charles H. Stoddard Papers, P1099:1, MHS.

140. Charles Stoddard, "New Program Direction in Bureau of Land Management: Briefing Statement for Secretary Udall and Assistant Secretary Carver," September 1964, Charles H. Stoddard Papers, P1099:1, MHS.

141. Stoddard, "Public Participation in Public Land Decisions," 79–80; Charles H. Stoddard and Jerry A. O'Callaghan, "Creative Federalism on the Retention or Disposition of Public Lands," *Arizona Law Review* 8, no. 1 (1966): 42.

142. Stoddard, "Public Participation in Public Land Decisions," 80.

143. Stoddard, "Public Land Management: 1963–1968," 8, UP, Muhn, BLML.

144. Robert A. Jones, interviewed by Hans Stuart and James Muhn, transcript, 1988. (BLM Library, Denver, CO), 27; Stoddard, "Public Participation in Public Land Decisions," 80–81. As Stoddard recalls, "when the chips were down and when their cards were called, where did they want this land to go? They wanted it to stay in federal ownership." Charles H. Stoddard, "Oral History Interview with Charles H. Stoddard," interviewed by Helen McCann White, 25.

145. Muhn and Stuart, *Opportunity and Challenge*, 111–15.

146. USDI, Bureau of Land Management, "Public Land Classification Progress," September 1, 1970. Cited in Frank Gregg, "Federal Land Transfers: The Case for a Westwide Program Based on the Federal Land Policy and Management Act" (Washington, DC: Conservation Foundation, 1982), 15.

147. Charles Stoddard, Address before the Portland City Club, Portland, OR, September 18, 1964, 2.

148. Ibid., 3.

149. Robert A. Jones, interviewed by Hans Stuart and James Muhn, 27; Muhn and Stuart, *Opportunity and Challenge*, 111–15; Charles H. Stoddard, interviewed by Helen McCann White, 25; Stoddard, "Public Participation in Public Land Decisions," 80–81; Stoddard and O'Callaghan, "Creative Federalism on the Retention or Disposition of Public Lands."

150. Gregg, "Federal Land Transfers."

151. Robert A. Jones, interviewed by Hans Stuart and James Muhn, 26.

152. Robert A. Jones, "Multiple Use Planning in BLM—Some Personal Recollections" (Denver, CO: Research Papers of James Muhn, 1988), 4.

153. Jones, interviewed by Hans Stuart and James Muhn, 31.

154. Robert A. Jones, "Developing a Planning System for Public Domain Lands: An Analysis of Organization Change in the Bureau of Land Management" (Master's thesis, University of Wisconsin, 1971), 13.

155. Ibid., 11.

156. Ibid., 12.

157. Ibid.

158. Ibid., 19.

159. Ibid., 20.

160. Nelson, *Public Lands and Private Rights*, 133–36.

161. Richard W. Behan, "The Irony of the Multiple Use/Sustained Yield Concept: Nothing Is So Powerful as an Idea Whose Time Has Passed" (paper presented at the workshop "Multiple Use and Sustained Yield: Changing Philosophies for Federal Land Management," Washington, DC, March 5–6, 1992); Perry R. Hagenstein, "Some History of Multiple Use and Sustained Yield Concepts" (paper presented at the workshop "Multiple Use and Sustained Yield: Changing Philosophies for Federal Land Management," Washington, DC, March 5–6, 1992); Christopher K. Leman, "Formal versus De Facto Systems of Multiple Use Planning in the Bureau of Land Management: Integrating Comprehensive and Focused Approaches," in *Developing Strategies for Rangeland Management: A Report Prepared by the Committee on Developing Strategies for Rangeland Management* (Boulder, CO: Westview Press, 1984); John A. Zivnuska, "The Multiple Problems of Multiple Use," *Journal of Forestry* 59, no. 8 (1961).

162. Dorotha M. Bradley and Helen M. Ingram, "Science vs. the Grass Roots: Representation in the Bureau of Land Management," *Natural Resources Journal* 26, no. 3 (1986).

163. Phillip O. Foss, "Problems in Federal Management of Natural Resources for Recreation," *Natural Resources Journal* 5 (1965).

164. Culhane, *Public Lands Politics*, 218.

CHAPTER FOUR. BLM ENTERS THE ENVIRONMENTAL DECADE

1. Irving Senzel, "Genesis of a Law, Part 1," *American Forests* 84, no. 1 (1978): 61.

2. *One Third of the Nation's Land: A Report to the President and to the Congress by the Public Land Law Review Commission* (Washington, DC: Public Land Law Review Commission, 1970).

3. Bradley and Ingram, "Science vs. the Grass Roots," 511; Lynton K. Caldwell, "An Ecosystems Approach to Public Land Policy," in *Public Land Policy: Proceedings of the Western Resources Conference*, ed. Phillip O. Foss (Boulder: Colorado Associated University Press, 1968); Lynton K. Caldwell, "Environment: A New Focus for Public Policy?" *Public Administration Review* 23, no. 3 (1963); R. McGreggor Cawley, *Federal Land, Western Anger: The Sagebrush Rebellion and Environmental Politics* (Lawrence: University Press of Kansas, 1993), 38; Grant McConnell, "The Environmental Movement: Ambiguities and Meanings," *Natural Resources Journal* 11, no. 3 (1971).

4. Richard N. L. Andrews, "Agency Responses to NEPA: A Comparison and Implications," *Natural Resources Journal* 16, no. 2 (1976); Dennis C. Le Master, *Decade of Change: The Remaking of Forest Service Statutory Authority during the 1970s* (Westport, CT: Greenwood Press, 1984); Richard A. Liroff, *A National Policy for the Environment: NEPA and Its Aftermath* (Bloomington: Indiana University Press, 1976); Robert H. Nelson, "The New Range Wars: Environmentalists versus Cattlemen for the Public Rangelands" (Washington, DC: Office of Policy Analysis, 1980), 52–58; Joseph Sax, *Defending the Environment: A Strategy for Citizen Action* (New York: Alfred A. Knopf, 1971); Richard

B. Stewart, "The Reformation of American Administrative Law," *Harvard Law Review* 88, no. 8 (1975). *Sierra Club v. Morton*, 405 U.S. 727 (1972), relaxed standing requirements substantially.

5. Quoted in Phillip O. Foss, *Recreation* (New York: Chelsea House Publishers, 1971), 401. The Forest Service's autonomy declined during this period after a number of key clear-cutting controversies. Nonetheless, the Forest Service was able to adapt to the new pressures more easily than the BLM.

6. Culhane, *Public Lands Politics*, 218–19. Paul Culhane shows that BLM field managers played these competing interest groups off of one another, allowing the agency to escape capture by the livestock industry. This development was, however, far less than BLM leaders wanted, and the BLM lagged behind the Forest Service in setting its own agenda in the 1970s.

7. Richard W. Behan, "The Succotash Syndrome, or Multiple Use: A Heartfelt Approach to Forest Land Management," *Natural Resources Journal* 7, no. 4 (1967): 482–83.

8. Fairfax, "Beyond the Sagebrush Rebellion"; Frank Falen and Karen Budd Falen, "The Rights to Graze Livestock on the Federal Lands: The Historical Development of Western Grazing Rights," *Idaho Law Review* 30, no. 3 (1994); Foss, *Politics and Grass*, 61–68; Bill Steven Stern, "Permit Value: A Hidden Key to the Public Land Grazing Dispute" (Master's thesis, University of Montana, 1998).

9. Memorandum, James R. Schlesinger to John C. Whitaker, "Grazing Fees," December 1, 1969, Folder: "Public Land Law Review Commission: Grazing," Box 96, John C. Whitaker, (Whitaker), Staff Member and Office Files (SMOF), White House Central Files (WHCF), Richard M. Nixon Presidential Materials Staff (Nixon Materials), College Park, MD. As early as 1959, the Comptroller General recommended to Congress that the BLM and the Forest Service conduct a joint study of grazing fees, and in 1959, the Bureau of Budget released a circular that stressed uniform fees. U.S. Congress, Senate, Committee on Interior and Insular Affairs, *Grazing Fees on Public Lands*, 115.

10. U.S. Congress, Senate, Committee on Interior and Insular Affairs, *Grazing Fees on Public Lands*, 114–21, Memorandum, Harrison Loesch, Assistant Secretary for Public Land Management, to John C. Whitaker, "Grazing Fees," November 13, 1969. Memorandum, James R. Schlesinger, Acting Deputy Director of the Bureau of Budget, to John C. Whitaker, "Grazing Fees," December 1, 1969, Folder: PLLRC, Grazing 2 of 2, Box 96, Whitaker, SMOF, WHCF, Nixon Materials. Information Report, From the Secretariat to the Director, "Grazing Fees for the 1971 Grazing Season," November 5, 1970. Folder: Department of the Interior 1970, 2 of 5, Box 73, Whitaker, SMOF, WHCF, Nixon Materials.

11. American National Cattlemen's Association, "The Livestock Grazing Permit—Its Economic Importance" (Denver: American National Cattlemen's Association, 1968), 2.

12. U.S. Congress, Senate, Committee on Interior and Insular Affairs, *Grazing Fees on Public Lands*, 118.

13. Rasmussen argued that small livestock operators, who paid a $10 minimum rather than $0.33 per AUM fee, wouldn't experience an actual fee increase for the first six years. The 5 percent of permittees who used 52 percent of the allotted forage would see their total grazing fees rise from $264 to $984 over a the ten-year period.

14. Published in the *Federal Register* on January 14, 1969.

15. As governor of Alaska, Hickel had emphasized natural resource development, and environmentalists turned his nomination hearing into a bitter five-day battle. Hickel's coach

for his nomination hearings was future secretary of the interior James Watt (1981–1983), who focused on training Hickel to deflect environmental questions and challenges. Despite this training, Hickel distanced himself from Alaskan development interests in the hearings and pledged his support for tough oil and water pollution standards. In the end, Nixon removed Hickel, in part for being too environmental. See U.S. Congress, Senate, Committee on Interior and Insular Affairs, *Hearings on the Nomination of Governor Walter J. Hickel, of Alaska, to be Secretary of the Interior*, 91st Cong., 1st sess., January 15–18, 20, 1969; Ron Arnold, *At the Eye of the Storm: James Watt and the Environmentalists* (Chicago: Regnery Gateway, 1982), 12–13; Walter J. Hickel, *Who Owns America?* (Englewood Cliffs, NJ: Prentice-Hall, 1971), 39–40.

16. See *Pankey Land & Cattle Company v. Hardin and Hickel*, 427 F.2d 43 (10th Cir., 1970). The Circuit of Appeals upheld existing precedent: "Although the permits are valuable to the ranchers, they are not an interest protected by the Fifth Amendment against the taking by the Government who granted them with the understanding that they could be withdrawn . . . without the payment of compensation." *United States v. Cox*, 190 F.2d 293, 296 (10th Cir.) cert. denied, 342 U.S. 867. This interpretation was also upheld in *Porter v. Resor*, 415 F.2d 764, 766 (10th Cir. 1969). Folder: "Public Land Law Review Commission: Grazing," Box 96, Whitaker, SMOF, WHCF, Nixon Materials.

17. Memorandum, Harrison Loesch, Assistant Secretary for Public Land Management, to John C. Whitaker, "Grazing Fees," November 13, 1969. Memorandum, James R. Schlesinger, Acting Deputy Director of the Bureau of Budget, to John C. Whitaker, "Grazing Fees," December 1, 1969, Folder: PLLRC, Grazing 2 of 2, Box 96, Whitaker, SMOF, WHCF, Nixon Materials. Information Report, From the Secretariat to the Director, "Grazing Fees for the 1971 Grazing Season," November 5, 1970.

18. Thomas L. Kimball to Fred E. Russell, Acting Secretary of the Interior, December 14, 1970, Folder: Grazing Fees, Department of the Interior, Box 70, Whitaker, SMOF, WHCF, Nixon Materials (emphasis added).

19. The Forest Service's average fee went from $0.60 to $0.78. Roger Fleming to Walter J. Hickel, October 14, 1970, Folder: Grazing Fees, Department of the Interior, Box 70, Whitaker, SMOF, WHCF, Nixon Materials.

20. The fee increases were postponed two more times in 1975 and 1977.

21. Since an O & C scandal had led to the resignation of Charles Stoddard in 1966, the O & C lands were a focal point for Director Rasmussen's efforts to rebuild the agency's professional credibility. Bureau of Land Management, "An Environmentally Based Allowable Cut Plan for Full Forest Production in Western Oregon," April 1970, Rasmussen, FHS; "The O & C Lands" (Eugene: Bureau of Governmental Research and Service, University of Oregon, 1981), 35; Richardson, *BLM's Billion-Dollar Checkerboard: Managing the O&C Lands*, 163.

22. Richardson, *BLM's Billion-Dollar Checkerboard: Managing the O&C Lands*, 163.

23. Ibid.

24. Muhn and Stuart, *Opportunity and Challenge*, 142–47. The romantic myth of wild horses received a boost from the 1961 film *The Misfits*, starring Marilyn Monroe and Clark Gable.

25. Ibid., 147–50. Bureau of Land Management, News Release: "Wild Horse Study Committee Named by Bureau of Land Management," October 1, 1968, Rasmussen, FHS.

26. P.L. 92-195.

27. Dana and Fairfax, *Forest and Range Policy*, 260; Muhn and Stuart, *Opportunity and Challenge*, 200; George L. Turcott, interviewed by Bob Stewart, transcript, March 18, 1980 (Nevada State Office, BLM Library, Denver, CO), 11.

28. These included landmark cases: *Kleppe v. New Mexico* in 1976 (426 U.S. 529) expanded the federal government's authority over wildlife; *American Horse Protection Association, Inc. v. Watt* in 1982 (694 F.2d 1310) dealt with the BLM's implementation of the act; and *Mountain States Legal Foundation v. Hodel* in 1986 (799 F.2d. 1423) dealt with the problem of excess horses.

29. Rothman, "'A Regular Ding-Dong Fight.'"

30. Christopher James Klyza, *Who Controls Public Lands? Mining, Forestry, and Grazing Policies, 1870–1990* (Chapel Hill: University of North Carolina Press, 1996).

31. Lloyd C. Irland, "Citizen Participation—A Tool for Conflict Management on the Public Lands," *Public Administration Review* 35, no. 3 (1975); Jones, "Developing a Planning System for Public Domain Lands," 4, 24.

32. Jones, "Developing a Planning System for Public Domain Lands," 47; Nelson, *Public Lands and Private Rights*, 137.

33. Jones, "Developing a Planning System for Public Domain Lands," 34.

34. Nelson, *Public Lands and Private Rights*, 37.

35. Jones, "Developing a Planning System for Public Domain Lands," 50.

36. Nelson, *Public Lands and Private Rights*, 138.

37. Jones, "Multiple Use Planning in BLM," 6–7; Leman, "Formal versus De Facto Systems of Multiple Use Planning," 1858.

38. Robert H. Nelson, "Basic Issues in Land Use Planning for the Public Lands" (Washington, DC: Office of Policy Analysis, 1980), Part 2, 38.

39. Irving Senzel, who was instrumental in BLM's classification and planning programs and who was serving as assistant director for Legislation and Plans at the time of the commission's report, wrote, "There wasn't much opportunity for the type of agency participation we had expected. The work we did proved to be more valuable after the commission published its report in June 1970. It was the basis for BLM's post-Commission drive for an organic act." Senzel, "Genesis of a Law, Part 1," 61.

40. "Public Land Management: Identification of Problems—Analysis of Causes" (Washington, DC: Department of the Interior, 1968), 2.

41. Ibid., 34.

42. "Comments by the Department of the Interior on Legislative and Administrative Alternatives in PLLRC Study Reports, 1968–1970" (Washington, DC, 1970), Tab 7, 1–2.

43. Flippen writes that Nixon's advisors tried to downplay the report to avoid antagonizing environmental groups. J. Brooks Flippen, *Nixon and the Environment* (Albuquerque: University of New Mexico Press, 2000), 95–97.

44. George L. Turcott, interviewed by Bob Stewart, 8.

45. Stewart L. Udall, "Conflicting Claims over *A Third of the Nation*," *Newsday*, July 8, 1970.

46. R. McGreggor Cawley argues, "Rather than a manifesto for open exploitation, the PLLRC offered a carefully crafted set of recommendations attuned to both traditional conservation and new conservation." Cawley, *Federal Land, Western Anger*, 36.

47. James R. Wagner, "CPR Report/Government Lands Study Stirs Public-Private Interest Debate," *CPR National Journal* 2 (1970): 1093.

48. Paul W. Gates, *Pressure Groups and Recent American Land Policies, The Carl*

Becker Lecture (Ithaca, NY: Department of History, Cornell University, 1980), 12; Schulte, *Wayne Aspinall and the Shaping of the American West*. Aspinall explained at the 1962 White House Conference on Conservation, "To me this is what conservation has meant: Accepting all the material resources that nature is capable of providing, taking those natural resources where they are, and as they are, and developing them for the best use of the people as a whole. . . . It is a disservice to the conservation movement that many people have come to think of conservation as meaning preservation alone, to the exclusion of other uses." Panel on Conservation and the Congress, White House Conference on Conservation, May 24–25 (Washington, DC: Government Printing Office, 1962), 62.

49. *One Third of the Nation's Land*, 53.

50. Ibid., 2.

51. Ibid., 3. There have been two basic definitions of multiple use in American conservation. The first, advocated by G. A. Pearson, 1940, was that "multiple use would be applied over large enough areas that portions of the area could be managed for a single use, but that overall the area would be managed for more than one use." The second, advocated by Samuel T. Dana, was that "more than one use would be made of each area of forest land." Hagenstein, "Some History of Multiple Use and Sustained Yield Concepts," 32.

52. *One Third of the Nation's Land*, 70–77; Hamilton K. Pyles, ed., *What's Ahead for Our Public Lands? A Summary Review of the Activities and Final Report of the Public Land Law Review Commission* (Washington, DC: Natural Resources Council of America, 1970), 4–12.

53. Elmer W. Shaw, "Selected Commentaries on the Report of the Public Land Law Review Commission, *One Third of the Nation's Land*" (Washington, DC: Congressional Research Service, 1970), 3, 24–25.

54. Quoted in ibid., 17–18.

55. *One Third of the Nation's Land*, 121 (emphasis in the orginal). One may hear echoes of Gifford Pinchot's statement, "Coal is in a sense the vital essence of our civilization." Gifford Pinchot, *The Fight for Conservation* (New York: Doubleday, Page & Company, 1910), 43.

56. The commission explained that in looking at mineral development policy, it focused primarily on the nation's overriding need for fuel and nonfuel minerals. *One Third of the Nation's Land*, 121–22 (emphasis in the original).

57. Ibid., 127 (emphasis in the original).

58. Ibid., 117.

59. *National Wool Grower* 60, no. 7 (1970): 5.

60. Quoted in Shaw, "Selected Commentaries on the Report of the Public Land Law Review Commission, *One Third of the Nation's Land*," 24, 26.

61. T. H. Watkins and Charles S. Watson, Jr., *The Land No One Knows: America and the Public Domain* (San Francisco: Sierra Club Books, 1975), 153.

62. Donald E. Phillipson, "*One-Third of the Nation's Land*: The Public Land Law Review Commission Report: A Summary Critique from the Environmental Perspective" (Denver: Rocky Mountain Center on Environment, 1971); Pyles, *What's Ahead for Our Public Lands?*

63. This effort was led by Irving Senzel and Michael Harvey, who was chief of the Division of Legislation and Regulation. Muhn and Stuart, *Opportunity and Challenge,* 167; Senzel, "Genesis of a Law, Part 1," 61.

64. Memorandum from Secretary Hickel to John C. Whitaker, July 31, 1970, Folder:

Public Land Law Review Commission, Grazing, Box 96, Whitaker, SMOF, WHCF, Nixon Materials.

65. Muhn and Stuart, *Opportunity and Challenge*, 167; Senzel, "Genesis of a Law, Part 1," 61. BLM and Interior Department officials pressed repeatedly for Congress to extend the CMUA for at least two years while they worked with the BLM's congressional committees to produce a new statute. This request is featured, for example, in the secretary's initial response to the report. Memorandum from Assistant Secretary for Policy Planning and Research to the Under Secretary, "Public Land Law Review Commission Report," July 20, 1970, File: Committees—Public Land Law Review Commission Part 4, January 22, 1970–August 7, 1970, Central Classified Files 1969–1972, RG 48, NAII.

66. Introduced by Senator Jackson in August as S. 2401.

67. U.S. Congress, Senate, Committee on Energy and Natural Resources, *Legislative History of the Federal Land Policy and Management Act of 1976 (Public Law 94-579)*, 95th Cong., 2nd sess., April, 1978, 1111–1202; Senzel, "Genesis of a Law, Part 1," 62.

68. Mike Harvey, "BLM's Response to the Public Land Law Review Commission's Report," UP, Muhn, BLML, 4.

69. Aspinall introduced H.R. 7211 on April 6, 1971.

70. Senzel, "Genesis of a Law, Part 1," 63.

71. *One Third of the Nation's Land*, 6.

72. Ibid., 284–85.

73. Gates, *Pressure Groups and Recent American Land Policies*, 15–16.

74. *Papers Relating to the President's Departmental Reorganization Program: A Reference Compilation* (Washington, DC: U.S. Government Printing Office, 1972), 111–85.

75. Wolf, interviewed by Claire Rhein, 227–50.

76. *Papers Relating to the President's Departmental Reorganization Program*, 8, 12.

77. Lynton K. Caldwell, "The Ecosystem as a Criterion for Public Land Policy," *Natural Resources Journal* 10, no. 2 (1970): 204–5.

78. Caldwell, "Ecosystems Approach to Public Land Policy," 44. See also, by the same author, "Ecosystem as a Criterion for Public Land Policy"; *Environment: A Challenge for Modern Society* (New York: National History Press, 1970); "Environmental Quality as an Administrative Problem," *Annals of the American Academy of Political and Social Science* 400 (1972); *Man and His Environment: Policy and Administration* (New York: Harper & Row, 1975); "Public Policy Implications of Environmental Control" (paper presented at the Social Sciences and the Environment Conference on the Present and Potential Contribution of the Social Sciences to Research and Policy Formation in the Quality of the Physical Environment, Boulder, CO, January 31, February 1, 2, 1967).

79. George Cameron Coggins, Charles F. Wilkinson, and John D. Leshy, *Federal Public Land and Resources Law*, 4th ed. (New York: Foundation Press, 2001), 253–87; Stewart, "Reformation of American Administrative Law."

80. Jones, "Developing a Planning System for Public Domain Lands," 50; Irving Senzel, "The Future of BLM" (paper presented at the Bureau of Land Management Planning Conference, San Francisco, August 10–14, 1970).

81. Theodore J. Lowi, *The End of Liberalism: The Second Republic of the United States*, 2nd ed. (New York: W. W. Norton, 1979), 62. Lowi criticized this system of interest-group politics, arguing that it led increasingly to ambiguous delegation of congressional authority and ultimately weakened the rule of law.

82. Jones, "Developing a Planning System for Public Domain Lands," 50.

83. For helpful treatments of participation related to federal lands and specifically the Forest Service and BLM, see Gail L. Achterman and Sally K. Fairfax, "The Public Participation Requirements of the Federal Land Policy and Management Act," *Arizona Law Review* 21, no. 2 (1979); Sally K. Fairfax, "Public Involvement and the Forest Service," *Journal of Forestry* 73, no. 7 (1975); Irland, "Citizen Participation"; Michael P. Smith, "Alienation and Bureaucracy: The Role of Participatory Administration," *Public Administration Review* 31, no. 6 (1971); Stoddard, "Public Participation in Public Land Decisions"; Ben W. Twight, "Confidence or More Controversy: Whither Public Involvement?" *Journal of Forestry* 75 (1977). Herbert Kaufman wrote in 1969, "substantial (though minority) segments of the population apparently believe the political, economic, and social systems have not delivered to them fair—even minimally fair—shares of the [current] system's benefits and rewards, and . . . they think they cannot win their appropriate shares in those benefits and rewards through the political institutions of the country as they are now constituted." Herbert Kaufman, "Administrative Decentralization and Political Power," *Public Administration Review* 29, no. 1 (1969): 4.

84. Marion Clawson, *Federal Lands Revisited* (Washington, DC: Resources for the Future, 1983), 251.

85. Quoted in Flippen, *Nixon and the Environment*, 50–51.

86. 42 U.S.C. §4321.

87. Ron Hofman, head of the Division of Environmental Planning Coordination, helped lead initial efforts to create a formal environmental education program in the agency. The BLM held a bureau-wide environmental education workshop in 1971, and growing out of its Earth Day presence in primary and secondary schools, the agency developed an environmental education curriculum entitled *All around You* in 1971, with subsequent editions in 1973, 1975, and 1977. It isn't clear how much teachers used the curriculum nationally, but the State of Pennsylvania adopted it as an official text for sixth graders. The agency also established environment study areas in numerous districts throughout the West to provide outdoor classrooms for environmental education, and in 1974 it published an environmental education inventory. See *All around You* (Washington, DC: Bureau of Land Management, 1971); Ron Hofman, interviewed by James Muhn, transcript, 1988 (BLM Library, Denver, CO), 2–6.

88. Memorandum, Morton to the President, March 1970, Folder: Alaska Pipeline 4 of 4, Box 25, Whitaker, SMOF, WHCF, Nixon Materials; John C. Whitaker, *Striking a Balance: Environment and Natural Resources Policy in the Nixon-Ford Years*, AEI-Hoover *Policy Studies* (Washington, DC: American Enterprise Institute for Public Policy Research, 1976).

89. News Release, "Be Part of the Solution—Not the Problem," University of Alaska, Fairbanks, April 22, 1970, Folder: Alaska Pipeline 4 of 4, Box 25, Whitaker, SMOF, WHCF, Nixon Materials.

90. Ibid.

91. Ibid.

92. Stewart L. Udall and Jeff Stansbury, "The Pipeline Fantasy," *Newsday*, March 17, 1971.

93. 42 USC § 4332.

94. Liroff, *National Policy for the Environment*, 85–89.

95. NEPA added to the mounting procedural regulation governing federal agencies, starting significantly with the Administrative Procedure Act of 1946 and its later amendments.

96. Even in the years 1975–1980, the BLM continued to lag well behind the Forest Service on the number of EISs that it filed. In those years the BLM filed an average of twenty-two, while the Forest Service filed an average of sixty-three. Environmental Law Institute, "NEPA in Action: Environmental Offices in Nineteen Federal Agencies" (Washington, DC: Council on Environmental Quality, 1981), 38, 193.

97. VTN Consolidated, Inc., "The National Environmental Policy Act Process Study: An Evaluation of the Implementation and Administration of the NEPA by the Forest Service and the Bureau of Land Management" (Washington, DC: Council on Environmental Quality, 1975), 10.

98. Jones, "Multiple Use Planning in BLM," 7–8.

99. In the first two years of NEPA implementation, agencies in the Interior Department produced 83 EISs, and agencies in the Department of Agriculture produced 141. This was due in part to ambiguity about what exactly constituted a "major federal action" that necessitated an EIS. During this same two-year period, the Army Corp of Engineers produced 435 EISs and the Department of Transportation produced 1,293, presumably because these agencies were focused on major, discrete projects like dams and highways. In FY 1974, the BLM spent $3,849,243, or 1.3 percent of its operating budget, on EIS preparation. The Forest Service, by contrast, spent $27,225,000, or 2.7 percent of its operating budget, on EIS preparation. Russell W. Peterson, "Environmental Impact Statements: An Analysis of Six Years' Experience by Seventy Federal Agencies" (Washington, DC: Council on Environmental Quality, 1976), 22, 46–47.

100. Ron Hofman, who directed the Division of Environmental Planning Coordination in 1970, writes, "The problem in BLM . . . was not that the policy was not accepted . . . some believed that BLM activities were in fact already creating and maintaining suitable conditions in which man and nature can exist in productive harmony." Ron Hofman, "Implementation of the National Environmental Policy Act," *Publius* 2, no. 2 (1972): 121.

101. Ibid., 122–24.

102. *Citizens for Reid State Park v. Laird*, 336 F.Supp. 783 (1972), 788.

103. Instruction Memorandum no. 71-88, quoted from U.S. Congress, House, Subcommittee on Fisheries and Wildlife Conservation, *Administration of the National Environmental Policy Act—1972, Appendix,* 99th Cong., 2nd sess., February 17, 25, and May 24, 1972, 142.

104. U.S. Congress, House, Subcommittee on Fisheries and Wildlife Conservation, *Administration of the National Environmental Policy Act—1972*, 6.

105. In 1975, the BLM produced 9,431 EAs, compared to 60 to 65 by the Fish and Wildlife Service and 150 by the National Park Service. Peterson, "Environmental Impact Statements," 18. As Ron Hofman later recalled, "And so that became almost the biggest selling point [for EAs]. Not the fact that we were going to look at the environmental impacts and mitigate them but the fact that oh boy, if we do this, we won't have to write so many environmental impact statements." Ron Hofman, interviewed by James Muhn, 8.

106. VTN Consolidated, Inc., "National Environmental Policy Act Process Study," 12 (emphasis in the original).

107. Ibid.

108. GAO, "Administration of Regulations of Surface Exploration, Mining, and Reclamation of Public and Indian Coal Lands" (Washington, DC: General Accounting Office, 1972).

109. Muhn and Stuart, *Opportunity and Challenge*, 187.

110. Ibid.

111. Letter from Secretary Hickel to President Nixon, March 5, 1970, Memorandum for the Secretary of the Interior from John C. Whitaker, February 24, 1970, Memorandum, Rogers C. B. Morton to the President, "The Political Significance of the Alaskan Situation and the Alaskan Pipeline," Folders: Alaska Pipeline 1, 2, and 4 of 4, Box 25, Whitaker, SMOF, WHCF, Nixon Materials.

112. *Wilderness Society v. Hickel*, 325 F.Supp. 422 (D.C. 1970).

113. Equally important, five native villages in Alaska sued Secretary Hickel to block the permits until their land claims could be resolved. Peter Coates, *The Trans-Alaska Pipeline Controversy* (Bethlehem, Toronto: Lehigh University Press, Associated University Press, 1991), 189; Flippen, *Nixon and the Environment*, 90.

114. Coates, *Trans-Alaska Pipeline Controversy*, 200.

115. Memorandum for the President from the Council on Environmental Quality, "Secretary of the Interior's proposed Alaskan Pipeline," Folder: Alaska Pipeline 4 of 4, Box 25, Whitaker, SMOF, WHCF, Nixon Materials. Hofman, "Interview with Ron Hofman: His Role Implementing NEPA in BLM," 9–10.

116. *Environmental Defense Fund, Inc. v. Resor, Citizens to Preserve Overton Park, Inc. v. Volpe, Environmental Defense Fund v. Ruckelshaus*, and *Wellford v. Ruckelshaus*. Memorandum from the Solicitor [Interior Department] to the Secretary of the Interior, "Final Section 102(2)(C) Statement on Proposed Trans-Alaska Pipeline," March 12, 1971, Folder: Trans Alaska Pipeline, Box 26, Whitaker, SMOF, WHCF, Nixon Materials.

117. Memorandum from Secretary Morton to John Ehrlichman, Peter Flanigan, and John Whitaker, "Timetable for the TAPS Environmental Statement," Folder: Trans Alaska Pipeline 1 of 3, Box 26, Whitaker, SMOF, WHCF, Nixon Materials.

118. Memorandum from John C. Whitaker to John D. Ehrlichman, "Alaska Pipeline," March 4, 1971, Folder: Trans Alaska Pipeline 1 of 3, Box 26, Whitaker, SMOF, WHCF, Nixon Materials.

119. News Release, "Interior Releases Final Environmental Impact Statement on Trans-Alaska Pipeline Proposal; No Decision Due Yet," March 20, 1972, Folder: Trans Alaska Pipeline 2 of 4, Box 26, Whitaker, SMOF, WHCF, Nixon Materials; "National Security Aspects of Alaskan Oil," Folder: Trans Alaska Pipeline 4 of 4, Box 26, Whitaker, SMOF, WHCF, Nixon Materials.

120. *Wilderness Society v. Morton*, 479 F.2d 842, 1973.

121. Coates, *Trans-Alaska Pipeline Controversy*, 246–50.

122. *NRDC v. Morton* (458 F.2d 827, D.C. Cir. 1972).

123. *Natural Resources Defense Council v. Morton*, 458 F.2d 827 (D.C. Cir. 1972). Matthew J. Lindstrom and Zachary A. Smith, *The National Environmental Policy Act: Judicial Misconstruction, Legislative Indifference, and Executive Neglect*, ed. Dan Flores, Environmental History Series (College Station: Texas A&M University Press, 2001), 122; Liroff, *National Policy for the Environment*, 168–70.

124. *Natural Resources Defense Council v. Hughes*, 437 F.Supp. 981 (D.D.C. 1977). This general moratorium would remain in effect until 1976, when Congress passed the Federal Coal Leasing Amendments Act. Carl J. Mayer and A. Riley George, *Public Domain, Private Domain: A History of Public Land Mineral Policy in America* (San Francisco: Sierra Club Books, 1985), 142.

125. See *Natural Resources Defense Council, Inc. v. Berklund* (U.S. Court of Appeals, D.C.C., 1979) 609 F.2d 553. Sally K. Fairfax and Barbara T. Andrews, "Debate Within

and Debate Without: NEPA and the Redefinition of the 'Prudent Man' Rule," *Natural Resources Journal* 19, no. 3 (1979).

126. GAO, "Reclamation of Public and Indian Coal Lands" (Washington, DC: General Accounting Office, 1973); Robert H. Nelson, *The Making of Federal Coal Policy* (Durham, NC: Duke University Press, 1983), 45.

127. Nelson, *Making of Federal Coal Policy*, 45.

128. Quoted from ibid., 60–61.

129. Ibid., 105.

130. 437 F.Supp. 981 (D.D.C. 1977); Coggins, Wilkinson, and Leshy, *Federal Public Land and Resources Law*, 532.

131. Nelson, *Making of Federal Coal Policy*, 114.

132. Nelson, "New Range Wars," 45–46. *Natural Resources Defense Council v. Morton*, 388 F.Supp. 829, 1974.

133. Quoted from Nelson, "New Range Wars," 48.

134. Ibid.

135. Ibid.

136. Ibid., 43–52.

137. *NRDC v. Morton* (388 F.Supp. 829, 1974).

138. Nelson, "New Range Wars."

139. George L. Turcott, "Beginning at Challis: What Happened at Challis May Help Revitalize the Public Range," *Our Public Lands* 26, no. 1 (1975): 10.

140. Nelson, "New Range Wars," 55.

141. One author writes, "the federal judiciary helped coax a conservation agenda from recalcitrant elements within the BLM, to legitimate agency requests for badly needed funding, and to accelerate and diversify the Bureau's professionalization." Robert F. Durant, *The Administrative Presidency Revisited: Public Lands, the BLM, and the Reagan Revolution* (Albany: State University of New York Press, 1992), 24.

142. Nelson, "New Range Wars," 116.

143. Quoted from ibid., 51–52.

144. See Hays, "Public Values and Management Response"; Gary D. Libecap, *Locking Up the Range: Federal Land Controls and Grazing* (Cambridge, MA: Ballinger, 1981); Nelson, "New Range Wars"; Rowley, "Historical Considerations in the Development of Range Science"; Sagoff, *Price, Principle, and the Environment*.

145. Quoted in R. McGreggor Cawley and John Freemuth, "A Critique of the Multiple Use Framework in Public Lands Decisionmaking," in *Western Public Lands and Environmental Politics,* ed. Charles Davis (Boulder, CO: Westview Press, 1997), 34–35.

146. Jones, "Multiple Use Planning in BLM," 9.

147. Hofman, "Interview with Ron Hofman: His Role Implementing NEPA in BLM," 6; Muhn and Stuart, *Opportunity and Challenge*, 215.

148. Sagoff, *Price, Principle, and the Environment*, 201–32.

CHAPTER FIVE. POLITICAL INERTIA UNDER A NEW STATUTORY MANDATE

1. 30 U.S.C.A. §§22–39, 30 U.S.C. §§181 *et seq.,* 43 U.S.C. §§315–3160, and 43 U.S.C. §1181, respectively.

2. 43 U.S.C. §§1701–1782, P.L. 94-579.

3. John A. Carver, Jr., "BLM Organic Act: Federal Land Policy and Management Act of 1976: Fruition or Frustration," *Denver Law Journal* 54, no. 3–4 (1977); Fairfax, "Coming of Age in the Bureau of Land Management," 1727.

4. Cawley, *Federal Land, Western Anger*, 34–91.

5. "Legislative History of the Federal Land Policy and Management Act of 1976 (Public Law 94-579)," 1111–1474; Eleanor Schwartz, "A Capsule Examination of the Legislative History of the Federal Land Policy and Management Act of 1976," *Arizona Law Review* 21, no. 2 (1979).

6. "Legislative History of the Federal Land Policy and Management Act of 1976 (Public Law 94-579)," 212, 716.

7. Schwartz, "Capsule Examination"; Irving Senzel, "Genesis of a Law, Part 2," *American Forests* 84, no. 2 (1978). Senator Jackson identified forty-five major differences between the two acts that the conference committee needed to address. D. Michael Harvey, "Exempt from Public Haunt: The Wilderness Study Provisions of the Federal Land Policy and Management Act," *Idaho Law Review* 16, no. 3 (1980): 495.

8. For example, Irving Senzel worked for the House Subcommittee on Public Lands, and Michael Harvey was deputy chief counsel for the Senate Committee on Interior and Insular Affairs. Senzel, "Genesis of a Law, Part 2."

9. Schwartz, "Capsule Examination."

10. Quoted in D. Michael Harvey, "Support Your Local Sheriff: Federalism and Law Enforcement under the Federal Land Policy and Management Act," *Arizona Law Review* 21, no. 2 (1979): 461.

11. Ibid., 462; Paul B. Smyth, "Federal Law Enforcement on Public Lands: Reality or Mirage?" *Arizona Law Review* 21, no. 2 (1979).

12. Schwartz, "Capsule Examination"; Senzel, "Genesis of a Law, Part 2."

13. Schwartz, "Capsule Examination," 288.

14. Ibid.

15. 43 U.S.C. §102.

16. Ibid.

17. Tom Arrandale, *The Battle for Natural Resources* (Washington, DC: Congressional Quarterly, 1983), 71.

18. Foss, ed., *Public Land Policy*, 130. George L. Turcott, interviewed by Bob Stewart, 6.

19. FLPMA, §202(c)(3), 43 U.S.C. §1712.

20. FLPMA, §202(a), 43 U.S.C. §1712.

21. Jones, "Multiple Use Planning in BLM."

22. FLPMA, §202(f), 43 U.S.C. §1712.

23. Achterman and Fairfax, "Public Participation Requirements of the Federal Land Policy and Management Act," 512.

24. Hays, "Public Values and Management Response," 1825; *Our Public Lands* 14, nos. 3–4 (1965); "Report and Summary of Actions in the Bureau of Land Management during the Directorship of Charles H. Stoddard," 15–16.

25. 43 U.S.C. §1751.

26. 43 U.S.C. §1752; Carver, "BLM Organic Act," 394.

27. George Cameron Coggins, "The Law of Public Rangeland Management IV: FLPMA, PRIA, and the Multiple Use Mandate," *Environmental Law* 14 (Fall 1983): 22, 24.

28. Ibid., 26.

29. 43 U.S.C. §1744; Cheryl Outerbridge and Don H. Sherwood, "Recordation and Filing of Unpatented Mining Claims and Sites with the Federal Government," *Arizona Law Review* 21, no. 2 (1979): 434–35.

30. Leshy, *Mining Law*, 81.

31. 43 U.S.C. §1732(b).

32. Ibid.

33. Leshy, *Mining Law*, 200, 202.

34. Clare Ginger, "Interpreting Wilderness Policy in the Bureau of Land Management" (Ph.D. diss., University of Michigan, 1995); Craig W. Allin, *The Politics of Wilderness Preservation* (Westport, CT: Greenwood Press, 1982).

35. Harvey, "Exempt from Public Haunt."

36. George L. Turcott, interviewed by Bob Stewart, 27–28.

37. Harvey, "Exempt from Public Haunt," 492–93.

38. Ibid., 498–99.

39. 43 U.S.C. §1702.

40. Schwartz, "Capsule Examination," 288–89.

41. Quoted in Perry R. Hagenstein, "Public Lands and Environmental Concerns," *Arizona Law Review* 21, no. 2 (1979): 454.

42. Ibid.

43. The BLM prepared its first reports jointly with the National Park Service. It released "The California Desert" in 1968 and "The California Desert—A Critical Environmental Challenge" in 1970. See J. Russell Penny's account of managing the California Desert in Muhn and Stuart, *Opportunity and Challenge*, 130.

44. 43 U.S.C. §1781.

45. Ibid.; Muhn and Stuart, *Opportunity and Challenge*, 193; Frank Wheat, *California Desert Miracle: The Fight for Desert Parks and Wilderness* (San Diego, CA: Sunbelt Publications, 1999), 1–48.

46. "Legislative History of the Federal Land Policy and Management Act of 1976 (Public Law 94-579)," vi.

47. Carver, "BLM Organic Act."

48. Richard O. Miller, "FLPMA: A Decade of Management under the BLM Organic Act," *Policy Studies Journal* 14, no. 2 (1985): 266.

49. Achterman and Fairfax, "Public Participation Requirements of the Federal Land Policy and Management Act," 509.

50. For a helpful explanation of how the Forest Service culture has adjusted to new environmental values, see Kennedy, "Evolution of USDA Forest Service Organizational Culture."

51. Arrandale, *Battle for Natural Resources*, 72.

52. Rocky Barker, "Cecil Andrus Knew How to Take a Stand," *High Country News* 27, no. 3 (1995).

53. Arrandale, *Battle for Natural Resources*, 72–73.

54. Cecil Andrus, interviewed by James Reston, April 6, 1977 (James B. Reston Papers, University of Illinois Archives, Urbana, IL).

55. President Carter released his infamous hit list of major dam projects on February 21, 1977. President Carter's budget proposal removed funding for a total of nineteen major water projects, eight of which were located in western states. Secretary Andrus warned the president not to attack all nineteen projects because of the inevitable political fallout, but

the president chose to side with principles over politics in this matter. The episode cost the Carter administration an enormous amount of political capital. Cawley, *Federal Land, Western Anger*, 82. Cecil Andrus, interviewed by the author, May 18, 2007, Boise, ID.

56. Dana and Fairfax, *Forest and Range Policy*, 345.

57. Arrandale, *Battle for Natural Resources*, 73.

58. Nelson, *Making of Federal Coal Policy*, 107; Nelson, "New Range Wars," 70.

59. Luther J. Carter, "Interior Department: Andrus Promises 'Sweeping Changes,'" *Science* 196, no. 4289 (1977): 507.

60. Clarke and McCool, *Staking Out the Terrain*, 157–78.

61. "President's Reorganization Project Office of Management and Budget: Proposal for Natural Resources Organization" (Washington, DC: Office of Management and Budget, 1979), 1.

62. Ibid., 5–6.

63. White House Press Release, March 1, 1979, Folder 17, Box 1, 140.1, Andrus Papers (AP), Boise State University Library (BSL), Boise, ID.

64. Ickes, "Why a Department of Conservation," 12.

65. U.S. Congress, House, Subcommittee on Public Lands of the Committee on Interior and Insular Affairs, *Matters Relating to the Public Lands*, 96th Cong., 1st and 2nd sess., November 27, 29, 1979; February 22, June 12, 1980, 12.

66. Ibid.

67. Paul J. Culhane and H. Paul Friesema, "Land Use Planning for the Public Lands," *Natural Resources Journal* 19, no. 1 (1979).

68. Ibid.

69. Jones, "Multiple Use Planning in BLM," 10.

70. Culhane and Friesema, "Land Use Planning for the Public Lands"; Jones, "Multiple Use Planning in BLM," 7, 9.

71. Jones, "Multiple Use Planning in BLM," 9.

72. *Natural Resources Defense Council v. Morton*, 388 F.Supp. 829, 1974; Muhn and Stuart, *Opportunity and Challenge*, 207; Nelson, "New Range Wars," 49–50.

73. Nelson, "New Range Wars," 64–65.

74. Ibid., 66.

75. F. E. Mollin, *If and When It Rains: The Stockman's View of the Range Question* (Denver: American National Live Stock Association, 1938).

76. For a broader treatment of range science, see Rowley, "Historical Considerations in the Development of Range Science."

77. Nelson, "New Range Wars," 39–40.

78. Hays, "Public Values and Management Response," 1825.

79. GAO, "Public Rangelands Continue to Deteriorate" (Washington, DC: General Accounting Office, 1977), 6–8.

80. Joseph M. Feller, "What Is Wrong with the BLM's Management of Livestock Grazing on the Public Lands?" *Idaho Law Review* 30, no. 3 (1994).

81. Nelson, "New Range Wars," 71.

82. Quoted in ibid., 74–75.

83. Robert H. Nelson, "Making Sense of the Sagebrush Rebellion: A Long Term Strategy for the Public Lands" (paper presented at the Association for Public Policy Analysis and Management, Washington, DC, October 23–25, 1981), 19.

84. Nelson, "New Range Wars," 78.

85. George L. Turcott, interviewed by Bob Stewart, 14.

86. Libecap, *Locking Up the Range*, 82, n.10.

87. 43 U.S.C. §§1901–1908; Arrandale, *Battle for Natural Resources*, 166–67; Coggins, Wilkinson, and Leshy, *Federal Public Land and Resources Law*, 756–58. In 1979, the BLM charged $1.89 per AUM, and in 1980 the fee rose to $2.36 per AUM. By 1985, however, the fee had fallen to $1.35, and over the next twenty years, the fee was an average of $1.56. Betsy A. Cody, "Grazing Fees: An Overview" (Washington, DC: Congressional Research Service, 1996), 48.

88. Nelson, "New Range Wars," 76.

89. Nelson, *Making of Federal Coal Policy*, 60–61.

90. President's Environmental Message, May 23, 1977. Quoted in ibid., 107.

91. Quoted in ibid., 110.

92. Ibid., 118–19. The BLM held additional responsibility for coal leasing in federal lands managed by other federal land agencies.

93. Statement of John W. Sprague, Associate Director, Energy and Minerals Division, General Accounting Office, before the House Subcommittee on Mines and Mining, September 20, 1979.

94. Nelson, *Making of Federal Coal Policy*, 122.

95. Muhn and Stuart, *Opportunity and Challenge*, 215.

96. William L. Graf, *Wilderness Preservation and the Sagebrush Rebellions* (Savage, MD: Rowman & Littlefield, 1990). It was the previous rebellion, led by congressmen like Senator McCarran, that led Congress to slash the BLM's initial grazing budget for FY 1947.

97. Quoted in Cawley, *Federal Land, Western Anger*, 96.

98. Bruce Babbitt, "Federalism and the Environment: An Intergovernmental Perspective of the Sagebrush Rebellion," *Environmental Law* 12 (Summer 1982): 853.

99. Ibid., 858.

100. There have been several excellent treatments of the Sagebrush Rebellion. The best is probably Cawley, *Federal Land, Western Anger*. Other useful studies include Arrandale, *Battle for Natural Resources*; Durant, *Administrative Presidency Revisited*; Richard D. Lamm and Michael McCarthy, *The Angry West: A Vulnerable Land and Its Future* (Boston: Houghton Mifflin, 1982); C. Brant Short, *Ronald Reagan and the Public Lands: America's Conservation Debate, 1979–1984*, ed. Martin V. Melosi, vol. 10, Environmental History Series (College Station: Texas A&M University Press, 1989).

101. Cawley, *Federal Land, Western Anger*.

102. Arrandale, *Battle for Natural Resources*; Clarke and McCool, *Staking Out the Terrain*, 24; Durant, *Administrative Presidency Revisited;* Lamm and McCarthy, *Angry West;* Short, *Ronald Reagan and the Public Lands*.

103. Durant, *Administrative Presidency Revisited*, 12–18; Graf, *Wilderness Preservation and the Sagebrush Rebellions*, 221.

104. Durant, *Administrative Presidency Revisited*, 103.

105. Graf, *Wilderness Preservation and the Sagebrush Rebellions*, 221; Pamela A. Ray and Craig R. Carver, "Section 603 of the Federal Land Policy and Management Act: An Analysis of the BLM's Wilderness Study Process," *Arizona Law Review* 21, no. 2 (1979): 373.

106. Harvey, "Exempt from Public Haunt," 499.

107. Ginger, "Interpreting Wilderness Policy in the Bureau of Land Management"; Harvey, "Exempt from Public Haunt," 505–6.

108. Muhn and Stuart, *Opportunity and Challenge*, 184–90.

109. "Sagebrush Rebellion," Memorandum to All District Managers from the Chief of Public Affairs, January 8, 1980, Folder 171: The Sagebrush Rebellion, Public Lands Foundation Archive (PLFA), Phoenix, AZ.

110. Reagan's First Inaugural Address.

111. Durant, *Administrative Presidency Revisited*, 52.

112. Michael E. Kraft and Norman J. Vig, "Environmental Policy in the Reagan Presidency," *Political Science Quarterly* 99, no. 3 (1984): 427.

113. Arnold, *At the Eye of the Storm*, 1–26; Arrandale, *Battle for Natural Resources*, 166.

114. Speech before the Outdoor Writers Association of America, Louisville, KY, June 15, 1981, Folder 15: Speeches: Watt, Box 49, 140.1, AP, BSL.

115. See, for example, Jay D. Hair and Patrick A. Parenteau, "Marching Backwards: The Department of Interior under James G. Watt" (Washington, DC: National Wildlife Federation, 1982).

116. *A Year of Change: To Restore America's Greatness: Department of the Interior, January 20, 1981–January 20, 1982* (Washington, DC: Department of the Interior, 1982).

117. George Cameron Coggins and Doris K. Nagel, "'Nothing Beside Remains': The Legal Legacy of James G. Watt's Tenure as Secretary of the Interior on Federal Land Law and Policy," *Boston College Environmental Affairs Law Review* 17, no. 3 (1990): 476.

118. Ibid.

119. Michael Moss, "Making the Most of the Public Lands," *High Country News* 13, no. 22 (1981).

120. Muhn and Stuart, *Opportunity and Challenge*, 262–63.

121. Durant, *Administrative Presidency Revisited*, 53.

122. Kraft and Vig, "Environmental Policy in the Reagan Presidency," 430.

123. Robert V. Bartlett, "The Budgetary Process and Environmental Policy," in *Environmental Policy in the 1980s: Reagan's New Agenda*, ed. Norman J. Vig and Michael E. Kraft (Washington, DC: CQ Press, 1984), 123.

124. Ibid., 129.

125. Moss, "Making the Most of the Public Lands," 1.

126. Leman, "Formal versus De Facto Systems of Multiple Use Planning."

127. Jones, "Multiple Use Planning in BLM," 11.

128. Leman, "Formal versus De Facto Systems of Multiple Use Planning," 1879.

129. Moss, "Making the Most of the Public Lands." See also the October 31, 1983, issue of *High Country News*, which provides a retrospective on the Watt years.

130. Moss, "Making the Most of the Public Lands," 11.

131. Coggins and Nagel, "'Nothing Beside Remains,'" 540; Nelson, "New Range Wars," 78.

132. Quoted in Leman, "Formal versus De Facto Systems of Multiple Use Planning," 1878.

133. Coggins and Nagel, "'Nothing Beside Remains,'" 540–41.

134. Arrandale, *Battle for Natural Resources*, 167.

135. Ibid.; Coggins and Nagel, "'Nothing Beside Remains,'" 540.

136. Coggins and Nagel, "'Nothing Beside Remains,'" 542.

137. Andrews, "Environment and Energy"; Coggins and Nagel, "'Nothing Beside Remains,'" 529, n.389.

138. Quoted in Mayer and George, *Public Domain, Private Domain*, 275.

139. "Washington Office Reorganziation," Informational Memorandum No. 81-237, July 21, 1981, Folder 136, PLFA.

140. Muhn and Stuart, *Opportunity and Challenge*, 225–28.

141. Quoted in Nelson, *Making of Federal Coal Policy*, 236.

142. Arrandale, *Battle for Natural Resources*, 93–99; Hair and Parenteau, "Marching Backwards," 18; John D. Leshy, "Natural Resource Policy," in *Natural Resources and the Environment*, ed. Paul R. Portney (Washington, DC: Resources for the Future, 1984), 23–26; Nelson, *Making of Federal Coal Policy*, 232–39.

143. Coggins and Nagel, "'Nothing Beside Remains,'" 529, 631.

144. Paul J. Culhane, "Sagebrush Rebels in Office: Jim Watt's Land and Water Politics," in *Environmental Policy in the 1980s: Reagan's New Agenda*, ed. Norman J. Vig and Michael E. Kraft (Washington, DC: CQ Press, 1984), 301–3.

145. Durant, *Administrative Presidency Revisited*, 207, 344–45, n.210.

146. Ibid., 207–8.

147. Coggins and Nagel, "'Nothing Beside Remains,'" 517.

148. Gregg, "Federal Land Transfers."

CHAPTER SIX. BLM IN THE 1990S: BUREAU OF LANDSCAPES AND MONUMENTS?

1. Beginning in 1994, Congress placed a moratorium on mining patents.

2. Michael P. Dombeck, interviewed by Harold K. Steen, transcript, May 15–18, 2003 (Forest History Society, Stevens Point, WI, Durham, NC), 26; Hair and Parenteau, "Marching Backwards."

3. John C. Hendee and Randall C. Pitstick, "The Growth of Environmental and Conservation-Related Organizations: 1980–1991," *Renewable Resources Journal* 10, no. 2 (1992); Norman J. Vig, "Presidential Leadership and the Environment: From Reagan to Clinton," in *Environmental Policy in the 1990s: Reform or Reaction?* ed. Norman J. Vig and Michael E. Kraft (Washington, DC: CQ Press, 1997).

4. Vig, "Presidential Leadership and the Environment," 101–4.

5. "Issues for the 90's: Bureau of Land Management" (Washington, DC: Bureau of Land Management, 1989).

6. Charles A. Bowsher, "Interior Issues" (Washington, DC: General Accounting Office, 1988); James Duffus, "Public Land Management: Issues Related to the Reauthorization of the Bureau of Land Management" (Washington, DC: General Accounting Office, 1991).

7. "Federal Land Management: Limited Action Taken to Reclaim Hardrock Mine Sites" (Washington, DC: General Accounting Office, 1987); "Public Lands: Limited Progress in Resource Management Planning" (Washington, DC: General Accounting Office, 1990); "Rangeland Management: BLM Efforts to Prevent Unauthorized Livestock Grazing Need Strengthening" (Washington, DC: General Accounting Office, 1990); "Rangeland Management: Interior's Monitoring Has Fallen Short of Agency Requirements" (Washington,

DC: General Accounting Office, 1992); "Rangeland Management: More Emphasis Needed on Declining and Overstocked Grazing Allotments" (Washington, DC: General Accounting Office, 1988); "Shortfalls in BLM's Management of Wildlife Habitat in the California Desert Conservation Area" (Washington, DC: General Accounting Office, 1989); Duffus, "Public Land Management"; GAO, "Federal Land Management: The Mining Law of 1872 Needs Revision" (Washington, DC: General Accounting Office, 1989).

8. Betsy A. Cody and Pamela Baldwin, "Bureau of Land Management Authorization" (Washington, DC: Congressional Research Service, 1995).

9. See Carver, "BLM Organic Act"; John A. Carver, Jr., and Craig R. Carver, "Federal Land Policy and Management Act of 1976," *Rocky Mountain Mineral Law Newsletter* 9, no. 10 (1976).

10. Mike Dombeck, Christopher Wood, and Jack E. Williams, *From Conquest to Conservation: Our Public Lands Legacy* (Washington, DC: Island Press, 2003), 40–41; Cy Jamison, interviewed by James Muhn (Denver, CO: BLM Library, 1991), 1–3, 8–9, 12–13.

11. Cy Jamison, interviewed by James Muhn, 3–4.

12. It should be noted that President Bush's environmental interest and commitment waned substantially over the course of his presidency, following a pattern very similar to that of President Nixon. During his unsuccessful reelection campaign in 1992, for example, he repeatedly attacked the Democratic environmental platform. Dennis L. Soden, ed., *The Environmental Presidency* (Albany: State University of New York Press, 1999), 117–18.

13. Michael P. Dombeck, interviewed by Harold K. Steen, 30.

14. Ibid., 26; Cy Jamison, interviewed by James Muhn, 4. During Jamison's first two and a half years as director, the BLM's budget rose by $165 million, and most of this went to programs like recreation, fish and wildlife, and so on.

15. Maitland Sharpe, David L. Ture, James E. Browns, J. Wayne Burkhardt, Stan Tixier, Bob McQuivey, Delmar Vail, H. James Fox, and Deen Boe, "Report of the Blue Ribbon Panel to the National Public Lands Advisory Council on Rangeland Program Initiatives and Strategies" (Washington, DC: National Public Lands Advisory Council, 1992), 1–2.

16. Ibid., 4.

17. Ibid.

18. Jamison's pledge came after a scathing GAO report suggested that BLM field managers were not supported in these efforts, and he encouraged cooperative agreements with conservation organizations to protect riparian areas. Dombeck, interviewed by Harold K. Steen, 36; Duffus, "Public Land Management," 5; GAO, "Public Rangelands: Some Riparian Areas Restored but Widespread Improvement Will Be Slow" (Washington, DC: General Accounting Office, 1988), 4.

19. "Change Urged in Mining Law," *New York Times*, September 24 1991; GAO, "Federal Land Management: An Assessment of Hardrock Mining Damage" (Washington, DC: General Accounting Office, 1988); GAO, "Federal Land Management: The Mining Law of 1872 Needs Revision."; John D. Leshy, "Mining Law Reform Redux, Once More," *Natural Resources Journal* 42, no. 3 (2002): 463.

20. Mike Dombeck, "Blueprint for the Future" (Washington, DC: Bureau of Land Management, 1994).

21. Cy Jamison, interviewed by James Muhn, 5. Draft Executive Order: Designation of National Trust Lands, June 28, 1989, BLM Library, Denver Service Center, Denver, CO. See also memoranda in "Names for the Public Lands–National Resource Lands, Etc.,"

Folder no. 168, Subject Code 1610, "Resource Management Planning," Public Lands Foundation Archive, BLM National Training Center, Phoenix, AZ.

22. The BLM and the Forest Service agreed to implement something called the "Oregon Spotted Owl Management Plan" in 1977. Jack Ward Thomas, Eric D. Forsman, Joseph B. Linit, E. Charles Meslow, Barry B. Noon, and Jared Verner, "A Conservation Strategy for the Northern Spotted Owl: Report of the Interagency Scientific Committee to Address the Conservation of the Northern Spotted Owl" (Portland, OR: USDA Forest Service, USDI Bureau of Land Management, USDI Fish and Wildlife Service, USDI National Park Service, 1990), 52–53.

23. Dombeck, Wood, and Williams, *From Conquest to Conservation*, 39–40; Dombeck, interviewed by Harold K. Steen, 44; Bruce G. Marcot and Jack Ward Thomas, "Of Spotted Owls, Old Growth, and New Policies: A History since the Interagency Scientific Committee Report" (Washington, DC: USDA Forest Service, 1997), 5–6; Brendon Swedlow, "Scientists, Judges, and Spotted Owls: Policymakers in the Pacific Northwest," *Duke Environmental Law and Policy Forum* 13 (2003): 265–67.

24. *Seattle Audubon Society v. Evans*, 771 F.Supp 1081 (W.D. Wash., 1991), and *Portland Audubon Society v. Lujan*, 784 F.Supp 786 (D. Or., 1992).

25. Dombeck, Wood, and Williams, *From Conquest to Conservation*; Marcot and Thomas, "Of Spotted Owls, Old Growth, and New Policies," 7.

26. Dombeck, Wood, and Williams, *From Conquest to Conservation*, 41–42.

27. Jamison, interviewed by James Muhn, 3.

28. Dombeck, Wood, and Williams, *From Conquest to Conservation*, 37–40.

29. Phillip A. Davis, "Critics Say Too Few Jobs, Owls Saved under 'God Squad' Plan," *Congressional Quarterly Weekly Report* 50, no. 20 (1992); Jon Healy, "Ten Environmental Nettles That Await the 103rd Congress," *Congressional Quarterly Weekly Report* 51, no. 7 (1992).

30. Quoted in Oliver Houck, "Reflections on the Endangered Species Act," *Environmental Law* 25, no. 3 (Summer 1995): 691.

31. "Presidential Elections 1988–2000," http://www.nationalatlas.gov, accessed May 1, 2006.

32. John D. Leshy, "Natural Resources Policy in the Clinton Administration: A Mid-Course Evaluation from Inside," *Environmental Law* 25 (Summer 1995): 679.

33. Jon Healy, "From Conflict to Coexistence: New Politics of Environment," *Congressional Quarterly Weekly Report* 51, no. 7 (1993): 309; Vig, "Presidential Leadership and the Environment," 106.

34. Bruce Babbitt, "The Future Environmental Agenda for the United States," *University of Colorado Law Review* 64, no. 2 (1993).

35. Valerie Richardson, "Alone on the Range," *National Review* 46, no. 10 (1994): 24.

36. Vig, "Presidential Leadership and the Environment," 107.

37. Bruce Babbitt, interviewed by Charles Wilkinson and Patricia Limerick, transcript, April 20, 2004, Center of the American West, Boulder, CO.

38. Alexander Cockburn, "'Win-Win' with Bruce Babbitt: The Clinton Administration Meets the Environment," *New Left Review* 201 (1993): 48.

39. One columnist for *High Country News* wrote, "He came in assuming that the West had changed character during the Reagan-Bush years, and that it wanted to reform grazing, mining, logging, and water development." Ed Marston, "Babbitt Is Trying to Nationalize the BLM," *High Country News* 26, no. 9 (1994); Ed Marston, "Jim

Baca Says the Department of Interior Is in Deep Trouble," *High Country News* 26, no. 3 (1994).

40. Catalina Camia, "Many Find Babbitt Too Valuable to Move from Cabinet to Court," *Congressional Quarterly Weekly Report* 51, no. 24 (1993).

41. Paul Larmer, "The Drill Starts to Change at Interior," *High Country News* 25, no. 4 (1993).

42. Quoted in Marston, "Jim Baca Says the Department of Interior Is in Deep Trouble."

43. Healy, "From Conflict to Coexistence," and "Ten Environmental Nettles That Await the 103rd Congress."

44. George Hager, "President Throws Down Gauntlet," *Congressional Quarterly Weekly Report* 51, no. 8 (1993); Ed Marston, "Interior View: Bruce Babbitt Took the Real West to Washington, DC: A *High Country News* Interview," *High Country News* 33, no. 3 (2001).

45. Elizabeth Palmer, "More Money Comes in under Plan for 'Savings' in Budget," *Congressional Quarterly Weekly Report* 51, no. 8 (1993).

46. John D. Leshy, "The Babbitt Legacy at the Department of the Interior: A Preliminary View," *Environmental Law* 31 (Spring 2001).

47. Babbitt explained, "I came into office that first day to find that the Office of Management and Budget had already penciled the grazing fee and the mining fee increases into the budget. They didn't even bother to consult with us, so we were stuck with opening that battle on a ground not of our choosing. . . . Then, to make matters worse two or three months later, the White House unilaterally—without talking to us—pulls the grazing fee off the table." Marston, "Interior View."

48. Michael P. Dombeck, interviewed by Harold K. Steen, 54.

49. Bruce Babbitt, interviewed by Charles Wilkinson and Patricia Limerick.

50. Marston, "Interior View."

51. Bruce Babbitt, interviewed by Charles Wilkinson and Patricia Limerick; Bruce Babbitt, "Science: Opening the Next Century of Conservation History," *Science* 267, no. 5206 (1995).

52. In one report, the GAO explains, "Currently, ecosystem management has no clear policy goal, and the term has come to represent different things to different people." GAO, "Ecosystem Management: Additional Actions Needed to Adequately Test a Promising Approach" (Washington, DC: General Accounting Office, 1994), 3.

53. Interagency Ecosystem Management Task Force, "The Ecosystem Approach: Healthy Ecosystems *and* Sustainable Economies" (Washington, DC: Task Force, 1995), 17.

54. John Freemuth, "The Emergence of Ecosystem Management: Reinterpreting the Gospel?" *Society and Natural Resources* 9, no. 4 (1996); GAO, "Ecosystem Management"; William M. Lewis, Jr., "The Ecological Sciences and the Public Domain," *University of Colorado Law Review* 65, no. 2 (1993).

55. John D. Leshy, "Is the Multiple Use/Sustained Yield Management Philosophy Still Applicable Today?" (paper presented at the workshop "Multiple Use and Sustained Yield: Changing Philosophies for Federal Land Management?" Washington, DC, March 5–6, 1992).

56. Behan, "Irony of the Multiple Use/Sustained Yield Concept."

57. Tom Marshall, "Ecosystem Management: Sustaining the Nation's Natural Resources Trust" (Washington, DC: Committee on Resources, U.S. House of Representatives, 1994), ix.

58. Interagency Ecosystem Management Task Force, "The Ecosystem Approach," 17.

59. Marshall, "Ecosystem Management."

60. Dombeck, Wood, and Williams, *From Conquest to Conservation*, 157.

61. Martha H. Brookes, ed, "The Northwest Forest Plan: A Report to the President and Congress" (Washington, DC: U.S. Department of Agriculture, Office of Forestry and Economic Assistance, 1996), 1; Dombeck, interviewed by Harold K. Steen, 43; Marcot and Thomas, "Of Spotted Owls, Old Growth, and New Policies."

62. Bruce Babbitt, interviewed by Charles Wilkinson and Patricia Limerick.

63. Brookes, "Northwest Forest Plan," 101–5; Catalina Camia, "Clinton's Forest Compromise Is Assailed from All Sides," *Congressional Quarterly Weekly Report* 51, no. 27 (1993); Dombeck, Wood, and Williams, *From Conquest to Conservation*, 44–48.

64. President Clinton promised a total of $1.2 billion for job retraining and other types of assistance. Ross W. Gorte, "The Clinton Administration's Forest Plan for the Pacific Northwest" (Washington, DC: Congressional Research Service, 1993).

65. Catalina Camia, "Administration Aims to Increase Grazing Fees, Tighten Rules," *Congressional Quarterly Weekly Report* 51, no. 33 (1993).

66. Ibid.

67. Catalina Camia, "Babbitt and Western Democrats Reach Pact on Grazing Fees," *Congressional Quarterly Weekly Report* 51, no. 40 (1993); Catalina Camia, "The Filibuster Ends; Bill Clears; Babbitt Can Still Raise Fees," *Congressional Quarterly Weekly Report* 51, no. 45 (1993); Catalina Camia, "Senate Votes to Block Increase in Grazing Fees Next Year," *Congressional Quarterly Weekly Report* 51, no. 37 (1993).

68. Hannah Gosnell, "Rangeland Reform '94 and the Politics of the Old West: An Analysis of Institutional and Ideological Barriers to Reforming Federal Rangeland Policy" (Master's thesis, University of Colorado, 1995).

69. Catalina Camia, "Babbitt Offers New Plan in Grazing Fee Dispute," *Congressional Quarterly Weekly Report* 52, no. 11 (1994).

70. Catalina Camia, "Democrats Lash Out at Babbitt over Revised Grazing Plan," *Congressional Quarterly Weekly Report* 52, no. 10 (1994).

71. U.S. Congress, Senate, Committee on Energy and Natural Resources, *Grazing*, 103rd Cong., 2nd sess., April 20, May 14, 1994, 20.

72. Ibid., 2–3.

73. Laura Michaelis, "Economic, Ecological Climate Favors Mining Law Overhaul," *Congressional Quarterly Weekly Report* 51, no. 12 (1993).

74. One author writes, "The 1872 Mining Law is a throwback to the frontier era when it was more important to settle the West and exploit its resources. The law does not charge royalties for the extraction of hard-rock minerals such as gold and silver, contains few rules for the repair of damaged lands and presumes that mining is acceptable on virtually any federal parcel." "Mining Law," *Congressional Quarterly Weekly Report* 52, no. 43 (1994).

75. Leshy, "Mining Law Reform Redux, Once More."

76. Palmer, "More Money Comes in under Plan for 'Savings' in Budget"; Daphine Werth, "Where Regulation and Property Rights Collide: Reforming the Hardrock Act of 1872," *University of Colorado Law Review* 65, no. 2 (1994).

77. Chip Giller, "Babbitt Protests a $1 Billion Giveaway," *High Country News* 27, no. 18 (1995); Leshy, "Babbitt Legacy at the Department of the Interior," 223.

78. Catalina Camia, "Senate OKs Mining Law Rewrite; Bill Is Backed by Industry," *Congressional Quarterly Weekly Report* 51, no. 22 (1993); Leshy, "Mining Law Reform Redux, Once More," 463.

79. Bob Benenson, "House Easily Passes Overhaul of 1872 Mining Law," *Congressional Quarterly Weekly Report* 51, no. 46 (1993).

80. "Action on Mining Law Awaits Babbitt's Grazing Fee Plan," *Congressional Quarterly Weekly Report* 52, no. 9 (1994); Marc Humphries, "Mining on Federal Lands" (Washington, DC: Congressional Research Service, 2002), 12–13.

81. Leshy, "Mining Law Reform Redux, Once More," 464.

82. Ibid., 464–65.

83. 43 U.S.C. §1732.

84. Leshy, "Mining Law Reform Redux, Once More," 475–76.

85. Ibid., 477. See "Hardrock Mining on Federal Lands" (Washington, DC: National Research Council, 1999).

86. These were consistent with the National Research Council's 1999 report: "Hardrock Mining on Federal Lands," 93–124.

87. Quoted in Leshy, "Mining Law Reform Redux, Once More," 479.

88. Leshy, "Babbitt Legacy at the Department of the Interior," 224.

89. Sanjay Ranchod, "The Clinton National Monuments: Protecting Ecosystems with the Antiquities Act," *Harvard Environmental Law Review* 25 (2001). For broader treatments of the Antiquities Act and national monuments, see David Harmon, Francis P. McManamon, and Dwight T. Pitcaithley, eds., *The Antiquities Act: A Century of American Archaeology, Historic Preservation, and Nature Conservation* (Tucson: University of Arizona Press, 2006); Paul Larmer, ed., *Give and Take: How the Clinton Administration's Public Lands Offensive Transformed the American West* (Paonia, CO: High Country News Books, 2004); Hal Rothman, *Preserving Different Pasts: The American National Monuments* (Chicago: University of Illinois Press, 1989).

90. 16 U.S.C. §431.

91. Rothman, *Preserving Different Pasts.*

92. Clare Ginger, "Discourse and Argument in Bureau of Land Management Wilderness Environmental Impact Statements," *Policy Studies Journal* 28, no. 2 (2000). It is interesting that the land included in the Grand Staircase–Escalante National Monument in 1996 was part of a National Park Service monument proposal in 1936, and some of the first people to oppose the monument were from one of the BLM's predecessor agencies, the U.S. Grazing Service. Elmo Richardson, "Federal Park Policy in Utah: The Escalante National Monument Controversy of 1935–1940," *Utah Historical Quarterly* 33, no. 2 (1965).

93. Bruce Babbitt, interviewed by Charles Wilkinson and Patricia Limerick.

94. Ibid.

95. The final monument plan included some 1.8 million acres of land. Doug Goodman and Daniel C. McCool, eds., *Contested Landscape: The Politics of Wilderness in Utah and the West* (Salt Lake City: University of Utah Press,1999).

96. Personal conversation with BLM staff.

97. Proclamation 6920.

98. Charles F. Wilkinson, "Clinton Learns the Art of Audacity," *High Country News* 28, no. 18 (1996).

99. Marston, "Interior View."

100. Bruce Babbitt, "From Grand Staircase to Grand Canyon Parashant: Is There a Monumental Future for the BLM?" (paper presented at the University of Denver Law School, February 17, 2000); Leshy, "Babbitt Legacy at the Department of the Interior," 219.

101. Paul Larmer, "Utah Counties Bulldoze the BLM, Park Service," *High Country News*, October 28, 1996; U.S. Congress, House, Subcommittee on National Parks and Public Lands, *Behind Closed Doors: The Abuse of Trust and Discretion in the Establishment of the Grand Staircase–Escalante National Monument*, 105th Cong., 1st sess., November 7, 1997.

102. Bruce Babbitt, interviewed by Charles Wilkinson and Patricia Limerick.

103. A. Jerry Meredith, "The BLM Planning Process," in *Visions of the Grand Staircase–Escalante: Examining Utah's Newest National Monument*, ed. Robert B. Keiter, Sarah B. George, and Joro Walker (Salt Lake City: Utah Museum of Natural History and Wallace Stegner Center, 1998).

104. Interior paid the Andalex Corporation $14 million to relinquish its seventeen leases, covering 35,000 acres, and it paid the Pacific-Corp $5.5 million to relinquish its one 18,000-acre lease. Gary C. Bryner, "What Does the Grand Staircase–Escalante Mean for Land Protection in the West? Resource Development and Ecological Protection," *Journal of Land Resources & Environmental Law* 21 (2001): 569–72. This was the largest federal land exchange since the Louisiana Purchase. The Interior Department exchanged 139,000 acres of land and mineral rights elsewhere in Utah along with $13 million in future coal royalties and $50 million in cash for 377,000 acres of state land, 177,000 of which were in the monument. Bryner, "What Does the Grand Staircase–Escalante Mean for Land Protection in the West?" 572–77.

105. Dean Reeder, "The Utah Travel Division and Tourism Planning," in *Visions of the Grand Staircase–Escalante: Examining Utah's Newest National Monument*, ed. Robert B. Keiter, Sarah B. George, and Joro Walker (Salt Lake City: Utah Museum of Natural History and Wallace Stegner Center, 1998). BLM field managers whom I interviewed in the summer of 2002 generally expressed distain for the National Park Service's more intensive management of recreation and tourism. They expressed a sense of pride that the BLM does not fence off its land or resources and does not provide visitors with extensive amenities within its national monuments.

106. Andy Kerr and Mark Salvo, "Evolving Presidential Policy toward Livestock Grazing in National Monuments," *Penn State Law Review* 10 (2001).

107. The increased scrutiny of grazing allotments encouraged the BLM, livestock operators, and environmental conservation groups to reduce grazing levels through private agreements and sales in order to avoid protracted grazing disputes between grazing permittees and the BLM. For example, the Grand Canyon Trust, a nonprofit organization, worked with the BLM and livestock operators in particularly sensitive areas of the monument. The trust reported that by compensating livestock operators for relinquishing grazing privileges to the BLM or by buying grazing privileges through a nonprofit grazing corporation it had eliminated grazing on more than 200,000 acres, or 10 percent, of the monument http://www.grandcanyontrust.org.

108. Michelle Nijhuis, "Change Comes Slowly to Escalante Country," *High Country News* 35, no. 7 (2003).

109. Bruce Babbitt, interviewed by Charles Wilkinson and Patricia Limerick.

110. The BLM identified areas that are now part of national monuments in 1965, when it released an inventory of 100 areas of natural, scientific, and historic value. The area now included in the Craters of the Moon National Monument expansion was among these sites. Donald B. Stough, "Wonders of the Public Domain," *Our Public Lands* 14, no. 3 (1965). Later, Secretary Udall designated sixteen of these areas as official scientific natural areas. *Our Public Lands,* 14, no. 4 (1965). In 1969, part of what is now Grand Staircase–Escalante National Monument was designated as one of the BLM's first two primitive areas, and a significant portion of what is now Vermillion Cliffs National Monument was designated a natural area. Robert B. Whitaker, "Keeping the Wild Lands Wild: BLM's First Primitive Areas," *Our Public Lands* 19, no. 2 (1969).

111. Mark E. Lawrence, "Pilot Rock: Ancient Guide of the Siskiyous," *Our Public Lands* 20, no. 4 (1970). Lawrence discusses a significant landform in what is now the Cascade-Siskiyou National Monument. Ivan B. Willis, "The Secret of Fifty Mile Mountain: Is It Lost Treasure?" *Our Public Lands* 18, no. 4 (1968). Willis discusses an area that is now part of the Grand Staircase–Escalante National Monument.

112. One author wrote in April 2000, "This time he is no passive observer of someone else's process. This time he comes West bearing a big stick and a small carrot. The stick is the Antiquities Act of 1906, and a threat to use it in a dozen or more places in the West to create national monuments, as President Bill Clinton did at Grand Staircase–Escalante in Utah, and more recently in Arizona and California. The carrot is a promise not to create another national monument if local interests and their congressional representatives come up with and pass a bill to protect the land." Ed Marston, "Beyond the Revolution," *High Country News* 32, no. 7 (2000); Stephen Stuebner, "Go Tell It on the Mountain," *High Country News* 31, no. 22 (1999).

113. "Public Rewards from the Public Lands, 2003" (Washington, DC: Bureau of Land Management, 2004), 3–4.

114. Bruce Babbitt, "Remarks by Secretary Bruce Babbitt" (paper presented at the BLM Interactive Townhall Meeting, Pheonix, AZ, March 24, 2000).

115. John Leshy, interior solicitor from 1993–2001, reiterated this challenge and threat in 2002: "The overall trend is inexorable. BLM has to become more conservation-oriented, or it will be effectively destroyed. If the NLCS does not thrive and grow inside BLM, it will ultimately be parceled out to the Forest Service, the FWS and the NPS." John D. Leshy, "BLM's Future" (paper presented at the Restoring and Managing Western Public Range and Grasslands: Public Lands Foundation 2002 Annual Meeting and Symposium, Sacramento, CA, September12–13 2002).

116. The author conducted interviews in seven BLM offices with national monument responsibilities in 2003.

117. Kirsten Bovee, "Monuments Caught in the Crosshairs," *High Country News* 33, no. 8 (2001).

118. See, for example, Durant, *Administrative Presidency Revisited*; Short, *Ronald Reagan and the Public Lands*; Soden, *Environmental Presidency*; Jacqueline Vaughn and Hanna J. Cortner, *George W. Bush's Healthy Forests: Reframing the Environmental Debate* (Boulder: University Press of Colorado, 2005); Vig, "Presidential Leadership and the Environment."

119. P.L. 103-433, October 31, 1994. BLM officials, particularly California State Director Ed Hastey, strongly opposed the California Desert Protection Act, which transferred land to the National Park Service to create Death Valley National Park, Joshua Tree

National Park, and Mojave National Preserve, and which transferred land to the State of California to create the Red Rock Canyon State Park. For a broader history of California Desert politics, see Wheat, *California Desert Miracle*.

120. Marston, "Babbitt Is Trying to Nationalize the BLM."

121. "Management Reform: Agencies' Initial Efforts to Restructure Personnel Operations" (Washington, DC: General Accounting Office, 1998); John M. Kamensky, "Role of the 'Reinventing Government' Movement in Federal Management Reform," *Public Administration Review* 56, no. 3 (1996).

122. Donald F. Kettl, "Reinventing Government: A Fifth-Year Report Card" (Washington, DC: Brookings Institution, 1998).

123. Compare the *Code of Federal Regulations* from 1993 and 2001. Dombeck, interviewed by Harold K. Steen, 50; Rogelio Garcia, "Federal Regulatory Reform: An Overview" (Washington, DC: Congressional Research Service, 2000).

124. Marston, "Jim Baca Says the Department of Interior Is in Deep Trouble." After serving as both BLM acting director and Forest Service chief, Mike Dombeck recalls, "the ideal Forest Service employee would aspire to be chief. But in BLM people aspire to be a state director. I think the view of the employees is that the power is in the field in BLM." Michael P. Dombeck, interviewed by Harold K. Steen, 69.

125. Glendon E. Collins and Marion Collins, "Historical Record of the Offices and Office Managers of the U.S. Bureau of Land Management and Its Predecessor Agencies, the Grazing Service, the General Land Office and the O&C Revested Lands Administration" (Phoenix, AZ: Public Lands Foundation, 1998); Marston, "Jim Baca Says the Department of Interior Is in Deep Trouble."

126. The Public Lands Foundation (PLF), an organization made up primarily of BLM retirees, objected strongly to some of the state director and district manager appointments during this time, arguing that many of the new appointees had no professional public lands experience. George Lea, PLF President, to Martha Hahn, Idaho State Director, February 14, 1996, PLF Advocacy Statements, Archive no. 116.01, Public Lands Foundation Archive, Phoenix, AZ; "BLM: The Next Generation," *High Country News* 26, no. 23 (1994); Chip Giller, "The BLM: New Faces and New Attitudes," *High Country News* 26, no. 23 (1994).

127. Nicholas J. Avdellas, "Use of Strategic Planning at the Bureau of Land Management" (Washington, DC: American Society for Public Administration: Government Accomplishment and Accountability Task Force, 1996), 5.

128. Marston, "Babbitt Is Trying to Nationalize the BLM."

129. Pinchot, *Fight for Conservation*, 48.

130. Bruce Babbitt, "Keynote Address" (paper presented at the Bureau of Land Management Summit, Incline Village, NV, 1994). This is the same basic idea that Forest Service chief Richard McArdle argued in 1953: "Let me make it completely clear that I think being in the middle is exactly where we ought to be. I believe that our inability to satisfy completely each and every group of national-forest users is a definite sign of success in doing the job assigned to us. When each group is somewhat dissatisfied, it is a sign that no one group is getting more than its fair share." Richard E. McArdle, "Multiple Use—Multiple Benefits," *Journal of Forestry* 51, no. 5 (1953).

131. Babbitt, "Keynote Address."

132. Marston, "Babbitt Is Trying to Nationalize the BLM."

133. Dombeck, "Blueprint for the Future."

134. Michael P. Dombeck, "Reality, Challenge, and Self-Confidence: Remarks by Mike Dombeck, Acting Director Bureau of Land Management" (Washington, DC: Bureau of Land Management, 1996), 2–3.

135. Ibid.

136. Babbitt, "Keynote Address."

137. Such as a 1:15 supervisor to employee ratio and a 8:2 field to administration ratio. Mike Dombeck, "Implementation of Field Organization Strategies, Instruction Memorandum No. 94-203, May 24, 1994, BLM Library, Denver, CO.

138. BLM employees responded to questions in nine key topic areas, and no topic area generated an approval rating over 50 percent. While resource management—what BLM field managers did in working directly with resources and resource users—got a 49 percent approval rating, management practices and policies earned only a 16 percent approval rating.

139. Jim Baca, director January 1993–February 1994; Mike Dombeck, acting director February 1994–January 1997; Sylvia Baca, acting director January 1997–July 1997; Pat Shea, director July 1997–November 1998; Tom Fry, director November 1998–January 2001. Hearings on BLM directors were contentious, and Congress refused to even hold hearings on Mike Dombeck's nomination. Stephen Stuebner, "The New Voice at BLM," *High Country News* 31, no. 7 (1999).

140. George Lea to Secretary Norton, January 30, 2001, File no. 406: PLF Correspondence/Testimony with BLM/DOI/Congress, Public Lands Foundation Archive, Phoenix, AZ.

CHAPTER SEVEN. NEOSAGEBRUSH POLITICS

1. President Clinton created the Sonoran Desert, Carrizo Plain, Pompey's Pillar, Upper Missouri River Breaks, and the Kasha-Katuwe Tent Rocks national monuments in January 2001. The Department of Agriculture published its final rule on roadless area protection in the *Federal Register* on January 12, 2001. It was set to take effect on March 13, 2001.

2. Jack M. Beerman, "Presidential Power in Transitions," *Boston University Law Review* 83 (2003): 948. Two years later, for example, District Judge Clarence Brimmer complained that the Roadless Rule was driven "through the administrative process in a vehicle smelling of political prestidigitation." *Wyoming v. U.S. Department of Agriculture,* 277 F.Supp. 2d 1197 (D.Wyo, 2003).

3. Joel Connelly, "Bush Would Seize Reins on Lands Policy," *Seattle Post-Intelligencer,* June 26, 2000.

4. B. Drummond Ayres, Jr., "The 2000 Campaign: Campaign Briefing," *New York Times,* August 25, 2000.

5. Connelly, "Bush Would Seize Reins on Lands Policy" (emphasis added).

6. Margie Kriz, "Bush on Environment: Leading Republican Candidate Reveals Team and Policies," *SEJournal* 9, no. 3 (1999): 19.

7. For an extended treatment of President George W. Bush's reframing of the environmental debate, see Vaughn and Cortner, *George W. Bush's Healthy Forests.*

8. "The Environment: A Cleaner, Safer, Healthier America" (Alexandra, VA: Luntz Research Companies, 2002).

9. Ibid. (emphasis in the original).

10. More controversial and/or openly ideological figures were generally placed one or two levels down the chain of command, where they would be out of the public spotlight. Consider, for example, the controversial work of Julie MacDonald, deputy assistant secretary of the interior for Fish, Wildlife and Parks; Water Robert Comer, associate solicitor for the Division of Land and Water; and Allan K. Fitzsimmons, fuel coordinator under the Healthy Forest Initiative. Earl E. Devaney, "Investigation of Settlement Agreement between BLM and Harvey Frank Robbins" (Washington, DC: U.S. Department of the Interior, Office of the Inspector General, 2005); Earl E. Devaney, "Investigative Report: On Allegations against Julie MacDonald, Deputy Assistant Secretary, Fish, Wildlife and Parks" (Washington, DC: U.S. Department of the Interior, Office of Inspector General, 2007); Earl E. Devaney, "J. Steven Griles: Report of Investigation" (Washington, DC: U.S. Department of the Interior, Office of Inspector General, 2004); Benjamin C. Dysert and Marion Clawson, eds., *Public Interest in the Use of Private Lands* (New York: Praeger,1989); Allan K. Fitzsimmons, *Defending Illusions: Federal Protection of Ecosystems* (New York: Rowman & Littlefield, 1999); Vaughn and Cortner, *George W. Bush's Healthy Forests.*

11. Kriz, "Bush on Environment," 19.

12. http://www.doi.gov/news/020422.html, accessed on February 1, 2008 (emphasis added).

13. Richard White, "Are You an Environmentalist or Do You Work for a Living?" in *Uncommon Ground: Toward Reinventing Nature*, ed. William Cronon (New York: W. W. Norton, 1995).

14. Emphasis added.

15. GAO, "Forest Service: Information on Appeals and Litigation Involving Fuels Reduction Activities" (Washington, DC: General Accounting Office, 2003); Vaughn and Cortner, *George W. Bush's Healthy Forests*, 28.

16. Interviews conducted by the author with BLM field managers in California, Arizona, Utah, and Colorado in July 2003.

17. Craig Welch, "Bush Switches Nation's Tack on Protecting Species," *Seattle Times*, September 27, 2004. Indeed, the U.S. Fish and Wildlife Service did not place a single plant or animal on the endangered species list in 2004. Mary H. Cooper, "Endangered Species Act: Is the Landmark Law in Need of Change?" *CQ Researcher* 15, no. 21 (2004): 497.

18. Matt Jenkins, "Two Decades of Hard Work, Plowed Under," *High Country News* 36, no. 1 (2004).

19. Devaney, "J. Steven Griles: Report of Investigation."

20. Letter, Joseph I. Lieberman to Gale Norton, April 29, 2004.

21. The investigator general reports: "According to DAS MacDonald, when she attended meetings at Western Regional Offices, it was not beyond the realm of possibility that she swore at field personnel when challenging them on their scientific/biological findings." Devaney, "Investigative Report," 10.

22. Ibid., 11.

23. Ibid., 16.

24. Dennis M. Roth, "The Wilderness Movement and the National Forests: 1964–1980" (Washington, DC: USDA Forest Service, 1984).

25. Devaney, "Investigation of Settlement Agreement Between BLM and Harvey Frank Robbins," 3.

26. Ibid., 5.

27. Ibid., 6–7.

28. Ibid., 10.

29. Ibid., 10–16.

30. Ibid.

31. Ibid.

32. U.S. Congress, House, Subcommittee on Energy and Resources, *Interior Department: A Culture of Managerial Irresponsibility and Lack of Accountability?* 109th Cong., 2nd sess., September 13–14, 2006.

33. Ibid.

34. http://bestplacestowork.org/BPTW/rankings/index.php?t=scores_subcomponent&c=index, accessed February 19, 2007.

35. Earl E. Devaney, "Evaluation: Conduct and Discipline" (Washington, DC: USDI Office of Inspector General, 2004).

36. "Quarreling over Monuments," *New York Times*, September 4, 2000.

37. Heather Abel, "Utah Wilderness Proposal Rises and Dies," *High Country News* 28, no. 7 (1996).

38. U.S. Congress, House, Subcommittee on National Parks and Public Lands, *Statement of Tom Fulton, Deputy Assistant Secretary for Land and Minerals Management*, 107th Cong., 2nd sess., July 17, 2001.

39. Committee on Resources, "Behind Closed Doors."

40. Eric Pianin, "White House Won't Fight Monument Designations: Norton Says Boundaries, Land Use Rules May Be Amended," *Washington Post*, February 21, 2001.

41. Ibid.

42. U.S. Department of the Interior Press Release, March 28, 2001.

43. Gale Norton, Letter, March 28, 2001.

44. John A. Kitzhaber to Secretary Norton, April 24, 2001.

45. 137 F.3d 1193 (10th Cir. 1998).

46. Brent Israelsen, "Land Deal Fought; Environmentalists Sue," *Salt Lake Tribune*, May 6, 2003.

47. 137 F.3d 1193 (10th Cir. 1998).

48. *Wilderness Inventory and Study Procedures Handbook* (Washington, DC: Bureau of Land Management, 2001).

49. Tom Wharton, "Norton Defends Settlement to Roll Back Land Protection," *Salt Lake Tribune*, June 18, 2003.

50. Anthony H. Gamboa, "Recognition of R.S. 2477 Rights-of-Way under the Department of the Interior's FLPMA Disclaimer Rules and Its Memorandum of Understanding with the State of Utah" (Washington, DC: General Accounting Office, 2004); Tim Westby, "Backcountry Road Deal Runs over Wilderness," *High Country News* (2003).

51. Gamboa, "Recognition of R.S. 2477 Rights-of-Way"; Westby, "Backcountry Road Deal Runs over Wilderness."

52. Matt Jenkins, "Norton Eases Road Claims," *High Country News* 38, no. 7 (2006).

53. "Ecosystem Management in the BLM: From Concept to Commitment" (Washington, D.C.: U.S. Department of Interior, 1994), 1–2.

54. Allan K. Fitzsimmons, "Ecosystem Management: An Illusion?" *PERC Reports* 17, no. 5 (1999): 4.

55. Fitzsimmons, *Defending Illusions*, 1, 6, 288.

56. "Department Hearings and Appeals Procedures; Cooperative Relations; Grazing Administration—Exclusive of Alaska," *Federal Register* 60, no. 35 (1995).

57. "BLM Considers 'Working Landscape' Grazing Policy Changes, Seeks Public Input in Developing Ideas" (Washington, DC: BLM, 2003).

58. "Grazing Administration—Exclusive of Alaska," *Federal Register* 68, no. 235 (2003).

59. Ibid.

60. "Final Environmental Impact Statement: Proposed Revisions to Grazing Regulations for the Public Lands" (Washington, DC: BLM, 2004).

61. "Grazing Administration—Exclusive of Alaska," *Federal Register* 68, no. 235 (2003): 68460.

62. Ibid.

63. For example, the Public Lands Foundation, a nonprofit organization composed primarily of BLM retirees, filed an amicus brief in the Supreme Court case to decide Harvey Frank Robbins's claims, recognizing that the case could have significant and detrimental repercussions on the BLM.

64. *Public Hearing to Receive Comments on the Draft Environmental Impact Statement on the Proposed Grazing Rule*, February 4, 2004, 22.

65. Joseph M. Feller, "Ride 'em Cowboy: A Critical Look at BLM's Proposed New Grazing Regulations," *Environmental Law* 34 (Fall 2004): 1123.

66. "The Bush Administration Altered Critical Portions of a Scientific Analysis of the Environmental Impact of Cattle Grazing on Public Lands," *Los Angeles Times*, June 18, 2005.

67. "Addendum to the Final Environmental Impact Statement FES 04-39: Proposed Revisions to Graizng Regulations for the Public Lands" (Washington, DC: BLM, 2006), 50.

68. *Western Watersheds Project v. Kraayenbrink*, Case No. CV-05–297-E-BLW (D.Idaho), 16–17.

69. Ibid., 10.

70. Ibid.

71. *Western Watersheds Project v. Kraayenbrink*, Case 4:05-cv-00297-BLW (D. Idaho), 1–2.

72. Glenns Ferry Grazing Association, Docket Nos. 096-04-014 and 096-04-09 (Interior Department Office of Hearings and Appeals, September 28, 2007), 70.

73. Ibid.

74. Ibid., 49.

75. Ibid., 47–48.

76. Ibid., 121.

77. Gary C. Bryner, "The National Energy Policy: Assessing Energy Policy Choices," *University of Colorado Law Review* 73 (2002): 344.

78. Mary H. Cooper, "Energy Policy," *CQ Researcher* 11, no. 20 (2001): 443.

79. Ibid., 444.

80. Bryner, "National Energy Policy," 344.

81. National Energy Policy Development Group, "National Energy Policy" (Washington, DC: Government Printing Office, 2001).

82. Joseph Kahn, "The Energy Plan: The Details," *New York Times*, May 18, 2001.

83. "National Energy Policy: Reliable, Affordable, and Environmentally Sound Energy for America's Future" (Washington, DC: National Energy Policy and Development Group, 2001), ix.

84. Ibid., xii.

85. Mike Soraghan, "Watt Applauds Bush Energy Strategy," *Denver Post*, May 16, 2001.

86. "National Energy Policy," xv.

87. See chapter five.

88. "Energy Task Force: Process Used to Develop the National Energy Policy" (Washington, DC: General Accounting Office, 2003).

89. Ibid., 5–9.

90. Peter Matthiessen, "Inside the Endangered Arctic Refuge," *New York Review of Books* 53, no. 16 (2006).

91. Cooper, "Energy Policy," 457.

92. Executive Order 13212, May 18, 2001.

93. Executive Order 13211, May 18, 2001.

94. "Scientific Inventory of Onshore Federal Lands Oil and Gas Resources and Reserves and the Extent and Nature of Restrictions or Impediments to Their Development" (Washington, DC: DOI, USDA, and DOE, 2003).

95. Ibid.

96. Timothy Egan, "Bush Administration Allows Oil Drilling Near Utah Parks," *New York Times*, February 8, 2002.

97. Theo Stein, "BLM to Ease Oil, Gas Access," *Denver Post*, March 19, 2002.

98. "Increased Permitting Activity Has Lessened BLM's Ability to Meet Its Environmental Protection Responsibilities" (Washington, DC: General Accounting Office, 2005), 5.

99. Matt Jenkins, "The BLM Wields Fork and Spatula over the West's Wildlands," *High Country News* 37, no. 2 (2005).

100. Tony Barboza, "Industry Embeds Its Own in the BLM," *High Country News* 37, no. 4 (2005).

101. "Increased Permitting Activity Has Lessened BLM's Ability," 5.

102. Ibid.

103. Brent Israelsen, "Governor Protests BLM Sale of Oil, Gas Leases in Wyoming," *Salt Lake Tribune*, June 9, 1994.

104. Tweetie Blancett, "The Coming Gas Explosion in the West," *Denver Post*, May 11, 2003.

105. Stein, "BLM to Ease Oil, Gas Access."

106. Kerry Brophy, "Split-Estate Rebellion: Ranchers Take on Energy Developers," *High Country News* 37, no. 2 (2005).

107. Timothy Egan, "Drilling in West Pits Republican Policy against Republican Base," *New York Times*, June 22, 2005.

108. Jennifer Frazer, "Great Divide Arguments Rage over Drilling in Red Desert," *Wyoming Tribune-Eagle*, April 10, 2005; Steve Lipsher, "Roan Drilling Takes Long Road: Concerned Public 'Looking over Our Shoulder,' BLM Official Says," *Denver Post*, February 13, 2004; Tania Soussan, "Oil Drillers Fight to Tap Otero Mesa," *Albuquerque Journal*, January 11, 2004.

109. Alan Prendergast, "Raiding the Roan," *Denver Westword*, January 1, 2004.

110. John Heilprin, "Bush Considers Rolling Back Mining Law," *Arkansas Democrat-Gazette*, March 21, 2001.

111. "Mining Claims under the General Mining Laws; Surface Management; Final Rule and Proposed Rule," *Federal Register* 66, no. 210 (2001): 54835.

112. Ibid.

113. 43 U.S.C. 1732(b).

114. Tom Kenworthy, "New Mining Rules Reverse Provisions," *USA Today*, October 26, 2001.

115. "White House Reverses Clinton Mining Decision," *Deseret News*, October 26, 2001.

116. John Freemuth, "Whatever Happened to Ecosystem Management" (paper presented at the American Society for Environmental History, Annual Conference, March 12–16, 2008, Boise, ID).

117. Scott Sonner, "BLM Chief Apologizes to Employees," *Las Vegas Review Journal* (2003).

118. Fitzsimmons, "Ecosystem Management."

CONCLUSION

1. Bruce Babbitt, *Cities in the Wilderness: A New Vision of Land Use in America* (Washington, DC: Island Press, 2005), 5.

2. Ibid.

3. Ibid., 51–52.

4. Ibid., 52–53.

5. Ibid., 53.

6. Ibid., 5–6.

7. James L. Huffman, "A New Era for the Western Public Lands: The Inevitability of Private Rights in Public Lands," *Colorado Law Review* 65 (Spring 1994).

8. Babbitt, *Cities in the Wilderness*, 51.

9. See Graf, *Wilderness Preservation and the Sagebrush Rebellions*, 139–264.

10. See chapter two. *Buford v. Houtz*, 133 U.S. 320 (1890), *Camfield v. United States*, 167 U.S. 518 (1897), *Light v. United States*, 220 U.S. 523 (1911), *United States v. Cox*, 190 F.2d 293 (10th Cir., 1951), *Porter v. Resor*, 415 F.2d 764 (10th Cir., 1969), and *Pankey Land & Cattle Company v. Hardin and Hickel*, 427 F.2d 43 (10th Cir., 1970).

11. Steve Lohr and John Markoff, "Windows Is So Slow, But Why? Sheer Size Is Causing Delays for Microsoft," *New York Times*, March 27, 2006.

12. For a brief overview of these commissions, see Milton A. Pearl, "Public Land Commissions," *Our Public Lands* 17, no. 2 (1967).

13. See Thomas Donaldson, "The Public Domain: Its History, with Statistics" (Washington, DC: Government Printing Office, 1884).

14. See James Alexander Williamson, Clarence King, Alexander Thompson Britton, Thomas Donaldson, and John Wesley Powell, "Report of the Public Lands Commission Created by the Act of March 3, 1879, Relating to Public Lands in the Western Portion of the United States and to the Operation of Existing Land Laws" (Washington, DC: Government Printing Office, 1880).

15. See "Report of the Committee on the Conservation and Administration of the Public Domain to the President of the United States" (Washington, DC: Government Printing Office, 1931).

16. See *One Third of the Nation's Land*.

17. Dave Foreman, "Wilderness: From Scenery to Nature," in *The Great New Wilderness Debate*, ed. J. Baird Callicott and Michael P. Nelson (Athens: University of Georgia Press, 1995).

18. "Forest Service to Bid Out Law Enforcement, Fire, and Environmental Positions—Group Decries 'Rent-a-Ranger,'" Public Employees for Environmental Responsibility, News Release, July 1, 2003; Greg Hanscom, "Outsourced," *High Country News* 36, no. 2 (2004); Gifford Pinchot III, "Outsourcing and the Alternatives," *Forest Magazine* (2003).

19. In some cases, environmental groups have been willing to pay ranchers for voluntarily retiring grazing permits that would be revoked without compensation otherwise. April Reese, "The Big Buyout," *High Country News* 37, no. 6 (2005).

20. Roger A Sedjo, "Streamlining Forest Service Planning," in *New Approaches on Energy and the Environment*, ed. Richard D. Morgenstern and Paul R. Portney (Washington, DC: Resources for the Future, 2004).

21. "Bureau of Land Management: 2006 Budget Justification," 22.

Bibliography

Abel, Heather. "Utah Wilderness Proposal Rises and Dies." *High Country News* 28, no. 7 (1996): 5.

Achterman, Gail L., and Sally K. Fairfax. "The Public Participation Requirements of the Federal Land Policy and Management Act." *Arizona Law Review* 21, no. 2 (1979): 501–39.

"Action on Mining Law Awaits Babbitt's Grazing Fee Plan." *Congressional Quarterly Weekly Report* 52, no. 9 (1994): 540.

"Addendum to the Final Environmental Impact Statement FES 04-39: Proposed Revisions to Grazing Regulations for the Public Lands." Washington, DC: BLM, 2006.

All around You. Washington, DC: Bureau of Land Management, 1971.

Allin, Craig W. *The Politics of Wilderness Preservation.* Westport, CT: Greenwood Press, 1982.

American National Cattlemen's Association. "The Livestock Grazing Permit—Its Economic Importance." Denver: American National Cattlemen's Association, 1968.

Andrews, Richard N. L. "Agency Responses to NEPA: A Comparison and Implications." *Natural Resources Journal* 16, no. 2 (1976): 301–22.

———. "Environment and Energy: Implications of Overloaded Agendas." *Natural Resources Journal* 19, no. 3 (1979): 487–503.

Argyris, Chris. *Organization of a Bank.* New Haven, CT: Yale University Labor and Management Center, 1954.

———. *Personality and Organization.* New York: Harper & Brothers, 1957.

———. *Understanding Organizational Behavior.* Homewood, IL: Dorsey Press, 1960.

Arnold, Ron. *At the Eye of the Storm: James Watt and the Environmentalists.* Chicago: Regnery Gateway, 1982.

Arrandale, Tom. *The Battle for Natural Resources.* Washington, DC: Congressional Quarterly, 1983.

Avdellas, Nicholas J. "Use of Strategic Planning at the Bureau of Land Management." Washington, DC: American Society for Public Administration: Government Accomplishment and Accountability Task Force, 1996.

Ayres, B. Drummond, Jr. "The 2000 Campaign: Campaign Briefing." *New York Times*, August 25, 2000.

Babbitt, Bruce. *Cities in the Wilderness: A New Vision of Land Use in America*. Washington, DC: Island Press, 2005.

———. "Federalism and the Environment: An Intergovernmental Perspective of the Sagebrush Rebellion." *Environmental Law* 12 (Summer 1982): 847–61.

———. "From Grand Staircase to Grand Canyon Parashant: Is There a Monumental Future for the BLM?" Paper presented at the University of Denver Law School, February 17, 2000.

———. "The Future Environmental Agenda for the United States." *University of Colorado Law Review* 64, no. 2 (1993): 513–22.

———. "Keynote Address." Paper presented at the Bureau of Land Management Summit, Incline Village, NV, 1994.

———. "Remarks by Secretary Bruce Babbitt." Paper presented at the BLM Interactive Townhall Meeting, Pheonix, AZ, March 24, 2000.

———. "Science: Opening the Next Century of Conservation History." *Science* 267, no. 5206 (1995): 1954–55.

Baker, Richard A. "The Conservation Congress of Anderson and Aspinall, 1963–64." *Journal of Forest History* 29, no. 3 (1985): 104–19.

Barboza, Tony. "Industry Embeds Its Own in the BLM." *High Country News* 37, no. 4 (2005): 3.

Barker, Rocky. "Cecil Andrus Knew How to Take a Stand." *High Country News* 27, no. 3 (1995): 14.

Bartlett, Robert V. "The Budgetary Process and Environmental Policy." In *Environmental Policy in the 1980s: Reagan's New Agenda*, edited by Norman J. Vig and Michael E. Kraft. Washington, DC: CQ Press, 1984.

Beerman, Jack M. "Presidential Power in Transitions." *Boston University Law Review* 83 (2003): 947–1016.

Behan, Richard W. "The Irony of the Multiple Use/Sustained Yield Concept: Nothing Is So Powerful as an Idea Whose Time Has Passed." Paper presented at the workshop "Multiple Use and Sustained Yield: Changing Philosophies for Federal Land Management?" Washington, DC, March 5–6, 1992.

———. "The Succotash Syndrome, or Multiple Use: A Heartfelt Approach to Forest Land Management." *Natural Resources Journal* 7, no. 4 (1967): 473–84.

Benenson, Bob. "House Easily Passes Overhaul of 1872 Mining Law." *Congressional Quarterly Weekly Report* 51, no. 46 (1993): 3191–92.

Binkly, Gail. "The BLM Stabs at a Tired Land." *High Country News* 34, no. 17 (2002): 3.

Blancett, Tweetie. "The Coming Gas Explosion in the West." *Denver Post*, May 11, 2003, 4.

"BLM Considers 'Working Landscape' Grazing Policy Changes, Seeks Public Input in Developing Ideas." Washington, DC: BLM, 2003.

"BLM: The Next Generation." *High Country News* 26, no. 23 (1994): 3.

Bovee, Kirsten. "Monuments Caught in the Crosshairs." *High Country News* 33, no. 8 (2001): 3.

Bowsher, Charles A. "Interior Issues." Washington, DC: General Accounting Office, 1988.

Bradley, Dorotha M., and Helen M. Ingram. "Science vs. the Grass Roots: Representation in the Bureau of Land Management." *Natural Resources Journal* 26, no. 3 (1986): 493–518.

Brookes, Martha H., ed. "The Northwest Forest Plan: A Report to the President and

Congress." Washington, DC: U.S. Department of Agriculture, Office of Forestry and Economic Assistance, 1996.

Brophy, Kerry. "Split-Estate Rebellion: Ranchers Take on Energy Developers." *High Country News* 37, no. 2 (2005): 4.

Brown, G., and C. C. Harris. "The U.S. Forest Service: Whither the New Resource Management Paradigm?" *Journal of Environmental Management* 58 (2000): 1–19.

Bryner, Gary C. "The National Energy Policy: Assessing Energy Policy Choices." *University of Colorado Law Review* 73 (2002): 341–412.

———. "What Does the Grand Staircase–Escalante Mean for Land Protection in the West? Resource Development and Ecological Protection." *Journal of Land Resources & Environmental Law* 21 (2001): 567–80.

"Budget Justifications and Performance Information: Fiscal Year 2006: National Park Service." Washington, DC: Department of the Interior, 2005.

"The Bureau of Land Management's National Landscape Conservation System." Washington, DC: Bureau of Land Management, 2004.

"Bureau of Land Management: 2006 Budget Justification." Washington, DC: Bureau of Land Management, 2005.

Bureau, U.S. Census. *Statistical Abstract of the United States: 2006.* Washington, DC: U.S. Government Printing Office, 2006.

"The Bush Administration Altered Critical Portions of a Scientific Analysis of the Environmental Impact of Cattle Grazing on Public Lands." *Los Angeles Times*, June 18, 2005.

Caldwell, Lynton K. "The Ecosystem as a Criterion for Public Land Policy." *Natural Resources Journal* 10, no. 2 (1970): 203–21.

———. "An Ecosystems Approach to Public Land Policy." In *Public Land Policy: Proceedings of the Western Resources Conference.* Edited by Phillip O. Foss. Boulder: Colorado Associated University Press, 1968.

———. *Environment: A Challenge for Modern Society.* New York: National History Press, 1970.

———. "Environment: A New Focus for Public Policy?" *Public Administration Review* 23, no. 3 (1963): 132–39.

———. "Environmental Quality as an Administrative Problem." *Annals of the American Academy of Political and Social Science* 400 (1972): 103–15.

———. *Environment as a Focus for Public Policy.* Edited by Robert V. Bartlett and James N. Gladden. College Station: Texas A&M University Press, 1995.

———. *Man and His Environment: Policy and Administration.* New York: Harper & Row, 1975.

———. "Public Policy Implications of Environmental Control." Paper presented at the Social Sciences and the Environment Conference on the Present and Potential Contribution of the Social Sciences to Research and Policy Formation in the Quality of the Physical Environment, Boulder, CO, January 31, February 1, 2, 1967.

Calef, Wesley. *Private Grazing and Public Lands: Studies of the Local Management of the Taylor Grazing Act.* Chicago: University of Chicago Press, 1960.

Camia, Catalina. "Administration Aims to Increase Grazing Fees, Tighten Rules." *Congressional Quarterly Weekly Report* 51, no. 33 (1993): 2223.

———. "Babbitt and Western Democrats Reach Pact on Grazing Fees." *Congressional Quarterly Weekly Report* 51, no. 40 (1993): 2723–24.

———. "Babbitt Offers New Plan in Grazing Fee Dispute." *Congressional Quarterly Weekly Report* 52, no. 11 (1994): 670.

———. "Clinton's Forest Compromise Is Assailed from All Sides." *Congressional Quarterly Weekly Report* 51, no. 27 (1993): 1726–27.

———. "Democrats Lash Out at Babbitt over Revised Grazing Plan." *Congressional Quarterly Weekly Report* 52, no. 10 (1994): 598.

———. "The Filibuster Ends; Bill Clears; Babbitt Can Still Raise Fees." *Congressional Quarterly Weekly Report* 51, no. 45 (1993): 3112–13.

———. "Many Find Babbitt Too Valuable to Move from Cabinet to Court." *Congressional Quarterly Weekly Report* 51, no. 24 (1993): 1473.

———. "Senate OKs Mining Law Rewrite; Bill Is Backed by Industry." *Congressional Quarterly Weekly Report* 51, no. 22 (1993): 1355.

———. "Senate Votes to Block Increase in Grazing Fees Next Year." *Congressional Quarterly Weekly Report* 51, no. 37 (1993): 2449–51.

Carter, Luther J. "Interior Department: Andrus Promises 'Sweeping Changes.'" *Science* 196, no. 4289 (1977): 507–10.

Carver, John A., Jr. "BLM Organic Act: Federal Land Policy and Management Act of 1976: Fruition or Frustration." *Denver Law Journal* 54, nos. 3–4 (1977): 387–444.

Carver, John A., Jr., and Craig R. Carver. "Federal Land Policy and Management Act of 1976." *Rocky Mountain Mineral Law Newsletter* 9, no. 10 (1976): 1–7.

Cawley, R. McGreggor. *Federal Land, Western Anger: The Sagebrush Rebellion and Environmental Politics.* Lawrence: University Press of Kansas, 1993.

Cawley, R. McGreggor, and John Freemuth. "A Critique of the Multiple Use Framework in Public Lands Decisionmaking." In *Western Public Lands and Environmental Politics*, edited by Charles Davis. Boulder, CO: Westview Press, 1997.

"Change Urged in Mining Law." *New York Times*, September 24 1991, 3.

Chapman, Oscar. "Comments of the Department of the Interior on the Recommendations of the Commission on Organization of the Executive Branch of the Government Concerning the Department of the Interior." Washington, DC: Department of the Interior, 1949.

Clarke, Jeanne Nienaber. *Roosevelt's Warrior: Harold Ickes and the New Deal.* Baltimore: Johns Hopkins University Press, 1996.

Clarke, Jeanne Nienaber, and Daniel C. McCool. *Staking Out the Terrain: Power and Performance among Natural Resource Agencies.* Albany: State University of New York Press, 1996.

Clawson, Marion. *The Bureau of Land Management.* New York: Praeger Publishers, 1971.

———. "The Crisis in Outdoor Recreation." *American Forests* 65, no. 3 (1959): 22–31, 40–41.

———. "The Crisis in Outdoor Recreation, Part II." *American Forests* 65, no. 4 (1959): 28–35, 61–62.

———. *Federal Lands Revisited.* Washington, DC: Resources for the Future, 1983.

———. *From Sagebrush to Sage.* Washington, DC: Ana Publications, 1987.

———. *Rebuilding the Federal Range.* Washington, DC: U.S. Government Printing Office, 1951.

———. *The Western Range Livestock Industry.* New York: McGraw-Hill, 1950.

Clawson, Marion, and Burnell Held. *The Federal Lands*. Baltimore: Johns Hopkins University Press, 1957.

Clawson, Marion, R. Burnell Held, and Charles H. Stoddard. *Land for the Future*. Baltimore: Johns Hopkins University Press, 1960.

Clawson, Marion, and Carlton S. Van Doren, eds. *Statistics on Outdoor Recreation*. Washington, DC: Resources for the Future, 1984.

Coates, Peter. *The Trans-Alaska Pipeline Controversy*. Bethlehem, Toronto: Lehigh University Press, Associated University Press, 1991.

Cockburn, Alexander. "'Win-Win' with Bruce Babbitt: The Clinton Administration Meets the Environment." *New Left Review* 201 (1993): 46–59.

Cody, Betsy A. "Grazing Fees: An Overview." Washington, DC: Congressional Research Service, 1996.

Cody, Betsy A., and Pamela Baldwin. "Bureau of Land Management Authorization." Washington, DC: Congressional Research Service, 1995.

Coggins, George Cameron. "The Law of Public Rangeland Management III: A Survey of Creeping Regulation at the Periphery, 1934–1982." *Environmental Law* 13 (Winter 1983): 295–365.

———. "The Law of Public Rangeland Management IV: FLPMA, PRIA, and the Multiple Use Mandate." *Environmental Law* 14 (Fall 1983): 1–131.

Coggins, George Cameron, and Margaret Lindberg-Johnson. "The Law of Public Rangeland Management II: The Commons and the Taylor Act." *Environmental Law* 13 (Fall 1982): 1–101.

Coggins, George Cameron, and Doris K. Nagel. "'Nothing Beside Remains': The Legal Legacy of James G. Watt's Tenure as Secretary of the Interior on Federal Land Law and Policy." *Boston College Environmental Affairs Law Review* 17, no. 3 (1990): 473–550.

Coggins, George Cameron, Charles F. Wilkinson, and John D. Leshy. *Federal Public Land and Resources Law*. 4th ed. New York: Foundation Press, 2001.

Collins, Glendon E., and Marion Collins. "Historical Record of the Offices and Office Managers of the U.S. Bureau of Land Management and Its Predecessor Agencies, the Grazing Service, the General Land Office and the O&C Revested Lands Administration." Phoenix, AZ: Public Lands Foundation, 1998.

"Comments by the Department of the Interior on Legislative and Administrative Alternatives in PLLRC Study Reports, 1968–1970." Washington, DC, 1970.

Connelly, Joel. "Bush Would Seize Reins on Lands Policy." *Seattle Post-Intelligencer*, June 26, 2000, A1.

Cook, Brian J. *Bureaucracy and Self-Government: Reconsidering the Role of Public Administration in American Politics*. Baltimore: Johns Hopkins University Press, 1996.

Cooper, Mary H. "Endangered Species Act: Is the Landmark Law in Need of Change?" *CQ Researcher* 15, no. 21 (2004): 493–516.

———. "Energy Policy." *CQ Researcher* 11, no. 20 (2001).

Culhane, Paul J. *Public Lands Politics: Interest Group Influence on the Forest Service and the Bureau of Land Management*. Baltimore: Johns Hopkins University Press, 1981.

———. "Sagebrush Rebels in Office: Jim Watt's Land and Water Politics." In *Environmental Policy in the 1980s: Reagan's New Agenda*, edited by Norman J. Vig and Michael E. Kraft. Washington, DC: CQ Press, 1984.

Culhane, Paul J., and H. Paul Friesema. "Land Use Planning for the Public Lands." *Natural Resources Journal* 19, no. 1 (1979): 43–74.

Dana, Samuel Trask, and Sally K. Fairfax. *Forest and Range Policy: Its Development in the United States.* 2nd ed. New York: McGraw-Hill, 1980.

Davis, Charles, and Sandra Davis. "Analyzing Change in Public Lands Policymaking: From Subsystems to Advocacy Coalitions." *Policy Studies Journal* 17, no. 1 (1988): 3–24.

Davis, Phillip A. "Critics Say Too Few Jobs, Owls Saved under 'God Squad' Plan." *Congressional Quarterly Weekly Report* 50, no. 20 (1992): 1334–35.

Dawson, William L. "Summary of the Objectives, Operations, and Results of the Commissions on Organization of the Executive Branch of the Government." Washington, DC: House Committee on Government Operations, 88th Congress, 1st Session, 1963.

"Department Hearings and Appeals Procedures; Cooperative Relations; Grazing Administration—Exclusive of Alaska." *Federal Register* 60, no. 35 (1995): 9894–971.

Devaney, Earl E. "Evaluation: Conduct and Discipline." Washington, DC: USDI Office of Inspector General, 2004.

———. "Investigation of Settlement Agreement between BLM and Harvey Frank Robbins." Washington, DC: U.S. Department of the Interior, Office of the Inspector General, 2005.

———. "Investigative Report: On Allegations Against Julie MacDonald, Deputy Assistant Secretary, Fish, Wildlife and Parks." Washington, DC: U.S. Department of the Interior, Office of Inspector General, 2007.

———. "J. Steven Griles: Report of Investigation." Washington, DC: U.S. Department of the Interior, Office of Inspector General, 2004.

DeVoto, Bernard. "Sacred Cows and Public Lands." In *The Western Paradox: A Conservation Reader*, edited by Douglas Brinkley and Patricia Nelson Limerick. New Haven, CT: Yale University Press, 2001.

———. *The Western Paradox: A Conservation Reader.* Edited by Douglas Brinkley and Patricia Nelson Limerick. New Haven, CT: Yale University Press, 2000.

"Digest of Federal Resource Laws of Interest to the U.S. Fish and Wildlife Service." Washington, DC: U.S. Fish and Wildlife Service, 1992.

Dombeck, Mike. "Blueprint for the Future." Washington, DC: Bureau of Land Management, 1994.

———. "Reality, Challenge, and Self-Confidence: Remarks by Mike Dombeck, Acting Director, Bureau of Land Management." Washington, DC: Bureau of Land Management, 1996.

Dombeck, Mike, Christopher Wood, and Jack E. Williams. *From Conquest to Conservation: Our Public Lands Legacy.* Washington, DC: Island Press, 2003.

Donaldson, Thomas. "The Public Domain: Its History, with Statistics." Washington, DC: Government Printing Office, 1884.

Duffus, James. "Public Land Management: Issues Related to the Reauthorization of the Bureau of Land Management." Washington, DC: General Accounting Office, 1991.

Durant, Robert F. *The Administrative Presidency Revisited: Public Lands, the BLM, and the Reagan Revolution.* Albany: State University of New York Press, 1992.

Dysert, Benjamin C., and Marion Clawson, eds. *Public Interest in the Use of Private Lands.* New York: Praeger, 1989.

"Ecosystem Management in the BLM: From Concept to Commitment." Washington, DC: U.S. Department of Interior, 1994.

Egan, Timothy. "Bush Administration Allows Oil Drilling Near Utah Parks." *New York Times*, February 8, 2002, 14.

———. "Drilling in West Pits Republican Policy against Republican Base." *New York Times*, June 22, 2005, 11.

"Energy Task Force: Process Used to Develop the National Energy Policy." Washington, DC: General Accounting Office, 2003.

"The Environment: A Cleaner, Safer, Healthier America." Luntz Research Companies, 2002.

Environmental Law Institute. "NEPA In Action: Environmental Offices in Nineteen Federal Agencies." Washington, DC: Council on Environmental Quality, 1981.

Fairfax, Sally K. "Beyond the Sagebrush Rebellion: The BLM as Neighbor and Manager in the Western States." In *Western Public Lands: The Management of Natural Resources in the Time of Declining Federalism*, edited by John G. Francis and Richard Ganzel. Totowa, NJ: Rowman & Allanheld, 1984.

———. "Coming of Age in the Bureau of Land Management: Range Management in Search of a Gospel." In *Developing Strategies for Rangeland Management: A Report Prepared by the Committee on Developing Strategies for Rangeland Management.* Boulder, CO: Westview Press, 1984.

———. "The Difference Between BLM and the Forest Service." In *Opportunity and Challenge: The Story of BLM*, edited by James Muhn and Hanson R. Stuart. Washington, DC: Bureau of Land Management, 1988.

———. "Public Involvement and the Forest Service." *Journal of Forestry* 73, no. 7 (1975): 657–59.

Fairfax, Sally K., and Barbara T. Andrews. "Debate Within and Debate Without: NEPA and the Redefinition of the 'Prudent Man' Rule." *Natural Resources Journal* 19, no. 3 (1979): 505–35.

Falen, Frank, and Karen Budd Falen. "The Rights to Graze Livestock on the Federal Lands: The Historical Development of Western Grazing Rights." *Idaho Law Review* 30, no. 3 (1994): 505–24.

"Federal Land Management: Limited Action Taken to Reclaim Hardrock Mine Sites." Washington, DC: General Accounting Office, 1987.

Feller, Joseph M. "Ride 'em Cowboy: A Critical Look at BLM's Proposed New Grazing Regulations." *Environmental Law* 34 (Fall 2004): 1123–41.

———. "What Is Wrong with the BLM's Management of Livestock Grazing on the Public Lands?" *Idaho Law Review* 30, no. 3 (1994): 555–602.

"Final Environmental Impact Statement: Proposed Revisions to Grazing Regulations for the Public Lands." Washington, DC: BLM, 2004.

Fitzsimmons, Allan K. *Defending Illusions: Federal Protection of Ecosystems.* New York: Rowman & Littlefield, 1999.

———. "Ecosystem Management: An Illusion?" *PERC Reports* 17, no. 5 (1999).

Flippen, J. Brooks. *Nixon and the Environment.* Albuquerque: University of New Mexico Press, 2000.

Foreman, Dave. "Wilderness: From Scenery to Nature." In *The Great New Wilderness Debate*, edited by J. Baird Callicott and Michael P. Nelson. Athens: University of Georgia Press, 1995.

Foss, Phillip O. *The Battle of Soldier Creek, Inter-University Case Program.* Tuscaloosa: University of Alabama Press, 1961.

———. *Politics and Grass: The Administration of the Public Domain.* Seattle: University of Washington Press, 1960.

———. "Problems in Federal Management of Natural Resources for Recreation." *Natural Resources Journal* 5 (1965): 62–95.

———. *Recreation.* New York: Chelsea House Publishers, 1971.

———, ed. *Public Land Policy: Proceedings of the Western Resources Conference.* Boulder: Colorado Associated University Press, 1970.

Frazer, Jennifer. "Great Divide Arguments Rage over Drilling in Red Desert." *Wyoming Tribune-Eagle*, April 10, 2005.

Freemuth, John. "The Emergence of Ecosystem Management: Reinterpreting the Gospel?" *Society and Natural Resources* 9, no. 4 (1996): 411–17.

Gamboa, Anthony H. "Recognition of R.S. 2477 Rights-of-Way under the Department of the Interior's FLPMA Disclaimer Rules and Its Memorandum of Understanding with the State of Utah." Washington, DC: General Accounting Office, 2004.

GAO. "Administration of Regulations of Surface Exploration, Mining, and Reclamation of Public and Indian Coal Lands." Washington, DC: General Accounting Office, 1972.

———. "Ecosystem Management: Additional Actions Needed to Adequately Test a Promising Approach." Washington, DC: General Accounting Office, 1994.

———. "Federal Land Management: An Assessment of Hardrock Mining Damage." Washington, DC: General Accounting Office, 1988.

———. "Federal Land Management: The Mining Law of 1872 Needs Revision." Washington, DC: General Accounting Office, 1989.

———. "Forest Service: Information on Appeals and Litigation Involving Fuels Reduction Activities." Washington, DC: General Accounting Office, 2003.

———. "Increased Permitting Activity Has Lessened BLM's Ability to Meet Its Environmental Protection Responsibilities." Washington, DC: General Accounting Office, 2005.

———. "Public Rangelands Continue to Deteriorate." Washington, DC: General Accounting Office, 1977.

———. "Public Rangelands: Some Riparian Areas Restored but Widespread Improvement Will Be Slow." Washington, DC: General Accounting Office, 1988.

———. "Reclamation of Public and Indian Coal Lands." Washington, DC: General Accounting Office, 1973.

Garcia, Rogelio. "Federal Regulatory Reform: An Overview." Washington, DC: Congressional Research Service, 2000.

Gates, Paul W. *History of Public Land Law Development.* Washington, DC: Government Printing Office, 1968.

———. *Pressure Groups and Recent American Land Policies, The Carl Becker Lecture.* Ithaca, NY: Department of History, Cornell University, 1980.

Giller, Chip. "Babbitt Protests a $1 Billion Giveaway." *High Country News* 27, no. 18 (1995): 5.

———. "The BLM: New Faces and New Attitudes." *High Country News* 26, no. 23 (1994): 3.

Ginger, Clare. "Discourse and Argument in Bureau of Land Management Wilderness Environmental Impact Statements." *Policy Studies Journal* 28, no. 2 (2000): 292–313.

————. "Interpreting Wilderness Policy in the Bureau of Land Management." Ph.D. diss., University of Michigan, 1995.

Goodman, Doug, and Daniel C. McCool, eds. *Contested Landscape: The Politics of Wilderness in Utah and the West*. Salt Lake City: University of Utah Press, 1999.

Gorte, Ross W. "The Clinton Administration's Forest Plan for the Pacific Northwest." Washington, DC: Congressional Research Service, 1993.

Gosnell, Hannah. "Rangeland Reform '94 and the Politics of the Old West: An Analysis of Institutional and Ideological Barriers to Reforming Federal Rangeland Policy." Master's thesis, University of Colorado, 1995.

Graf, William L. *Wilderness Preservation and the Sagebrush Rebellions*. Savage, MD: Rowman & Littlefield, 1990.

"Grazing Administration—Exclusive of Alaska." *Federal Register* 68, no. 235 (2003): 68452–74.

Gregg, Frank. "Federal Land Transfers: The Case for a Westwide Program Based on the Federal Land Policy and Management Act." Washington, DC: Conservation Foundation, 1982.

Gulick, Luther. *Administrative Reflections from World War II*. Birmingham: University of Alabama Press, 1948.

Gulick, Luther, and Lyndall Urwick, eds. *Papers on the Science of Administration*. New York: Columbia University, Institute of Public Administration, 1937.

Hagenstein, Perry R. "Public Lands and Environmental Concerns." *Arizona Law Review* 21, no. 2 (1979): 449–59.

————. "Some History of Multiple Use and Sustained Yield Concepts." Paper presented at the workshop "Multiple Use and Sustained Yield: Changing Philosophies for Federal Land Management?" Washington, DC, March 5–6, 1992.

Hager, George. "President Throws Down Gauntlet." *Congressional Quarterly Weekly Report* 51, no. 8 (1993): 355–58.

Hair, Jay D., and Patrick A. Parenteau. "Marching Backwards: The Department of Interior under James G. Watt." Washington, DC: National Wildlife Federation, 1982.

Hanscom, Greg. "Outsourced." *High Country News* 36, no. 8 (2004): 7–12.

"Hardrock Mining on Federal Lands." Washington, DC: National Research Council, 1999.

Hardt, Scott W. "Federal Land Management in the Twenty-First Century: From Wise Use to Wise Stewardship." *Public Land and Resources Law Digest* 32, no. 1 (1995): 47–105.

Harmon, David, Francis P. McManamon, and Dwight T. Pitcaithley, eds. *The Antiquities Act: A Century of American Archaeology, Historic Preservation, and Nature Conservation*. Tucson: University of Arizona Press, 2006.

Harvey, D. Michael. "BLM's Response to the Public Land Law Review Commission's Report." 1988. Uncatalogued Papers. Compiled by James Muhn. BLM Library. Denver Service Center. Denver, CO.

————. "Exempt from Public Haunt: The Wilderness Study Provisions of the Federal Land Policy and Management Act." *Idaho Law Review* 16, no. 3 (1980): 481–510.

————. "Support Your Local Sheriff: Federalism and Law Enforcement under the Federal Land Policy and Management Act." *Arizona Law Review* 21, no. 2 (1979): 461–83.

Hays, Samuel P. *Beauty, Health and Permanence: Environmental Politics in the United States, 1955–1985*. New York: Cambridge University Press, 1987.

————. *Conservation and the Gospel of Efficiency: The Progressive Conservation Movement, 1890–1920*. Cambridge, MA: Harvard University Press, 1959.

———. "Public Values and Management Response." In *Developing Strategies for Rangeland Management: A Report Prepared by the Committee on Developing Strategies for Rangeland Management*, 1811–43. Boulder, CO: Westview Press, 1984.

Healy, Jon. "From Conflict to Coexistence: New Politics of Environment." *Congressional Quarterly Weekly Online* (February 13, 1993): 309.

———. "Ten Environmental Nettles That Await the 103rd Congress." *Congressional Quarterly Weekly Online* (February 13, 1993): 310-11.

Healy, Robert G., and William E. Shands. "A Conversation with Marion Clawson: How Times (and Foresters) Have Changed." *Journal of Forestry* 87, no. 5 (1989): 18–24.

Heclo, Hugh. "The Issue-Network and the Executive Establishment." In *The New American Political System*, edited by Anthony King. Washington, DC: American Enterprise Institute for Public Policy Research, 1978.

Heilprin, John. "Bush Considers Rolling Back Mining Law." *Arkansas Democrat-Gazette*, March 21, 2001, A3.

Hendee, John C., and Randall C. Pitstick. "The Growth of Environmental and Conservation-Related Organizations: 1980–1991." *Renewable Resources Journal* 10, no. 2 (1992): 6–11.

Hickel, Walter J. *Who Owns America?* Englewood Cliffs, NJ: Prentice-Hall, 1971.

Hofman, Ron. "Implementation of the National Environmental Policy Act." *Publius* 2, no. 2 (1972): 119.

Hoover, Herbert, Dean Acheson, Arthur S. Flemming, James Forrestal, George H. Mead, George D. Aiken, Joseph P. Kennedy, John L. McClellan, James K. Pollock, Clarence J. Brown, Carter Manasco, and James H. Rowe, Jr. "Reorganization of the Department of the Interior: A Report to the Congress by the Commission on Organization of the Executive Branch of the Government." Washington, DC: Commission on Organization of the Executive Branch of the Government, 1949.

Houck, Oliver. "Reflections on the Endangered Species Act." *Environmental Law* 25, no. 3 (Summer 1995): 689–702.

Huffman, James L. "A New Era for the Western Public Lands: The Inevitability of Private Rights in Public Lands." *Colorado Law Review* 65 (Spring 1994): 241–77.

Humphries, Marc. "Mining on Federal Lands." Washington, DC: Congressional Research Service, 2002.

Ickes, Harold L. *The Secret Diary of Harold L. Ickes.* 3 vols. Vol. 1, *The First Thousand Days, 1933–1936*. New York: Simon & Schuster, 1954.

———. "Why a Department of Conservation." Washington, DC: Government Printing Office, 1938.

Interagency Ecosystem Management Task Force. "The Ecosystem Approach: Healthy Ecosystems *and* Sustainable Economies." Washington, DC: Task Force, 1995.

Irland, Lloyd C. "Citizen Participation—A Tool for Conflict Management on the Public Lands." *Public Administration Review* 35, no. 3 (1975): 263–69.

Israelsen, Brent. "Governor Protests BLM Sale of Oil, Gas Leases in Wyoming." *Salt Lake Tribune*, June 9, 1994, 11.

———. "Land Deal Fought; Environmentalists Sue." *Salt Lake Tribune*, May 6, 2003, A1.

"Issues for the 90's: Bureau of Land Management." Washington, DC: Bureau of Land Management, 1989.

Jenkins, Matt. "The BLM Wields Fork and Spatula over the West's Wildlands." *High Country News* 37, no. 2 (2005): 21.

———. "Norton Eases Road Claims." *High Country News* 38, no. 7 (2006): 6.

———. "Two Decades of Hard Work, Plowed Under." *High Country News* 36, no. 1 (2004): 7–10, 12, 15.

Johnson, Lyndon B. "Special Message to Congress on Conservation and Restoration of Natural Beauty," February 8, 1965. In *Public Papers of the Presidents of the United States: Lyndon B. Johnson, 1965*. Washington, DC: Government Printing Office, 1966.

Jones, Robert A. "Developing a Planning System for Public Domain Lands: An Analysis of Organization Change in the Bureau of Land Management." Master's thesis, University of Wisconsin, 1971.

———. "Master Unit Classification." *Our Public Lands* 11, no. 3 (1962).

———. "Multiple Use Planning in BLM—Some Personal Recollections." Denver, CO: Research Papers of James Muhn, 1988.

———. "The New Look in Public Lands Management." Paper presented at the BLM District Managers Conference, Denver, CO, April 20, 1964.

Kahn, Joseph. "The Energy Plan: The Details." *New York Times*, May 18, 2001.

Kamensky, John M. "Role of the 'Reinventing Government' Movement in Federal Management Reform." *Public Administration Review* 56, no. 3 (1996): 247–55.

Kaufman, Herbert. "Administrative Decentralization and Political Power." *Public Administration Review* 29, no. 1 (1969): 3–15.

———. "Emerging Conflicts in the Doctrines of Public Administration." *American Political Science Review* 50, no. 4 (1956): 1057–74.

———. *The Forest Ranger: A Study in Administrative Behavior*. Baltimore: Johns Hopkins University Press, 1960.

Keiter, Robert B. "Change Comes to the Public Lands: New Forces, Directions, and Policies." *Rocky Mountain Mineral Law Institute* 46, no. 3-1 (2000).

Kennedy, James J., and Thomas M. Quigley. "Evolution of USDA Forest Service Organizational Culture and Adaptation Issues in Embracing an Ecosystem Management Paradigm." *Landscape and Urban Planning* 40, no. 1 (1998): 113–22.

Kennedy, John F. "Special Message to the Congress on Conservation." In *Public Papers of the Presidents of the United States: John F. Kennedy, 1962*. Washington, DC: Government Printing Office, 1963.

———. "Special Message to Congress on Natural Resources." In *Public Papers of the President of the United States: John F. Kennedy, 1961*. Washington, DC: Government Printing Office, 1962.

———. Speech delivered at the Shrine Auditorium, Billings, MT, September 22, 1960.

———. Speech delivered at the White House Conference on Conservation, Washington, DC, May 24–25, 1962.

Kenworthy, Tom. "New Mining Rules Reverse Provisions." *USA Today*, October 26, 2001, 8A.

Kerr, Andy, and Mark Salvo. "Evolving Presidential Policy toward Livestock Grazing in National Monuments." *Penn State Law Review* 10 (2001): 1–12.

Kettl, Donald F. "Reinventing Government: A Fifth-Year Report Card." Washington, DC: Brookings Institution, 1998.

Klyza, Christopher James. "Patterns in Public Lands Policy: The Consequences of Ideas and the State." Dissertation, University of Minnesota, 1990.

———. *Who Controls Public Lands? Mining, Forestry, and Grazing Policies, 1870–1990*. Chapel Hill: University of North Carolina Press, 1996.

Klyza, Christopher McGrory, and David Sousa. *American Environmental Policy, 1990–2006*. Cambridge, MA: MIT Press, 2008.

Kraft, Michael E., and Norman J. Vig. "Environmental Policy in the Reagan Presidency." *Political Science Quarterly* 99, no. 3 (1984): 415–39.

Kriz, Margie. "Bush on Environment: Leading Republican Candidate Reveals Team and Policies." *SEJournal* 9, no. 3 (1999): 1, 19–20.

Lambert, Darwin. *The Undying Past of Shenandoah National Park*. Boulder, CO: Roberts Rinehart, 1989.

Lamm, Richard D., and Michael McCarthy. *The Angry West: A Vulnerable Land and Its Future*. Boston: Houghton Mifflin, 1982.

Landstrom, Karl S. "Program for the Public Lands and Resources." Washington, DC: U.S. Department of the Interior, Bureau of Land Management, 1962.

Larmer, Paul. "The Drill Starts to Change at Interior." *High Country News* 25, no. 4 (1993): 3.

———. "Utah Counties Bulldoze the BLM, Park Service." *High Country News* 28, no. 20 (1996): 3.

———, ed. *Give and Take: How the Clinton Administration's Public Lands Offensive Transformed the American West*. Paonia, CO: High Country News Books, 2004.

Lawrence, Mark E. "Pilot Rock: Ancient Guide of the Siskiyous." *Our Public Lands* 20, no. 4 (1970): 19.

Leman, Christopher K. "Formal versus De Facto Systems of Multiple Use Planning in the Bureau of Land Management: Integrating Comprehensive and Focused Approaches." In *Developing Strategies for Rangeland Management: A Report Prepared by the Committee on Developing Strategies for Rangeland Management*. Boulder, CO: Westview Press, 1984.

Le Master, Dennis C. *Decade of Change: The Remaking of Forest Service Statutory Authority during the 1970s*. Westport, CT: Greenwood Press, 1984.

Lerner, William, ed. *Historical Statistics of the United States, Colonial Times to 1970*. Washington, DC: U.S. Bureau of the Census, 1975.

Leshy, John D. "The Babbitt Legacy at the Department of the Interior: A Preliminary View." *Environmental Law* 31 (Spring 2001): 199–227.

———. "BLM's Future." Paper presented at the Restoring and Managing Western Public Range and Grasslands: Public Lands Foundation 2002 Annual Meeting and Symposium, Sacramento, CA, September 12–13, 2002.

———. "Is the Multiple Use/Sustained Yield Management Philosophy Still Applicable Today?" Paper presented at the workshop "Multiple Use and Sustained Yield: Changing Philosophies for Federal Land Management" Washington, DC, March 5–6, 1992.

———. "Mining Law Reform Redux, Once More." *Natural Resources Journal* 42, no. 3 (2002): 461–90.

———. *The Mining Law: A Study in Perpetual Motion*. Washington, DC: Resources for the Future, 1987.

———. "Natural Resource Policy." In *Natural Resources and the Environment*, edited by Paul R. Portney. Washington, DC: Resources for the Future, 1984.

———. "Natural Resources Policy in the Clinton Administration: A Mid-Course Evaluation from Inside." *Environmental Law* 25 (Summer 1995): 679–87.

Leunes, Barbara Laverne Blythe. "The Conservation Philosophy of Stewart L. Udall, 1961–1968." Ph.D. diss., Texas A&M University, 1977.

Lewis, William M., Jr. "The Ecological Sciences and the Public Domain." *University of Colorado Law Review* 65, no. 2 (1993): 279–92.

Libecap, Gary D. *Locking Up the Range: Federal Land Controls and Grazing*. Cambridge, MA: Ballinger, 1981.

Lindblom, Charles E. "The Science of Muddling Through." *Public Administration Review* 19, no. 2 (1959): 79–88.

Lindstrom, Matthew J., and Zachary A. Smith. *The National Environmental Policy Act: Judicial Misconstruction, Legislative Indifference, and Executive Neglect*. Edited by Dan Flores, Environmental History Series. College Station: Texas A&M University Press, 2001.

Lipsher, Steve. "Roan Drilling Takes Long Road: Concerned Public 'Looking over Our Shoulder,' BLM Official Says." *Denver Post*, February 13, 2004, B01.

Liroff, Richard A. *A National Policy for the Environment: NEPA and Its Aftermath*. Bloomington: Indiana University Press, 1976.

Lohr, Steve, and John Markoff. "Windows Is So Slow, But Why? Sheer Size Is Causing Delays for Microsoft." *New York Times*, March 27, 2006, 1.

Lowi, Theodore J. *The End of Liberalism: The Second Republic of the United States*. 2nd ed. New York: W. W. Norton, 1979.

"Management Reform: Agencies' Initial Efforts to Restructure Personnel Operations." Washington, DC: General Accounting Office, 1998.

March, James G., and Herbert Simon. *Organizations*. New York: Wiley, 1958.

Marcot, Bruce G., and Jack Ward Thomas. "Of Spotted Owls, Old Growth, and New Policies: A History since the Interagency Scientific Committee Report." Washington, DC: USDA Forest Service, 1997.

Marshall, Tom. "Ecosystem Management: Sustaining the Nation's Natural Resources Trust." Washington, DC: Committee on Resources, U.S. House of Representatives, 1994.

Marston, Ed. "Babbitt Is Trying to Nationalize the BLM." *High Country News* 26, no. 9 (1994): 1.

———. "Beyond the Revolution." *High Country News* 32, no. 7 (2000).

———. "Interior View: Bruce Babbitt Took the Real West to Washington, DC: A *High Country News* Interview." *High Country News* 33, no. 3 (2001): 8.

———. "Jim Baca Says the Department of Interior Is in Deep Trouble." *High Country News* 26, no. 3 (1994): 3.

Matthiessen, Peter. "Inside the Endangered Arctic Refuge." *New York Review of Books* 53, no. 16 (2006): 33–36.

Mayer, Carl J., and A. Riley George. *Public Domain, Private Domain: A History of Public Land Mineral Policy in America*. San Francisco: Sierra Club Books, 1985.

McArdle, Richard E. "Multiple Use—Multiple Benefits." *Journal of Forestry* 51, no. 5 (1953): 323–25.

McConnell, Grant. "The Environmental Movement: Ambiguities and Meanings." *Natural Resources Journal* 11, no. 3 (1971): 427–35.

———. *Private Power and American Democracy*. New York: Vintage Books, 1966.

McCormick, Robert L. L. "Management of Public Land Resources." *Yale Law Journal* 61 (1951).

Meredith, A. Jerry. "The BLM Planning Process." In *Visions of the Grand Staircase–Escalante: Examining Utah's Newest National Monument*, edited by Robert B. Keiter,

Sarah B. George, and Joro Walker. Salt Lake City: Utah Museum of Natural History and Wallace Stegner Center, 1998.

Merrill, Karen R. *Public Lands and Political Meaning: Ranchers, the Government, and the Property between Them.* Berkeley: University of California Press, 2002.

Michaelis, Laura. "Economic, Ecological Climate Favors Mining Law Overhaul." *Congressional Quarterly Weekly Report* 51, no. 12 (1993): 662–63.

Miller, Leslie A., Horace M. Albright, John Dempsey, Ralph Carr, Donald H. McLaughlin, Isaiah Bowman, Gilbert White, Samuel T. Dana, and Ernest S. Griffith. "Organization and Policy in the Field of Natural Resources: A Report with Recommendations Prepared for the Commission on Organization of the Executive Branch of the Government." Washington, DC: Commission on Organization of the Executive Branch of the Government, 1949.

Miller, Richard O. "FLPMA: A Decade of Management under the BLM Organic Act." *Policy Studies Journal* 14, no. 2 (1985): 265–73.

"Mining Claims under the General Mining Laws; Surface Management; Final Rule and Proposed Rule." *Federal Register* 66, no. 210 (2001): 54834–62.

"Mining Law." *Congressional Quarterly Weekly Report* 52, no. 43 (1994): 3169–70.

Mollin, F. E. *If and When It Rains: The Stockman's View of the Range Question.* Denver: American National Live Stock Association, 1938.

Moss, Michael. "Making the Most of the Public Lands." *High Country News* 13, no. 22 (1981): 1, 10–11.

Muhn, James, and Hanson R. Stuart. *Opportunity and Challenge: The Story of the BLM.* Washington, DC: U.S. Government Printing Office, 1988.

National Energy Policy Development Group. "National Energy Policy: Reliable, Affordable, and Environmentally Sound Energy for America's Future." Washington, DC: Government Printing Office, 2001.

Nelson, Robert H. "Basic Issues in Land Use Planning for the Public Lands." Washington, DC: Office of Policy Analysis, 1980.

———. *The Making of Federal Coal Policy.* Durham, NC: Duke University Press, 1983.

———. "Making Sense of the Sagebrush Rebellion: A Long Term Strategy for the Public Lands." Paper presented at the Association for Public Policy Analysis and Management, Washington, DC, October 23–25, 1981.

———. "The New Range Wars: Environmentalists versus Cattlemen for the Public Rangelands." Washington, DC: Office of Policy Analysis, 1980.

———. *Public Lands and Private Rights: The Failure of Scientific Management.* Lanham, MD: Rowman & Littlefield, 1995.

Nicholson, Rex L. "Reorganization Plan No. 3 as Proposed to J. A. Krug, Secretary of the Interior." Washington, DC: Bureau of Land Management, 1946.

Nienaber, Jeanne, and Aaron Wildavsky. *The Budgeting and Evaluation of Federal Recreation Programs.* New York: Basic Books, 1973.

Nijhuis, Michelle. "Change Comes Slowly to Escalante Country." *High Country News* 35, no. 7 (2003).

"The O & C Lands." Eugene: Bureau of Governmental Research and Service, University of Oregon, 1981.

One Third of the Nation's Land: A Report to the President and to the Congress by the Public Land Law Review Commission. Washington, DC: Public Land Law Review Commission, 1970.

Outerbridge, Cheryl, and Don H. Sherwood. "Recordation and Filing of Unpatented Mining Claims and Sites with the Federal Government." *Arizona Law Review* 21, no. 2 (1979): 433–47.

Palmer, Elizabeth. "More Money Comes in under Plan for 'Savings' in Budget." *Congressional Quarterly Weekly Report* 51, no. 8 (1993): 370–77.

Papers Relating to the President's Departmental Reorganization Program: A Reference Compilation. Washington, DC: U.S. Government Printing Office, 1972.

Paskus, Laura. "Up in Smoke: Obama Administration Will Inherit a Beleaguered Forest Service." *High Country News* 40, no. 23 (2008): 10.

Paulsen, David Frederick. "An Approach to Organizational Analysis: A Case Study of the Bureau of Land Management." Ph.D. diss., University of Washington, 1966.

Pearl, Milton S. "Public Land Commissions." *Our Public Lands* 17, no. 2 (1967): 14–17.

Peffer, E. Louise. *The Closing of the Public Domain: Disposal and Reservation Policies 1900–50*. Stanford, CA: Stanford University Press, 1951.

Peterson, E. K. "Recreation on the National Land Reserve." *Our Public Lands* 11, no. 3 (1962): 5–6.

Peterson, Gene. *Pioneering Outdoor Recreation*. McLean, VA: Public Lands Foundation, 1996.

Peterson, Russell W. "Environmental Impact Statements: An Analysis of Six Years' Experience by Seventy Federal Agencies." Washington, DC: Council on Environmental Quality, 1976.

Phillipson, Donald E. "*One-Third of the Nation's Land*: The Public Land Law Review Commission Report: A Summary Critique from the Environmental Perspective." Denver, CO: Rocky Mountain Center on Environment, 1971.

Pianin, Eric. "White House Won't Fight Monument Designations: Norton Says Boundaries, Land Use Rules May Be Amended." *Washington Post*, February 21, 2001, A07.

Pierson, Royale K. "Cooperative Agreement on Recreation." *Our Public Lands* 3, no. 2 (1953): 3.

Pinchot, Gifford. *Breaking New Ground*. Washington, DC: Island Press, 1998.

——. *The Fight for Conservation*. New York: Doubleday, Page & Company, 1910.

Pinchot III, Gifford. "Outsourcing and the Alternatives." *Forest Magazine* (2003).

Poyner, Ann Marie. "Fighting Over Forgotten Lands: The Evolution of Recreation Provision on the United States Public Domain." Ph.D. diss., University of Bristol, 1999.

Prendergast, Alan. "Raiding the Roan." *Denver Westword*, January 1, 2004.

"President's Reorganization Project Office of Management and Budget: Proposal for Natural Resources Organization." Washington, DC: Office of Management and Budget, 1979.

Press, Daniel. *Democratic Dilemmas in the Age of Ecology: Trees and Toxics in the American West*. Durham, NC: Duke University Press, 1994.

Public Hearing to Receive Comments on the Draft Environmental Impact Statement on the Proposed Grazing Rule, Bureau of Land Management, Washington, DC, February 4, 2004.

"Public Land Management: Identification of Problems—Analysis of Causes." Washington, DC: Department of the Interior, 1968.

"Public Land Meeting." *American Cattle Producer* 28, no. 4 (1946): 8–13.

"Public Land Statistics, 1961," Washington, DC: Bureau of Land Management, 1962.

"Public Land Statistics, 1962," Washington, DC: Bureau of Land Management, 1963.

"Public Land Statistics, 2003," Washington, DC: Bureau of Land Management, 2004.

"Public Land Statistics, 2007," Washington, DC: Bureau of Land Management, 2008.

"Public Lands: Limited Progress in Resource Management Planning." Washington, DC: General Accounting Office, 1990.

"Public Rewards from the Public Lands, 2003." Washington, DC: Bureau of Land Management, 2004.

Pyles, Hamilton K., ed. *What's Ahead for Our Public Lands?: A Summary Review of the Activities and Final Report of the Public Land Law Review Commission*. Washington, DC: Natural Resources Council of America, 1970.

"Quarreling over Monuments." *New York Times*, September 4, 2000.

Ranchod, Sanjay. "The Clinton National Monuments: Protecting Ecosystems with the Antiquities Act." *Harvard Environmental Law Review* 25 (2001): 535–89.

"Rangeland Management: BLM Efforts to Prevent Unauthorized Livestock Grazing Need Strengthening." Washington, DC: General Accounting Office, 1990.

"Rangeland Management: Interior's Monitoring Has Fallen Short of Agency Requirements." Washington, DC: General Accounting Office, 1992.

"Rangeland Management: More Emphasis Needed on Declining and Overstocked Grazing Allotments." Washington, DC: General Accounting Office, 1988.

Ray, Pamela A., and Craig R. Carver. "Section 603 of the Federal Land Policy and Management Act: An Analysis of the BLM's Wilderness Study Process." *Arizona Law Review* 21, no. 2 (1979): 373–94.

Reeder, Dean. "The Utah Travel Division and Tourism Planning." In *Visions of the Grand Staircase–Escalante: Examining Utah's Newest National Monument*, edited by Robert B. Keiter, Sarah B. George, and Joro Walker. Salt Lake City: Utah Museum of Natural History and Wallace Stegner Center, 1998.

Reese, April. "The Big Buyout." *High Country News* 37, no. 6 (2005): 10–12, 19.

"Report of the Committee on the Conservation and Administration of the Public Domain to the President of the United States." Washington, DC: Government Printing Office, 1931.

Richardson, Elmo. *BLM's Billion-Dollar Checkerboard: Managing the O&C Lands*. Santa Cruz, CA: Forest History Society, 1980.

———. "Federal Park Policy in Utah: The Escalante National Monument Controversy of 1935–1940." *Utah Historical Quarterly* 33, no. 2 (1965): 109–33.

Richardson, Valerie. "Alone on the Range." *National Review* 46, no. 10 (1994): 24–25.

Roth, Dennis M. "The Wilderness Movement and the National Forests: 1964–1980." Washington, DC: USDA Forest Service, 1984.

Rothman, Hal. *Preserving Different Pasts: The American National Monuments*. Chicago: University of Illinois Press, 1989.

———. "'A Regular Ding-Dong Fight': The Dynamics of Park Service–Forest Service Controversy during the 1920s and 1930s." In *American Forests*, edited by Char Miller. Lawrence: University Press of Kansas, 1997.

Rowley, William D. "Historical Considerations in the Development of Range Science." In *Forest and Wildlife Science in America: A History*, edited by Harold K. Steen. Durham, NC: Forest History Society, 1999.

Rudzitis, Gundars. *Wilderness and the Changing American West*. New York: John Wiley & Sons, 1996.

Sabatier, Paul A., ed. *Policy Change and Learning: An Advocacy Coalition Approach.* Boulder, CO: Westview Press, 1993.

Sagoff, Mark. *Price, Principle, and the Environment.* New York: Cambridge University Press, 2004.

Sax, Joseph. *Defending the Environment: A Strategy for Citizen Action.* New York: Alfred A. Knopf, 1971.

———. "Do Communities Have Rights? The National Parks as a Laboratory of New Ideas." *University of Pittsburgh Law Review* 45, no. 3 (1984): 499–511.

———. "Perspectives Lecture: Public Land Law in the 21st Century." *Rocky Mountain Mineral Law Institute* 45, no. 1-1 (1999).

———. "The Trampas File." *Michigan Law Review* 84, no. 7 (1986): 1389–414.

Schroth, Thomas, ed. *Congress and the Nation, 1945–1964: A Review of Government and Politics in the Postwar Years.* 1st ed. Washington, DC: Congressional Quarterly Service, 1965.

Schulte, Steven C. *Wayne Aspinall and the Shaping of the American West.* Boulder: University Press of Colorado, 2002.

Schwartz, Eleanor. "A Capsule Examination of the Legislative History of the Federal Land Policy and Management Act of 1976." *Arizona Law Review* 21, no. 2 (1979): 285–300.

"Scientific Inventory of Onshore Federal Lands Oil and Gas Resources and Reserves and the Extent and Nature of Restrictions or Impediments to Their Development." Washington, DC: DOI, USDA, and DOE, 2003.

Sedjo, Roger A. "Streamlining Forest Service Planning." In *New Approaches on Energy and the Environment,* edited by Richard D. Morgenstern and Paul R. Portney. Washington, DC: Resources for the Future, 2004.

Selznick, Philip. *TVA and the Grass Roots.* Berkeley: University of California Press, 1949.

Senzel, Irving. "The Future of BLM." Paper presented at the Bureau of Land Management Planning Conference, San Francisco, August 10–14, 1970.

———. "Genesis of a Law, Part 1." *American Forests* 84, no. 1 (1978): 30–32, 61–64.

———. "Genesis of a Law, Part 2." *American Forests* 84, no. 2 (1978): 32–39.

Sharpe, Maitland, David L. Ture, James E. Browns, J. Wayne Burkhardt, Stan Tixier, Bob McQuivey, Delmar Vail, H. James Fox, and Deen Boe. "Report of the Blue Ribbon Panel to the National Public Lands Advisory Council on Rangeland Program Initiatives and Strategies." Washington, DC: National Public Lands Advisory Council, 1992.

Shaw, Elmer W. "Selected Commentaries on the Report of the Public Land Law Review Commission, *One Third of the Nation's Land.*" Washington, DC: Congressional Research Service, 1970.

Shipman, George A., and David F. Paulsen. "The Bureau of Land Management: United States Department of the Interior: The Organization of the Washington Office." Seattle: University of Washington, Institute for Administrative Research, 1963.

———. "The Bureau of Land Management: United States Department of the Interior: The Program Action System." Seattle: University of Washington, Institute for Administrative Research, 1964.

Short, C. Brant. *Ronald Reagan and the Public Lands: America's Conservation Debate, 1979–1984.* Edited by Martin V. Melosi. Vol. 10, Environmental History Series. College Station: Texas A&M University Press, 1989.

"Shortfalls in BLM's Management of Wildlife Habitat in the California Desert Conservation Area." Washington, DC: General Accounting Office, 1989.

Simon, Herbert. *Administrative Behavior: A Study of Decision-Making Processes in Administrative Behavior.* 4th ed. New York: The Free Press, 1997.

Skillen, James R. "Closing the Public Lands Frontier: The Bureau of Land Management,
1961–1969." *Journal of Policy History* 20, no. 3 (2008): 417–43.

Smith, Michael P. "Alienation and Bureaucracy: The Role of Participatory Administration." *Public Administration Review* 31, no. 6 (1971): 658–64.

Smith, Thomas G. "John Kennedy, Stewart Udall, and New Frontier Conservation." *Pacific Historical Review* 67, no. 3 (1995): 329–66.

Smyth, Paul B. "Federal Law Enforcement on Public Lands: Reality or Mirage?" *Arizona
Law Review* 21, no. 2 (1979): 485–99.

Soden, Dennis L., ed. *The Environmental Presidency.* Albany: State University of New
York Press, 1999.

Sonner, Scott. "BLM Chief Apologizes to Employees." *Las Vegas Review Journal*
(2003).

Soraghan, Mike. "Watt Applauds Bush Energy Strategy." *Denver Post*, May 16, 2001, 1.

Soussan, Tania. "Oil Drillers Fight to Tap Otero Mesa." *Albuquerque Journal*, January 11,
2004, B1.

Stein, Theo. "BLM to Ease Oil, Gas Access." *Denver Post*, March 19, 2002, B04.

Stern, Bill Steven. "Permit Value: A Hidden Key to the Public Land Grazing Dispute."
Master's thesis, University of Montana, 1998.

Stewart, Richard B. "The Reformation of American Administrative Law." *Harvard Law
Review* 88, no. 8 (1975): 1667–813.

Stoddard, Charles H. "Administration of Federal Lands." In *America's Public Lands: Politics, Economics and Administration*, edited by Harriet Nathan. Berkeley: University of
California Press, 1972.

———. "Public Land Management: 1963–1968." Washington, DC: Bureau of Land Management, 1968.

———. "Public Participation in Public Land Decisions." In *Public Land Policy: Proceedings of the Western Resources Conference*, edited by Phillip O. Foss. Boulder: Colorado
Associated University Press, 1968.

———. "Report and Summary of Actions in the Bureau of Land Management During the
Directorship of Charles H. Stoddard—June '63 to June '66." Uncatalogued Papers,
compiled by James Muhn, Bureau of Land Management Library, 13.

Stoddard, Charles H., and Jerry A. O'Callaghan. "Creative Federalism on the Retention or
Disposition of Public Lands." *Arizona Law Review* 8, no. 1 (1966): 37–45.

Stough, Donald B. "Wonders of the Public Domain." *Our Public Lands* 14, no. 3 (1965):
4–7.

Strosnider, Fred, Irving H. Cowles, Walter M. Gilmer, Gordon Griswold, Ernest H. Gubler,
E. R. Marvel, R. T. Marvel, J. A. Wadsworth, and R. A. Yelland. "A Study of the Hoover
Commission's Recommendation for a New Forest and Range Service in the Department of Agriculture." Reno, NV: Central Committee of Nevada State Grazing Boards,
1949.

Stuebner, Stephen. "Go Tell It on the Mountain." *High Country News* 31, no. 22
(1999): 5.

———. "The New Voice at BLM." *High Country News* 31, no. 7 (1999).

Swedlow, Brendon. "Scientists, Judges, and Spotted Owls: Policymakers in the Pacific Northwest." *Duke Environmental Law and Policy Forum* 13 (2003): 187–278.

Thomas, Craig W. *Bureaucratic Landscapes: Interagency Cooperation and the Preservation of Biodiversity*. Cambridge, MA: MIT Press, 2003.

Thomas, Jack Ward, Eric D. Forsman, Joseph B. Linit, E. Charles Meslow, Barry B. Noon, and Jared Verner. "A Conservation Strategy for the Northern Spotted Owl: Report of the Interagency Scientific Committee to Address the Conservation of the Northern Spotted Owl." Portland, OR: USDA Forest Service, USDI Bureau of Land Management, USDI Fish and Wildlife Service, USDI National Park Service, 1990.

Turcott, George L. "Beginning at Challis: What Happened at Challis May Help Revitalize the Public Range." *Our Public Lands* 26, no. 1 (1975): 10–15.

Twight, Ben W. "Confidence or More Controversy: Whither Public Involvement?" *Journal of Forestry* 75 (1977): 93–95.

Udall, Stewart L. *Annual Report of the Secretary of the Interior*. Washington, DC: U.S. Government Printing Office, 1963.

———. "Conflicting Claims over *A Third of the Nation*." *Newsday*, July 8, 1970.

———. *The Quiet Crisis*. Salt Lake City: Peregrine Smith Books, 1988.

———. "Resources for Tomorrow: 1961 Annual Report of the Secretary of the Interior." Washington, DC: Department of the Interior, 1961.

———. *The Third Wave . . . America's New Conservation*. Vol. 3, *Conservation Yearbook*. Washington, DC: Department of the Interior, 1966.

Udall, Stewart L., and Jeff Stansbury. "The Pipeline Fantasy." *Newsday*, March 17, 1971.

"The United States Department of the Interior Budget Justifications and Performance Information Fiscal Year 2004: Bureau of Land Management." Washington, DC: Bureau of Land Management, 2003.

U.S. Congress. House. Committee on Expenditures in the Executive Departments. *Reorganization Plans Nos. 1, 2, and 3 of 1946: Hearings on H. Con. Res. 151, H. Con. Res. 154, H. Con. Res. 155*, 79th Cong., 2nd sess., June 4, 5, 6, 7, 11, 12, 13, 1946.

———. Committee on Government Operations. *Summary of the Objectives, Operations, and Results of the Commissions on Organization of the Executive Branch of the Government*. Prepared by William L. Dawson. 88th Cong., 1st sess., 1963.

———. Committee on Interior and Insular Affairs. *Policies, Programs, and Activities of the Department of the Interior*. 87th Cong., 1st sess., February 15, 21, 27, 1961.

———. Committee on Interior and Insular Affairs. *Policies, Programs, and Activities of the Department of the Interior*. 88th Cong., 1st sess., February 5, 1963.

———. Committee on Natural Resources. *Ecosystem Management: Sustaining the Nation's Natural Resources Trust*. Prepared by Tom Marshall. 103rd Cong., 2nd sess., April 1994.

———. Subcommittee on Energy and Resources. *Interior Department: A Culture of Managerial Irresponsibility and Lack of Accountability?* 109th Cong., 2nd sess., September 13–14, 2006.

———. Subcommittee on Fisheries and Wildlife Conservation. *Administration of the National Environmental Policy Act—1972, Appendix*. 99th Cong., 2nd sess., February 17, 25 and May 24, 1972.

———. Subcommittee on National Parks and Public Lands. *Behind Closed Doors: The Abuse of Trust and Discretion in the Establishment of the Grand Staircase–Escalante National Monument*. 105th Cong., 1st sess., November 7, 1997.

————. Subcommittee on National Parks and Public Lands. *Statement of Tom Fulton, Deputy Assistant Secretary for Land and Minerals Management.* 107th Cong., 2nd sess., July 17, 2001.

————. Subcommittee on Public Lands. *Matters Relating to the Public Lands.* 96th Cong., 1st and 2nd sess., November 27, 29, 1979; February 22 and June 12, 1980.

————. Subcommittee on Public Lands. *Public Lands Policy: Hearings Pursuant to H. Res. 93, Committee Hearing No. 30.* 80th Cong., 1st sess., April 21 and May 10, 1947.

U.S. Congress. Senate. Committee on Energy and Natural Resources. *Grazing.* 103rd Cong., 2nd sess., April 20 and May 14, 1994.

————. Committee on Energy and Natural Resources. *Legislative History of the Federal Land Policy and Management Act of 1976 (Public Law 94-579).* 95th Cong., 2nd sess., April 1978.

————. Committee on Expenditures in the Executive Departments. *Hearings on S. 1149: A Bill to Provide for the Reorganization of the Department of Agriculture in Accordance with the Recommendations of the Commission on Organization of the Executive Branch of the Government.* 82nd Cong., 1st sess., August 28–29 and September 5–7, 10–12, 18, 1951.

————. Committee on Expenditures in the Executive Departments. *Reestablishing Registers of Land Offices.* 80th Cong., 1st sess., March 10, 1947.

————. Committee on Interior and Insular Affairs. *Grazing Fees on Public Lands.* 91st Cong., 1st sess., February 27–28, 1969.

————. Committee on Interior and Insular Affairs. *Hearings on the Nomination of Governor Walter J. Hickel, of Alaska, to be Secretary of the Interior.* 91st Cong., 1st sess., January 15–18, 20, 1969.

————. Committee on Interior and Insular Affairs. *National Resource Policy.* 81st Cong., 1st sess., January 31 and February 1–4, 7, 1949.

————. Committee on the Judiciary. *President's Plan for Reorganization of Executive Departments: Hearings on S. Con. Res. 64, 65, and 66 Concurrent Resolutions Disapproving Reorganization Plans 1, 2, and 3.* 79th Cong., 2nd sess., June 14, 15, 18, 19, 20, 21, 25, 26, 27, 1946.

————. Committee on Public Lands and Surveys. *Administration and Use of Public Lands.* 79th Cong., 1st sess., 1945.

————. Committee on Public Lands and Surveys. *Granting Remaining Unreserved Public Lands to States.* 72nd Cong., 1st sess., March 15, 16, 19, 24, 29, 31, and April 1, 5, 1932.

————. Committee on Public Lands and Surveys. *Hearings Pursuant to S. Res. 241: Resolutions Authorizing the Committee on Public Lands to Make a Full and Complete Investigation with Respect to the Administration and Use of the Public Lands.* 79th Cong., 1st sess., January 22–23, 1945.

————. Committee on Public Lands and Surveys. *Nomination of Julius A. Krug for Appointment as Secretary of the Interior.* 79th Cong., 2nd sess., March 5, 1946.

"U.S. Forest Service: 2006 Budget Justification." Washington, DC: U.S. Forest Service, 2005.

Vaughn, Jacqueline, and Hanna J. Cortner. *George W. Bush's Healthy Forests: Reframing the Environmental Debate.* Boulder: University Press of Colorado, 2005.

Vig, Norman J. "Presidential Leadership and the Environment: From Reagan to Clinton." In *Environmental Policy in the 1990s: Reform or Reaction?* edited by Norman J. Vig and Michael E. Kraft. Washington, DC: CQ Press, 1997.

Voight, William, Jr. *Public Grazing Lands: Use and Misuse by Industry and Government.* New Brunswick, NJ: Rutgers University Press, 1976.

VTN Consolidated, Inc. "The National Environmental Policy Act Process Study: An Evaluation of the Implementation and Administration of the NEPA by the Forest Service and the Bureau of Land Management." Washington, DC: Council on Environmental Quality, 1975.

Wagner, James R. "CPR Report/Government Lands Study Stirs Public-Private Interest Debate." *CPR National Journal* 2 (1970): 1088–96.

Wallace, H. A. "The Western Range." Washington, DC: Government Printing Office, 1936.

Watkins, T. H. *Righteous Pilgrim: The Life and Times of Harold L. Ickes, 1874–1952.* New York: H. Holt, 1990.

Watkins, T. H., and Charles S. Watson, Jr. *The Land No One Knows: America and the Public Domain.* San Francisco: Sierra Club Books, 1975.

Welch, Craig. "Bush Switches Nation's Tack on Protecting Species." *Seattle Times*, September 27, 2004.

Wengert, Norman. "The Ideological Basis of Conservation and Natural Resources Policies and Programs." *Annals of the American Academy of Political and Social Sciences* 344 (1962): 65–75.

———. *Natural Resources and the Political Struggle.* New York: Random House, 1955.

Werth, Daphine. "Where Regulation and Property Rights Collide: Reforming the Hardrock Act of 1872." *University of Colorado Law Review* 65, no. 2 (1994): 427–58.

Westby, Tim. "Backcountry Road Deal Runs over Wilderness." *High Country News* 35, no. 9 (2003): 5.

Wharton, Tom. "Norton Defends Settlement to Roll Back Land Protection." *Salt Lake Tribune*, June 18, 2003, A1.

Wheat, Frank. *California Desert Miracle: The Fight for Desert Parks and Wilderness.* San Diego, CA: Sunbelt Publications, 1999.

Whitaker, John C. *Striking a Balance: Environment and Natural Resources Policy in the Nixon-Ford Years, AEI-Hoover Policy Studies.* Washington, DC: American Enterprise Institute for Public Policy Research, 1976.

Whitaker, Robert B. "Keeping the Wild Lands Wild: BLM's First Primitive Areas." *Our Public Lands* 19, no. 2 (1969): 12–13.

"White House Reverses Clinton Mining Decision." *Deseret News*, October 26, 2001, A02.

White, Richard. "Are You an Environmentalist or Do You Work for a Living?" In *Uncommon Ground: Toward Reinventing Nature*, edited by William Cronon. New York: W. W. Norton, 1995.

Wichelman, Allan F. "Administrative Agency Implementation of the National Environmental Policy Act of 1969: A Conceptual Framework for Explaining Differential Response." *Natural Resources Journal* 16, no. 2 (1976): 263–300.

Wilkinson, Charles F. "Clinton Learns the Art of Audacity." *High Country News* 28, no. 18 (1996).

Williamson, James Alexander, Clarence King, Alexander Thompson Britton, Thomas Donaldson, and John Wesley Powell. "Report of the Public Lands Commission Created by the Act of March 3, 1879, Relating to Public Lands in the Western Portion of the United States and to the Operation of Existing Land Laws." Washington, DC: Government Printing Office, 1880.

Willis, Ivan B. "The Secret of Fifty Mile Mountain: Is It Lost Treasure?" *Our Public Lands* 18, no. 4 (1968): 16–17.

Winter, Charles E. *Four Hundred Million Acres: The Public Lands and Resources.* New York: Arno Press, 1979.

Zivnuska, John A. "The Multiple Problems of Multiple Use." *Journal of Forestry* 59, no. 8 (1961): 555–60.

COURT CASES

American Horse Protection Association, Inc. v. Watt, 694 F.2d 1310 (D.C.Cir.1982)

Burford v. Houtz, 133 U.S. 320 (1890)

Camfield v. United States, 167 U.S. 524 (1897)

Citizens for Reid State Park v. Laird, 336 F. Supp. 783 (1972)

Citizens to Preserve Overton Park, Inc. v. Volpe, 401 U.S. 402 (1971)

Environmental Defense Fund v. Resor, 325 F.Supp. 749 (E.D.Ark.1971)

Environmental Defense Fund v. Ruckelshaus, 439 F.2d 584 (D.C.Cir.1971)

Grimaud v. United States, 220 U.S. 506 (1911)

Kleppe v. New Mexico, 426 U.S. 529 (1976)

Light v. United States, 220 U.S. 523 (1911)

Mountain States Legal Foundation v. Hodel, 799 F.2d 1423 (10th Cir.1986)

Natural Resources Defense Council, Inc. v. Berklund, 609 F.2d 553 (D.C.Cir.1979)

Natural Resources Defense Council, Inc. v. Hughes, 437 F.Supp. 981 (D.D.C.1977)

Natural Resources Defense Council, Inc. v. Morton, 458 F.2d 827 (D.C.Cir.1972)

Natural Resources Defense Council, Inc. v. Morton, 388 F.Supp. 829 (D.D.C.1974)

Pankey Land and Cattle Company v. Hardin, 427 F.2d 43 (10th Cir.1970)

Porter v. Resor, 415 F.2d 766 (10th Cir.1969)

Portland Audubon Society v. Lujan, 784 F.Supp. 786 (D.Or.1992)

Seattle Audubon Society v. Evans, 771 F.Supp. 1081 (W.D.Wash.1991)

United States v. Cox, 190 F.2d 293 (10th Cir.1951)

Wellford v. Ruckelshaus, 439 F.2d 598 (D.C.Cir.1971)

Wilderness Society v. Hickel, 325 F.Supp. 422 (D.D.C.1970)

Wilderness Society v. Morton, 479 F.2d 842 (D.C.Cir.1973)

INTERVIEWS

Andrus, Cecil. Interviewed by James Reston. April 6, 1977. James B. Reston Papers, University of Illinois Archives, Urbana, IL.

———. Interviewed by James R. Skillen. May 18, 2007. Boise, ID. Audiorecording in author's possession.

Aspinall, Wayne. Interviewed by Charles T. Morrisey. Transcript. November 10, 1965. Oral History Interviews. JFK Library, Boston, MA.

Babbitt, Bruce. Interviewed by Charles Wilkinson and Patricia Limerick. Transcript. April 20, 2004. Center of the American West, Boulder, CO.

Beasley, D. Otis. Interview by William W. Moss. Transcript. December 15, 1969. Oral History Interviews. JFK Library, Boston, MA.

Beaty, Orren. Interviewed by William W. Moss. Transcript. October 10, 24, 31, 1969, November 7, 14, 21, 1969, December 19, 1969, January 9, 16, 1970, February 13, 20, 27, 1970. Oral History Interviews. JFK Library, Boston, MA.

Carr, James A. Interviewed by William W. Moss. Transcript. November 18,1970. San Francisco, CA. Oral History Interviews. JFK Library, Boston, MA.

Carver, John A. Interviewed by John F. Stewart. Transcript. August 19, 1968, September 20, 1968. Oral History Interviews. JFK Library, Boston, MA.

———. Interviewed by William W. Moss. September 11, 23, 1969, October 7, 21, 1969. Oral History Interviews. JFK Library, Boston, MA.

Chapman, Oscar L. Interviewed by Jerry N. Ness. 1972–1973. Truman Library, Independence, MO.

Clawson, Marion. Interviewed by James Muhn. Transcript. Undated. BLM Library, Denver, CO.

Dombeck, Michael P. Interviewed by Harold K. Steen. Transcript. May 15–18, 2003. Forest History Society Stevens Point, WI, Durham, NC.

Goldy, Daniel L. "Oral History Interview with Daniel L. Goldy." Edited by Raymond L. Geselbracht and Dennis E. Bilger. 1994. Truman Library, Independence, MO.

Harvey, Mike. Interviewed by Hans Stuart and James Muhn. Transcript. May 26, 1988. BLM Library, Denver, CO.

Hofman, Ron. Interviewed by James Muhn. Transcript. 1988. BLM Library, Denver, CO.

Jamison, Cy. Interviewed by James Muhn. Transcript. January 10, 1991. BLM Library, Denver, CO.

———. Interviewed by James Muhn. Transcript. December 15, 1992. BLM Library, Denver, CO.

Jones, Robert A. Interviewed by Hans Stuart and James Muhn. Transcript. 1988. BLM Library, Denver, CO.

Landstrom, Karl. Interviewed by Hans Stuart and James Muhn. Transcript. May 23, 1988. BLM Library, Denver, CO.

Senzel, Irving. Interviewed by Hans Stuart and James Muhn. Transcript. March 3, 1988. BLM Library, Denver, CO.

Stoddard, Charles H. Interviewed by Helen McCann White. Transcript. November 29, 1967. Charles H. Stoddard Papers. Minnesota Historical Society, St. Paul, MN.

Turcott, George. Interviewed by Bob Stewart. Transcript. March 18, 1980. Nevada State Office. BLM Library, Denver, CO.

Udall, Stewart. Interviewed by William W. Moss. Transcript. January 12, February 16, March 12, April 7, May 20, June 2, and July 6, 1970. Oral History Interviews. JFK Library, Boston, MA.

Wolf, Robert. Interviewed by Claire Rhein. Transcript. April 17, 1989–March 2001. Robert Wolf Oral History Project. Maureen and Mike Mansfield Library and K. Ross Toole Archives, Missoula, MT.

ARCHIVES AND MANUSCRIPT COLLECTIONS

Andrus, Cecil. Papers, Secretary of the Interior 1977–1981. Special Collections. Boise State University, Boise, ID.

Beaty, Orren. Personal Papers. John F. Kennedy Library, Boston, MA.

Carver, John A. Personal Papers. John F. Kennedy Library, Boston, MA.

Forsling, Clarence Luther. Papers. Library and Archives. Forest History Society, Durham, NC.

Kennedy, John F. White House Central Subject Files. JFK Library, Boston, MA.

Morton, Rogers C. B., Collection, 1939–1976. 84M1. Special Collections and Archives. University of Kentucky Libraries, Lexington, KY.

Nixon, Richard M. Presidential Materials Staff. National Archives Building II, College Park, MD.

Public Lands Foundation Archive. Bureau of Land Management National Training Center, Phoenix, AZ.

Rasmussen, Boyd. Papers. Library and Archives. Forest History Society, Durham, NC.

Records of the Bureau of Land Management: Record Group 49 (RG 49). National Archives Building, Washington, DC.

Records of the Office of the Secretary of the Interior: Record Group 48 (RG 48). National Archives Building II, College Park, MD.

Stoddard, Charles H. Papers. Minnesota Historical Society, St. Paul, MN.

Uncatalogued Papers. Compiled by James Muhn. BLM Library, Denver Service Center, Denver, CO.

Whitaker, John C. Staff Member and Office Files. White House Central Files. Richard M. Nixon Presidential Materials Staff. National Archives Building II, College Park, MD.

Index